A History of Ottoman Poetry Volume 4

لِلّٰهِ كُنُوزٌ تَحْتَ ٱلْعَرْشِ مَقَاتِيمُهَا ٱلْسِنَةُ ٱلشُّعَرَاهِ

'God hath Treasuries aneath the Throne, the Keys
whereof are the Tongues of the Poets.'

Hadís-i-Sheríf.

A

HISTORY

OF

OTTOMAN POETRY

BY

THE LATE

E. J. W. GIBB, M. R. A. S.

VOLUME IV

EDITED BY

EDWARD G. BROWNE, M. A., M. B.,

SIR THOMAS ADAMS' PROFESSOR OF ARABIC AND FELLOW OF PEMBROKE
COLLEGE IN THE UNIVERSITY OF CAMBRIDGE; FELLOW
OF THE BRITISH ACADEMY.

LONDON
LUZAC & CO., GREAT RUSSELL STREET
1905

PRINTED BY E J. BRILL LEYDEN.

EDITOR'S PREFACE.

With the completion of this fourth volume of my late friend's *History of Ottoman Poetry*, which brings us to the end of the *ancien régime*, and almost into our own times, the character of what remains of my task undergoes a material change. Up to this point I have had before me a manuscript, which, however much the author, had he lived, might have modified or added to it, was essentially complete, and needed only trifling alterations and occasional notes. For the period which remains, the period, that is to say, of the New School, who deserted Persian for French models, and almost re-created the Turkish language, so greatly did they change its structure and the literary ideals of their countrymen, only three chapters were to be discovered amongst my friend's papers. Of these, the first, entitled "the Dawn of a New Era", treats of the character and inception of the movement, and, in a general way, of its chief representatives, viz. Shinásí Efendi, Ẓiyá Pasha, Kemál Bey, 'Abdu'l-Ḥaqq Ḥámid Bey, Aḥmed Midḥat Efendi, Aḥmed Vefíq Pasha and Ebu'ẓ-Ẓiyá Tevfíq Bey; the second discusses the life and work of Shinásí Efendi (A. D. 1826—1871); and the third is devoted to Ẓiyá Pasha (A. D. 1830—1880). There are, it is true, besides this fragment of the last volume, a good many notes and translations on loose sheets of paper and in note-books included amongst my friend's very

numerous papers, as well as some indications in his fine collection of printed and lithographed Turkish books (generously
presented by Mrs. E. J. W. Gibb to the Cambridge University Library) of the course which he intended to follow
in writing of the Modern School; but the most valuable
document of this sort which has come into my hands is an
outline of the whole history of Turkish poetry, containing
the names of the most eminent poets, the titles of their
principal works, and observations on their characteristics,
which was drawn up by Mr. Gibb for a friend, who has
most kindly placed it at my disposal. As the notes on the
Modern School are of great importance as an indication of
the plan which the author would have followed, had he
lived to complete his work, in the last volume, and as they
are also very short, I here print them in full.

"THE MODERN SCHOOL (A. D. 1859—).

"*(The inspiration now comes from Europe, chiefly from France).*

"*Shinásí* (died A. D. 1871). Occasional verses; translations
from the French Poets (1859); Fables in verse. The
translations are the first renderings of poetry ever
made into Turkish from a European language, and
their appearance marks an epoch.

"*Kázim Pasha. Diwán; Maqálid-i-ʿAshq*, or 'Garners of
Love'; *Báz u Khunfesá*, or 'the Hawk and the Beetle'.
The 'Garners of Love' is a series of elegies on Ḥuseyn,
the Prophet's grandson, who was killed at Kerbelá.
'The Hawk and the Beetle' is a satire on two Pashas.

"*Ḥaqqi Bey. Diwán.* He wrote in Nefʿí's style.

"*Hersekli ʿÁrif Ḥikmet Bey.*

"*Nevres. Diwán.* These four poets wrote in the old style,
not in the modern.

Edhem Pertev Pasha (died A. D. 1873). Translations from Victor Hugo and Jean Jacques Rousseau.

Ẓiyá Pasha (died A. D. 1880). *Díwán; Ẓafer-náme,* or 'the Book of Victory'; *Kharábát,* or 'the Tavern', an Anthology. A great poet. The *Ẓafer-náme* is a satire on ʿAlí Pasha, the grand Vezír, who was a personal and political enemy of Ẓiyá.

ʿAbdu'l-Ḥaqq Ḥámid Bey. Many occasional poems, and also the following dramas in poetry: *Nesteren; Tezer; Eshber* (these are all proper names). His first volume of poems is *Ṣaḥrá* ('the Country'); others are *Beldé* ('the Town', *i.e.* Paris); *Ḥajle* ('the Bridal'); *Maqber* ('the Tomb); *Ülü* ('Death'); *Bunlar O dur* ('These are she'). The four poems last mentioned are in memory of his late wife. *Bir Sefílenin Ḥasb-i-Ḥáli* ('The Cry of an Unfortunate'). Ḥámid Bey was the first to introduce the European verse-forms into Turkish. He has written several dramas in prose as well as those mentioned above, which are in verse. He has many works still in manuscript which have never yet been published.

Kemál Bey (died A. D. 1888). Many occasional poems, chiefly patriotic. He wrote in the European forms after Ḥámid had published his *Ṣaḥrá* in 1879. He is perhaps the greatest literary genius ever produced by Turkey, but his work, which is of every kind, is mostly in prose.

Ekrem Bey. Occasional poems. He has a collection in three parts called *Zemzeme,* or 'the Ripples'. He is the

best of Ḥámid Bey's followers, and is now [1] looked
upon by the young Turkish writers as their master.
He has written a good deal, but many of his poems
are scattered about in magazines and other periodical
publications, and have never yet been collected.

"*Muʿallim* (Professor) *Nájí* (died A. D. 1893). A distinguished poet and critic of the Modern School. Several
collections of his poems have been published, including
one called *Átesh-pára* ('Scintillations'), and another
entitled *Shiráre* ('sparks').

"Ḥámid, Kemál, Ekrem and Nájí are the real founders
of the Modern School of Poetry. They soon had a large
following of young poets and poetesses, but I have not yet
examined the works of these in detail. Some two or three
years ago two young men, Dr. Jenáb Shihábu'd-Dín Bey [2]
and Tevfíq Fikret Bey [3], struck out a new line of poetry,
modelled on the work of the French impressionist and sym-
bolist poets. With the exception of Ḥámid Bey and Ekrem
Bey, these two innovators are probably the best living Turkish poets."

The above extract will serve to indicate the ground which
the concluding volume of Mr. Gibb's *History of Ottoman
Poetry* was intended to cover, though he would doubtless
have made mention of others of the most modern Turkish
writers, such as Fá'iq ʿAlí, Ismaʿíl Ṣafá, Ḥasan Suʿád, Jalál
Sáhir and Qádir, together with some of the most talented
novelists, such as Sezá'í Bey, the son of Sámí Pasha, author

---

[1] [These notes are dated 1897. ED.]
[2] [I am informed that he was living in Rhodes a few months ago. ED.]
[3] [I believe that he is now a professor at the American College at Rumeylí Ḥiṣár. ED.]

of *Kúchuk sheyler* ("Little Things"), Khálid Ẓiyá Bey, author of *°Ashq-i-memnú°* ("Forbidden Love"), Ḥusayn Raḥmí, author of *°Iffet* ("Chastity"), and Muḥammed Re'úf, author of *Eylúl* ("September"). [1] It is a matter of deep regret that this particular portion of the History should have remained unwritten, for no European, so far as I know, even approached the late Mr. Gibb either in knowledge of or sympathy with the Modern School of Turkish writers, in the value of whose work he had a profound belief, and whose aims and ideals he appreciated to a degree never reached, I should think, by any other foreigner. In the four volumes of his *History* now before the public he has said what will for very many years, if not for ever, remain the final word on the Old School of Turkish poets; but who can complete, with any approach to his learning and sympathy, the volume which he intended to devote to the wonderful transformation — almost unique, perhaps, in literary history — effected by the New School? Here is a question which has constantly occupied my mind during the time while I was engaged in editing these volumes, and especially this last one; nor have I yet discovered any way which justifies me in hoping that it may be made worthy of its predecessors.

Be this as it may, the end of my task is now in view. Two more volumes are still to appear; the fifth, which will contain the above mentioned three chapters written by Mr. Gibb on the Modern School, supplemented by such additional information as I can collect as to its subsequent history (and here I rely especially on the kind offers of help which I have received from several of my Turkish friends), together with the Index of the whole work, on which my colleague Mr. R. A. Nicholson has been for some

[1] [For this list I am indebted to some of my Turkish friends resident in Paris. ED.]

time engaged; and the sixth and last, which will contain
the Turkish texts of all the poems translated in the preceding volumes, and will in itself constitute an almost unique
Anthology of the best and most typical Ottoman poetry of
all time.

It remains only for me to speak briefly of two other
matters, to which reference is made in my Preface to vol.
II of this work, pp. XXXI—XXXII, and again in the Preface
to vol. III, pp. X—XII, *viz.* the late Mr. Gibb's library,
and the Gibb Memorial Fund established by his mother,
Mrs. Jane Gibb.

As regards my friend's library, his valuable collection of
manuscripts, ultimately destined for the British Museum,
still remains in my keeping, for reasons explained on pp. IX—
X of the Preface to vol. III, and will not be transferred
to the Museum until this work is completed. As regards
his printed books, which I spoke of in vol. II, p. XXXI,
as "destined to be dispersed", many volumes were given
by his widow, Mrs. E. J. W. Gibb, to her late husband's
friends and fellow-workers, while a very fine selection of
European works on Turkey was presented by her to the
library of the British Embassy at Constantinople. Almost
the whole collection of Turkish (together with a small number
of Persian) printed and lithographed books was, however,
generously presented by her, as already mentioned, to the
Cambridge University Library. This valuable collection, which
is particularly rich in *Edebiyyât*, or Belles Lettres, comprises
some 300 volumes (many of them very rare, and containing,
in many cases, notes and comments in Mr. Gibb's hand),
and is kept apart by itself; and I have just completed the
list of its contents, which, I hope, will soon be published.

Mrs. Jane Gibb, the mother of my friend, and the generous
Foundress of the Memorial destined to commemorate and

carry on his work, died on November 26 of last year (1904), and did not, alas! live to see either the completion of this book, in the progress of which, until the end of her life, she showed the keenest interest, or the first fruits of her munificent endowment of the studies to which her son's life was devoted. In her will she left for the further endowment of the Memorial an additional large sum of money, which should enable the Trustees to do much for the promotion of Arabic, Persian and Turkish studies, and especially to publish many important texts and translations. Seven or eight volumes of the Memorial Series are now in preparation or in contemplation, and two — Mrs. Beveridge's *Bábar-náma* and my abridged translation of Ibn Isfandiyár's *History of Tabaristán* — are almost ready for publication. The Trustees will be glad to receive communications from scholars who desire to publish works coming within the scope of the Trust, that is to say works dealing with the history, litera- ture, philosophy and civilisation of the Turks, Arabs and Persians. All communications intended for the consideration of the Trustees should, in the first instance, be addressed to Mr. Julius Bertram, Clerk of the Trust, 14, Suffolk Street, Pall Mall East, London, S. W.

May 7, 1905.   EDWARD G. BROWNE.

CONTENTS OF THE FOURTH VOLUME.

BOOK V.

THE FOURTH, OR TRANSITION PERIOD.

A. D. 1700—1850.

CHAPTER I.

The Early Transition Age Ahmed III.
1115—1143 (1703—1730).

Sábit. Nedím.

In the Archaic Period we observed how Turkish poetry
was moulded into shape and started on its course under the
direction and influence of Persia, in the Classic we have
seen how for a long time that influence was paramount and
absolute, exclusive also to the last degree, raising a barrier
unsurmountable by anything alien to itself, in that on which
we have now entered, and which for want of a better name
I have called the Transition, we shall have to watch the
gradual decline of this influence, its replacement by a more
national spirit, and finally its disappearance before the Occidentalism of the present day.

The Transition Period is thus the last of the four stages
through which the Older or Asian School of Ottoman poetry
passed. In some repects it is the most interesting of all the
Periods, for in it Turkish poetry is most truly Turkish In
the Archaic and Classic Ages the all-powerful domination of
Persia had stifled whatever was of native growth and made
Turkish poetry little better than a reflection or shadow, a
thing that might have been produced almost equally in any
country; while in Modern times the poetry, partly because
it is the work of men whose culture is practically that of

Western Europe, and partly because it is the production of
an epoch in which the old Asiatic civilisation of Turkey is
fast disappearing, though it is characterised by a refinement
and nobility beyond anything that has gone before, has
almost of necessity lost somewhat of national individuality.
But in the Transition Period, and especially towards the
end of the eighteenth and the beginning of the nineteenth
centuries, when the Persian fetters had been fairly broken
and the lessons of the West were as yet unlearned, Turkish
poetry, untrammelled by any foreign influence, was free to
shape its own course, and glows with a brightness of local
colour unequalled at any other stage of its progress. The
Ottoman muse, whom during the Classic Period we pictured
as a pretty Turkish girl arrayed in Persian garments, now
casts aside her foreign finery, dons the entari and shalwar,
and wears the fez of her native land, and she looks all the
better for the change

Allusions to the customs of the people, references to the
costumes of the time, and similar little touches inspired by
the familiar sights and doings of every day life, not only
invest the poetry of this Period with a picturesque element
unknown in the past, but render it more interesting and
endow it with an air at once livelier and more natural.
Although most pronounced about the time which I have
mentioned, this local colouring more or less pervades the
whole Period, and forms one of the most marked, as well
as the most attractive of its characteristics. From Nedím,
whose verses mirror the gay times of Ahmed the Third,
down to ʿOsmán Nevres, the friend of Ziyá Pasha and the
bête noire of Kemál Bey, who brings into his ghazels the
theatre and the steamboat, we have a succession of poets
whose writings spread before us, like a panorama, the life
of Constantinople during these hundred and fifty years For

we are entering on a period when men will no longer hesitate till they get the lead from Shíráz or Isfahán ere they write about the things that really interest them in the manner which they deem the best, they have even invented a verse-form of their own, to which is affixed the imprimatur of no Iránian master. Truly the Ottomans have at last grown weary of being the parrots of the Persians!

The question at once arises. how came this great change, the most revolutionary, so far, in the history of Ottoman poetry, to occur at this particular juncture? Remembering how in the past each fresh development in Turkish poetry has been the reflection of a similar movement in that of Persia, our first impulse would be to look for some corresponding evolution in the literature of Irán to supply the answer to this question. But when we turn to the works of 'Urfí and Feyzí, whose influence was supreme in Turkey at the time when the first signs of the coming change appeared, we fail to discover any trace of that objective spirit which gives its special stamp to the poetry of the Transition, and of which the local colouring just referred to is a conspicuous manifestation. Turkish poetry has, indeed, ceased to derive its direct inspiration from Persia, so we must look elswhere for the answer to our question.

The first step is to see whether we can discover why the Ottoman poets should, at this particular point, sever a connection which has existed since the very foundation of their literature, and break away from a tradition which has from the beginning been the pivot on which has turned the whole aesthetic culture of their race. When Turkish poetry started on its career early in the fourteenth century, Persian literature was, with the single exception of Italian, the greatest living literature in the world, and, apart from any accidental or local circumstances, was well worthy to serve as model

to a people possessing no literary traditions and endowed
with no great artistic originality. This pre-eminence was fairly
maintained up to the age of Jámí, and did not entirely
disappear until after the time of Sá'ib ' The period subsequent
to the death of that author, which occurred about 1088
(1677), is known in the history of Persian poetry as that of
the Decadence, and although writers not altogether unworthy
of the past still continued to appear from time to time, the
literature of Trán now sank into a state of decrepitude from
which there has as yet been no revival. [1] Having thus lost
her own inspiration, the Persian muse was no longer able
to inspire her neighbour, and this the Turkish poets must
have felt, though they may never have recognized, or even
realised, the fact.

Again, just as the Turks were thus compelled to abandon
the practice of modelling their poetry on the contemporary
work of Persia through the insufficiency of the latter, they
were prohibited from continuing to imitate the productions
of Trán's earlier and happier days, in as much as the spirit
which animated those belonged to a past age, and was no
longer adequate to express the tendencies and ideals of a
new time Moreover, Turco-Persianism had, as we have seen,
said its last word in the poems of Nef'í and Nábí, it was
impossible to go farther than the first of these writers in the
direction of technical excellence, or than the second in that
of downright imitation. No advance was therefore possible
along the old lines, and so the Turkish poets found themselves

[1] [I have already repeatedly expressed my dissent from this view. Qa'ání of
Shíráz, who was living not much more than half a century ago, is alone sufficient, in my opinion, to disprove it The fact is that no careful study of
modern Persian poetry has yet been made in Europe It was the good fortune
of the Turks to find so faithful a friend, so appreciative an admirer, and so
diligent a student of their literature of all periods, ancient and modern, as
the Author of this work This good fortune has hitherto been denied to the
Persians. ED.]

confronted with the necessity of shaping some new course for themselves, unless they wished to see their work lose whatever vitality it possessed and degenerate more than ever into the position of a mere academic exercise What they actually did was the very best thing they could have done, they turned their attention to the life they saw about them, and brought what they could of the national spirit into their work.

This takes us to the second point in our enquiry, namely, why the Turkish poets, when deprived of the guidance of Persia, should have turned for inspiration to that well-spring of national sentiment which they had hitherto contemptuously ignored. The answer seems to be that they had no choice. The writings of ancient Greece and Rome, together with the modern European literatures which derive so much from these, were for the Turks of those times practically as non-existent as the Sanscrit Vedas, or as the poems of Jámí and Báqí for the contemporary scholars of the West, and even had the case been otherwise, racial pride and religious bigotry were still too strong to permit of any lesson being taken from the Frankish paynim. There was indeed available the vast literature of the Arabs, but, apart from the fact that the two races have always been antipathetic in genius, Arabic poetry was at this moment in a yet more atrophied condition than that of Persia, [1] and to have substituted the former for the latter would simply have been, while slightly varying its character, to have intensified the nature of the evil it was sought to remedy.

And so the poets were compelled to fall back upon their native resources, and to the student of Ottoman literature it can only be a matter of regret that this necessity did not

[1] [I am inclined to think that much of what I said in the last note about modern Persian poetry is applicable, *mutatis mutandis*, to that of the Arabs ED.]

arise earlier, not that the Turkish genius is superior to the Persian, for, as a matter of fact, the converse is true, but because a literature which really expresses the feelings of those who formed it is more interesting and more valuable than one which but reflects the mind of another, albeit a more gifted, race.

For the sake of convenience I have begun the Transition Period with the year 1115 (1703), which is the date of the accession of Ahmed III. But, of course, this date is only an approximation, here, as in all similar cases, there is a certain amount of overlapping, many poems, as we have already seen, inspired by a sentiment quite in accordance with that of the Transition were written during the Classic age, while many more, as we shall shortly see, produced during the later period are in full sympathy with the spirit of the earlier period Thus the sharqí, which is the distinctive verse-form of the Transition, made its appearance, as we know, in the díwán of the Classic poet Nazím.[1]

I call the sharqí the distinctive verse-form of the Transition, because, although it was introduced some few years before Sultan Ahmed ascended the throne, it is itself the symbol and embodiment of the great change then accomplished. The sharqí is the sign that the Turk is no longer in tutelage to the Persian; its outward form is of native growth, and the spirit which animates it is the native spirit, and this is the spirit that creates the Transition Period.

Persian forms, it is true, remain, ghazel and qasída and mesneví continue with us as before, but it is no longer only an echo of the voice of Írán that is heard through these The old familiar accents are certainly not wanting, but with them have begun to mingle the tones of another voice, less soft and caressing it may be, but stronger, clearer, and more

[1] [See vol. III, pp 319—323 ED.]

manly, in the ever-increasing volume of which those gradually melt away till they are lost

Persianism had struck root too deeply to be easily or quickly done away. Its influence, indeed, lasts all through the Transition, which is the period of its decline, not of its disappearance, To bring about that consummation, to deal the coup de grace to the incubus which had for so many centuries oppressed the poetry of Turkey, a new force was needful, a force as yet undreamed of, but in due course to be born of the intellectual alliance of the Ottoman poets with the West

The native Turkish spirit, the presence of which thus differentiates the Transition from the preceding Periods, is most clearly seen, as I have often had occasion to remark, in the folksongs and national ballads known as Turkis As presented in these, it is in direct antithesis to that Persian spirit which till now has animated well-nigh the whole mass of the literary poetry. It is as simple as that is affected, and as spontaneous as that is artificial, while the intense subject- ivity of the latter is paralleled by the remarkable objectivity of the former

The Turk is of a more practical nature than the Persian, he is not so much of a dreamer, left to himself, he rarely sits down to weave romances or speculate as to the mystery of existence. Consequently we find, comparatively speaking, but little more avowedly mystic poetry Every true Persian is more or less of a mystic, but the average Turk finds greater satisfaction in turning his attention to things that lie more immediately to his hand.

A natural result of this is that as the Turkish spirit ousts the Persian, the tone of the poetry becomes less and less spiritual and more and more material. Thus the object of the poet's love who, when Persianism was at its best, was

conceived as a sexless being, the ideal of youthful beauty,
now becomes frankly a human creature, generally a girl,
whose charms are sometimes described in terms such as would
have made the elder poets shroud their faces with their sleeve
When Persianism was not at its best we have seen that the
beloved was, through a variety of motives already sufficiently
indicated, most often pictured as a boy. But this was contrary to Turkish popular taste, so, as the native spirit began
to assert itself and gain strength, we find the girl beginning
to compete with the boy, then gradually pushing him farther
into the background until at last she has the stage entirely
to herself, a victory the permanence of which has been
secured to her by the Occidentalism of the Modern School
The magnitude of the change in this respect will be appreciated if we call to mind the bitter and uncompromising
misogyny of the Classic Age, when the mere mention a
woman (outside the fictitious world of romance) was an
outrage on decorum, while to suggest that such a creature
could possess any charm was to evoke a hurricane of oppro-
brium and obloquy.

Although the national spirit was able thus profoundly to
modify the aims and the tone of poetry, the case was otherwise with regard to outward form. Never having been cultivated, the Turkish folksong had but little to offer in this
direction; turkis, varying slightly in rime-arrangement, but
all more or less rugged and uncouth, were its sole medium
of expression These the literary poets took up and elaborated
into the existing varieties of the sharqí; but beyond this
nothing was possible.

The other verse-forms continue much as heretofore. There
is a tendency in the ghazel, especially as the Period advances,
to lose something of its discursiveness and to confine itself
to a single subject. Long mesnevís become rarer, but there

is a large number of shorter poems of this class, generally descriptive or narrative The táríkhs or chronograms show a marked increase, which culminates in the extraordinary díwán of Surúrí Possibly the growing favour of this style of poem may in some measure be accounted for by the fact that it has always for subject some definite event, a circumstance which would be likely to recommend it to the practical and somewhat uninventive Turkish mind.

A corresponding change becomes perceptible in the vocabulary of the poets. This ceases to be so exclusively Persian as formerly, and many Turkish words and idioms which have hitherto been regarded as outside the literary pale begin to find their way into the díwáns As time goes on, more and more of such are introduced, and their presence does much to heighten that national Turkish air which not only distinguishes the more interesting poetry of this Period, but gives it well-nigh whatever it possesses of originality.

During the reign of Ahmed III, which lasted from 1115 (1703) to 1143 (1730), the Ottoman court reached the zenith of its splendour. At first, indeed, the horizon was dark with war-clouds, but these passed away, and the Sultan who cared little for military glory gave himself up, heart and soul, to the realisation of his dreams of luxury and magnificence. But Ahmed was no sensual despot like Ibráhím, he was a refined and appreciative lover of all things beautiful, who found his chief delight in laying out enchanting gardens, building gay kiosques and pavilions, and organising brilliant fêtes for the delectation of himself and his friends and of the bevy of fair women with whom he loved to surround himself. All the great men of the court followed his example, and scarce less splendid than his own were the pleasaunces and palaces of his son-in-law the Grand Vezír Ibráhím Pasha and of the

Grand Admiral Mustafá Pasha. With these two high officers
the Sultan was on the most intimate terms, he would often
invite them to special entertainments at his palaces, and
would even at times honour the Vezír by accepting his
hospitality in return It was a careless pleasure-loving age
when the great world of Constantinople had no thought but
to enjoy life to the uttermost, when morals were naturally
far from rigid and many things were done openly which in
former times would have been discreetly veiled. The love
of pomp and show which seized upon the court found expression not alone in the many pleasure gardens and palaces
which sprang up on every side, but in the magnificent
pageants that were organised on all available occasions. The
historian Ráshid and the poet Seyyid Vehbí give glowing
accounts of the brilliant processions and countless entertainments when princesses were married or princes circumcised,
while some idea of the sumptuous decoration of the apart-
ments and the costly magnificence of the dresses of the great
ladies may be gathered from the letters of the English "am-
bassadress" Lady Mary Wortley Montague, who visited Turkey
during this reign, and who was happily a careful observer
and a faithful recorder of what she saw. Saʿd-ábád on the
Sweet Waters of Europe, where a fair palace was now built,
became the favourite resort of the pleasure-seeking Constantinopolitans, and is henceforward to the Ottoman poets what
the fields of Musallá and the banks of the Ruknábád were
to Háfiz of Shíráz. Illuminations and tulip-fêtes, garden-parties
and banquets, excursions and pageants, followed one another
in endless succession, until at length the people grew weary
of the extravagance and carelessness of a government whose
chiefs thought of nothing beyond their own enjoyment. And
so it came about that in the autumn of 1730 the janissaries
mutinied, dragged the Grand Admiral from his garden on

the Bosphorus where he was planting tulips, strangled him along with the Grand Vezír and another high officer, and compelled Ahmed to abdicate in favour of his nephew Mahmúd.

Sultan Ahmed and the great men of his court, more especially Ibráhím Pasha,[1] were, as we should have expected, intelligent and enthusiastic patrons of literature. The Grand Vezír encouraged letters by every means in his power. On at least two occasions he formed committees consisting of the most learned and accomplished men in Constantinople for the purpose of translating some of the great Arabian and Persian classics, which had hitherto never appeared in a Turkish dress. The plan of translation adopted by these committees was singular, each member was told off to translate a certain number of pages of the work in hand, which when completed were bound up together, and thus, we are told, a work which it would have taken a single scholar years to accomplish was finished within a little time. No doubt it was; but this celerity of execution must have been dearly purchased if unity of style is of any account

A brilliant group of poets, with the illustrious Nedím at their head, sang the splendours of the court, and lavished all the wealth of their Eastern imaginations in extolling the glories of the great Sultan and his ministers. At such a time, when the court was the centre of all things, it was but natural that court-poets should abound, all the more as the grandees were most generous in their encouragement of men of letters, and as there was really much to stimulate and inspire impressionable natures in the dazzling magnificence displayed upon every side. And thus, although at all times court-poetry has been considerably in evidence in Turkey,

[1] [In a pencil note on this passage the Author observes "He is often praised in the same qasída as the Sultan, which is, I think, quite unprecedented." ED]

it was never cultivated with so much success, and never
achieved such brilliancy and distinction, as during the later
years of the reign of Aḥmed the Third

But while the court thus attracted to itself several of the
best poets of the day, including the most gifted of them all,
there were many writers who, either because their lot was
cast elsewhere than in the capital, or because a retiring
temperament led them to shun publicity, stood altogether
outside the ranks of the court-poets, — an attitude which,
be it said to his honour, did not prevent Ibráhím Pasha
from extending to them such encouragement and assistance
as they required and were willing to accept. Two or three
of these writers have since attained a renown greater than
that of any of the court-poets, save only Nedím himself;
and it is with one of such that we shall begin the Transition
Period.

There are few educated Turks who are unfamiliar with
the name of Sábit; for though by no means a great poet,
this author was a man of unusual versatility, and possessed
a happy knack of presenting well-known proverbs and other
familiar phrases and expressions in a neat and epigrammatic
form, often enlivened by a dash of humour, which at once
gained for him a large share of popular favour, of which the
shadow at least remains to the present day.

Born in what the biographers call 'the town of Úzicha in
Bosnia,'[1] Sábit, whose personal name was ʿAlá-ud-Dín, began
his studies under a certain Khalíl Efendi who had a reputation
for learning in those parts In due time he made his way to
Constantinople, where he continued his studies, until, having
passed through the several classes of the muderrisate, and

---

[1] This is probably the Ushitza or Usicza of our maps, which is now included
in the Kingdom of Servia

served as judge-substitute at Rodosto, he entered the second
or devriyye order of the magistracy and was appointed molla
of Bosna-Seráy, Qonya, and Diyár-Bekr successively. He received the mollaship of the last-named city in 1119 (1707—8),
but before his death, which occurred in 1124 (1712—3), he
had retired from public life. The only personal note that I
find recorded of Sábit is that he was afflicted with a stutter
or stammer in his speech which made him say on occasions,
'I cannot speak, but thank God my pen can speak a little,
were it too unable to speak, I should split.'

Sábit died too early to come under the influence of Sultan
Ahmed's court, which did not attain the full height of its
splendour until some years later. A considerable portion of
his work, indeed, must fall within the Classic Period, he has
a chronogram on the accession of Suleymán II in 1098 (1686)
But in spirit he is a thorough-going Transitionist, so Turkish
is his language at times that Kemál Bey cites him as one
of the two old writers who most endeavoured to develop a
new and national style, the other being Kání who flourished
somewhat later. The cause of Sábit's failure in this direction
we shall consider by and bye; but first we must note that
this poet has a style of his own which though occasionally
approaching that of Nábí, is in reality essentially different.

The characteristic which distinguishes Sábit not only from
Nábí but from all his predecessors is his humour. None of
the earlier Turkish poets seriously attempted humorous verse;
the only approach to it had been in the works called Shehr-
engíz, and it is hard to say how much in these was jest and
how much was earnest This has not happened because the
Turks are destitute of the sense of humour, but because this
sense, like most other native traits, has up till now been
regarded as beneath the dignity of poetry. But in the new
condition of affairs humour begins to assert itself, and it is

16

worthy of note that the more humorous a poem is in purpose,
the more Turkish it is in vocabulary and idiom. Sábit may
fairly claim to be the first to introduce the spirit of humour
into Ottoman poetry, others followed in his footsteps and
in some respects improved upon his work, but the glory of
the pioneer is his.

The way in which he introduces those proverbs and popular
sayings to which I have already referred and which abound
in his writings, bears witness to this tendency of Sábit's temper,
for he presents those phrases and locutions, with which everyone is familiar, in a manner so neat and at the same time
so whimsical that it is impossible to refrain from smiling
when reading his verses. The setting of proverbs in this
comic fashion appears to have been what afforded him the
greatest pleasure in writing poetry, and many of his verses
were no doubt composed merely for the point which the
humorously introduced citation enabled him to make. This
was perceived by his contemporary Nábí who, as we have
seen, sometimes tried his own hand in this direction, and
was gracefully acknowledged by him in more than one of
his poems. Thus he says.

> "Nabi, in this age no one can rival
> "Sábit Efendi in the citation of proverbs." [1]

And again

> "Nábí, everyone cannot be like Sábit Efendi,
> "A proverb for proverbs among the witty " [2]

If Nábí had Sábit in his mind when he wrote the following

[1]
ضرب المثل ايرادنـه بـو عصرده نـابـى
كمسه اولـهمـار ثـابـت افـندى به رسـمـده

[2]
نـابى اولـهمـار ثـابت افندى كمى هر كس
صـرب امـثـل بكـنـهوران صـرب مـثـلـده

couplet, a gentle and not unjust criticism must have been intended, but possibly he may have been thinking only of himself.

"There is nothing against quoting proverbs in one's speech;
"But true speech is such that there shall remain from what thou
[sayest a proverb to the world." [1]

Sábit on his part refers to Nábí in a couple of ghazels which he wrote naziras to two of the elder poet, who was then residing at Aleppo. In the first the reference is entirely complimentary

"Is there any man of eloquence like Sábit in Aleppo
"Who can write a nazíra to his reverence the master Nábí?" [2]

In the second, Sábit betrays some jealousy of the favour shown to Nábí's poetry in the capital, at the same time unintentionally demonstrating how popular was the master's work even then:

"At present, O Sábit, there is no demand in Constantinople
"For the new silk of talent if the Aleppo stamp be not thereon" [3]

Besides his love of quoting proverbs, Sábit had an extraordinary craze for punning in season and out of season; and it is this more than anything else that disqualified his work from becoming an example to his successors. Other Turkish poets, as we know well, were fond of equivoques, but they sought after such purely as rhetorical embellishments, and

[1]

سـوزده صـرب المثل ابرادبمه سور بوی امّا
سـور اودر عـالمه سندن قاله بر صرب مثل

[2]

حـصـرت ثابتّی استـاده نـظـمـه دبمکه
ثابت آسا حلبك مرد سخندانـسمی وار

[3]

ثـمـاش دو طـهـور مـعـرفـتـده شمدبلك ثابت
دولنهازسه حلب بمعاسی اسناـسولده رغبت بوی

2

used them in a manner which, in their eyes at any rate, in no wise lessened the dignity of their work Sábit on the other hand scatters his puns broadcast through his verses with but scant regard to either propriety or taste, and most often with no other purpose than that of provoking a smile. And this chiefly when he is most Turkish, when he uses Arabic and Persian he can be as sedate as any of his predecessors, but he seems to have considered the Turkish idiom as unworthy of serious cultivation and fitted only to be a medium for jokes and whimsicalities And herein lies the reason why the genius of this poet failed of its due effect. He did indeed show his contemporaries and successors that it was possible to write verses in simple and vigorous Turkish; but while he did so he was laughing at the whole thing and hinting to them with a wink of the eye and a shrug of the shoulders that burlesque, if not buffoonery and ribaldry, was the only proper subject for such a style Had Sábit turned to more account the great talent he undoubtedly possessed, and striven seriously to write poetry in that natural and familiar idiom he knew so well how to use, his work would probably have had a powerful and beneficent influence upon the subsequent literature of his country; as it is, he but set a fashion of writing facetious verse in a language bordering more or less on the vernacular.

When he chose, this poet could write in a strain both elevated and noble, as he clearly proved on more occasions than one Scattered throughout his poems are many graceful and pleasing passages and many witty and amusing sallies, but the continual straining after puns and other word-plays wearies the reader, and the complete absence of taste with which these are introduced displeases and eventually disgusts And so Professor Nájí, speaking of his poems, says that the beauties which now and then occur are wonderfully great and such as to render imitation impossible, while the commonplaces are tasteless to the last degree and such that they are altogether unworthy of imitation.

Ziyá Pasha declares Sábit to be a vigorous poet in the style of Yahyá Efendi and Nedím (i e of the Transition), and with true discrimination selects his Na‘t, or Hymn in honour of the Prophet, and his Mi‘rájiyya, or Ascension-song, for special mention. His language is said to be often technical, though his thoughts are worth jewels, while his thraldom to proverbs sometimes drives him to commit prosodial errors. In another part of the preface to his anthology the Pasha charges Sábit, along with Sámí, who wrote a little later, with introducing into Turkish poetry two other prosodial laxities which subsequent writers adopted on their authority. But, as Kemál Bey points out, one of these was in general use long before Sábit's time, while the Pasha himself takes advantage of the other in his own poetical work.

Sábit's díwán opens with what is called a Mi‘rájiyya, that is, a poem descriptive of the Mi‘ráj or Ascension of Muhammed, the vision in which that Prophet saw himself transported to Heaven and introduced into the immediate presence of God It had been the custom from early times to devote one of the prefatory cantos or sections of the romantic mesnevís to this subject, but separate poems, dealing exclusively with it, though not unknown in the Classic Period, only now became at all frequent There are but one or two passages in the Koran where the vision is referred to, but an immense mass of legend grew up round these in after times, and it is the story in this amplified form that supplies the text for the Mi‘rájiyyas or Ascension-Songs. These, which often go into great detail, are written with all the splendour of diction and wealth of fancy which the poet can command. Sábit's poem, which is in qasída form, is one of the best of his

works, and although the imagery is often too extravagant
and fantastic to please modern taste, it contains some passages
which may be justly termed sublime According to the author
of the Caravan of the Poets, Sábit wrote this work as a
nazíra to a similar poem by Nádirí, an author who died in
1036 (1626—7).

In his Naʿt, which, along with the Miʿrájiyya, shares the
honour of Ziyá Pasha's special praise, Sábit writes in his
most erudite style and with a dignity which he reaches
nowhere else Some passages in certain of his qasídas and
ghazels are good, though in the latter especially he gives
the rein to his passion for quoting proverbs and making puns

Sábit, it would appear, at one time meditated writing a
Khamsa in emulation of that of ʿAtáʾí, but he got no further
than the first poem, and this he only finished, and in a
somewhat perfunctory manner, at the suggestion of a friend,
long after it had been begun and laid aside. The work is
a romantic mesneví, and is entitled Edhem and Humá. The
narrative portion of the poem, which is much shorter than
the prefatory, is claimed by Sábit as his own invention, and
may very well be so. In any case it is of the slightest, and
contains hardly any plot at all. [1]

---

[1] The following is an outline of the story which is scarcely worth relegating
to the Appendix Edhem is a beautiful and pious youth of Balkh, who spends
his days distributing water among the people, and his nights in worshipping
God in a cave in the cemetery He has a friend who looks after him during
the night and acts as a barber during the day One day Edhem, while
going to fill his water-skin at a fountain near the king's palace, raises his
eyes to the building, and sees at a window a lovely girl with whom he at
once falls passionately in love When she perceives that she is being watched,
the girl closes the window and retires, whereupon Edhem falls down in a
faint. He is borne to his cave where he tells his friend what has happened.
The friend tells him that the girl is the king's daughter Humá and that as
his love is quite hopeless he had better banish it altogether from his mind
Thus Edhem cannot do, so he straightway dies broken-hearted but happy in
that he is giving his life for love Von Hammer is mistaken in saying that
this poem is in honour of the saint Ibráhím Edhem

The Zafer-Náme or Victory-Book is a poem in mesneví
verse in honour of Selím Giráy the Khán of the Crimea, and
records the exploits of that Prince in the war waged by
Suleymán II against the Austrians In both the Edhem u
Humá and the Zafer-Náme there is much that can be read
with pleasure, and in both there is the usual wealth of proverbs.

Sábit has finally two mesnevís the intention of which is
wholly humorous. It is in these that he finds freest scope
for his puns and proverbs, which here crowd upon one
another's heels so that there is scarce a line but contains
some joke or quibble. Apart from the puns and the comical
connections in which the proverbs are introduced, the humour
of the two works consists merely of the most audacious
ribaldry. The first, which is variously entitled Hikáye-i Khoja
Fesád, or The Story of Fesád, and Dere-Náme or The Valley-
Book, is the tale of a trick played upon an Armenian woman
by a ruffian of Rodosto. The second, called the Berber-Náme
or Barber-Book, is worse, it details the treachery which an
infamous reprobate and his associates practised towards a
coquettish young barber.[1] These works and others like them
— for they do not stand alone — probably reflect accurately
enough the worst features of the vilest section of the rabble
of those days, but their true interest lies exclusively in their

[1] In the several subjects of these two poems is exemplified one characteristic
of the Transition — the competition of the girl and the boy on equal terms,
which occurs throughout in Sábit Thus the following quatrain would have
been impossible in the previous age, the verse, though it cannot well be
translated, is clever in its way and a good example of one side of the poet's
humour

احـوال زناق كجه بـر سـمـكـه كـوزیمنس

دیرمش که بو مصمونله درلر كلن ایش دار

در طبه معصدن دوكدسورلر انکی طوبله

م قلۀسـنـه صو فیوسنـدن سورنش دار

language. This is invariably the raciest and the most idiomatic
Turkish of which the author is capable, and is in the strongest
possible contrast to the artificial Persianised dialect of conventional literary poetry And so these otherwise contemptible
productions preserve for us something of the colloquial language of their day, which but for them would have passed
altogether into oblivion; for the prose literature is as affected
and unnatural as the poetic and has equally little in common
with the speech of everyday life. There are, however, in
such humorous poems very frequently a number of allusions
to localities bearing significant names in the neighbourhood
of the places where the work is written, which together with
local and sometimes now obsolete expressions and a crowd
of playfully introduced technicalities connected with the trades
or professions of the actors in the stories, combine to render
it often extremely difficult to fully understand all that the
author meant.

The first of the two following passages from the Mi'rájiyya
opens the poem and describes the night when the Ascension
took place The second relates what happened to the Prophet
when in his Celestial journey he reached 'the Lote-Tree
beyond which none may pass,' and had to leave behind his
guide Gabriel and his steed Buráq.

From the Mi'rájiyya [311]

All hail to thee! O happy-starred, O favoured and most blessed night,
The title of whose fame's the head-line of the chapter 'Esrá' hight [1]
Before the sun-bride's radiant face the evening hung a rosy veil,
The stellar largesse [2] yielded matchless gems untold and infinite
'Twas ne'er the lunar disc, the gloomy deep of night did surge and swell,

[1] The seventeenth chapter of the Koran is entitled "Esrá," because the
word esrá, meaning, 'he transported by night,' occurs in the opening verse.
[2] [Sachi, like the Arabic nithár, denotes coins cast about on occasions of
rejoicing ED]

Whereon the raying waves cast up a fish with golden scales and bright.
The hour had o'er its gold-embroidered raimenture of orange-hue
A flowered cloak of ambergris with flashing jewelled buttons dight [1]
Th' Efrásıyáb-night laid beneath his hand the Khusrev-day's domain, [2]
And let illumine all the skies in honour of his conquering might.
* . *
What time they reached unto the Lote-Tree [3] still the Bird Celestial [4] bode,
For unto him the Lote-Tree formed the term of his permitted flight
The heaven-scouring steed Buráq [5] did likewise cease to prance and play,
For this that neither horse nor steed had part on yonder peerless site.
Thereon the Refref [6] came anear with lowly reverence to serve,
And sky-like gave its heart as station for yon Sun of beauty bright [7]
Therewith he passed through many an hundred thousand veils of light and dark,
Then stopped the Refref too, and Ahmed [8] went alone without affright
He reached unto a region where the six directions were no more,
Where earth and sky were not, and where all roof and floor were lost to sight.
A wondrous world was yonder world, with no beginning and no end,
Where voice and ear and speech and mind and reason were forgot outright
* *

The Naʿt opens as follows·

From the Naʿt. [312]

O heart, come, let us rouse the soul and raise the eye to see,
Enough of this blind trifling with to be or not to be [1]
Enough, in following this vain, deceitful flesh hast thou

[1] The starry night succeeding the sunset.
[2] Efrásıyáb was the legendary Turanian King whose wars with Rustem and other Persian heroes in the time of Key-Káʾús and Key Khusrev fill so large a portion of the Sháh-Náme.
[3] The Lote-Tree which marks the spot in Heaven beyond which even the angels may not pass, hence called Sıdretuʾl-Muntehá, "the Lote-Tree of the Limit "
[4] I. e. Gabriel the Archangel
[5] Buráq, 'the Flashing Steed,' that bore the Prophet from earth to this point in Heaven.
[6] The Refref, presumably a kind of throne, is the name of the last vehicle which bore the Prophet on this famous journey
[7] I e. the Prophet
[8] Ahmed = Muhammed

The dales and mountain-paths of lust traverséd wearily
What means this wildered wandering through the vale of covetise?
What means this mazed confusion mid the qualms of agony?
Remove forthright the bursting boil from off the foot of quest,
What profiteth this vain and purposeless futility?
While all this two-day's life [1] our foot is stirruped to depart,
What mean these endless, anxious cares anent futurity?
This pillory, the body, 'tis that holds thee fast ensnared
From winning to the fearful things and grand of Deity
O wash it pure with tears of penitence and let us lay
The face in prayer amid the dust, and worship earnestly
'Tis time the stony heart were molten through distress and dole,
That forth from out the eyne might pour the tears of cramoisie [2]
Enough the idols of desire have made the spirit-shrine
An Indian Somnáth, [3] a Holy Tomb of paynimne [4]
They say that 'tis the lustings of the stubborn flesh that fling
Yon fluttering bird, the heart, into the snare of vanity.
No likelihood of rescue, nay, nor any hope of 'scape,
Not e'en desire to win from out these chains to liberty
Within my heart the senseless sophistry of lust of days,
Within my head the cheating cares of coin and property
* * * * * * * * * * * * * * * * * * * *

The couplets that follow are taken from a qasída addressed
to Ahmed III on the occasion of the defeat of Peter the
Great by the Grand Vezír Baltají Mehemed Pasha

From a Qasída. [313]

* * * * * * * * * * * * * * * * * * * *
Holding high the Prophet's standard, forward swept the Grand Vezír,

[1] 1 e this ephemeral life
[2] Let the hard heart be melted and turned to blood, so that it may supply tears of blood, i e bitter tears of penitence
[3] Somnáth, the famous idol temple in India which was destroyed by Mahmúd of Ghazna.
[4] That is, the Church of the Holy Sepulchre in Jerusalem. We have seen that the statues, images, and paintings with which the Christians decorate their churches are looked upon as idols by the Muslims

On before him like to guides did Victory and Triumph go
Lion-like he chased that crafty fox, the Czar of Muscovy,
Will he nill he, swift he drave him straight into the hole of woe
On the one hand showered the muskets venom even like to snakes,
On the other did the cannons, dragon-fashion, fire throw
* * * * * * * * * * * † * * * * * * * * *
Thou hast finished off the Russian, Sovran mine, though dead he be,
Yet for fear of thee his carcase quaketh in its pit below.
Down he falleth into hell's abyss when once thy musket flames,
Needless here to draw the sabre as against another foe
Yea, the glory of the ruddy ruby on thy sabre-hilt
Burns the paynim all unsmitten, makes him ember-like to glow,
* *

Here are three ghazels.

Ghazel. [314]

To bring that youngling to his school the pedagogue strives night and day;
He well may get himself prayed o'er, [1] he's clean gone daft, ah welaway!

Ay, let her quaff the wine pomegranate-hued from out the pear-shaped glass,
For e'en as far as the Red Apple [2] yon pomonic chin [3] holds sway

Unbuttoning my love's attire, I looked to see the hour last night,
Lo, morn had broke, the world was light, and scattered all the stars' array. [4]

According to his taste vouchsafe to each, cupbearer, at this feast,
Give salep [5] to the zealot, ay, and red wine to the toper gay.

[1] As a mad or sick person has a prayer or incantation recited over him They say, Kendını oqut, 'go and have yourself prayed over,' i e you have gone mad.

[2] The Red Apple is an old name for the city of Rome, and is said by some to have been derived from the gilt globe over St. Peter's which is visible from the sea.

[3] The chin is often compared to an apple

[4] The morn broke, i. e. the beauty's white body was exposed and its brightness illumined the world· the stars were scattered, i. e the gold or silver buttons of her dress were unfastened.

[5] Salep (for Arabic Sa'leb) is a drink made from the powdered root of the orchis mascula, and is not, like wine, forbidden by the Law.

O Sábit, what although I pour the molten ruby of my soul
The sweet cupbearer's lip will form a spinel bowl therefor in fay

Ghazel. [315]

Fain to hide his wine, the zealot passioned to his bosom's core
Hangs his prayer-rug as a curtain there before the tavern-door.

In his night-clothes sweat the lover as 'twere with the sweat of doom
While he stripped that wanton beauty even to the shift she wore

Casting down her hook-like tresses, searcheth she her chin's sweet well [1]
For the heart therein that's fallen of her lover all foilore

That she looks not on her lover comes of her abounding grace,
From her eyen's shafts she guardeth him who doth herself adore

Loosen not thy locks, let not them fall, by that fair head of thine!
Bind not Sábit's still free spirit in the chains of anguish sore

To the next ghazel, in which the poet describes his sweetheart's silver belt, Sámí has written a nazíra.

Ghazel [316]

Full heavy it is clear to see's thy belt,
Let's unbind it, for a load to thee's thy belt

Of that cup of milk, thy navel, sore athirst,
A snake with drooping head perdie's thy belt.

To encircle with adornment union's realm,
A cordon of orfeverie's thy belt.

In this city do they laud the Silver Stream, [2]
But the vaunt of all the century's thy belt

Let us add thereto the circlet of our eye,
All too narrow for thy waist maybe's thy belt

[1] The well of the chin is the dimple
[2] Gumush Suyu = the Silver Stream, is the name of a little river in the
vicinity of Constantinople

By magic hath it clomb the Crystal mount, [1]
A witch that rides the vault, ah me's thy belt.

It is even as the rainbow, Sábit, look,
A-glitter with all brilliancy's thy belt

The following from the Edhem u Humá is the dying
speech of the hero to his friend.

From the Edhem u Humá. [317]

O friend as Messiah kind, (quoth he),
Forgive me if e'er I have injured thee
In the cave of my love is delight the light,
And death unto me seemeth passing bright.
Surrendered for Love be all that is!
A thousand lives for a death like this!
Think not this is death whereto I'm doomed,
'Tis to be in the nuptial couch entombed
With many a Khizr's life I'd buy
For a Fount of Life like this to die
Good sooth, if I give my life for her,
My bones shall nourish the Humá fair [2]
If union with her I ne'er may gain,
A joy to my soul will be parting's pain
The dule of her love will suffice for me,
And in union's stead shall her mem'ry be
Of her mole doth the memory haunt my eye
Which is turned to her garden-close thereby.
The heart is the vase for her jacinth hair,
How might the lily find entrance there?
My soul with the hosts of parting drear
Doth battle, each hair on my frame's a spear
Breathed on my breast hath Love's ancient sage,
And for dole of Humá are my bones a cage.

[1] Kúh-i Billúr, "the Crystal Mount," is the name of a mountain in Central
Asia (Mt. Beloor on the maps), here it is a metaphor for the girl's hips
[2] Playing on the lady's name and alluding to the legend of the humá-bird
living upon bones

If aught with the Lord thou mayest gain,
Pray that my soul e'en now be ta'en
A disciple true of the Path I'd be,
Let me pay my debt and wander fiee
Ah¹ where is the sword⁇ I am ready now,
And my blood-stained shift will be shroud enow.

The Zafer-Náme begins as follows, the poet calling upon
his reed-pen to abandon love themes and describe the glories
of war He enumerates the favourite romances in order to
disparage them, omitting only that of Joseph and Zelíkhá,
probably because of its sacred origin.

From the Zafer-Náme. [318]

Arise, reed, thou war-steed of rhetoric's fray,
And o'er speech's field make the battle-dust play
A stoure do thou raise upon poesy's plain,
And pluck from the meadows of fancy thy strain
The tale of the rose and the lily forswear,
And bring to us tidings of sabre and spear
Enow of the musk-scented tresses, enow¹
We'd cast up and catch the lasso and the bow ¹
Enow of the locks falling loop upon loop¹
As the links of the mail are mine eyen a-hoop
Enow of the glance dealing anguish and bane¹
That tale let the sword keen of edge cleave atwain
Enow of the graces and charms of the fair¹
Let wave in its beauty that sapling, the spear
At length let the horsemen of fantasy's plain
Betrample these things in the mire of disdain
For ancient this building of dolour is grown,
'Tis ruined, there resteth not stone upon stone ²
We've heard all these stories a thousand times o'er,

¹ One of the military games or exercises of the Turks in old times used
to consist in throwing up and catching their weapons while riding at full speed
² طاش طاش اوسننه قالمسون 'Set not one stone remain upon another,'
is a proverb in Turkish as in other languages

To listen thereto is permitted no more.
Why then to the legend of Qays [1] be heart-bound
Since, thanks be to Allah, our reason is sound'
Repeat not of Leylá and Mejnún the song,
Nor throw words to madmen, let be, pass along
Or what art and part with a navvy hast thou'
Then run not with Ferhád thy head into woe,
To tell of that rock of distress and dismay
Were reminding the madman of stones, in good fay [2]
Or wherefore recount thou of Wámiq the tale?
Nor look thou for devils nor lá havla wail [3]
Beware, nor the praises of Pervíz sing thou,
So great a fire-server would burn one I trow
If the name of Shírín on thy tongue thou dost take,
The taste of thy palate thou'lt ruin, alack [4]
Then seek, O thou reed-pen, a tract unbeknown,
Disport in a land where no footstep hath gone,
Go, find thee a realm where none other hath been,
Untrodden of Ferhád, of Mejnún unseen

I regret that the nature of the two humorous poems is
such as to render it impossible to offer an example, for it
is precisely in those passages which are most characteristic
that these works are most offensive.

The light-hearted mirth and the gorgeous luxury of the
gay and brilliant days of Ahmed the Third live for us still
in the ghazels and qasídas of Nedím, of Nedím 'the Boon-

[1] Qays was the real name of Leylá's lover, who was nicknamed Mejnún
'the Possessed,' 'the madman,' on account of his passion for the lady
[2] طاش ملا دى له 'Do not remind the madman of stones,' is a proverb
which is variously applied it is often used to mean, 'do not remind one of
unpleasant things,' referring to village children sometimes throwing stones at
idiots, or it means, 'do not remind him of stones, lest he be moved to pelt
you with them' The rock alluded to in the text is the precipice of Mount
Bí-sutún over which Ferhád flung himself.
[3] Lá havla ve lá quvveta illá bi'lláh, 'There is no strength nor power save
in God!' an Arabic phrase uttered in times of danger
[4] The name Shírín meaning 'sweet'

Companion,' the third, and in some respects the greatest, of those four poets who stand fore-eminent among the legions of old time.

The materials for forming a biography are as scanty in the case of Nedím as in those of his three great companions. We know little beyond the facts that Ahmed Nedím of Constantinople was the grandson of a certain qádí-ᶜasker called Mustafá Efendi; that he was himself a member of the ᶜulemá and at one time officiated as cadi in the tribunal in the court of the mosque of Mahmúd Pasha, that he became the librarian and boon-companion of the Grand Vezír Ibráhím, and that he met his death on the occasion of the fall of his patron. This tragedy, which happened in the middle of the First Rebíᶜ of 1143 (the beginning of October 1730), occurred under the following circumstances. On the outbreak of the revolution which cost Ibráhím his life and Ahmed his throne, Nedím, who chanced to be in the Vezír's palace, hoping to escape the furious mob, got out on to the roof, and, while endeavouring to jump to the roof of an adjoining building, missed his footing, fell, and was killed, thus unwillingly bringing his career to a close on the very day that saw the break up of that gay court whose doings he had so often and so eloquently sung.

'Nedím is the greatest poet in our language,' and again, 'let whoso will be the greatest in prose, Nedím is the strongest of the Ottomans in poetry,' says Kemál Bey This is high praise, but it is not wholly undeserved, Nedím is at any rate the most original of the Ottoman poets of the Old School Boldly advancing along that road which Yahyá and his followers had but pointed out, he opened for himself a new path in literature,—one which no Persian had ever trod His ghazels and sharqís stand out from the mass of artificial work which has preceded them by the freshness of their inspiration and the joyous individuality of their note. For never was there poet who reflected more faithfully his day, the love of pleasure which was then predominant. is the keynote of all his work, the passion for beautiful things which distinguished the court of Sultan Ahmed finds its counterpart in the graceful and dainty fancies which dressed in the prettiest words in the language, abound in his ghazels, while the all-pervading love of magnificence is mirrored in his qasídas which in splendour rival those of Nef'í, and in sheer beauty leave them far behind

Joyousness of tone and daintiness alike of fancy and expression are the two great characteristics of Nedím, and in these he has no rival among the Ottoman poets. He has nothing of the passion of Fuzúlí, neither have his verses the majestic roll of Nef'í's qasídas, but for grace and lightness of touch, and for that happy faculty of evoking by a few well-chosen words the mental atmosphere of a situation, neither Fuzúlí nor Nef'í nor any other of all the vast host of Turkish singers can stand beside him.

Yet Nedím never looked upon his poetry as a serious matter, his art was to him always a plaything, but one diversion the more for his companions and himself. Ekrem Bey thinks that it may be for this reason that he never wrote a fakhriyya after the usual manner of Turkish poets; for the self-laudatory couplets that occur in some of his ghazels are evidently but an echo of the fashion of his day and have none of the earnestness of Nef'í's poems of this class.

In the díwán of this poet there is a happy absence of that oppressive sense of labouredness so conspicuous in many others, for although his style is highly artistic and his every word is chosen for its beauty and fitness, his work appears perfectly spontaneous, the quaint and pretty fancies seem to arise quite naturally and to fall of themselves into graceful and appropriate words with an ease-that-has somewhat the air of the inevitable.

Scarcely less distinguished is Nedím for the richness of his imagination than for the delicacy of his imagery and the beauty of his language, of the former gift he was himself aware, and he alludes to it with equal grace and truth in one of his poems where he speaks of his imagination as a gardener who when desired to bring a rose offers the wealth of a whole garden

One of Nedím's greatest merits lies in the fact that he consistently wrote in an idiom as close to the genius-of-the Turkish language and as far removed from that-of-the Persian as was possible under the circumstances. For this he deserves to take rank above either Fuzúlí or Nefí who preceded him or Sheykh Ghálib who came after. Each of these poets surpassed Nedím in one direction or another, but he surpassed them all in the success with which he imparted a national tone to his work. That this must have been a conscious and deliberate act, and not the result of any want of familiarity with Persian, is proved by the poems he wrote in that language which show him to have been as well versed therein as the most scholarly of his countrymen.

As Nedím writes of all manner of pretty things, he naturally often mentions those which some persons think ought never to be heard of It is this that makes Ekrem Bey declare that, though most of those maidens, his fancies, are graceful and charming as the fairies of old romance, they are yet but light o' loves, and it is this that makes Kemál Bey say of his díwán that it is like the picture of a lovely girl stript naked as when born of her mother, and that, though the grace and beauty of it may captivate the fancy of men of taste, it is an enemy to morality, and so should not be made the companion [1] of our thoughts This concluding

---

[1] Alluding to the poet's name which means the Boon Companion.

remark of Kemál may or may not be true, for it must greatly
depend upon the mental attitude of the reader; but the simile
with which he begins is certainly apt enough. Yet had Nedím
been more reticent, he would have been false alike to himself and to his age which adored all things beautiful that
ministered to pleasure, and cared for nothing else. Outspokenness of this kind was new in Ottoman lyric poetry, but
it became usual as time went on, though not every subsequent
writer shared the refinement of Nedím, from whose temperament coarseness was as far removed as prudery.

When he sings of such things and of the pleasures of wine,
and these are among the most usual of his themes, Nedím
is perfectly frank and straightforward, and means what he
says in as literal and downright a fashion as ever did Burns
or Byron. There is nothing of the mystic about him; he is
a true Turk, by no means in the clouds, but very certainly
on the earth, writing in the gladness of his heart of the
merry life around, but with a lightsomeness and grace unknown before in Turkish poetry.

If there is, remarks Ekrem Bey, anything about Nedím to
which exception might be taken, it is that he devoted his
great and unique talent entirely to such subjects and never
wrote a helpful word encouraging to high purpose or noble
endeavour, devotion to duty or love of country, which would
have been at once a thank-offering for his own brilliant gifts
and a precious heritage bequeathed to his successors. In reply
to this criticism of the Bey Efendi's which, as he himself
admits, refers only to the subject-matter of the poems and
in no wise reflects upon their style, we can only say that
Nedím was an artist and not a prophet, and held that his
mission was to please by the creation of beautiful things, and
not to teach by the administration of moral lessons sugared
for their greater palatableness with a coating of sweet words.

There is a legend that when Nedím used to present to
Ibráhím Pasha his brilliant qasídas and dainty sharqís describing those gay pavilions and lovely gardens, those dazzling
illuminations and merry parties amid which their lives were
passed, the Grand Vezír in his delight would fill the poet's
mouth with jewels. Although, as Ekrem Bey who tells it
says, this story is most probably apocryphal, it is altogether
in harmony with the spirit of the age and in keeping with
the munificence and wealth of Ibráhím In all likelihood it
is but a fanciful interpretation of the not unfamiliar figure
of speech by which it is said that the mouth of a poet who
sings so sweetly is a treasury of gems.

The modern critics are loud in their praises of Nedím. I
have already quoted the eulogistic verdict of Kemál Bey who
so greatly admired this poet (some of whose verses he maintained were worthy of a place beside the poetry of the Arabs
and of the West) that when Ebu-z-Ziyá Tevfíq Bey was
meditating the issue of an annotated anthology, he requested
to be allowed to make the selection from Nedím, promising
himself to write and sign the 'appreciation' Again in his
criticism of the Kharábát he fulminates against Ziyá Pasha
for pronouncing Nedím to be an imitator of Yahyá, reminding
the Pasha how ⁽Arif Hikmet Bey, a late Sheykh-ul-Islám and
well-known poet, whom he had himself highly but not unjustly eulogised in one of his qasídas, used constantly to
declare that there was no Ottoman-poet-except Nedím who
was wholly innocent of copying the Persians or Arabs and had
formed for himself an entirely original style. Another proof
of Kemál's admiration is furnished by his avowed selection
of Nedím as the model for his Sáqí-náme a poem which he
wrote before Hámid Bey had inaugurated the Modern School.

In his little pamphlet on the great poets of the olden time
Ekrem Bey has an eloquent chapter on Nedím. In this, to

which I have more than once referred, he does ample justice
to the brilliant talents of the poet and the admirable qualities
of his work, saying that although it is now more than a
century and a half since he passed away, those bright and
joyous poems of his are still fresh and fragrant as a posy
of sweet flowers culled this morning.

Ebu-z-Ziyá Tevfíq Bey also, in his Examples of Literature,
speaks of the poems of Nedím as being truly miracles by
reason of the beauty of imagery and grace of fancy displayed
in them, and says that his work is in a literary idiom apart,
peculiar to himself alone.

Next, Jelál Bey, youngest and latest-comer of them all,
takes up the song of praise, and in glowing language declares
this wonderful poet to have united in himself the eloquence
of Nef'í, the delicacy of Fuzúlí, and the sublimity of Sheykh
Ghálib, and maintains that were he alive to-day, he would
stand the foremost in the world of letters, and that all the
poets of modern Turkey would fain be amongst his followers.

Ziyá Pasha does not think so much of Nedím as do the
critics of the Modern School, for although he allows that he
added fresh brilliancy and lustre to the language, he charges
him with copying Yahyá and Behá'í, and asserts that he
pushed exaggeration to the borders of the ridiculous. With
regard to the last count, it is undeniable that Nedím did
occasionally transgress the bounds of sobriety and indulge
in metaphors and similes which, if judged by a modern
standard, must be pronounced absurd. But so did every
Turkish poet until very recent times. The first charge, that
of copying Yahyá and Behá'í, is denied with indignation by
Kemál and with moderation but no less firmly by Ekrem
Bey. These writers will not admit that a poet whom they
regard as unique in Ottoman literature is at all indebted to
any of his predecessors.

When critics so distinguished speak with such emphasis it must appear somewhat presumptuous for any foreigner to dispute their judgment, and it is with considerable diffidence that I venture to state my own views upon this question Nedím, it seems to me, is indeed no imitator of Yahyá or Behá'í, his tone, his language, and his style are essentially his own, they have been borrowed from no previous writer, and they have been successfully copied by no after-comer. So far I am in perfect accord with Kemál and Ekrem Beys. But unless I have altogether misread the development of Ottoman poetry, Nedím did indeed take up the struggle against Persianism and conventionality, which had been begun by Yahyá, and, by carrying the same to a triumphant issue, secure the success of that movement in the evolution of this poetry to which I have given the name of the Transition I believe that Ziyá Pasha likewise was conscious of this, and that it is to it that he alludes when he speaks of Nedím being an imitator of Yahyá. Had he used the word 'successor' in place of 'imitator,' he would, in my opinion, have accurately defined the relationship.

I look upon Nedím as the typical poet of the Transition, whatever is characteristic of that Period, or, to be more exact, of the movement which constitutes it, is present in his work. Objectiveness of view, absence of mysticism, local colour, materialism of tone, a more definite recognition of the 'eternal feminine,' as well as such external matters as the use of the sharqí-form and the employment of native words and idioms, all in short that differentiates the later poetry from the earlier will be found to distinguish this poet's díwán This is to me Nedím's first and greatest charm; he is the most truly national of the great literary poets of old. His second charm lies in the unapproached, and apparently unapproachable, beauty of his language, he has shown, as no one else, the subtle harmony of music and the exquisite delicacy in expression of which the Turkish language is capable. But, these things apart, his work is valueless save as a faithful picture of his age, the subjects which he treats are-as limited as they are trivial, and were I asked to convey in a single word the impression which his work leaves upon my mind, it would be on Daintiness that my choice would fall.

It is curious to note how Von Hammer, who devotes pages to mediocrities and nonentities whose names are now well-nigh forgotten, disposes of this great poet in a few lines, dismissing him with the extraordinary remark that neither his qasídas nor his ghazels possess anything of distinction. But the critical faculty has never been reckoned among the many endowments of this illustrious scholar.

Nedím's poetical works are all comprised in his Díwán. He has some thirty or forty qasídas, mostly to the honour and glory of his patron the Grand Vezír Ibráhím Pasha and Sultan Ahmed III, though a few of the earlier ones are in praise of the Grand Vezír ʿAlí Pasha of Chorli who fell in battle at Peterwaradin These are followed by a few short poems in mesneví form, and by a number of chronograms. The printed edition of his book contains one hundred and fourteen ghazels in Turkish and fifteen in Persian, twenty sharqís, and a few quatrains and single couplets in Turkish and Persian. In prose he made a translation of the historical work of the Munejjim Bashi, which in its own way is scarcely less meritorious than his verse. [1] That he had a high reputation as a translator is shown by the circumstance of his forming one of the committee appointed by Ibráhím Pasha to translate the great biographical work known as the ʿIqd-

[1] This is an universal history, beginning with the creation of Adam and coming down to the year 1083 (1672—3) It was written in Arabic by Ahmed Dede the Munejjim Bashi or Chief Astrologer Nedím began his translation in 1132 (1719—20) and finished it in 1142 (1729—30)

ul-Jumán or Necklet of Pearls, written in the fifteenth century by the Imám Bedr-ud-Dín el-ʿAyní Haníf-záda Ahmed, the continuer of Hájjı Khalífa's bibliographical dictionary, gives us the names of the thirty members of this committee, which included three poets besides Nedím, namely, Vehbí, Neylí and ʿAsım

It has been said of Chinese poetry that to attempt to translate it is like endeavouring to copy a miniature in chalk. The same remark might be applied with the greatest justice to Turkish poetry, and above all to the poetry of Nedím. An English poet of equal skill could indeed write English verses of equal grace, but I doubt whether even he could give an adequate rendering of Nedím and at the same time preserve all the delicate lightness of his touch and the magic music of his language I must therefore pray my readers to accept my assurance that though the following translations convey the meaning of what Nedím wrote, the lovely and cunningly wrought setting — here far the more precious thing — has almost altogether disappeared, and so to refrain from passing judgment on the poet from the renderings I am about to offer.

Ghazel [319]

But a glass or two she gave us, yet she drave our thoughts astray,
Out on yonder wine-retailing, wit-assailing paynim may!

Brighter far her breast and clearer than the bowl she holds in hand,
Ruddier her cheeks than any fragrant wine her hands convey

All aglow thy son hath promised to bestow one kiss on us,
Ay, thy daughter, master vintner, chewed that mastic yesterday [1]

[1] That is, yesterday she too promised me something nice in the same direction جـكـنـمـسـك سـاقـر رو 'to chew a piece of mastic,' is a proverbial locution meaning spontaneously to promise one something pleasant, without saying definitely what it is

Quiet nook and brimming wine-crock, dainty mate and lusty pate,
Woe is me for ye, O patience and restraiment, welaway!

O Nedím, I weet not, lives there any other like to her,
Murderess of unction, thief of piety, and foe of fay?

Ghazel. [320]

Her every curl a thousand heart-enchanting tangles bears,
And every tangle in each curl a thousand souls ensnares

A sly and roguish glance hath she, and a soft smile and sweet,
A dulcet and a graceful speech, and dear seductive airs.

Behold those locks of ambergris beneath her fez of white,
And see a wallflower sweet a vest of jasmine leaves that wears.

I may not tell the tale of her bright charms, nor mayst thou hear,
Yet naught but lack of some small troth her sweetest self impairs.

An eye she hath that knoweth many an hundred thousand tongues;
A thousand mates who understand its speech hath she for feres. [1]

My lord, thou wert with envy torn, an if thou did but know
What manner of adventure now Nedím in joyance shares

Ghazel [321]

Yea, her fair and lucent neck as white as shining camphor glows;
Yea, her eyebrows and her eyes surpass the black the sable knows.

Dazzled every eye whene'er it looks upon her beauty's ray;
Ever and anon she cometh, stands, and like a glory shows.

Sheen they say and fragrant all thy dainty body bloometh fair,
All, from head to foot, like crystal bright, and lovesome like the rose

Wherefore droops thine eye so languid, O thou wanton sweet and free?
One would deem thine eyen drunken since the Primal Banquet's close [2]

[1] That is, her eyes are more eloquent of love than a hundred thousand tongues.
[2] This phrase, an echo from the mystic poets, is here used conventionally.

O my Princess, never shall I wish for others' grief or teen,
E'en as one of sickness smitten, groans Nedím for passion's woes.

Ghazel. [322]

O my wayward fair, who thus hath reared thee sans all fear to be?
Who hath tendered thee that thus thou shamest e'en the cypress-tree?

Sweeter than all perfume, brighter than all bloom, thy dainty frame,
One would deem some rose had nursed thee in her bosom, love o' me.

Thou hast donned a rose-enwroughten rich brocade, but sore I fear
Lest the shadow of the broidered rose's thorn make thee to dree. [1]

Holding in one hand a bowl, in one a rose, thou camest, sweet,
Ah, I knew not which thereof to take, the bowl, the rose, or thee

Lo, there springs a jetting fountain from the Stream of Life, methought,
When thou lettest me that lovely lissom shape o' thine to see

While the mirror of my bosom clear was as thy frame, alas,
For that even once I clipped thee not, thou darling fair and free

Whensoe'er I ask it, saying Who hath bowed thy body so?
Theeward ever points the beaker at the feast of mirth and glee. [2]

Ghazel. [323]

Thy bosom bright hath worked the sun's pavilion dire dismay,
Thy leg diaphanous hath wrought the shaft of dawn's deray [3]

The vitals of the bud are torn with bitter pangs whene'er
Thy rose-like navel peepeth forth from neath thy shift, my may

Astound thereat, with mouth agape, e'en like the slipper, bode
The cordwainer what time he saw thy lustrous ankle ray.

[1] So delicate is thy skin that even the shadow of a thorn embroidered on
thy robe may hurt it A delicate skin is regarded as a great beauty
[2] This must refer to the shape of some vessel, or it may refer to the handle
of the decanter. 'Shiráb size báqiyor' ('the wine is looking at you') means
'Pass the bottle'
[3] The shaft or column of the dawn is the ray or beam of light that shoots
up from the sun not yet visible in the eastern horizon

Belike thy lips once more have shown how sweetest speech should flow;
For all around thee, lo, the grains of sugar [1] strew the way

Nedím, unless a silvern mirror sparkle therewithin,
What glory hath the bravest wede of gold-enwroughten say? [2]

Ghazel [324]

Love-distraught, my heart and soul are gone for naught to beauties fair;
All my patience and endurance spent on torn and shredded spare

Once I bared her lovely bosom, whereupon did calm and peace
Forth my breast take flight, but how I wist not, nay, nor why, nor where.

Paynim mole, and paynim tresses, paynim eyes, I cry ye grace;
All thy cruel beauty's kingdom is but Paynimrie, I swear.

Kisses on her neck and kisses on her bosom promised she,
Woe is me, for now the Paynim rues the troth she pledged while-ere.

Such the winsome grace wherewith she showed her locks aneath her fez,
Whatsoever wight beheld her gazed bewildered then and there.

'Sorrowing for whom,' thou askest, 'weeps Nedím so passing sore?'
Ruthless, 'tis for thee that all men weep and wail in drear despair

Ghazel. [325]

To Moorish Fez her locks and cap have wroughten mickle woe; [3]
Her bright blue eyes have forayed in Circassian lands, I trow [4]

Her dusky tresses hang across her cheek, alack, O heart,
How passing fair doth sable [5] o'er yon blush-pink satin show?

How should not roses, when they see her, rend their verdant wedes?
One glance upon that sendal green, that crimson fez bestow

[1] That is, sweet speeches or pretty verses
[2] However richly wrought, the case or bag derives its true lustre from the mirror it is designed to hold; and so the most splendid garments are vain unless they clothe some silvery-bodied beauty
[3] The typical Moor is dark, but her locks are darker, and her fez prettier than anything that the city of Fez can show
[4] The typical Circassian is blue-eyed.
[5] Sable is a favourite figure for dark hair

The flautist alway views askance the songster at the feast, [1]
Whence comes this rivalry betwixt the twain, I ne'er can know

Her curling tresses overfall her eyebrows, O Nedím,
And deck yon Ferrand Dome with Chinese pictury arow. [2]

Ghazel [326]

Her legs and hips, her chin and lips, are e'en to mine own heart,
In brief she's all, from head to foot, I ween, to mine own heart

The youthful Magian proffered me both cup and ruby lip
The Magian elder may he be' He's clean to mine own heart'

O Sphere, let not thine eye alight upon my Plenilune,
For mid the feast were mirth and cheer this e'en to mine own heart

I'm fain to urge the plea of quaffing wine and, like the cup,
To kiss the sweetest mouth of my fair quean to mine own heart

On truth, I may not quit the place where flows the wine, Nedím,
For mirth is to my mind, and joyous mien to mine own heart

Ghazel [327]

The realm of sufferance thou'st laid waste, Hulágú Khán [3] art hight, Paynim,
Have ruth' thou'st set the world aflame, art thou a burning light, Paynim?

A maiden's winsome air, thine air, a youthful gallant's tone, thy tone,
A Torment thou' I wist not, art thou youth or maiden bright, Paynim?

What meaning bears that wede of flame-hued satin o'er thy shoulders thrown?
Art thou the soul-consuming leam of grace and love-delight, Pagnim?

[1] That is, he bends his head to one side while playing
[2] The term Táq-ı muqarnes, which is the special name of the throne of Solomon, is applied to a dome that rises by stages to the centre Here the forehead represents the dome, the eyebrows are the stages or galleries, and the locks the Chinese pictures which decorated these
[3] Hulágú Khán, grandson of Chingíz Khán, was in command of the Mongol horde which, having devastated Persia with fire and sword, captured and sacked Baghdad and murdered the last 'Abbásıd Caliph, al-Musta'sım, in 656 (1258) Hence generally the name is used to denote a cruel and blood-thirsty Tyrant, as we might say 'an Attila.'

Ah what may be those secret, secret sighs, and what that rended spare?
Art thou, e'en thou, the wailing lover of some wanton wight, Paynim?

A many say to thee 'My Life,' another many say 'My Love,'
What art thou? Art thou Life, or art thou Love? declare aright, Paynim.

The flame-hued wine hath flushed thee, dear, and set thy sweetest face aglow;
Art thou become the lamp wherewith the topers' circle is dight, Paynim?

O wherefore in the burnished mirror lookest thou so oft, my fair?
Art thou likewise astound of thine own dazzling beauty's sight, Paynim?

I've heard a Paynim hath made thrall of hapless and forlore Nedím,
Art thou that foe unto the Faith, that adversaire of right, Paynim?

Ghazel. [328]

Is't the chirp of the harp, cupbearer, that hath stol'n my wits away,
Or the rose-red bowl, I marvel, that thy dainty hands convey?

Those glances so bright and keen are the prelude to all thine airs,
Are thine eye and thy viol attuned, O minstrel blithe and gay?

Can it be thy rubies bright and pure, or a precious bale
By the rieving zephyr's hand untied in the garden-way?

Thou hast drawn the veil of shame from before thy dazzling cheek;
O child of the grape, [1] wouldest filch from that roseate face the say?

Doth it hide not away, O love, in a little secret smile,
That mouth o' thine that it shows so small? by Allah, say.

How comes it thou meltest not for delight of that fresh spinel? [2]
Alack, is thy heart of stone, O ruby cup, I pray?

What limner of strange device may this be, Nedím, unless
The Erzheng pencil [3] hath taught to thy reed its own display?

---

[1] The child of the grape, the daughter of the vine, i. e wine
[2] i. e. for delight of touching her lips.
[3] Erzheng or Erteng is the name of the studio and also of the collected paintings of Máni, or Manes, whom the Persians suppose to have been a most skilful artist. The idea here is of course that the poet's fancies are as beautiful as the pictures of this renowned painter

Ghazel. [329]

A sacred rite and holy 'tis become to weep for thy dusk hair,
Our hearts' wails rise, the bells of caravans that forth to China fare [1]

Two streamlets flowing from the Fount of Life were frozen, and now form
The crystal legs of my sweet silver-bodied wanton debonair.

What time soever that we haste to loose the knot that binds our soul,
The eyebrows of yon froward Idol many a frown of anger wear

The clearness of our soul hath but increased thy beauty's proud disdain,
For gazing in that mirror, naught but thine own self thou seest there.

Alack, the flame of love hath brought my spirit scant relief, Nedím,
My sleepful fortune's flower-wrought pillow is the wound my heart doth bear

In the sharqís, four examples of which I give, the new
note is even more emphatic than in the ghazels. The theme
of the first is one which afterwards became very popular,
namely, an invitation to the beloved to join the poet in
an excursion to Saʿd-ábád [2] The song contains several allusions to the summer-palace which had recently been con-
structed there

Sharqí. [330]

Let us deal a little kindly by this heart fulfilled of woe,
　　Let us go to Saʿd-ábád, waving cypress, let us go ـ
See, the six-oared caique [3] waits us at the landing-stage below.
　　Let us go to Saʿd-ábád, waving cypress, let us go

Let us go and let us play, and the time let us redeem,
From the new-made fountain there let us drink of sweet Tesním, [4]

---

[1] China, the land of fragrance, here the scented hair.
[2] Saʿd-ábád, the Home of Felicity, is the literary name of the Sultan's
summer-palace in the valley of the Sweet Waters of Europe, in common
parlance the place is called Kághid-kháne, 'the Paper-Mill'
[3] The public caiques, plying for hire, had two or three pairs of oars
[4] Tesním, one of the rivers of Paradise, to which some fountain at Saʿd-
ábád is here compared

Let us watch the drops of life from the dragon's mouth that stream? [1]
  Let us go to Sa^cd-ábád, waving cypress, let us go.

Let us go and wander there by the lakelet's margin bright, [2]
Let us gaze upon the palace, on the fair and goodly sight,
Let us sharqís sing at times and at times ghazels recite
  'Let us go to Sa^cd-ábád, waving cypress, let us go

Get thy mother's leave, pretending 'tis for Friday's holy prayer,
And we'll filch a day, my darling, from the cruel-hearted sphere.
We shall slip through quiet streets to the landing-stage, my dear
  Let us go to Sa^cd-ábád, waving cypress, let us go

Only thou and I, my love, and a minstrel sweet of say,
Though we'll take forlorn Nedím if my dearest sayeth yea,
And forego all other feres, wanton beauty, for the day
  Let us go to Sa^cd-ábád, waving cypress, let us go.

Sharqí. [331]

Sweet a castanetist maid hath pierced my bosom sore to-day;
  Rosy-cheeked and roseate-vested, prankt with violet watered say;
Silvery-necked and sunny-visaged, fair beseen with moles a tway,
  Rosy-cheeked and roseate-vested, prankt with violet watered say

Round her head a broidered crenate turban had my lady tied,
And her attar-scented eyebrows black with surma had she dyed.
I should reckon she was only fifteen years of age this tide
  Rosy-cheeked and roseate-vested, prankt with violet watered say.

Pride of balconies [3] and glory of all clasping arms were she,
Since she parted from her nurse's charge it scarce a year can be.
O my loved one, joyance of my heart, and source of life to me.
  Rosy-cheeked and roseate-vested, prankt with violet watered say.

---

[1] An allusion to the Water of Life, the 'dragon's mouth' must refer to some ornamental fountain

[2] There is an artificial lake, or rather canal, under the windows of the palace of Sa^cd-ábád

[3] She was meet to sit in a balcony (in Turkish, a seat for a king) which would be graced by her presence.

All, her winsome ways, her airs, her smiles, her voice, beyond compare;
Beautiful her eyes, and mole-besprent her neck exceeding fair·
Silver-necked and slender-waisted, bright with ruffled golden hair, [1]
  Rosy-cheeked and roseate-vested, prankt with violet watered say.

Naught I'll say of yonder fairy-face's anguish-dealing eye,
Neither shall I speak of how Nedím for love of her doth sigh,
I may sing her ways and charms, but tell her name, that, ne'er will I.
  Rosy-cheeked and roseate-vested, prankt with violet watered say

Sharqí. [332]

Come forth afield, 'tis now the time o'er mead and plain to stray,
  O sapling of the lawn, [2] restore to ancient spring his sway
Let fall thy tresses, like the sable, round about thy cheek,
  O sapling of the lawn, restore to ancient spring his sway.

Come, Rosebud-mouth, for all thy nightingales are seeking thee,
Come to the bower, and that the rose is o'er forget shall we,
Come forth ere trod 'neath winter's foot the garden-kingdom be,
  O sapling of the lawn, restore to ancient spring his sway

Around those ruddy cheeks o' thine thy dusky locks unbind,
And let thy sable be this year with crimson camlet lined [3]
Take thou in hand the bowl, if ne'er a tulip thou canst find.
  O sapling of the lawn, restore to ancient spring his sway.

Again with many fruits and fair is earth like Paradise;
O wilt thou not vouchsafe to us thy union's fruit likewise?
A kiss bestowing secretly on each who lovelorn sighs
  O sapling of the lawn, restore to ancient spring his sway

[1] This is perhaps the first instance of a golden-haired beauty in Turkish poetry. Till now the loved one has, in accordance with Persian taste, always · been described as black-haired Such still continues to be the general rule till we reach the Modern Period when the ideal beauty is very often fair-haired.

[2] That is, the graceful beloved one; the song is an invitation to her to come into the garden, the season being autumn.

[3] Line thy sable cloak with crimson, i.e cover thy red cheeks with thy dark hair

I heard a verse, O wanton bright who mak'st the heart to beam,
I knew not well the meaning that it bore, but yet I deem
'Twas not withouten reason it was chanted by Nedím.
O sapling of the lawn, restore to ancient spring his sway

The next Sharqí is so far irregular that it has a refrain
of two lines

Sharqí [333]

O my Queen of beauties, make thee for that frame so fair that shows,
Shift of odour of the jasmine, wede of tincture of the rose.
Thou'rt a cypress, well beseem thee camlet vest that verdant glows,
Shift of odour of the jasmine, wede of tincture of the rose.
Bloom, O rosebud-mouth, O roseate-body, deck the garden-close.

O my hair-waist,[1] yonder cincture gleameth on thee fair to see,
Ay, and eke that royal kerchief graceth thee right wonderly.
Thou'rt a rosebud, sue the zephyr so that he may waft to thee
Shift of odour of the jasmine, wede of tincture of the rose
Bloom, O rosebud-mouth; O roseate-body, deck the garden-close.

Thou hast veiled thy radiant visage with thy long and fragrant hair,
Hail unto thy coyness, O thou bud of virtue's garden fair,
Thou'rt coquetry's nursling, meet it were, did they for thee prepare
Shift of odour of the jasmine, wede of tincture of the rose.
Bloom, O rosebud-mouth; O roseate-body, deck the garden-close,

She hath donned a crimson silken tunic, pictured angel gay,
Meet it were, were it but worthy of her frame of sheeny ray.
Tulip-like I saw her blossom in the garth at break of day.
Shift of odour of the jasmine, wede of tincture of the rose.
Bloom, O rosebud-mouth, O roseate-body, deck the garden-close.

The following mukhammes in praise of the Grand Vezír
Ibráhím Pasha was written on the occasion of a visit which
that functionary paid to the Lord High Admiral

---

[1] A slender waist, which is esteemed a great beauty, is often compared
by Eastern poets to a hair

Mukhammes. [334]

Fair welcome to thee, O Lord benign,
Our hearts are blithe in the grace that's thine,
For joy of thy deeds is earth a-shine,
And all of thy works alway combine
    To deck the field of the world most gay

Beloved and glorious Vezír,
In thy time doth the earth like Heaven appear
With thee is Bounty a servant dear,
And splendour watcheth thy door anear,
    Of thy threshold-dust the nurslings they

She vanquished earth by thy wisdom's word
Whom the folk to entitle Fate accord,
For thy craft and device, most noble Lord,
In the hand of the sphere are a naked sword
    And an iron bow for his arm to sway

O sapient Asaph, [1] dread of might,
To Zál the golden or Rustem wight [2]
Can ever we liken thee with right,
For while that the world thy works doth sight,
    Of them there is naught but a tale or lay

The ancient world hath found once more
Adornment gay of thy grace and glore,
This truth is known of the men of lore,
And they hint at a story of days of yore,
    'His bounty would Ja'fer beseem,' they say. [3]

---

[1] Asaph, Solomon's minister and councillor, the type of the ideal Vezír.

[2] Zál and his son Rustem, are two of the chief of the ancient Persian heroes whose exploits are recounted in the Sháh-Náma.

[3] Ja'fer el-Bermekí (or the Barmecide), the famous vezír of the caliph Hárún-ur-Reshíd, and the hero of many stories in the Arabian Nights, was especially renowned for his munificence.

The world repairs to thy favour's gate,
And earth is proud upon thee to wait.
Vezír through whom is the world elate,
Thy visit maketh this hall of state
   The envy of Heaven above, in fay.

Thy kinsman dear thou hast honoured free,
And thine advent filleth his soul with glee,
And since he hath gained this grace of thee
The star of his luck is come to be
   The bridle-fere of the sun alway. [1]

Before thy face it were meet the Sky
Lit up as a censer the sun on high,
While Jupiter, girding his skirts, stood nigh, [2]
And the shining Moon watched the curtain by,
   Whose glory it were this part to play.

While all of these do attend with cheer,
Is the hour not come when the aged Sphere
Should likewise worthy and bold appear?
And so, an he think a new world to rear,
   'Twere sure a befitting time to-day.

And smiling Venus is come again,
Her viol she into her hand hath ta'en;
And struck on Newá a passing strain,
Although from Nehávend its prelude fain
   And in Isfahán it doth fade away. [3]

May feast and assembly for aye abide,
And mirth and liesse attend thy side,
And favour and fortune and happy tide;
And each moment a thousand joys provide.
   To God be thanks, He doth this purvey.

---

[1] A bridle-fere is one who rides alongside of another, the heads of the two horses being on a level; it implies an equal in rank.

[2] As a servant ready to attend.

[3] Newá, Nehávend, and Isfahán are all names of melodies.

At length my reed from its task may rest,
This service to me did it first suggest.
From his portal stir not, or east or west,
Let it be in this world thy refuge blest.
'Tis e'en as the gate of Heaven's array

I have translated almost the whole of the next poem, including the panegyric This is quite the same as in the qasídas, but on account of the almost insuperable difficulty of finding a sufficient number of suitable riming-words for the satisfactory rendering of these, I have preferred to illustrate the style from the following mesneví The subject is a garden, called Bágh-ı Wefá, or the garden of Constancy, which had been laid out by the grand Admiral Mustafá Pasha. Nedím imagines himself giving a description of it to his beloved cupbearer.

A Description of the garden of Constancy the same being in Laudation of the Admiral Mustafa Pasha. [335]

O cupbearer, where is the bowl turkis-blue?
No time this, no time this for sloth, an thou knew!
Bespeed thee, so thou be my life, now's the tide,
Then lose not the chance, for we're mounted to ride [1]
Nor patience is left me, nor sufferance, nor might;
Have ruth, O have ruth, passing woesome my plight.
That sdeign-flushed demeanance, those blood-spilling eyne,
Those languorous fashions, that dark eye o' thine,
On such wise have wrought to inebriate me
That drunk, an it heard, e'en the wine-bowl would be
Whoe'er might behold thee nor heart-smitten bow?
A Torment, thou Tyrant, a Torment art thou!
Ah what might I say? when my eyes fell on thee
Anon passed away lore and language from me

[1] That is, our life is fleeting by

51

So let me bethink me, my mistress, I pray,
And hand thou the beaker, and list what I say.
* * * * * * * * * * * * * *
O come thou, the soul's darling wayward and free,
O come thou, remede of the sick heart, to me.
Come hither, I pray thee, thou wanton and gay,
In accord like the harp and the lute let us play.
I'll tell thee a tale full of wonder, my dear,
Do thou to this marvel attend and give ear.
I passed by a garden so beauteous to-day,
That amazed and confounded, my wits went astray.
The world it illumed with decore and adorn,
But nay, 'twas not this world, a new world was born!
Aloft and alow, upon left, upon right,
Were splendour and radiance, delice and delight.
The jasmine and jacinth and rose round me shone,
And lawn upon lawn upon lawn upon lawn.
Amaze came upon me what garth this might be,
What loved one bedecked and beprankt artfully;
Who fashioned this rose-garden, Eden's despair;
And who reaps the harvest of these meadows fair;
And what may his name be who wrought all this grace;
For whom smileth sweet this herbere's winsome face.
With thoughts like to those wandered I all around,
When lo, writ before me these verses I found:
O fair for a pleasaunce as Eden divine,
In whose dust all the virtues of Heaven combine!
May this be a lawn or a rose-garden fair,
Or a mart where the venders of sweet smiles repair?
Its air is the breath of Messiah amene,
Its sight is the theriac of drunkards, I ween.
As clear as the cock's eye [1] its bright waters glide,
Its red rose is sweet as the blush of the bride;
(That tall lissom cypress, that fair-blooming plain,
As bounteous as joyance, as wide as the main!)
The brocade of the sun o'er its lawn is dispread,
The locks of the houris do besom its stead;

[1] Cock's eye is a term for red wine.

A sun fallen earthward, its each dew-drop leams,
Its red tulip bright as the moon's halo gleams,
The spring holdeth revel so high on its plain,
To deem that the Wheel wantoned wild thou wert fain.
On all sides the roseres are rangéd arow,
With their file is arrived bloom and odour, I trow;
Like beauties embracing each other, appear
The parterre, the orchard, the lawn, the herbere,
A chip of the moon is the marge of its pond,
The spray of its fount casts the Pleiads around,
There gleams in its marble such lustre and sheen
That the sun as a taper by daylight is seen;
Its water, aloft springing, toucheth the sky,
The which like a bowl is hung o'er it on high,
Its fountain lassoeth the heart of the meet,
Its wavelet entangleth life's swift-speeding feet,
With fretwork the runnels its rose-garden tire,
Or elsewise they draw through the gauge silver wire.
O fair for a pond full of sheen and of light,
What belle hath a navel so clear, and so bright!
A Selsebîl, [1] source whence doth purity rise,
Each ripple a beam of the light of the eyes
So jubilant ringeth the laugh of the rose,
The herbs may not rest them in sleepful repose.
The rose and the tulip make merry in fere,
In attune sing the cushat and nightingale clear.
There climbs o'er the trellis the white jessamine,
Methought 'twas Canopus of Yemen did shine
Irradiate glitters the hyacinth's hair,
With the new moon belike it hath combed it so fair
In its midst doth an ornate pavilion arise,
Whose portals and roofs flash as noon to the skies.
Therein was there seated a far-famed Vezír,
A noble illustrate, a valorous Peer,
A glorious Lord, Heaven-fair of display,
A Captain victorious, of star-bright array,
A Sage, Aristotle might serve with acclaim,

[1] One of the rivers of Paradise

A glorious Chieftain, of name and of fame;
The sheen of noblesse on his brow beameth bright,
And glore and renown to his signet are plight;
The grand Admiral, Heaven-high of abode,
The namesake of him, Mustafá, sent of God. [1]
As naught in his court is the eagle of the skies, [2]
The símurgh appeareth a gnat to his eyes; [3]
At his banquet is Bounty the Minstrel-man brave,
In his palace is Favour a house-nurtured slave.
Yon garden was made by this valiant Vezír,
Like himself, on the earth without rival or peer.
They smile for his kindliness, blossom and bloom;
His virtue the season of vere doth perfume.
The hyacinth curls as his destrier's mane;
The cypress hath he for his flag-bearer ta'en.
Yon garth is a draft by his pen written fair,
The violet blooms, his sign-manual there.
His bounty of soul hath pervaded the earth,
That all of these florets and treen blossom forth.
O God, for the love of Thy Heaven on high,
Preserve Thou this garden from Autumn, I cry.
May its Lord aye abide in secure sojourning,
May his garth be for ever the home of the Spring;
May envy the heart of his foe rend in tway
As Nedím chants his praises for aye and for aye.

I give next the exordiums of three qasídas, portions of all of which are quoted with high approval by Ekrem Bey, the first as an example of figurative language, the second as a specimen of the ornate in style, and the third as a model of artistic treatment.

The first is from a poem in praise of Sultan Ahmed who had addressed a complimentary verse to Ibráhím Pasha;

[1] Mustafá, 'the Elect', is a title of the Prophet.
[2] The constellation Aquila.
[3] The símurgh like the 'Anqá is a fabulous bird of gigantic size said to inhabit Mount Elburz or Mount Qáf.'

and the poet adroitly manages to eulogize the latter also
in the course of his panegyric.

Qasída. [336]

O springtide, come, from thee's the dreamful rest that doth my life console,
My bosom-friend art thou, the hope of my sad heart fulfilled of dole
Yea, ope the rosebud's mouth, and moisten thou the lily's parchéd tongue,
Thou art mine advocate for him who fails to keep his vows in whole.
O Cypress, stand aloft amidst the garth e'en like a noble thought,
That balanced shape of thine I shall as mine own chosen verse enroll
O Winter-Season, leave the bowers, I pray, and let the roses bloom,
And sing, thou Nightingale, for thou'rt my minstrel, rebeck, and citole.
Thou'st waved on such a wise, O Juniper, that thou hast burned my heart,
For when I looked on thee, methought 'twas mine own charmer high of soul
I'm wont to say unto my love. 'My Rose is this,' 'My Rose is that:'
My darling loves thee well, O Rose, for by thy name I her extol
And thou, O heart-expanding Tulip, ne'er far from the garden be,
Hilarity through thee I gain, in sooth thou art my wine-filled bowl
How wondrous strange, the while I gaze on thee, O Brook, my life ebbs not,
'Twould seem thou art a chain which held my life that flits toward its goal
＊ ＊

The next passage is from a qasída glorifying a sea-side
palace built by the Lord High Admiral Mustafá Pasha.

Qasída. [337]

'Tis the home of grace and beauty, no mere tower to glad the spright,
E'en as Highest Heaven the garniture and gear wherewith 'tis dight
When that I beheld the novel fashion of its roofing high,
' 'Tis of earth the World Above, if such there be,' said I forthright
'Nay, nay,' quoth the soul of Plato, 'greatly hast thou erred indeed,
'Mid the universe of splendour 'tis a new world come to light '
Then said I 'It is a mansion glorious of Paradise '
Answered Rizwán : [1] 'Paradise is e'en this house, if read aright '
Yea, the world is dolour's dwelling, but the dust before this gate

[1] Rizwán is the angel gate-keeper of Paradise.

Is the one, the sole exception to that truth that meets our sight.
Shírín's Castle is its mother, and its sire is Kisrá's Dome; [1]
This their new-born child in whom all beauties of the twain unite.
Sea and mountain-land embrace it round about on either hand,
'Tis as though the sea its nurse were, and its guardian yonder height.
There the mountain careful shields its cheek what time the sun doth rise,
Here the sea displays the mirror 'fore its dazzling visage bright.
O how fair a sea-side palace! such that spring doth bloom and scent
Borrow from the beauteous rosebud mid its bowers of fair delight.
Yonder gentle heart-rejoicing wind-waft from its fragrant meads
Is the Jesus of the kingdom of the spring and garden-site. [2]
O how fair a garth of beauty, mid whose wonder-lovely shows
Were the Eightfold Bower of Heaven [3] but a lonely nook by night!
Thou hast reached the topmost summit of the peak of error wild
When, O smiling reed, thy fancy bade thee 'lonely nook' to write.
How may there be aught of lonely in that noble palace where
Dwelleth yonder glorious Asaph girt with splendour, pomp and might?
* *

The third qasída describes a palace which had been restored by one of the grandees of the capital.

Qasída. [338]

O wanderer illustrate through fancy's world of dreaming,
Hast e'er beheld a mansion that bore the springtide's seeming?
Come, if thou ne'er hast seen such; but take good heed thou err not,
Nor deem yon gilded trellis the moonbeams gently streaming.
The tiring-maid perfection's all-beautifying pencil
Hath touched the bride Adornment's eyebrows with gold beseeming.

[1] 'Shírín's Castle' (Qasr-i-Shírín), and 'Kisrá's Palace' (Aywán, or Táq-i Kisrá) are names given to two Sásánian palaces, the ruins of which are still extant near the site of Ctesiphon.

[2] That is, breathes life into the springtide and the garden.

[3] [Frequent reference has been already made to the Eight Paradises. Everything else, the Heavens, the Earths, the Planets, even the Hells, are, according to the orthodox Muslim belief, arranged in Sevens. That God should have increased the number of Paradises to Eight is regarded as symbolic of His Mercy. ED.].

Behold that heart-rejoicing fair ground of musky odour,
And view yon radiant ceiling with gold and paintings gleaming.
'Twould seem as though that nature had levelled all earth's surface,
Had lowered the hills of Tibet and raiséd China's seeming [1]
There shine amid its courtyards such sort of grace and bounty,
That there the Age's glory reposeth, all are deeming.
Quoth I, 'The pleasant-savoured glad days of joyous Jemshíd
Have hither come and tarried, thereby the past redeeming'
Think not that 'tis with gilding its radiant walls coruscate,
For over all reflected, 'tis Eden's garden beaming.
Right strange and wondrous surely that thus a view of Heaven
Should be by earthly objects disclosed to our esteeming
This side, a bed of tulips, the sown of Jemshíd's beaker,
That side, a bower of roses, the mine-possessor, leaming
* * * * * * * * * * * * *\,* * * * * * * *

Nedím did not write many rubá'ís, but such as he has
are good. The following is quite in his own manner:

Rubá'í. [339]

Thy glances, O cup-bearer, overbore me,
They darkened all the face of earth before me
   God on thee! prate not of the wine, I pray thee,
   Those drooping eyes wrought all that hath come o'er me!

In the next he appears in the unwonted guise of a satirist
and lays his finger on what had all along been the darkest
blot on the record of the 'ulemá: there is of course a *double
entendre* in the 'maiden fancy', maiden being the recognised
term for original, so that Nedím here further twits his contemporaries with their lack of originality.

Rubá'í. [340]

The learned are enamoured all of boys,
Not one remains who female love enjoys,
The most part of the poets of this age
With no new fancy — for 'twere virgin-toys.

[1] Tibet referring to the musk-scented ground, China to the painted ceiling.

The following pretty little thing is very characteristic of the poet.

Rubá'í. [341]

O dancer, are these dainty poses part and parcel of thy game?
Content art thou to bear alone of all thy lover's sins the blame?
 'Tis e'en as on the nights o' fast, I've ne'er enow on nights wi' thee; [1]
Dost hide the radiant dawn within thy bosom, O thou silver-frame?

[1] During the night throughout the month of Ramazán they eat and drink (and sometimes make merry) to compensate for the rigorous fast which prevails all day from the breaking of dawn.

CHAPTER II.

The Third Persian School, or School of Sáʾib
and Nábí. Sámí. Ráshid. Hámí Rahmí.
ʿAsim. Independent Persianists: Nahífí.
Neylí. Sheykh Rizá.

In this chapter we shall consider the more noteworthy
members of the Third Persianist School, that group of poets
who look to Nábí as their leader and through him to the
Persian Sáʾib as their master, as well as some of the Independent Persianists, leaving Rághib Pasha, the last and
greatest of the former, who occupies an important position
in the history of Ottoman poetry, for fuller consideration
at the end of the chapter.

Mustafa Sámí Bey, famous alike as historian and poet,
was the son of one ʿOsmán Efendi who held the position
of Arpa Emíni or Intendant of the Barley, as the comptroller of the supplies of barley for Constantinople and the
Sultan's stables used to be called in olden times. Sámí, who
entered the civil service and became a Clerk of the Divan,
was during the reign of Ahmed's successor, Mahmúd I,
appointed Wáqiʿa-nevís or Imperial Annalist, and as such
wrote the chronicles of the Empire from 1143 (173$\frac{0}{1}$) till
1146 (173$\frac{3}{4}$) in which year he died.

Sámí is one of the most brilliant, and certainly the most artistic, of the followers of Nábí. His most individual work is characterised by an absence of spontaneity which he makes no attempt to conceal, by an undisguised laboriousness eloquent of the midnight oil. None the less is his work highly successful; he contrived to get on very well, in spite of the dictum anent the supereminent virtue that lies in the concealment of art, for it is precisely through the artistic quality of his work that his success is achieved. Well-weighed thoughts and carefully-elaborated imagery, conveyed in fastidiously selected language, distinguish his most important writings, which thus rather resemble good Classic work than productions of the Transition. Sámí indeed is quite out of touch with the current Romanticism; he deals with abstractions in preference to actualities, there is but little local colour in his verses, and his vocabulary and idiom are remarkable for the absence of Turkicisms. In like manner his themes, except in the chronograms which perforce deal with current events, are almost always philosophic or at least meditative, the musings of a thoughtful reflective mind; he rarely condescends to the mundane and at times risky subjects which interest so many of his contemporaries, and knows nothing of the sprightly grace of Nedím or of the bolder humour of Sábit. [1]

Although Sámí's poetry is thus lacking in the picturesqueness and vivacity characteristic of his period, there is much in his díwán which merits our attention; for this poet

[1] And yet among the mufreds or independent couplets at the end of Sámí's díwán occurs the following verse which, though hardly translatable, shows that the poet did not remain altogether uninfluenced by the realism and unconventionality of the Transition.

بنـد شلوارين چوزوب اوپسم كس نرمى نوله

بارمـه شفعانوسى باغ وصلتك غـايـت لـذيـذ

is ever careful to give us of his best, and many of the
things he says are well worth the saying, and are moreover
said in the most eloquent and expressive language which
an accomplished scholar could command.

Sámí is not an easy writer, his thoughts are often profound, his language is often painfully learned, and his style
is not unfrequently elliptical and recondite, but I do not
agree with Ziyá Pasha in finding confusion the rule in his
verses or in thinking that his words and expressions are ill
assorted. When the Pasha goes on to say that he sometimes
writes things in a manner so distorted that the Primal Intelligence itself would fail to comprehend them, I presume
that he is referring to certain passages where the ellipses
are so violent as to render the precise meaning of the verse
undeterminable The Pasha's remarks concerning Sámí are,
on the whole, rather unfortunate, for he declares him to
have versified in the same style as Nazím, and Nazím, as
we have already learned, [1] wrote in as simple and unpe-
dantic a fashion as was possible under the conditions of the
Old School, while Sámí, as we have just seen, chose a manner
which was exactly the reverse.

It is true that our author was so far influenced by the
Romanticist spirit of his time as to write a few pieces in
the playful tone which Nedím was making fashionable, but
although he has one or two extraordinarily happy verses
of the kind, it is more than doubtful whether he possessed
the lightness of touch requisite for sustained success in this
direction.

Ziyá Pasha again, while admitting that Sámí is now and
then a brilliant writer, declares him to be so only when
he throws aside his laborious artificiality; but we have the

[1] [See vol III, pp 319—323. ED.].

authority of Kemál Bey for saying that it is just in his most artificial poems that the author's mastership is most clearly shown. I have already referred to the Pasha's charge against Sámí and Sábit of introducing certain prosodial errors. [1]

Fatín Efendi, the author of the latest Tezkere, that which comprises the poets who flourished from about 1700 to about 1850, though he rarely commits himself to anything in the way of criticism beyond a conventional compliment or two, departs from his usual reticence to laud the genius of Sámí, and to defend him against the attacks of certain poetasters of the day who, it seems, were seeking to belittle him. This biographer, who declares that Sámí's eloquent díwán will immortalise his name on the record of the world, pronounces him to be the greatest of the Ottomans in the ghazel, even as Nef'í is the greatest in the qasída — a manifest and absurd exaggeration. Fatín adds that our poet was an elegant calligraphist.

Jelál Bey, too, has a good word for Sámí whose philosophic thoughts and masterly style, he says, entitle him to be ranked amongst poets of distinction.

Sámí's poetical works are all included in his Díwán, which comprises a number of qasídas dedicated to Sultan Ahmed and his vezírs, a Nazíra (praised by Kemál Bey) to Rúhí's famous Terkíb-bend, a few pieces in mesneví, a series of chronograms on events of the day, a collection of ghazels, a section of quatrains, and a large number of mufreds or unrelated couplets.

In the following ghazel, which is a good example of the moralising tone that characterises much of Sámí's work, the influence of Nábí is very apparent; in the closing couplet, as elsewhere in his díwán, the veneration of the writer for his master finds expression.

[1] [See p. 19 *supra*. ED.].

Ghazel [342]

Within this mart so soon to close [1] what boots it after wealth to strain?
The borrowed [2] gear the broker [3] bears can never yield contentment's gain

The Shewwál [4] shout of 'Drink full deep!' from those who've broke the
[vows they plight
Hath rent the robe of pietism's ear, on bubble wise, atwain

The dullard souls of zealotry may hope to soar on wings of works
Doth ever van of barndoor-fowl unto the grace of flight attain?

Should ocean's head uplifted be to smite the clouds, as rain 'twould fall
Abasement ever follows hard in o'er-propitious Fortune's train

Belike my eyelash-thorn doth wound thy fair and tender foot, my sweet,
Forgive, if not myself, that trod of thee, O Rosebud fresh and fain

E'en though he silent bide, the fool's unseemly ways may ne'er be borne,
The dumb man's signs and gestures naught beyond his foolish words explain.

The sorting good and bad is evil's self to the fault-finding crew
This care it is that pierceth all the body of the sieve with pain

The patient bearing of distress doth purchase still to live at peace
According to his burden's weight increaseth aye the porter's gain.

May any follow in the master Nábi's footsteps, O Sámí?
A scrawl untimely is the verse that childhood's pen to write is fain.

This next ghazel is in a somewhat similar strain.

Ghazel. [343]

Surge in waves my streaming tears, e'en like a rushing flood once mo,
Like the volume of an hundred Niles their smallest drop would show.

---

[1] The world.
[2] All earthly possessions are 'borrowed', being enjoyed only for a season.
[3] The broker who carries about goods for sale in the bazaars
[4] Shewwál, the tenth month of the lunar year, which, coming immediately
after Ramazán, the month of fast, may be supposed to be a season of more
than usual licence. It is ushered in by the Shekker Bayrámí, or „Feast of
Sweetmeats", which may be described as the Muhammedan Easter.

Yea, the raging of the tearful flood would whelm the spirit's barque,
Did the mem'ry of her visage, like the fanal, radiance throw.

In the eyes of fools the splendid subtleties my pen indites
Are as radiance to the sightless, or the blinding-needle's glow. [1]

One the beggar's bowl would be with the tiara of the king
Were its diadem-like figure but reversed, full well I know. [2]

Though his origin be rushen, he will mount the shoulder's throne
Like the wattle-basket, who doth bread of charity bestow. [3]

'Yonder hair-waist have I clasped', bragging did the rival say.
Nay, he lieth, and as feeble as the hair his vauntings show.

O thou prideful wight, behold the dolour wroughten Nimrod's head
By the gnat's sting which was elephantine trunk to work him woe. [4]

[1] Sámí here refers to the obscurity of some of his lines which are, he says, to the ignorant or unlearned what brilliancy is to the blind man, that is an unknown and therefore hateful and hostile thing like the needle which of old was used for blinding certain prisoners or criminals. The point of the second line is made by a hint at the proverb اعـايـه الـوائـدن يحث اولـلـمـاز "one does not discuss colours with the blind," that is, one ought not to speak to a man of things that are beyond his comprehension. So the brilliancy and lustre of Sámí's verses are to the unlearned as colours are to the blind, i. e. unperceived and therefore incomprehensible. The unlearned will consequently hate them, for the well-known Arabic proverb says الـمـرء عـدوّ مـا جـهـل "man is the enemy of that he knoweth not," and hating them, will regard them as hostile to himself, even as the blinding-needle is to the sight.

[2] There is here a reference to the shape of the head-dress, modelled after the tiara of the ancient Kings of Persia, which was introduced by Selím I, and worn with certain modifications as the state-turban by all the Sultans down to the middle of the eighteenth century.

The basket in which bread is carried for distribution to the poor, though it be made but of coarse rushes, is elevated to a post of honour on the bearer's shoulder, is borne 'shoulder-high;' so will a charitable man be honoured, however mean his origin. The figure of the basket is an example of husn-i ta'líl.

[4] Referring to the following legend: Nimrod, by his cruel persecution of Abraham, and arrogant insolence in building the Tower of Babel to wage war with God, drew upon himself the Divine wrath. To punish his pride, God chose the meanest of His creatures, the gnat, as the instrument of His vengeance. A vast army of these insects was sent against the tyrant's men, whom they compelled to flee, for they consumed their flesh and ate the eyes

Through the blooming flowers of fancy, Sámí, it is thine intent
Paradise itself to image in this eightfold rime, I trow. [1]

The ghazel which follows is typical of that want of spontaneity successfully combined with highly artistic execution
which I have spoken of as being a feature of this poet's
work; Jelál Bey says that no one has yet been able to
write a successful nazíra to it.

Ghazel. [344]

Beauty's feast adorn beyond compare yon curl and mole and cheek,
Fume, and ambergris, and censer's flare, — yon curl and mole and cheek.

O'er thy crystal neck they show them, as 'twere in a glass empight
Hyacinth, wall-flower, and rosebud rare, yon curl and mole and cheek.

Ne'er may vanish scar of sorrow or the woe that clouds the soul,
For within the heart are graven e'er yon curl and mole and cheek

Like the night-adorning taper and the moth of scorchéd wing,
Ever warmest friends together fare yon curl and mole and cheek [3]

Rue besprinkled on the sigh's flame is the heart's core whensoe'er
'Fore the mind arise in beauty fair yon curl and mole and cheek [4]

out of their heads Nimrod himself fled to a thick-walled tower, but a gnat
entered with him, and worked its way through his nostril into his brain
which it commenced to devour. The pain it caused was so great that Nimrod
could find no relief save by dashing his head against the wall, or by getting
some one to strike his forehead with a hammer But the gnat grew continually
larger till on the fortieth day Nimrod's head burst open, and the insect, which
had attained the size of a pigeon, flew out

[1] Alluding to the Eight gardens or Mansions of Paradise, and the eight
couplets contained in this ghazel.

[2] The curl = the fume; the mole = the ambergris, the cheek = the bright
censer· similarly in several of the verses

[3] Here again the taper corresponds to the cheek, the curl and mole to the moth
Moth and Taper, as we have already seen, are constantly associated

[4] Sipend, or rue, is a black seed, burned to counteract the effects of the
evil eye. Here the suweyda, or black core of the lover's heart, is compared
to the rue, which he burns in his burning sighs to protect the beauty of
his beloved from the evil eye

By the gin and grain of fascination spread in beauty's garth
Fain are they this bird, the heart, to snare, — yon curl and mole and cheek.

Yearning's ardour still will banish sleep from out the eye the while
Deck the visage of that beauty rare yon curl and mole and cheek.

Sámí, lo how they have doubled all the charmer, Verse's, grace,
Since in my refrain did I declare yon curl and mole and cheek.

This little fragment is in Sámí's lighter vein.

Verses. [345]

Deem not that the heart's desire is reached through the Kevser-fountain's praise;[1]
O preacher, the tale of the mouth bekissed it is that delights always.

Whenever that I of tobacco drink,[2] bemusing her rubies red,
The nárgíl's[3] a flask of wine, the bowl is a jacinth before my gaze.

From this learn thou of the virtue rare that e'en in its dust resides,
Stamboul he greets before Mekka's shrine who in Adrianople prays.[4]

I give in conclusion the first stanza of the Terkíb-Bend
which Sámí wrote as a nazíra to Rúhí's famous poem in
the same form.

Terkíb-Bend. [346]

Deem not we're Súfí-like,[5] our hands the rosary enshrine,
We tell the jewel-beads of yonder Primal Pact divine.[6]

[1] The Paradisal stream so often mentioned.
[2] The Turks speak of 'drinking' tobacco where we should now say 'smoking;' but terms such as 'to drink tobacco' and 'tobacco-drinker' were in constant use in England during the first half of the seventeenth century.
[3] The nárgíl is the cocoanut-shaped vessel that contains the water in the Persian pipe known in England as a hookah or hubble-bubble. The bowl is the receptacle for the tobacco, the smoke arising from which is here fancied as a hyacinth.
[4] As Constantinople lies to the south of Adrianople, and between that city and Mekka, a worshipper in Adrianople bowing towards the Ka'ba, would be bowing at the same time towards Stamboul, which being the nearer is here supposed to receive the salutation first.
[5] The 'Súfí' here replaces the 'zealot' as the type of pietism.
[6] The Pact of E-lest, see Vol. I, pp. 22—23.

Ay, in the faces of the hypociites we fling the dregs,
We're drunken with the brimming, beaker of Love's heady wine
The stibium, shade-like, for the solar eye in sooth are we,   1
For that beneath their feet who deal reproach we're dust supine 1
Equal we bow us low in Ka'ba and in idol-house,
For God it is we worship still within the spirit's shrine
What though the self-beholding zealot know not of our worth 3
Yon mirror we which broken is in Ethiop's hand malign 2
Wildered we wander since our passing from our far-off source,
And like the desert-stream no place of rest may we divine
We've lost the track upon the way of Love's bewilderment
In yonder waste we traverse hand in hand with Khizr digne
    Within the tavern of God's love the beaker-holders we,
    The beggars mad who strew the dregs on the Sphere's crown we be

Muhammed Ráshid was, like Sámí, both an historian and
a poet, but unlike his contemporary, he has acquired a
greater fame through his annals than through his verses,
so that he is known in Ottoman literature as Ráshid-i Mu'-
errikh or Ráshid the Historian. Born at Melatiya [3] in the
province of Kharput to a molla named Mustafá Efendi,
Ráshid in due time adopted his father's profession, and
entered the ranks of the 'ulemá ' In 1134 (1721—2) he was
appointed Molla of Aleppo, and some seven years after-

---

[1] Because we are dust beneath the feet of (i e are humble before) the
pietists who reproach us, we are exalted to become as it were collyrium for
the eye of the sun, the type of splendour The black shadow which is inse-
parable from the bright sunlight is compared to the black collyrium which
is used to adorn the bright eye
[2] There may here be an allusion to some story, but no doubt the meaning
of the verse is something like this the negro, on looking at himself in the
mirror, is so enraged at its showing him to be black and ugly that in his
fury and resentment he smashes it, heedless alike of its innocence and of its
real worth in showing a true reflection Similarly, the zealot who imagines
himself to be a pious man, on looking at us sees by comparison how far
such is from being really the case, it is then but natural that he too, in
his envy and disappointment, should wish to injure us and break our heart
[3] The Melitene of ancient times.

wards was sent on a diplomatic mission to Persia. On his return he was promoted to the rank of Judge in Constantinople, and after a period of banishment which he passed in Brusa, he was recalled and raised to the Anatolian Qadi-ʿAskership in 1147 (1734—5), in which same year he died.

Ráshid held the office of Vaqʿa-Nevís or Imperial Annalist for many years, and his history, in two large volumes, though written in a rather laboured style, is highly esteemed and is our best authority for the greater part of Ahmed the Third's reign. [1]

In his poetry Ráshid is, like Sámí, a disciple of Nábí, and moralises in the sententious fashion of his school from the beginning to the end of a complete Díwán.

The following is the best-known, and probably also the best, of his ghazels.

Ghazel. [347]

Ne'er will skill or talent cause the braggart crew [2] respect to meet;
Robe of gold makes none with lowly reverence the crier greet. [3]

The abasing of the cultured do not thou for honour deem;
Though upon the ground the sunbeams lie, they're trod not under feet. [4]

Since 'tis word of eld, it is the shaft of penetration's bow;
Like the elif of bent figure, ne'er is it a dál, I weet. [5]

---

[1] Ráshid's History contains the annals of the Empire from 1071 (1660—1) to 1134 (1721—2).

[2] Literally, they who sell themselves, i. e. the ostentatious and conceited.

[3] The crier in the bazaar may bear about (for sale) a robe of gold brocade such as is worn by the great, but no one bows before him in consequence.

[4] As Jelál Bey points out, there is probably here an echo of Fuzúlí's couplet :

سعـادت ازلـی قـابـل زوال اولمــاز   ضيا بر أوستنه دوشمكله پايمال اولماز

'The eternal felicity is incapable of declination;
By falling on the ground, light is not trodden under foot.'

[5] In this couplet the advice of old age is first compared to a penetrating arrow; then the poet suggests that even as the upright letter elif, ا, though sometimes written in a curved or bent form, as in ﻻ, nevertheless always remains an elif, and never degenerates into the crooked letter dál, د, so wise men though bent with age, do not lose their essential rectitude.

68

If the meaning of the sentence be not pure as virgin gold,
Ne'er is it refined in crucible of phrase or fair conceit

Ráshid, where amiss the vow abstemious of the month of fast,
Since it never doth the circling of the Shevvál bowl defeat? [1]

The next poet to claim our attention is that Mustafá
Efendi known in Ottoman literature as Antákiyali Muníf
or Muníf of Antioch. Arriving at Scutari in 1130 (1717—8),
this poet, who then wrote under the pen-name of Hezárí
which he very soon afterwards abandoned in favour of Muníf, made the acquaintance of Ráshid Efendi, the famous
historian and poet whom we have just been discussing and
was fortunate enough at once to win his good graces and
be received as a guest in his villa on the Bosphorus. Muníf
knew how to retain the favour of his patron and in 1141
(1728—9), when the latter was sent to Persia to treat with
Eshref Khan the Afghan, he accompanied him among the
members of his suite. [2]

On his return to Constantinople, Muníf found another good
friend in the influential Defterdár or Finance Minister 'Átif
Efendi By the help of this new protector he was enrolled
among the Clerks of the Dívan, and was quickly promoted
till he reached the post of Máliyya Tezkirejisi, an important
position in the office of the Ministry of Finance But in

[1] Shevvál, the month succeeding the fast of Ramazan, is naturally, like
Easter after Lent, a time of social festivity and relaxation See p 62 n 4 *supra*
[2] This playful couplet embodying one of Muníf's Persian experiences is
well-known,

بر رمان رومده دریاکش ایدك ای ساقی
سمدی ایرانده ساعت الدرر حای ایله بر

'Once upon a time in Turkey we used to drink oceans, O cupbearer,
'Now in Persia we content ourselves with a chay (brooklet, cup of tea)
The point lies in the double signification of the Turkish word 'chay,' which
means at once 'brooklet' and 'tea' or 'cup of tea' The allusion is of course
to the Persian custom of drinking tea

1156 (1743—4) ᶜAtif Efendi died; and the loss of his kind friend so preyed upon the affectionate heart of the poet that he fell into a profound melancholy and resigned his office which had now grown distasteful. Brooding in retirement over his sorrow soon told upon his health, and within a couple of mouths of ᶜAtif's death he followed that beloved patron to the grave. Muníf lies in the Scutari cemetery beside the road by the Sea that leads to Hayder Pasha.

Muníf is described as having had, in addition to his accomplishments as a poet, the charms of a gentle and modest nature. That he must have been a man of amiable character is proved by the way in which he won and retained the friendship and esteem of Ráshid and ᶜAtif, while the grief that overwhelmed him when the latter passed away, a grief that could find no comforter but death, is evidence enough of a tender, loving heart.

As a poet Muníf, while a loyal follower of Nábí, does not tread quite so closely in the master's footsteps as do most of his fellow-disciples. In his qasídas Ziyá Pasha pronounces him to have surpassed Nábí himself, a judgment confirmed by Professor Nájí. Two of these qasídas are singled out by the critics as being of special merit, and superior to all those of Nábí alike in dignity and lucidity. Indeed the Professor says that had Muníf lived to the same age as his master, there is little doubt that his superiority would have been proved elsewhere. As it is, Muníf is not a poet of even the second rank, but he stands well in front of the mediocre.

One of the qasídas eulogised by Ziyá Pasha and Professor Nájí begins as follows: it is a visionary picture of the interconnection of all things from the hour when God spake the creative word.

Qasída [348]

When the reed-pen of the edict 'Be' the sum of all did write, [1]
Bounden by the laws of Being were all things soe'er forthright,
Over yonder draught, the patent of Nonentity to rule,
Was there drawn the line of cancel by the pen of Heavenly might
Borne away was that thick blackness of the night of cecity,
Every darkling nook and cranny spread a spacious plain in sight
He, the Everlasting Master, decked the veil of things beheld,
One by one all kinds of forms and figures shone there wonder-bright
Broken though appears the sequence of the pictures of things seen,
Yet their true selves, hidden inward, each to other joined, unite.
Through the pencil of yon Manes, Power Divine, earth's every page
Straight became like leaves of that fair volume Engelyún that hight [2]
One of hue appear to them who see with vision clear and keen
All these shows so strange and wondrous with chameleon tints bedight

This ghazel was written by Muníf after the death of ʿÁtif
Efendi.

Ghazel [349]

But rust upon the mirror-heart's the solar ray withouten thee,
A burden for the spirit's back the moonbeam's say withouten thee.

What though its circling billows form an anklet round the ʿArsh's leg [3]
An ocean is the Sphere through tears of my dismay withouten thee

No wonder if they silent be who look upon the words I write,
The reed I hold is speech's surme-style to-day withouten thee [4]

It ne'er sets foot beyond the circle of the pupil's ring, in sooth
Mine eyen's sight is like the compass-circuit aye withouten thee [5]

[1] God's fiat to creation, in itself involving all that has been, is, and shall be.
[2] Engelyún is another name for the Erteng or collection or pictures painted by Mání (Manes) the ancient Persian heresiarch and reputed artist
[3] The ʿArsh or Throne of God in the Empyrean See vol I, pp 35—36, etc.
[4] Writing is here compared to surma, both being black and both assisting the vision (bodily or spiritual), while the reed-pen is compared to the style with which it is applied There is also an allusion to a popular belief that if one eats surma, one becomes dumb
[5] i e without thee my vision is limited to the circle of the pupil of my

Though every mote within the world a mirror of delight became,
Would each myself to me as rival loathed display withouten thee.

The cord of Unity and eke the lambent flaming of its lamp
Within my spirit's shrine doth paynim cord portray withouten thee. [1]

With flambeau-lights the sun must pass, if e'er it pass, through Muníf's soul,
So dark and narrow there is grown the bitter way withouten thee.

Few particulars are forthcoming concerning the life of
Hámí Efendi who is usually called Hámí of Ámid, from his
native city of Ámid or Diyárbekr. He is said to have been
for a time Divan-secretary to certain vezírs, and as in some
of his poems he refers to what he saw in Constantinople,
he must have visited the capital, if he did not reside there.
He died, however, in 1160 (1747—8) in his native city, to
which, and to places in the neighbourhood of which, he at
times refers in his Díwán.

Hámí's poetry, which is marked by the usual characteristics
of the last Persianist school, has but little individuality.
Ziyá Pasha couples this poet with Rúhí of Baghdad who
died a century before and with whom he has nothing in
common, apparently for no better reason than that they
were both born in the Eastern provinces. Hámí has a riming letter or petition which Kemál Bey looks upon as the
best thing he did. His ghazels are often unusually long, and
not infrequently he opens them with two matla's or riming-

eye, round which it revolves like the moving leg of a pair of compasses; in
other words, now that thou art gone, I look at nothing and am interested
in nothing.

[1] Allusion is here made to a very favourite symbol whereby the mystics
illustrate the illusory nature of plurality, viz. the apparent circle of fire formed by a revolving spark. The cord with ignited end so whirled round is
the "Cord of Unity" in this verse, while the "paynim cord" is the zunnár,
or sacred zone, of the Magians and Hindús. Here the poet wishes only to
say that without his friend the true and the false, the real and the apparent,
appear equally indifferent.

couplets, an irregularity which was occasionally affected about this time

The following is the best-known of his ghazels, the signet referred to throughout is the seal-ring engraved with the owner's name, the impression of which used to replace the signature in the East

Ghazel [350]

Furrowed still the heart by dolorous dismay on signet wise, [1]
Oh that I might ever hold the beaker gay on signet wise! [2]

An thou seek to print thy name on earth for aye on signet wise,
Show thee resolute within thy stead to stay on signet wise [3]

Like the beazle to the ring, completing its adornment fair,
On the saddle yonder silver-frame doth ray on signet wise.

Whoso seeketh yonder stony-hearted Idol to embrace,
Needs must he a snare of gold and silver lay on signet wise

All the graver's cruel harrowing he still must patient thole
Who is fain to win him gold and silver prey on signet wise.

Ne'er did king of name and fame withouten rending of the breast [5]
Mount the eager-longed-for golden throne of sway on signet wise.

White would come forth thy device, and black would be thy face's hue;
Do not then to all thy secret thoughts bewray on signet wise [6]

---

[1] As the seal is cut into by the letters forming the inscription, so is the heart cut into by grief.

[2] i. e. would that I might make the beaker my signet, be always merry

[3] As the stone is firmly fixed in the ring

[4] The gold or silver of the ring holds captive the stone

[5] i. e. without trouble, the stone's breast is rent or cut when engraved

[6] نوشی ساصه جعدی 'Its (his) device has come out white,' is a proverb meaning that a person's secret failings or vices have come to light, the figure is derived from the impression of a seal, where the engraved inscription, which is difficult to decipher when one looks only at the stone, comes out clear and white against the black background formed by the ink Blackness of face, of course, typifies disgrace

Like a stoneless ring is he who strains not to his bosom fast
One with ruby lips and almond eyes in fay on signet wise.

Be not barren like to stoneless ring or like to stone engraved,
But to all the folk thy favours boon convey on signet wise.

Take it back, Hámí, our gain; 'tis nought but blackness of the face;
In our fancy had we won to fame the way on signet wise. [1]

Another member of this group of poets is Rahmí Efendi, the Qirímí Rahmí or Crimean Rahmí of the Turkish writers, so styled from his having been born in the Crimea, which country was still an independent Tartar Khanate under the nominal suzerainty of the Ottoman Sultan. Rahmí, who had devoted his life to study, made his way in the course of time to Constantinople where he was appointed to the secretaryship of the Bullet Magazine in the Imperial Arsenal. In 1160 (1747) he accompanied Hajji Ahmed Pasha, in the capacity of chief secretary, on his mission to Persia, of which journey he has left a record in an itinerary of the route from Scutari to Hamadán. Rahmí died of the plague in Constantinople in the year 1164 (1750—1).

These four lines are probably the best thing he has written:

Rubá'í. [351]

Soon as the star of morn appears the night is put to flight,
And when the rout is o'er, the sun of triumph beameth bright.
The nights are, all of them, with joyance and with dolour big;
Ere day is born what may not issue forth the womb of night! [2]

[1] In this couplet the poet fancies himself to have made his name, but finding such glory vain, will have none of it.
[2] There is here an allusion to a famous Arabic proverb, الليلة حبلى, 'night is pregnant,' i. e. we know not what the morrow may bring forth. Sábit quotes it in one of his ghazels where he says:

دلداری بو شب غائله جامه دوشوردك
الليلة حبلى ديو اخشامه دوشوردك

Ghazel. [352]

When the wildered heart reclineth prostrate in the cell of woe
Though the hour of death should come, 'twould find it not, it lies so low

O'er the heart's expanse there lieth vast an ocean, Love yclept,
Such that should it surge, its billows would the forms of all things show.

Ope the inward eye and go and gaze upon non-being's waste,
Dust is many an Alexander, many a Dárá lies below.

Though the king of earth should come, no foot aneath the skirt would draw
Rahmi, so unfearful lies he self-sufficing here, I trow

One of the best of the poets who form the present group
is the Sheykh-ul-Islám Isma'íl 'Asim Efendi. This legist,
who was known as Chelebi-záde 'Asim, was born in Constantinople, and was the son of the Re'ís Efendi, Chelebi
Mehemmed. He began his professional career as mulázim
in 1100 (1688—9), becoming muderris in 1120 (1708—9)
Fifteen years later he was appointed Imperial Annalist in

'To-night we have persuaded the loved one to the excitement of the bowl,
'Saying, 'night is pregnant,' we have persuaded her (to come) to our even-
[ing (party)'
Here the second line means I have persuaded her to join me in my evening
carouse, saying 'whatever may happen on the morrow, let us enjoy ourselves
to-night ' Sometimes the proverb appears in the Turkish form of كيجهلر كبدر.
Wásif Bey, a distinguished poet of the early nineteenth century has this couplet

اسدر السبنته تـوڭـد ولـد امـمـمـدك
واصعا صرب مثلدر كمكهلر حاملدر

'Of a certainty the child, thy hope, will be born;
'O Wásif, the proverb says 'the nights are pregnant '
[The same proverb is very well known in Persian, and runs شب آبسمى
است، فردا چه زايد, "The night is pregnant what will To-morrow bring
forth?" From a passage in the *Yatimatu'd-Dahr* (Vol IV, p. 23 of the
Damascus edition), I am inclined to think that it passed into Arabic from
Persian ED]

succession to Ráshid. [1] He was subsequently Molla of Larissa, Brusa, and Medína, successively. In 1160 (1747) he
was promoted to the Judgeship of Constantinople, and ten
years afterwards to the Qadi-ʿaskerate first of Anatolia, then
of Rumelia. Towards the close of 1172 (1759) he reached
the goal of the Ottoman legist's ambition, the seat of the
Sheykh-ul-Islám; but he held this lofty post for eight months
only, as he died over ninety years of age in the Latter
Jemází of 1173 (1760).

Much of 'Asim's poetry was written during the reign of
Ahmed III, the period when the brilliant genius of Nedím
was determining the issue of the struggle between Romanticism and Persianist tradition; and as Ekrem Bey, who
devotes a few pages to him, points out, the influence of his
illustrious contemporary is from time to time perceptible in
his work. But the lightness of touch and delicacy of fancy
essential to success in that direction are absent here, and
'Asim seems to have felt that Romanticism was not for
him. He therefore turned or reverted to that style which
was more in harmony alike with his temperament and his
education, and as a poet of the Third Persianist School
succeeded in winning for himself a position of considerable
eminence. If his poetry is, in common with that of most
of the followers of Nábí, inspired by no very lofty sentiments or high ideals of beauty, it is at least lucid and
straightforward, and comparatively free from trivial or far-
fetched conceits. Ekrem Bey, who speaks of 'Asim's philosophic views and vigour of character, declares that this poet
is more correct in his use of language than most of his
contemporaries, and maintains that Ziyá Pasha is wrong in

[1] 'Asim's work, which is entitled Tárikh-i Chelebi-záde, deals with the
history of the Empire from 1135 (1722) to 1141 (1728).

altering the number of syllables in words in order to force them into compliance with prosodial requirements. Like the other members of his school, 'Asim displays great partiality towards the irsál-i mesel, that rhetorical trick which we have already described as consisting in the citation of a proverb or brief allegory in one line of a couplet and the application of it in the other.

The whole of 'Asim's poetical work is comprised in his Díwán, from which the following pieces have been translated.

Ghazel. [353]

Nor earth nor sky would bear the burden of Love's heart-tormenting pain,
But though the world itself would bear not what I bear, I'll ne'er complain. [1]

The spring is come, why suffer still the topers in this lovesome tide?
'Tis they alone whose heads are light who dare no heavy beaker drain. [2]

Distraction cometh from the cares of ordering our case, elsewise
He suffers not the dread of loss who giveth up the hope of gain

From him of crooked ways he much endures whose walk on earth is straight,
The bow doth bear not in this archer-court the dole that bears the plane [3]

[1] In the Koran (XXXIII, 72) we read 'Verily we offered the trust unto the heavens and the earth and the mountains, but they refused to bear it and shrank from it, but man bore it, verily he was passing cruel and passing foolish.' To explain this, a legend is told to the effect that when God created the heavens and the earth and the mountains, these were endowed with reason, and God offered them 'the trust,' that is, entire obedience to His Law with the promise of Paradise if observed, but with the penalty of Hell if neglected The material universe shrank from a responsibility so terrible, but man undertook it, and in so doing was 'passing foolish' and 'passing cruel' to himself. Here 'Asim, adopting the view held by the poets, takes 'the trust' to be Love, and declares that however grievous the burden may be, it is unworthy of a man to groan under it
[2] The heads of seasoned topers are not easily turned, such may drink deeply, so have no excuse for sadness during the festive season
[3] The bow, which is crooked or curved, does not suffer the same harsh treatment as does the straight arrow which it drives afar off, similarly, the man whose conduct is straightforward is apt to suffer wrong at the hands of him whose ways are crooked.

Secure Is Fortune from the wounds the noble-hearted's tongue might deal;
To bare the sword against a hag the Rustem-soul would never deign.

The palate of my fond desire is tender, 'Asim, yea, in sooth
'Tis smitten of catarrh and may not taste the savour of disdain. [1]

Ghazel. [354]

For ne'er a moment is this house of mourning void of wails and sighs, [2]
Nor leaves the sphere's inverted bowl to ring with sad despairing cries.

Adaptability to place is the condition of success;
Behold, not every drop of April rain becomes a pearl of price. [3]

The seekers after God no mention make of Paradise or Hell;
The heart of lover true no standing-room for 'This' and 'That' supplies. [4]

Of none effect will counsel prove upon the hardened heart; 'tis like
The wax which till it melted be can ne'er receive the seal's device.

O 'Asim, for this curtained bride, my gracious heart-desired verse,
Shall ne'er another noble bridegroom like to 'Izzet Bey arise. [5]

Ghazel. [355]

'This can suffer Love,' within the Primal conclave did they say;
Then they called a flame 'a heart,' and set it in my breast straightway.
Shall not they, the earth-born crew, he heartened of the glow of Love?
Store they not the cheering grape-juice in the jar because it's clay?
From my riven bosom proffered is this bleeding heart of mine
To the youthful Magian, saying, 'This for Wine's athirst alway.'
Hasten, then and part those lashes, O thou fell, death-dealing glance!

[1] That is, I am tender-hearted; my loved one's coquetries only vex me,
I can derive no pleasure from them, as other poets say they do.

[2] The 'house of mourning' is the world.

[3] In order to succeed one must fulfil the conditions on which success
depends; thus, not every rain-drop becomes a pearl, but only such as comply
with the necessary condition of falling into the oyster-shell.

[4] Here 'This and That' refers specially to Paradise and Hell, but generally
to individuality as opposed to Unity, or to all things other than the Beloved.

[5] This 'Izzet Bey is probably the poet of that name who flourished under
Ahmed III. He and 'Asim may have written 'parallels' to one another's verses.

Yonder languid eye they'd prison, crying, 'It is drunken, yea!'
So long from mine eyes 'tis fallen that I heed no more its case, [1]
Saying 'yes, this flood of blood-stained tears is naméd "current" aye!'
Deem not those be moles the scribe of Beauty's Díwán marked the dots
Of the dear one's hemistichal eyebrows, so uneath are they.
Good and bad, the sum of either world, it all is flashed therein;
In my breast they've set a mirror which they call the heart, in fay
Ever surgeth, resting never, Love's pale martyr's guiltless blood,
Crying 'Murdress she!' it seeketh still to seize on yonder may.
Such as crave it are right welcome thereunto, but 'Asim, hark,
Naught will I of this world's glory, seeing it doth fade away!

Here is 'Asim's version of 'to err is human, to forgive
divine.'

Rubáí [356]

O Lord, this truth is known to all who be
To err is ours, 'tis Thine to pardon free.
　Lo, I have failed not to perform my part,
So Heaven forefend there be not grace with Thee!

Suleymán Nahífí of Constantinople began life as a calligraphist. In those days penmanship was reckoned among
the fine arts in Turkey, and the proficient in the craft was
held in honour and esteem. Nahífí's teacher was the distinguished penman Háfiz 'Osmán under whom he studied in
the first instance to acquire mastery of the varieties of
handwriting known as suls and neskh [2] Having taken his
diploma in these, he turned his attention to the beautiful
ta'líq hand in which are written most of the fine manuscript
díwáns of old times, and in this too, we are told, he attained
considerable skill.

---

[1] ı e I have wept so long that I have ceased to think any thing of my
tears. The word سَيْل means both "current", "flowing", and also "a beggar",
"asking".

Suls is a kind of large-text, neskh is the small-text round hand used in
transcribing books other than those of poetry

. Though still continuing to work at his art, Nahífí entered the government service, and in 1100 (1688—9) went to Persia in the suite of the ambassador Mehemmed Pasha. On his return he held one or two appointments of some importance, and later on, in 1130 (1717—8), he visited Hungary in company with another ambassador, Ibráhím Agha. When he came back to Constantinople he received a high position in the Ministry of Finance, which, however, he soon resigned, and retired upon a pension. He died in 1151 (1738—9), and was buried near the sepulchre of Sari 'Abdulláh Efendi in the cemetery of Mal-Tepe outside the Cannon Gate of Constantinople. This simple chronogram was carved upon his tomb stone:

'This (is) Suleymán Nahífí: (recite) the Fátiha for his soul.'[1]

Nahífí made his mark both as an original poet and as a translator. The Díwán, which contains all his original work except some religious poems, is characterised by a tenderness of tone such that Jelál Bey compares it to a mirror reflecting all manner of gentle feelings and loving thoughts.

But Nahífí's most important work is his masterly translation of the Mesneví of Mevláná Jelál-ud-Dín. This is perhaps the best translation of a great Persian classic that has ever been made into Turkish. The earlier poets, when writing their romantic mesnevís, used to paraphrase Persian works, not translate them. But Nahífí has given us a literal and line for line rendering of Jelál's wonderful poem, the metre and, as far as possible, the phraseology of which he has been careful to preserve, anticipating thus the system of translation adopted by myself in the present History. We may ask with Professor Nájí whether it was necessary to make such a translation at all; but however this question

بو سليمان نحيفى روحنه الفاتحه ١.

may be answered, there can be no dispute as to the ability
and success with which Nahífí has accomplished his self-
imposed task. The poet certainly deserves the applause which
Ziyá Pasha bestows on his untiring industry and application.

In a prose preface prefixed to the first volume of his
translation Nahífí gives some interesting particulars concerning the circumstances under which he began his work.
He tells us that on his way to Egypt in 1092 (1681), when
he must have been quite a young man, he visited the tomb
of Jelál-ud-Dín at Qonya, where he was affiliated to the
Mevleví brotherhood by the then general of the order It
is presumably from this visit that he dates his interest in
Jelál and his great poem, but the idea of translating this
into Turkish did not occur to his mind until many years
later, not till 1124 (1712), when influenced by what he
regarded as a Divine inspiration, was he constrained to
begin his task He was calling on one of his friends, when
the latter's grandson, a clever and intelligent lad, came
into the room, and knowing Nahífí to be familiar with the
Mesneví, asked him to read some verses along with him
This he did, and choosing the Proem, explained to the boy
the meaning of the Persian lines. But when he returned to
his home, Nahífí was haunted by the third couplet, the
two lines of which continually recurring to him, suggested
others, whereupon came the notion of trying to turn them
into Turkish So he began with the Proem, and before
nightfall had translated the first eighteen couplets. That
night was the night of the first Friday [1] in Rejeb 1124
(August 1712), and the mosques were lit up for the evening
service when Nahífí bowed down and prayed to God to

---

[1] That is the night preceding the Friday, what we should call the Thursday night

bless him in the long and arduous work he then determined
to undertake.

In another preface, prefixed to the fourth volume, the
translator informs us that when the third was drawing towards
a close he fell into want; but Sultan Ahmed having happily
heard of his work asked Ibráhím Pasha to make enquiries
concerning it. The translation was accordingly laid before
the Sultan who, Nahífí says, applauded it and encouraged
him; and, though the poet is silent here, no doubt saw
that he was suitably provided for. [1]

Nahífí has fared well at the hands of the critics; thus
Fatín speaks of him as a unique poet whose words are inspired by love and whose works are masterly in style. Ziyá
Pasha, as we have already seen, praises his application, and
describes him as a powerful and artistic poet; while Professor Nájí goes so far as to say that of all the poets whom
Constantinople has yet produced, Nahífí is the one most
highly gifted with strength of nature. As the Professor appeals to the translation of the Mesneví in justification of
this assertion, it is to be presumed that singleness of purpose and steady devotion to a work once undertaken enter
largely into the moral or intellectual quality which he thus
defines.

The religious work to which I have alluded as forming,
along with the Díwán, the sum of Nahífí's original contri-
butions to literature, is called Hilyet-ul-Enwár, 'The Jewel

---

[1] The Mesneví of Jelál-ud-Dín consists of six books all of which Nahífí
translated; but to these six there is often added an apocryphal seventh which
is generally regarded as the work of the commentator Isma'íl of Angora — died
1041 or 1042 (1631—2 : 32—3) — who professed to have discovered it in
a MS. dated 814 (1411—2). This seventh book was translated into Turkish
by a certain Isma'íl Ferrukhí who died in 1256 (1840—1), and is printed
at the end of the superb Búláq edition of 1268 (1851—2) in which the
Persian original of Jelál and the Turkish translation of Nahífí are printed
side by side.

of Lustres,' and consists of a series of those hymns in honour
of the Prophet which are known as Naʿts.

Haníf-záde, the continuer of Hájjí Khalífa's bibliographical
encyclopaedia, says that Nahífí (whom he calls Mustafá instead
of Suleymán) [1] made further a Turkish takhmís on the famous
Arabic poem called the Qasídat-ul-Burde, or 'Mantle-Poem'
and a translation of the first fifteen Séances of the Maqámát
of Harírí which he dedicated to Ibráhím. He also wrote,
according to Professor Nájí, a prose work entitled Risále-ı
Khizriyya.

The following ghazel is an example of Nahífí's original work:

Ghazel. [357]

Ne'er may any's store of peace of mind be borne as spoil away!
Ne'er may any o'er the waste of ignominy helpless stray!

'Mid the garth I saw a noble charmer,' sayst thou, breeze of dawn;
That it be not yonder cypress-form' thou sawest, sore I pray

Cup on cup affliction's poison have I drunken through thy love
Oh what at thy hands I've suffered! yet no plaint shall me bewray. -

'Sorrow not, one day thou'lt win to union with me,' sayest thou,
Look thou lest thy promised season be the Resurrection-Day!

Ready standeth he, full ready, here to rend his garment's spare,
May no signal reach Nahífí from thy merry eye and gay!

The subjoined English version of the famous Proem of
the Mesneví, which I have made from Nahífí's Turkish translation, will satisfy every reader acquainted with the Persian

---

[1] There is some confusion in Haníf-záde's remarks about this poet He
attributes the Takhmís on the Burde to Mehemmed Suleymán Nahífí, and
the translations of the Mesneví and the Maqámát to Mustafá Nahífí, who
was, he adds, one of the members of Ibráhím Pasha's committee for the
translation of the Persian universal history called Habíb-us-Siyer written by
Khwánd Amír. In the preface to his Mesneví the poet calls himself Nahífí
Mehemmed Suleymán, the son of ʿAbd-ur-Rahmán, the son of Sálih

original as to the faithful manner in which the Ottoman scholar has rendered the great poem of Jelál-ud-Dín. The reed-flute mentioned at the beginning of this Proem is the sacred instrument of the Mevleví dervishes, whose order was, as we know, founded by Mevláná Jelál-ud-Dín the poet of the Mesneví. It is to the sound of this reed-flute that certain members of the order perform, in their special public services of commemoration, the peculiar religious waltz, which has caused them to be known in Europe as the Dancing Dervishes. Thy look upon this instrument with love and veneration as the symbol of the sighing parted lover, who in his turn is the symbol of the human soul yearning after its Divine source.

The Proem of the Mesneví. [358]

Harken how the flute doth plaintive chant its tale,
How for separation's dolour rings its wail:
'From the reedy swamp they tore me,' doth it cry,
'Oft my moan hath bidden man and woman sigh.
'Sore let stress of absence still my bosom wring,
'So that I full ardently my yearning sing.
'Whoso from his home is banished far away
'Longeth for the hour of union night and day.
'I, who am the wailer where'er folk unite,
'Comrade am to all the sad and all the bright.
'Every one regards me from his own estate,
'Seeking aye the secret in my sad debate.
'Though my secret is not distant from my sigh,
'Yet the light of grace comes not to every eye.
'Soul and body each from other are not hid,
'Yet to body is the sight of soul forbid.'
    So, the reed-flute's voice is fire; deem not 'tis air:
Woe for him in whom this fire up-flareth ne'er!
Fire of Love it is that doth the flute empower;
Stress of Love it is that doth the wine endower.

Fore of parted lovers, wails the flute forlorn,
By the flute the veil of flesh in twain is torn.
Antidote and bane like to the flute is none,
Comrade fond and fain like to the flute is none
Tidings of a blood-stained path [1] the flute doth show,
All the tale it tells of Mejnún's love and woe
They who lose their hearts do reason's secrets hear;
None may purchase of the tongue except the ear.
All untimely for our anguish pass the days,
Many a sorrow fareth with the days always.
Though the days thus pass away, 'tis naught of pain,
So that Thou, O Purest one, do still remain [2]

Oceans can not sate the fish that swims the sea,
But the day sans daily bread is long to dree [3]
Of th' initiate's state how should the untutored tell?
Brief then let our paileyings be, and fare thee well!

Break thy bonds, O youth, and win to freedom sweet,
Until when shall gold and silver bind thy feet?
Though thou pour into a pitcher all the sea,
Nought beyond a one day's store therein may be
How should aught that pitcher fill — the eye of greed?
Sans content pearls form not in the shells, indeed. [4]
Yonder robe that Love hath never rent atwain

---

[1] The bitter path of Love

[2] Mr. Whinfield, who has given us an admirable epitome of Jelál's Mesneví, 'Masnaví i Ma²naví,' translated and abridged by E H Whinfield, M A London, Trubner and Co 1887, commenting on this line, says, Self-annihilation leads to eternal life in God — the universal Noumenon, by whom all phenomena exist [Under the title of 'the Song of the Reed' a very graceful and spirited translation of this Proem was published in 1877 by the late Professor E H Palmer ED.]

[3] The meaning seems to be that though the adept cannot have too much of an esoteric discourse like the present, the uninitiated, for whom no provision is made, will find it dreary, I shall therefore be brief

[4] [Reference has already been frequently made to the Oriental belief as to the formation of pearls The oysters come open-mouthed to the surface of the sea in the month of April [Nísán], each seeking to catch a rain-drop, but as soon as the rain-drop is received, the oyster must close its shell and sink to the bottom, in order that the transformation may proceed It must be 'contented' with the one rain-drop ere it can hope for the pearl ED.]

Bideth still uncleansed of greed and passion's stain.

Joyous smile, O Love, sweet-fashioned, all our own!

Leech by whom our woes and ills away are done!

O thou Medicine of our pride and self-conceit!

Thou who art our Plato and our Galen meet!

High aloft doth soar the earthly frame through Love; [1]

Dance the hills, inebriate with joy thereof.

When the light of God's own face illumed Sinai,

There the tidings: 'Moses fell and swooned away.' [2]

Had I found a comrade leal, a friend at need,

Fain had I revealed my secret like the reed.

Whosoe'er is twinned from them that ken his speech

Speechless is, however much he talk or preach.

When the rose is past, the garden's beauty gone,

In the plaining bulbul bides nor wail nor moan.

All is the Beloved, the lover's but a veil; [3]

Living the Beloved, the lover dead and pale.

He in whom the fire of Love doth burn not high

Is a bird withouten wings, that may not fly.

How may sense or reason find whereon to stand

Till the Loved One's radiance reach a helping hand?

This the work of Love, the Secret to unveil.

Look in burnished mirror, that will tell the tale.

Is the Secret shown not in thy mirror-soul?

Then its face is rubbed not clear of rust in whole.

Were it cleansed of every stain of rust indign,

Thence would flash the radiance of the Sun Divine!

Let it deck the ear of them who walk aright;

Passing well hath this discourse portrayed our plight. [4]

---

[1] Alluding to Christ's or the Prophet's Ascension.

[2] The quotation is from Koran VII, 139; the allusion is to God's giving the law to Moses on Mount Sinai.

[3] The following is Mr. Whinfield's note on this line: 'All phenomenal existences (man included) are but 'veils' obscuring the face of the Divine Noumenon, the only real existence, and the moment His sustaining presence is withdrawn they at once relapse into their original nothingness.'

[4] This last couplet refers to the story of the King and the Handmaid, which immediately follows.

Ahmed Neylí Efendi, the poet at whose suggestion Seyyid Vehbí changed his pen-name, was the son of a Judge of Constantinople called Mírzá-záde Mehemmed, and was born in 1084 (1673—4). The truth of the adage, 'learn young, learn fair,' was well exemplified in the case of this accomplished man of letters, who began his professional studies when a little child six years of age. Neylí, thus early started on his course, gradually made his way, and when little more than forty found himself in the important position of Molla of Smyrna After a time he was promoted to the Mollaship of Cairo, which was soon followed by the further step to that of Mekka. In due course the Cadi-'Askerate, first of Anatolia, then of Rumelia, was reached. The latter office was held twice by Neylí; but before he had completed his second term, his health gave way, and he was compelled to resign. His resignation was followed in a few days by his death, which occurred in 1151 (1738—9).

Neylí was a poet of some eminence who, according to Professor Nájí, has not met with the recognition he deserves. Several of his couplets are, says the Professor, current among the people, who quote them without knowing whose they are. This ignorance the critic attributes partly to the fact that Neylí's Díwán has never been printed, a circumstance which serves him as the text for a not unmerited rebuke of modern Turkish Scholars for their neglect of their older writers.

Neylí, the Professor continues, is really to be preferred to many of the early poets, as he thinks well and speaks clearly, and although he inclines rather too much towards embellishment, his verses do not in consequence lose their attractiveness. At times, however, he errs, with so many of his fellows, in too closely imitating the Persians, while occasionally the triviality of his conceits accords but little

with the dignity of poetry. But such cases are not very
frequent, and do not seriously detract from the merit of
his Díwán.

Although a Persianist, Neylí has nothing in common with
the school of Nábí; his affinities are rather with the age of
Nef°í, of whose genius he seems to have had a due appreciation. His philosophy is of a deeper kind than that of the
contemporary school, and he rarely endeavours to make a
point by the happy introduction of some well-known saw.
On the other hand, he is just as little influenced by the
Romanticist movement. His love passages, which are often
graceful, are quite conventional and very Persian in tone,
while there is not the slightest trace of local colour in his
ghazels. His language too is unaffected by the Turkicising
tendency of the age, and resembles that of the later Classicists or early Neo-Persianists.

One of Neylí's prettiest poems is a little tale in mesneví verse of a Christian girl and a Muslim youth. The tale
is supposed to be told by a converted monk to a wandering
dervish in reply to the latter's enquiry as to how he came
to embrace the Faith of Islam. The monk relates how one
day a young Muslim came to his monastery and chanced
to be seen by a Christian maiden who became deeply enamoured of him. As he would not respond to her advances,
she endeavoured to console herself by getting a skilful artist
to paint his portrait. This she placed in her room, and constantly sitting before it, would speak to it as though it were
her beloved himself. By and bye the youth died; and a
few days later, when the monk went to console the girl,
he found her lying dead before the picture, underneath which
she had written some verses saying that she had accepted
Islam in the hope of being united to her dear one in Heaven.
When the monk returned a day or two afterwards, he saw

to his amaze that the girl had come back from Paradise to add a few more verses to the effect that through her adoption of Islam all her sins had been forgiven and that she was joined for ever with her beloved in the presence of God. On seeing this miracle the monk followed her example and entered the Faith.

Neylí's qasídas are for the most part in praise of Sultan Ahmed and Ibráhím Pasha, and are not very remarkable. He has a good many ghazels in Persian, and the usual number of chronograms, quatrains, and single verses

This poet was a very learned man who, besides translating several Arabic books, wrote a large number of professional works. He was also famous for his generosity.

Here are two ghazels from his Díwán

Ghazel. [359]

'Tis thy life-bestowing liplet that of joy's the store for me,
Cupbearer, the festal beaker's mouth may speak no more for me

Nature's marvellous arithmic mid the garden pondered I,
Every leaf became a volume fraught with wonder-lore for me

Yonder wanton's œillad signals naught but parting's lonely cell,
How from one so harsh should hope of union come o'er for me?

From the dust of longing's anguish washeth it my garment clean,
Yea, the kindly soul is lucent Tesním evermore for me.

Cribbed and cramped within the strait defile of eaith had been my heart,
Had not poesy's wide plateau, Neylí, stretched before for me.

Ghazel [360]

Wouldst thou the soul without the body see?
Behold that Angel when unclad is she!

Be yonder wanton's roaming o'er the mead
With folk unmeet forbid withouten me

For rivals be not sore against thy love;
O heart, no rose without a thorn may be. [1]

Would any lover at the meanest grain
Buy all earth's treasure sans that belamy?

Although a sun were every mote, would earth
Be dark to me, Light of my eyes, sans thee.

'How sinned I?' asketh Neylí of the fair,
'My heart ye've ta'en, and will not set it free.'

When we open the Díwán of Nejjár-záde Sheykh Mustafá
Rizá we find ourselves once again in the dervish convent,
where the philosophisings of the disciples of Nábí and the
love-songs of the followers of Nedím alike are silent, and
where the litanies of the devotee alone are heard.

Rizá was born in Constantinople in 1090 (1679—80), and
was the son of a man named Ibráhím. This Ibráhím would
appear to have been something of a military engineer; at
least he accompanied the artillery when on active service
and superintended the construction of such bridges as it

---

[1] That there is no rose without a thorn is a saying common doubtless to
most languages. In Turkish it assumes several slightly different forms; thus we have
چنكلسز گل اولماز انكلسز يار اولماز and گل چنكلسز يار انكلسز اولماز,
both of which mean, there is no thornless rose and no rivalless sweetheart,
that is, no sweetheart whom one may love without having rivals. This proverb is naturally a favourite one with the poets: Fuzúlí says:

سينه چاكمدن اكسك ايتمه تير غمزه‌يى .
اى گوكل رعنا بيلورسك كم گل اولماز خارسز

'Let not my riven bosom lack the dart of her glance;
'O heart, well thou knowest how there is no rose without a thorn.'
And Rúhí of Baghdad:

بويله ايتمش حكمت اى بلبل ازلدن اقتضا
كيم نه يار اغيارسز اوله نه غنچه خارسز

'Thus hath wisdom ruled from all eternity, O nightingale,
'That there may be neither rivalless sweetheart nor thornless rosebud.'

was necessary to build upon the line of march. On this account he was' playfully nicknamed Nejjár or Carpenter, whence Rizá came to be known as Nejjár-záde or Ibn-un Nejjár, both of which mean the Carpenter's son. In 1123 (1711—2) Rizá, who had spent his youth in study, entered the Naqshbendí order of dervishes, and by and bye became Sheykh or abbot of the convent at Beshik-Tash.

When the Grand Vezír Hakím-oghlı ʿAlí Pasha built his mosque at Altı-Mermer, the poets of the day were invited to compose chronograms on the event That of the Sheykh won the Vezír's approbation by its simplicity and directness, it was nothing more than Jámíʿ-ur-Rizá, that is, the Mosque of Rizá or of Acquiescence (to God's will), for the word rizá — which was the Sheykh's name — signifies 'acquiescence.' Naturally enough there were not lacking those who said that this was no proper chronogram, but a barefaced hint for an appointment in the mosque. But ʿAlí Pasha did not heed such detractors, and after a time, when the first holder of the office had for some reason been banished from the capital, he appointed Sheykh Rizá, who was famous for his eloquence, to the office of preacher. After a while, the original holder of this office returned from his exile, and set about, though with little hope of success, endeavouring to recover his post by appealing to the Vezír and other persons of influence As soon as Rizá heard of this, he sent the patent of office to his predecessor, saying as he did so, 'I performed those services only as his substitute; since he so wishes, let him return to his place.'

Sheykh Rizá died in 1159 (1746—7), and was buried in the court of his own convent.

Although Rizá was a dervish Sheykh, his poems are religious rather than mystical, and like those of Nazím are almost entirely devoted to the praise of the Prophet. Western readers

will agree with Von Hammer in finding that on the whole
they possess but little interest, although, as Professor Nájí
says, they are at times inspired by the ardour of religious
love. This is notably so in the case of the verses written
by Rizá while a pilgrim at the sacred shrines of Islam. Thus,
when he was leaving the Ka'ba he composed the following
lines which are the evident outcome of deep feeling:

> The sparks that from my burning sighs mount at the farewell hour
> It is that blacken yonder curtain o'er the Temple drawn.
> The darkling night of parting to joy's dayspring turneth he
> Who makes his ardent bosom-sigh to flame, the torch of dawn. [1]

Rizá's Díwán used to enjoy considerable reputation, perhaps because contemporary works of the kind were not very
common during the eighteenth century; but its poetical merit
is not high. It consists of what are really four separate díwáns
bound up together. There is no apparent reason why the
poems comprised in these should not have been arranged
as a single díwán; probably it is as Von Hammer suggests,
and the four díwáns represent four successive collections of
the poet's works. [2] Between the four Rizá has no fewer than
one hundred and seventy ghazels with the redíf 'O Apostle
of God!' so much was his poetic talent spent in the glorification of the Prophet.

In prose he made a translation of the Persian treatise

وقتِ وداع آتـش آغـم شراريـدر رنكِ قباى بيت حرامى سياه ايدن [1]
ديجور هجرى مطلع نور سرور ايدر آه درونى مشعلهٔ صباحگاه ايدن

[1] The allusion in the second line is to the Kiswet, or covering of rich black
damask, adorned with an embroidered band of gold, which is draped outside
the Ka°ba, and which is renewed every year at the expense of the Sultan.

[2] Each of the four díwáns bears a special title; these are in their order:
(1) Tuhfet-ul-Irshád = The Gift of Guidance: (2) Wáridát-i Ghaybiyya = Inspirations from the Unseen: (3) Zuhúrát-i Mekkiyye = Mekkan Manifestations:
(4) Khátimat-ul-Wáridát = The Postscript to the Inspirations.

called Mukhtasar-ul-Viláye by the great Naqshbendí Sheykh, Khoja Abu-ʿAbdulláh of Samarcand.

The following ghazel is a favourable example of Rızá's work, it occurs in the first of the four díwán's.

Ghazel. [361]

Within the realm of heart is none who kens my speech, I trow;
There is no dragoman on earth who doth Love's language know.

Why press the steed of my desire to bear the prize away,
When on this plain is none who may his bridle-comrade go?

On Faith's high way is ne'er a youth to be the staff of eld
Unto the teacher of the Truth when feeble he shall grow.

What I have held the ill I now behold to be the good,
Than mine own self there is none other ill on earth below

Within this factory dust-grimed not any booth is there
Which to the merchantman, emprize, can goods of value show

This garden-land can on the humá [1] fair, Rızá's high soul,
No corner meet to serve as nest of sweet repose bestow.

With Mehemmed Rághıb Pasha, who is the last and, save the founder, by far the most illustrious member of the School of Nábí, closes the long catalogue of the Persianist poets of Turkey.

Qoja Rághıb or Old Rághıb, as he is popularly styled, was the son of a secretary in the Defter-Kháne or office of the Rolls of the Exchequer, called Mehemmed Shevqí, and was born in Constantinople in 1110 (1698—9). Following in his father's footsteps, Rághıb entered the same government office, where his exceptional talents and abilities soon made him a marked man He was consequently appointed in the

---

[1] The humá, a mythical bird corresponding more or less to our Phoenix, has already been repeatedly noticed.

first place mektúbji or chief secretary to 'Arifí Ahmed Pasha
the Ottoman governor of Erivan (then momentarily incorpor-
ated in the Empire); next, agent of the Defter Emíni, as
the chief permanent official in the Finance Department is
styled, in the suite of ʿAlí Pasha who commanded the Imperial forces operating on the north-eastern frontier; and
then in 1140 (1727—8) defterdár or financial Commissary-
general of Erivan. A year later he returned to Constantinople,
but was soon sent to Hamadán (then likewise in Turkish
hands) as agent of the Re'ís Efendi, and charged with the
division of the recently acquired Persian territories into
feudal fiefs. In 1143 (1730—1) he was made defterdár of
Baghdád, and when three years later he returned to the
capital he was promoted to the important financial office
of máliyye tezkerejisi. The following year he was again
despatched as military defterdár and agent of the Re'ís
Efendi in the suite of Ahmed Pasha the ex-governor of
Baghdád, who had been put in command of the Erzerum
army-corps. The next step was in 1149 (1736—7), when
Rághib was made chief secretary to the Grand Vezír. Four
years later he became Re'ís Efendi, and in 1157 (1744—5)
he was elevated to the vezírate, and at the same time appointed governor of Egypt. He remained some three years
in that country which he ruled with much success, but which
at last proved irksome to him, if we are to take as literal
what he says in one of his ghazels:

> 'Full weary we of governing the Mother of the world;
> 'Enow this care of Cairo, let us hence to Rúm again.' [1]

[1] حكلال كلدى تـصـرفـدن أم دنـيـسـايـسى
يتـر شـو قاهرهنك قهـرى عـزم رم ايـدهلر
'The Mother of the world' is an Arabic surname of Cairo.

The desire here expressed was gratified, for in 1160 (1747—8) he was made collector of Aydın, then in 1163 (1749—50) governor of Raqqa, and then in 1168 (1754—5) governor of Aleppo At last, in 1170 (1756—7), Rághıb Pasha became Grand Vezír, and for six years he held this lofty office, the onerous duties of which he discharged in a manner worthy of the long and faithful services he had already rendered to his country. During his tenure of the grand vezírate peace was preserved abroad, and many important public works were carried out at home. Rághıb, who had married the Princess Sálıha, [1] a sister of Sultan Mustafá III, was honoured and esteemed by all, and his death on the 24th of Ramazán 1176 (8th April 1763) was in more ways than one a grievous loss to Turkey.

Being one of the greatest scholars of his time, his society was naturally much sought after by men of learning, and his house in Constantinople was a favourite resort of the literary world of the day The distinguished poetess Fitnet Khanım is mentioned as being among his literary friends.

---

[1] The following little story about this Princess is most probably apocryphal, but it is widely known in Constantinople In Rághıb's household there was, it is said, a beautiful slave-girl called Nerkıs (Narcisse) to whom the Pasha was much attached, and there was also an exceedingly ill-favoured Armenian man-servant named Serkıs. The Princess having discovered that the Pasha had arranged to visit Nerkıs on a certain night, ordered the girl to vacate her bed and bade Serkıs take her place At the appointed time Rághıb entered Nerkıs's room and, imagining of course that the pretty slave-girl was there, he improvised aloud the line·

خـواب نازدں قالقدى راعب عـزم نرکس قویـسه

'Up from slumber sweet awoke Rághıb and sought his Nerkıs' breast,'
and went up to the bed when he suddenly discovered that he was making love to the hideous Armenian, and at the same time heard the Princess, who had followed him unobserved, cap his line with the following

بر محالف روزگار اسدى آنـدى سرکس قویـمنه

'When an adverse wind arising cast him upon Serkıs' breast'

Prominent among Rághib Pasha's good works is the public library which he built in the Qosqa quarter of Constantinople for the reception of the fine collection of books which he had got together during the course of his life. Beside this library he built a fountain and likewise a mansoleum within which he lies buried.

Rághib Pasha's poetical work is not extensive, [1] it is all contained within the covers of a slender díwán. But this little volume is stuffed with good things, and well deserves the popularity which it has for long enjoyed, a popularity which has manifested itself in what is perhaps the most conclusive of all fashions, that of having supplied many of the lines and phrases which are current as proverbs in the language of daily life.

I have said that with the single exception of the master himself, Rághib is the most brilliant member of the school founded by Nábí. Within his limits, the later poet is perhaps even stronger than his predecessor; he has indeed nothing of Nábí's marvellous versatility, but his notes on life have more pith in them, and are expressed in language more direct and more forcible. In his language, indeed, Rághib is singularly modern, going straight to his point and eschewing all bombast, shunning even what is merely decorative. Many of the illustrations which he uses to drive home his maxims and comments are vividly drawn direct from nature, and have something of the air of the unpremeditated, so simply and naturally are they presented.

---

[1] He wrote a good deal of prose, but this being all in the pedantic fashion of his time, has now fallen out of notice; it never possessed any very great merit. The best known of his prose productions is not an original work but a huge compilation of untranslated extracts from many Arabic authors bearing on scientific and ethical matters, which he called Sefínet-ur-Rághib, that is, The Ship of Rághib, or of the Desirous One, for such is the meaning of the name Rághib.

While a convinced Persianist and a loyal — a too loyal —
follower of the Classic Tradition, Rághıb was too great a
man and too genuine a poet to remain unaffected by the
most vital and active of the literary forces working in his
day. As Nábí before him, though the founder of a Persianist
school, had been at bottom half a Romanticist, so now Rághıb
Pasha, his most illustrious and most gifted disciple, is in many
of his poems as Turanian in vocabulary and as idiomatic in phraseology as the most pronounced of contemporary Turkicists.

I have just said that the Pasha was too loyal a follower
of the Classic Tradition. Had he been content with Sá'ıb,
there might have been no great reason for regret; but unluckily he turned his attention to the Persian poet Shevket,
who just about this time was becoming fashionable, and
who, eventually displacing Sá'ıb as the load-star of those who
still turned Irán-ward [1] for light, was destined, after a brief
season of popularity, to pass from favour, the last and least
worthy of the series of Persian poets who for over three
hundred years were guides and models for the Ottomans.
Shevket's verses had really little to recommend them beyond
a certain gracefulness of fancy. This quality, such as it was,
Rághıb failed to assimilate; and many of his ghazels are
marred by the presence of tasteless conceits and the introduction of unreasonable subjects, the direct results of his
unfortunate choice of model [2]

[1] [As Shevket, or Shawkat, according to Persian pronunciation, was a native
of Bukhárá, which is Turkish or Turkí rather than Persian, "Irán-ward" seems
hardly a suitable expression, though I have let it stand It is worthy of note
that all the most turgid and florid Persian writing emanates from Transoxania,
whence, with Báber, it made its way into India ED]

[2] Rághıb was evidently proud of his efforts in the direction of this writer,
for he says at the close of a ghazel:

شعر پاکم گور نجمه طالبنور شوکتلدور

'See how my bright poetry Tálıbizes and Shevketizes.'

To a philosopher and lover of the truth like Rághib Pasha there would be but scant pleasure in composing panegyrics on the great, consequently we find in his Díwán but one qasída. This is followed by a few chronograms, after which come six takhmíses on as many ghazels of the Pasha's several masters; Shevket, Sáʾib, and Nábí being each represented by two poems. Those on the ghazels of Shevket and Sáʾib are in Persian, while those on Nábí's are of course in Turkish.

Rághib's claim to poetic distinction rests exclusively on his ghazels. He is essentially a moralizing poet of the school of Sáʾib and Nábí, and his writings, in common with those of the entire group, partake in considerable measure of the nature of a proverbial philosophy. Sound common-sense and sterling integrity of purpose, together with a frequent felicity of illustration, are the qualities that have done most to win his verse its high reputation. So long as he confines himself to this his proper field, he is always safe, often successful beyond his neighbours; but occasionally under some unlucky inspiration he tries his hand at a love passage, and then he always fails. The 'Moons' and 'Cypresses' seem singularly out of place in a string of brief reflections on the ways of the world and little maxims for the conduct of life.

As has been already said, the vocabulary of Rághib bears very distinctly the impress of the age. Although all the members of the Third Persianist School were more or less influenced by the tendency to introduce native Turkish words and phrases into poetry more freely than had hitherto been the rule, no one of the group went so far in this direction as did the Pasha. He seems indeed to have encouraged and fostered this movement, the development of which

Here the Pasha coins Turkish verbs from the names of Tálib and Shevket, the Tálib in question being another not very excellent Persian poet who was popular in Turkey about this time.

was, as we know, one of the foremost articles of the Romanticist faith. In so doing the Pasha showed himself at once
a liberal-minded scholar and an enlightened worker in the
nationalizing of literature.

Rághib's literary style, while terse, vigorous and admirably
suited to the message he has to give, is, as we should expect,
well nigh devoid of elegance and grace The delicate verbal
craftsmanship of the Classicists formed no part of the heritage of the last Persianists. A variety of offences against the
technical rules of the poetic art mark the verses of Rághib
This must be the result of deliberate purpose, for the Pasha
was a very learned man, and is even said to have written
a treatise on prosody. Perhaps he considered such matters
as trivial and beneath the notice of a philosopher, and chose
such phraseology as came readiest to his hand without troubling
to consider whether it bore the academic stamp. But all
such little matters may well be forgiven a writer whose
wholesome manly envisagement of life and duty is still a
living and helpful force, while the work of many a more
artistic poet which had little beyond its craftsmanship-to
boast of, has faded from the public mind, and is remembered
only by the antiquary or the student.

The modern critics are not slow to recognise the old
Vezír's worth. Ziyá Pasha, while admitting the flaws in his
workmanship, speaks highly in his favour He couples him
with 'Asim, but justly declares him to be the stronger He
goes perhaps a little too far when he says that there is no
padding in his verse, but his statement that while the poet
has many sentiments that are noble, he has very few that
are mean, will be echoed by every one who has glanced over
that little Díwán which Kemál Bey could describe as a
volume of wisdom filled full of choicest things

Professor Nájí, careful and just as usual, while pointing

out in considerable detail the solecisms of which Rághib is
guilty, pays a high tribute to the many merits of the old
Pasha who, as in statesmanship he gained for himself the
title of the Wise Vezír, has won likewise in literature the
honourable surname of the Wise Poet. Nájí maintains that
though the Pasha's prose writings have been forgotten owing
to the literary revolutions that have since occurred, there
is no chance of any such fate befalling his poems, so many
passages from these have become part and parcel of the
living language that an immortality appears to be ensured
to them commensurate with that of the Turkish tongue.
Most of Rághib's better verses, the critic continues, are
worth remembering because of the wisdom they contain; a
remark which, as the Professor adds with much truth, could
be made of hardly any other among the old poets.

Apart from its own intrinsic merits, real though these be,
the tiny Díwán of Rághib Pasha possesses a unique, almost
a pathetic, interest; it is the last word of a great literary
tradition, of a tradition that taught its followers to look up
to and learn from a poetry which, to whatever futilities and
ineptitudes it may have at times descended, was originally
and essentially inspired by the most sublime conception
which the human soul has ever formed. And so this little
book is one of the landmarks of our story. From the day,
more than two centuries and a half ago, when by tendering
allegiance to Mír 'Alí Shír, Ahmed Pasha established the
Classic Tradition as a fundamental principle for Ottoman
poetry, we have seen reflected in this poetry, in true and
unbroken sequence, each successive phase of that of Persia.
But this shall be no longer. The Turk now takes leave of
his Persian guide, who indeed can guide him no farther,
can only misguide him. Henceforward he must work out
his own salvation as best he may. And it is here, in this

Díwán of Rághib Pasha, that Turk and Persian say farewell.

Here is a selection of ghazels from Rághib Pasha's Díwán:

Ghazel. [362]

Austerity wraps not the Truth before the Mimic's trivial mind;
The pictured ocean's waves are never ruffled by the stormy wind

The benefactor's stately mien the needy deem not hard to bear,
The merry topers ne'er the jar of wine a weary burden find

The flambeau of the Moth's [1] renown doth shine until the Judgment Day,
For silence ne'er the flaming tongue that speaks the silent's fame shall bind.

The hests of Fate thou shalt obey, be wise or heedless, as thou wilt,
For ne'er with Destiny may cope the schemes of wit, howe'er designed

Regard with heed the fair relationship 'tween loveliness and love,
No ear like to the rose's o'er the bulbul's burning song's inclined

Abstention from display is e'er the true adornment of the great,
Unblazoned is the garment round about the Fleckless sphere entwined. [2]

The time is not propitious, else the place, else the cupbearer Fate,
Within this tavern, Rághib, ne'er are all the heart's desires combined

Ghazel. [363]

Each one who sees the tavern doth a diff'rent phase thereof debate,
The zealot tells its irksomeness, the toper sings its joys elate.

Whene'er the bulbul lifts his voice to chant the splendour of the rose,
The gurgle of the flask doth mid the feast the wine s delights relate.

May ever sybarite conceive the ecstasy the Vision [3] brings?
Whene'er of Paradise they speak, of feasting doth the zealot prate [4]

[1] The moth which courts destruction in its beloved flame is a favourite type of the fearless, devoted and uncomplaining lover

[2] The Empyrean, or Primum Mobile, is the Ninth and outermost of all the Ptolemaic Spheres, it is the Starless Heaven, being beyond that of the Fixed Stars; so Rághib speaks of its robe as unblazoned

[3] The Beatific Vision vouchsafed to the Saints in ecstasy

[4] Alluding sarcastically to the purely sensual pictures of Paradise which certain popular preachers were wont to present

Nor Reason's seigniory, nor yet the lordship of the Sacred Law,
The peace of Frenzy's clime it is the wand'rers o'er it celebrate.

In midst of converse doth the evil-natured let his vice be seen;
When bragging of his valour 'tis the gipsy doth his thefts narrate. [1]

In sooth the voice of wisdom friendly unto sanity appears:
Although he knows it false, the leech is fain the patient's health to state. [2]

The soul's distraction still remains like to an oracle obscure;
The sense whereof no man doth understand, nor doth Rághib translate.

Ghazel. [364]

The freed from fetters of desire may hold the head on high,
And he who knows nor wish nor want may flout the rolling sky.

The dark-hued troublous zágh it is unto the eyebrow-glaive, [3]
Whene'er sweet slumber's stibium-dust is drawn across thine eye.

[1] This is one of the most widely known of those lines of Rághib that
have passed into proverbs. In connection with it Professor Nájí mentions a
little incident which he says happened in Constantinople not long before
he wrote. A certain gentleman, 'Abd-ul-Ghaffár by name, who claimed to come
from Bukhárá, and who was a man of parts, though a terrible talker and
braggart, was present one day at a gathering of literary men, where he contrived as usual to monopolize the conversation. The others, by way of a
joke, kept perfectly silent, and gave the Bukhariot the field entirely to himself.
When he had at last tired himself out talking of his own accomplishments
and successes, someone in the party quietly said, 'God's blessing on him
who sleeps in the dust of Qosqa,' whereupon a general titter went through
the room, all present, including 'Abd-ul-Ghaffár, at once recalling this line
of Rághib.

[2] Eastern doctors generally make light of the ailments of their patients so
as to keep up their spirits. As the leech's statement parallels 'the voice of
wisdom' in the preceding line, this second hemistich repeats the dictum of
the first, though in a perverted sense.

[3] Zágh زاغ is the name of a vitriolic substance, a solution of which is (or
was) used by the sword-cutlers in Turkey for the purpose of bringing out
the grain or damascening of sword-blades. That this may be done, the blades
are basted with the zágh, which is apparently of a dark colour, as the poets
of this period are fond of comparing to it the dark-coloured ointment, called
vesme or rastiq, wherewith Eastern beauties intensify the blackness and improve
the shape of their scimitar-like eyebrows. Thus Neylí says:

He makes the bosom-nook a home where naught is grudged him e'er,
Can any win the heart as doth the friend in misery?

Th' elation from the grace of Jesu's breath abideth still,
The tavern's air restores the sick to healthful sanity

Of him to whom the garden's spring and autumn come the same,
The length of life shall even with the lofty cypress vie

At first the trav'ller crosseth o'er the Bridge of carnal love,
The Typal is the starting-point on road of Verity. [1]

O Rághib, he who tames his passion's wild and restive steed
Shall valiant gallop o'er the field with none to come him nigh

اولدلر ابرولرسه ومه‌که‌ش خوان شهر

راغلمدردی نه شمشمرسی سمائلر

'The beau'ies of the city have painted their eyebrows with vesme.
'The sword-dealers again have had their scimitars zághed.'
And Hashmet

ومه حکمه ابروانه راع حسمک آکه سس

ابتمه پاس‌الون تعک دسدم ای غداره آچ

'Paint not thine eyebrows with vesme, the zágh of thy beauty suffices them,
'Rust-stain not thy glaive, I say, Oh bare the broadsword'

An interesting account of Turkish sword-cutlery is given in an article in the 5th. volume of the Mines de l'Orient (that for 1816) by Mr John Barker, then British Consul at Aleppo. In this article, which is entitled 'Method of Renewing the Giohare (i e. Jevher, or Gevher), or Flowery Grain of Persian Swords, commonly called Damascus Blades,' there are several interesting particulars concerning the zágh, which is not adequately described in any of the dictionaries

In the present verse Rághib says that when the surme of sweet sleep is applied to the eyes of the beloved, it is the dark-coloured zágh of trouble (to the lover) for her sword (-shaped) eyebrows Both surme and zágh are dark-coloured sleep is compared to surme because of its beneficial effect on the eyes, but when sleep, closing the eyes of the beloved, hides them from sight, it augments the power of the eyebrows to cause trouble by relieving these of the rivalry of the eyes, and in this way it may be said to enhance their efficacy, as zágh does that of the scimitars whose shape and wound-dealing power they share.

[1] For 'The Typal is the Bridge to the Real' (المجاز قنطرة الحقيقة).

Ghazel. [365]

The rakish heart doth not himself in every circumstance extol,
Unless indeed it be anent the rosy wine and brimming bowl.

Yea, let the mansion of the heart adornment find through wisdom's base;
The worry over couch and cushion is but vain and needless dole.

Were't strange an I should brand my bosom o'er with wounds for love of thee,
When many a signet-stamp is meetly printed on petition-roll? [1]

What help thine if the youthful fair be for the other service used? [2]
For lo, they may nor barber nor shampooer for such work enrol.

An so thine object be to leave thy mark, one noble line's enow;
Bewilderment at Alexander's dyke doth ever fill my soul. [3]

The eye of yearning is bewitched by world-consuming beauty bright,
So none regards his comrade's heart what time some charmer is the goal.

For eloquent and wise Wahíd [4] the hands must form a veil, Rághib,
More surely now before this new-designed and freshly fashioned scroll.

Ghazel. [366]

Abject cringing to the creature will not gain thine object e'er;
God it is who gives, nor Bey nor Pasha; O my heart, beware!

[1] The impressions of the petitioner's seals taking the place of their sig-natures. The poet compares his yearning bosom to a scroll containing a petition for mercy, each of the scars he has inflicted thereon in the frenzy of love being the seal-stamp of a mute petitioner.

[2] This is directed against the pederast.

[3] Sedd-i Iskender or Alexander's Dyke, otherwise called Sedd-i Ye'júj u Me'júj or the Dyke of Gog and Magog, is the name of a vast rampart said to have been built by Alexander the Great to defend his dominions from the incursions of the wild northern tribes. The idea was probably derived from some confused account of the Great Wall of China. Rághib here exclaims upon the uselessness of so huge a monument when a single line of noble verse is sufficient to ensure immortality.

[4] Diláver ᶜOsmán Wahíd was a literary man of those days and a personal friend of Rághib Pasha, who seems to have written the present ghazel as a parallel to one of his poems. Wahíd wrote a continuation to ᶜOsmán-záde Tá'ib's history of the Grand Vezírs called Hadíqat-ul-Vuzerá or The garden-close of the Vezírs.

Yea, 'twas a celestial vision gave the hand to Moses there,
For the bushes of Sinai give not aye white hands to share. [1]

Well I know thou art the lover fain of freedom from Love's yoke,
But such liberty the heart distraught will grant unto thee ne'er

Ne'er without the dews and rains of bitter weeping groweth ripe
Yearning's fruit, for barren longing naught of worth produceth there.

Imitation, howsoever fair it be, hath naught of grace,
Never bush in pictured garden sweetly scented rose doth bear.

Stretched the helmet not to blow of battle-axe and sword its breast,
High upon the head in honour ne'er the valiant would it wear

Howsoever much the hair-splitters may talk and prate thereof,
No one can thy down [2] decipher like to Rághib, clear and fair.

Ghazel. [367]

Inward striving shows its presence in the troubled bosom's throes,
From the ore that makes the mirror is it that the rust-stain grows.

No untimely fret is needful for to win the heart's desire,
In its own good time will fortune come without or stress or woes

Never may Love's world-consuming lightning bide 'neath honour's veil,
Inebriety unstinted heedless doth itself expose.

Beauty's scene of revelation unto none its grace denies,
So upon the quailing mountain once the Face of God arose [3]

Difference betwixt good and evil hinders not their mingling, nay,
See, the thorn undying showeth 'neath the shadow of the rose

Fair and foul effects are mirrors showing true the deeds of men,
'Tis himself the wizard showeth, whatsoe'er his trick or pose

[1] Alluding to the miracle at the Burning Bush when Moses, at the bidding of the Voice that issued thence, drew his hand from his bosom 'white as snow '
[2] The down on thy cheek, or thy lines of writing — either the lines thou hast written, or the written lines that tell of thee.
[3] Alluding to the Theophany on Mount Sinai

Souls the mirrors are where Beauty's radiancy reflected shines;
Unto whichsoe'er he turn the Friend doth there Himself disclose. [1]

Deeds are so requited, Rághib, that one might as proverb say:
Ask the tyrant of his victim, and 'twill be himself he shows.

Ghazel. [368]

Although ambition will not let thee bide in privacy,
For rank and office hanker not, lest peace abandon thee.

A singleness of heart acquire meet for the Presence Pure;
For ritual ne'er will bring thee, zealot, Paradise to see.

From 'neath the veil of bashfulness, O moon-bright, show thyself;
For fame will ne'er permit thee in seclusion's vale to be.

The heart of thee will surely wander wildered for some Moon;
This nature will not let thee dwell self-centred, verily.

Can there be any pleasure sweet as vengeance on the foe?
Yet, Rághib, thou'rt forbid this joy by magnanimity.

Ghazel. [369]

Deem not abstinence and virtue e'er will wisdom's patent gain;
'Tis the feast of Jem, the ruler here's the bowl that drowneth pain.

Through the toil of Ferhád now is Bísitún a travelled tale;
E'en the steadfast mountain moveth 'fore the lover's mighty strain. [2]

Hard it is betwixt the fleeting and the permanent to tell;
To declare the shore is moving they within the ship are fain.

E'en though she avile his rival, yet on gracious wise she speaks;
Only 'gainst her lover raileth yonder cruel sans restrain.

[1] This couplet is purely mystic. The Súfís sometimes illustrate the doctrine of the Unity reflected in the multiplicity of contingent beings by the example of a person surrounded on every side by innumerable mirrors of different shapes and sizes. Each one of these mirrors will shew a different aspect of the One Person who alone is reflected in all.

[2] The toils of Ferhád have made of Mount Bísitún a story that travels passing from mouth to mouth.

E\er temperate the balmy climate of the World Aquose, [1]
Through the summer as the winter aye the wine-skiff [2] sails the main.

In this Seaport [3] is there traffic in all manner wares that be,
Now for patience is the market, now coquetry, now disdain

East and west from end to end the fame of her fair face hath filled;
All on earth, not only Rághib, yonder moon-bright's praise sustain

[1] ᶜAlem-ı Áb, 'the World Aquose', represents topers (alike of the literal
and mystic varieties) as a class, as we speak of the 'literary world,' the
'political world', and so on. The expression, which sometimes signifies also a
wine-party, is in constant use with the later poets. Thus Sáᵓib says

مـرا بـعــالم آب اى خـضـر هـدايـت كى

كه سوحت معر من أر راهلان و صحبت حشاى

'Guide me, O Khızr, to the World Aquose, for my brain is consumed by
[reason of the ascetics and their dry conversation'"
Similarly Shevket

يـهـمـام مـكشادـم بـادةّ نـاب دگـر بـاشـد

سـلام حـشـك مسمان عالم آب دگـر بـاشـد

[2] Zevraq-i Sahbá, 'the wine-skiff' i. e. the bowl, is another favourite expression of this period.
[3] That is, the Seaport of Love

CHAPTER III.

Seyyid Vehbí. Belígh. Nevres.

In this chapter we shall consider the work of the poets Seyyid Vehbí, Belígh, and Nevres, the three most prominent members (other than Nedím) of the Romanticist group contemporary with the Third Persianist School. The period covered by their activity extends from the reign of Ahmed III to 1175 (1761—2), the year immediately preceding that of the death of Rághib Pasha.

Huseyn Efendi, who is celebrated in Ottoman literature as Seyyid Vehbí, was, like his great contemporary Nedím, a native of Constantinople. His father Hajji Ahmed, who had been steward to an ex-cadi of Yeni-Shehir, called Imám-záde, claimed seyyidship or descent from the Prophet, through one Husám-ud-Dín, in honour of whom the young Huseyn, when he started on his literary career, chose for himself the pen-name of Husámí. It was the poet Neylí, whom we have already considered in the last chapter, who induced him to abandon this name for that under which he has become famous. 'How comes it,' said the poet, who was not slow to recognise the young Seyyid's talent, 'that you have chosen that name? You have come to add the lustre

of poetry to the honour of seyyidship which hitherto has
been the one glory of the race of Husám-ud-Dín, seeing
that no poet has arisen among them up till now. This is
the especial gift of God to you, so surely it were more
seemly that you called yourself Vehbí.' [1] And from that
day, we are told, Huseyn used no other pen-name than
Vehbí. Ever since the time of the great poet Sumbul-záde
Vehbí (himself the Seyyid's namesake) who flourished some
forty or fifty years later, it has been the custom to call
this earlier writer Seyyid Vehbí for distinction's sake

Vehbí was a member of the 'ulemá, and eventually rose
to become molla of Aleppo, in which city he was residing
at the time of the birth of his assistant's son, the little
Sumbul-záde who was destined to render yet more famous
their common name. Having served his term, Vehbí made
the pilgrimage to Mekka. On his return to Constantinople
he died in the year 1149 (1736—7), and was buried in the
court of the Rope-dancer's Mosque which is near the great
mosque of Jerráh Pasha.

Like Nedím, Seyyid Vehbí was in large measure a court
poet, and some of his best work was written to the honour
and glory of Sultan Ahmed and his ministers. Best of all
is reckoned the qasída in which he celebrates the completion
of the lovely fountain built by the Sultan in the square
outside the Seraglio gate, and which may still be read inscribed in golden letters on a ground of blue on the sides
of that most charming example of old Turkish art. The
story runs that Sultan Ahmed desiring to commemorate
the completion of his work in a chronogram, hit upon a
line which means

In the name of God drink of the water and pray for the

---

[1] The name Vehbí meaning 'He of the Gift.'

Khán Ahmed. [1] This, however, would not do, as, on addition,
the numerical value of the letters came out four short of
the required total. Thereupon Vehbí suggested that the word
Ach, meaning, 'Begin,' the letters forming which have the
value of four, should be prefixed to the Sultan's line, thus
making the chronogram perfectly correct. The poet then
composed his qasída in the rime and metre of the Sultan's
line thus amended which he introduced as the last of the
poem.

Although the Romanticist spirit breathes in much of Vehbí's
work, this poet is in no sense an imitator of Nedím. Indeed
neither he nor any of the Romanticists copied their master
as Nábí's disciples copied him; partly because the former's
lightness of touch was probably less easy to acquire than
the sententiousness of the latter, but no doubt also partly
because free play of individuality was of the essence of
Romanticism.

But while in the main a Romanticist, Vehbí never sought
to shun the influence of Nábí, many traces of which are
apparent in his Díwán. It may even be said that he unites
in a measure the characteristics of both contemporary Schools;
with Nedím he writes of the things about him in the manner
in which he sees and feels them, with Nábí he philosophises
in the most approved fashion of the neo-Persianists.

Ziyá Pasha says of Vehbí that he was versed in the
subtleties of language, which is true, and that he was the
chief of the poets of his age, which is not, and then proceeds
to tell us that in accordance with the tendencies of that
age he was enamoured of talking, so that his Díwán is
made up of padding and bad prosody, and finally, that if
all his ghazels were spread out before us, not a dozen of

[1] بسملهيله ايچ صويبى خان احمده ايله دا

them would be worth choosing. This seems an undeservedly
harsh judgment Kemál Bey, whose opinion as a critic is
worth a good deal more than Ziyá Pasha's, declares Vehbí
to have been a real poet, and adds that this assertion is
more than proved by the qasída on the Seraglio fountain.
Professor Nájí too speaks of the Seyyid's God-given talents
and says that he must be reckoned among the greatest of
Ottoman poets of the second rank. The Professor adds that
Sumbul-záde Vehbí surpasses the Seyyid only in the extent
of his work.

Besides his Díwán, Vehbí is said to have completed or
continued the romantic mesneví on the loves of Leylá and
Mejnún begun but left unfinished by the poet Qáf-záde Fá'izí
who died in 1031 (1621—2).

He has farther an interesting work in prose, with a good
deal of verse interspersed, which he called Súr-Náme or
The Book of the Festival It is a very detailed account of
the elaborate festivities given by Ahmed III on the occasion
of the circumcision of his four sons in 1132 (1720). This
gorgeous festival lasted for fifteen days, and Vehbí's careful
and sympathetic description of it throws an important side-
light on the gay doings of those brilliant times.

The following is a translation of the qasída that Vehbí
wrote for Sultan Ahmed's fountain:

Chronogrammatic Qasída for the Fountain erected by Sultan Ahmed outside the Seraglio Gate. [370]

The King of Kings of lineage high, the Sultan lauded far and nigh,
The Lord of Rúm and Araby, Khán Ahmed, victor everywhere,
The Source of equity and grace, the Sun of Saintship's rising-place.
Each portal in whose court doth trace the pinion of the humá fair,
His self the pride of every king, his sabre triumph's fountain-spring,

His reed [1] doth water ever bring to glad the Empery's parterre;
Doth Emperor and Saint is he, discovered in his person be
The grace of ꞌOmar and ꞌAlí, the virtues of Muhammed rare; [2]
The seal of empire in his hand hath conquered every realm and land,
For God hath made the Name Most Grand the legend that his brow
should bear; [3]

A hundred Cæsars he dismays, a thousand Alexanders slays,
His mandate every region sways, and king and beggar serve him e'er;
The Guardian of the Holy Shrine, [4] the Servant of the King Divine,
Arabia, Persia, Rúm supine beneath his lordship debonair;
Commander of the Faithful he, the Shade of God who aideth free,
By the sublime Koran's decree [5] must all to him obedience swear;
For him do kings their realms forego, while he doth crowns on kings bestow,
Before his sabre bows the foe when wave his horse-tails in the air.
Be yonder Source of bounty sweet who deals to all whate'er is meet
Of earth's high monarchs the retreat until the Judgment-Day is here!
Iskender, seeking far and wide, strayed in the gloom a weary tide, [6]
But he [7] the Royal Gate beside hath made the Stream of Life appear.
This bright device of mirthsome cheer suggested hath the Grand Vezír, [8]
The Royal Kinsman lief and dear whose name the Prophet's sire bare. [9]
Yon minister of haught array in this good service showed the way,
And made Zemzem [10] the fountain-spray, and won the Monarch blessings e'er.
The Sultan boon who scatters gold, expending riches vast, untold,
Hath reared this fountain ye behold: in Heaven may he be guerdoned fair!
Adorned hath he this noble site in winsome fashion fair and bright,

[1] Sultan Ahmed wrote verses.
[2] Muhammed, the Prophet; ꞌAlí, his son-in-law and the fourth Caliph;
ꞌOmar, the second Caliph.
[3] The Most Great Name of God was graven on the Seal of Solomon, and
in virtue thereof his rule extended over all created things.
[4] The Kaꞌba at Mekka.
[5] The reference is to súra IV, verse 62 of the Koran, which enjoins obedience
to Kings and governors.
[6] Alluding, of course, to Alexander the Great's quest of the Water of Life.
[7] He, i. e. Sultan Ahmed.
[8] Ibráhím Pasha.
[9] The Qureysh tribe to which the Prophet belonged is said to have been
directly descended from Abraham (Ibráhím) through Ishmael.
[10] Zemzem, the sacred spring in the Kaꞌba.

Rejoicing Huseyn's blessed spright, [1] hath raised this fount of water clear
O pure of soul, [2] unto this stream reach forth thy hand, 'twill Kevser [3] seem,
Its every lucent drop I deem to be of health a fountain rare
Its water passing sweet doth flow, and like the sphere its dome doth show,
Explore the heavenly vault below, may any pile with this compaie?
While bide on high the sun and moon may still this King adorn the throne!
And may the Vezir wise and boon, O God, be parted from him ne'er!
O Chosroes [4] of lofty line, untold these noble works of thine,
But yet this gracious fount doth shine right wonderful and passing fair
Its cups of gold and silver gleam; behold its life-restoring stream,
A silver almoner [5] 'twould seem who watcheth by thy postal e'er.
Within the palace-square wide hast thou unto the thirsting cried
In Heaven by Kevser-river's side a castle hast thou builded rare.
Thou'st bidden flow a stream of gold, as fount we Selsebil behold, [6]
For every act a thousand-fold may God reward thee, is our prayer
Be silent, Vehbi, nor let fall a word, but hold thy peace withal,
Before thee have the poets all with one accord essayed them here.
To tell the tale hereof full fain hath many a poet tried in vain,
At length the King of lustrous reign hath won its glory to declare.
To find the chronogram here-for the learned were bewildered sore,
When lo, the Sovereign of glore achieved this line beyond compare.
Its every word an ocean flows, as Aden's pearl its meaning glows,
So thou wouldst see how fair it shows, O thirster after beauties rare
The Sultan Ahmed's chronogram doth flow upon the fountain's tongue
'Begin, in name of Allah drink; and breathe for Ahmed Khán a prayer'

[1] Huseyn the Prophet's grandson, who died suffering of thirst at the battle
of Kerbelá The 10th of Muharrem, the 'Ashúrá, which is the anniversary
of that tragedy, is observed as a day of mourning and lamentation in Persia
and wherever there are Shí'ite Muhammedans Fountains (Sebíl) are often
erected in the name and to the memory of Huseyn

[2] The reader of the inscription on the fountain is here addressed

[3] Kevser, the Paradisal stream so often mentioned

[4] Chosroes or Khusrev, i.e King

[5] Literally, a water-carrier who distributes (or scatters) silver, alluding to
the silvery drops of the water

[6] It is as it were, the Heavenly stream Selsebíl turned into a fountain
Literally, 'thou hast made its golden water a charity (Sebíl) and hast con-
structed the founts of Selsebíl (each runnel of water being a fount) may
God reward thee for each of these!'

The following extracts from Vehbí's Díwán will give an idea of his usual style. The first is a Takhmís built on a ghazel of Nedím, in which the Seyyid has endeavoured to catch something of the master's manner.

Takhmís on a Ghazel of Nedím. [371]

The daughter of the grape [1] whose blushing cheek doth rosy ray
An English maiden is, [2] a slave-girl, thrall to pleasure's sway;
A lovesome chatterer is she whose airs delight convey.
  'Deem not the daughter of the vine hides with the rake away;
  'His Reverence the Sheykh and she as sire and daughter play.'

Whenas the daughter of the grape behind the glass is seen
She yoketh with the cupbearer as soul and body e'en;
What then if hence a hint of blending's virtues rare we glean? [3]
  'The daughter of the vine is e'en the youthful Magian sheen;
  'She's sooth a light o' love, a frolic-hearted Scioan may. [4]

Whene'er he sees the prancing of thy gallant courser fleet,
Whene'er he looks upon thy motions ravishing and sweet,
He makes collyrium of the dust upon thy road, I weet;
  'Thy prostrate one, until he kiss the prints of thy dear feet,
  'Will never quit thy path, O Sapling; well he knows his way.'

The elder's hand's a-tremble through his drunkenness, I trow,
And fasting is the name whereby His Grace doth feasting know;

[1] I. e. the red wine.

[2] The term 'English,' which is introduced by Vehbí for the sake of the rime, is not very appropriate here; as, seeing that no wine was made in this country, the daughter of the grape could not possibly be English. Perhaps the rosy cheeks typical of English girls may have been in the poet's mind, but one would imagine his knowledge of such matters must have been extremely limited.

[3] It is usual in the East to dilute the wine (which is very strong) with water. Here Vehbí means to say that the wine and the cupbearer, being each charming, consort well together, which gives a hint of the advantage of blending things.

[4] The word Saqiz means 'mastic,' and Saqiz Adasi or Mastic Isle is the name given to the Isle of Scio or Khios. Scioan wine, Scioan girls, and Scioan roses are all praised by the Romanticist poets.

8

114

He makes the-fear of God his rule of life to outward show
'The zealot drains the Scioan wine in secret, whispering low. —
'Let ne'er a stranger drink of this, 'tis mastic-mixed, I say.' [1]

By Love becomes the longing lover's eye the sea of tears;
The Sphere's a bubble on its face made by the sea of tears,
O'erwhelmeth all the ships of far and nigh the sea of tears;
'The eyne of weeping lovers blancheth aye the sea of tears;
'Yon wanton poop-levend [2] must hie from White Sea [3] shores, in fay.

The tiring-maiden, spring, hath all in blithesome fashion dight,
And made the blooming bower of earth the home of fair delight,
And set the dew for diamonds in the ring that sealeth plight [4]
'What though the bulbul bring as dower the roral mintage bright,
'The virgin rose is portioned rich with many a garden gay'

Blood is the script upon the heart that may not bear with pain;
The yearning for thy locks shall never leave the soul again,
Although the mansion of our life be burned by thy disdain,
'Although the frame be turned to ashes, yet will there remain
'The secret of thy tresses hid within the heart for aye.'

O Vehbí, sing Sipáhí-wise, for how should e'er Selím
Achieve upon this way to string the jewels of Nazím,

[1] Playing upon the two meanings of Saqız 'Mastic' and 'Scioan.'
[2] The Levends (Levantines) were a corps of naval gunners in old times, recruited chiefly from the maritime provinces. The Romanticist poets often speak of the youthful levend much as do the earlier writers of the Shah-suwár or cavalier, that is, as the type of a graceful and gallant, though heedless, youth Thus the Romanticists select their type from what they have seen, while the Persianists choose theirs from what they have read about in the Tránian poets The term qıch levendi means properly a levend or marine who fights from the stern of the ship, here there is a secondary meaning suggested
[3] What we call the Mediterranean Sea is by the Turks called the White Sea, in opposition to the Black Sea In mentioning the White Sea here the poet recalls the 'blanching' of the lover's eyes through excess of weeping which he has spoken of in the preceding line.
[4] The 'engagement ring' given on betrothal, the dower in the following line refers to that given by the husband in Muslim marriages.

E'en though his name be lifted to the nines [1] like to Kelím? [2]
'Octupled by these couplets eight the signatures, Nedím,
'Thy reed's certificate for eloquence can now display.

Ghazel. [372]

Yon Moon with beauty flushed doth ne'er the ground before her sight;
We're trodden heedless under foot, dismayful is our plight.

Did she behold the angels at her shoulders when she prays,
She ne'er would give the greeting on the left hand and the right. [3]

If thus she bide, yon Fairy on the Resurrection-Day
Will wave aside Rizwán if her to Kevser he invite. [4]

Inebriate with the torrent-wild tumultuous wine of pride,
'Tis wondrous naught of scathe doth e'er her honour's palace smite.

Let not that queen be hot with arrogance, for passing soon
Doth sickness from such wine its brave hilarity requite.

Will not that Fairy look and see how faded beauties strive,
The while their hearts for lovers yearn, excuses still to cite?

Vehbí, thou hast made o'er the humbling of the empery
Of yonder Torment's grace to that which down and cheek shall smite. [5]

---

[1] The Turkish term طقومجيسنه طقوزه 'to rise to the nine,' is a popular phrase much like our 'to be praised up to the nines,' and has much the same signification.

[2] Sipáhí, Selím, Nazím, and Kelím are all poets, of more or less repute, who flourished about this time. Nazím has been mentioned in a previous chapter (Vol. III, pp. 319—323).

[3] This alludes to the following practice: each person is believed to be attended by two guardian angels, the Kirámu'l-Kátibín or Noble Scribes, as they are called; and at the conclusion of prayer, before rising from the knees, it is the custom to salute these angels by inclining the head first over the right shoulder, then over the left, repeating at the same time the formula: Es-selámu ʿaleykum wa rahmetu-lláh, 'Peace be on you and the mercy of God!' Vehbí's young lady is so haughty that if she could see these angels, she would refuse to salute them.

[4] Rizwán the angel guardian of Paradise and the Kevser river or stream therein have often come under our notice.

[5] That is, Time.

The ghazel just translated is inspired by a haughty beauty, the next one describes a youthful lover.

Ghazel. [373]

While yet a tender youth, o'er him did Love his thraldom fling;
A bondsman he became while yet of grace and beauty king.

Betrodden of the steed of some fair Torment's pride was he,
While yet a child reed-mounted [1] who of love knew ne'er a thing

Athirst was he to sip the luscious rubies of some Moon,
The while he was himself the source of sweetness' fountain-spring.

He wept a-yearning to embrace some fair coquettish Palm,
And he himself a tendril on a sapling burgeoning.

He watched the heavens to espy some Star of beauty bright,
While he himself the pang that heart of sun and moon did sting.

Distraught he gazed upon his knee as 'twere a mirror sheen
And silent bode, while he a parrot sweet of tongue to sing. [2]

He smitten was of some bright Fairy lovely e'en as he,
His reason reft, himself a charmer reason-ravishing.

So, Vehbí, was e'en he distraughten of some Torment fair,
While he himself the age's Woe that dule to earth did bring

Ghazel. [374]

May any hope to scape from forth thy darkling tresses' chain?
How may the spirit-bird from yonder springe [3] deliv'rance gain?

---

[1] In Eastern lands children ride on a long reed for a horse, as they do on a stick in England.

[2] There is here an allusion to the method said to be employed in the East to teach parrots to speak. The parrot is held before a mirror, while the teacher utters from behind it the word or phrase which he wishes the parrot to learn; and the bird, seeing its own reflection, and imagining that the words proceed from it, tries to imitate it

[3] The word qalláb, here translated 'springe,' ordinarily means a hook, but also a curved perch to which a bird is tied by the leg By the 'springe,' the curls of the beloved are here intended

Torn were the heart, an it should sight that radiant cheek of thine,
Unrent beneath the lunar beams how should the flax remain? [1]

Who finds immunity from yonder wheeling of the Skies?
May any win to shun the fury of the raging main?

The rude assault of death will surely lay man low at last;
May ever sparrow from the eagle's clutch release obtain?

That he may scape alike from rage of foes and grace of friends,
O God, to succour hapless Vehbí of Thy mercy deign.

The poet Mehemmed Emín Belígh of Larissa must not
be confounded with the biographer of the same pen-name,
the Seyyid Isma'íl Belígh of Brusa, whose 'Posy from the
Garths of Culture' we have so often quoted. [2]

This poet Belígh is eminently typical of the period. He
shares something of Nedím's love of beautiful things and
also of his grace and delicacy of touch; he inherits from
Sábit a feeling for humour and a certain vigour of handling;
while at the same time he possesses a boldness and originality of his own which enable him to invent a new variety
of poem.

The meagre biography given by Fatín tells us very little.
Belígh, we are informed, was a member of the legal profession, and more than usually solicitous about promotion,
a characteristic to which he is himself supposed to refer in
the following couplet:

[1] A certain kind of cloth or gauze made of flax is (or was) supposed to
go into shreds if exposed to the moonlight; it is hence sometimes represented by the poets as being enamoured of the moon. Certain amorous princes
of old are fabled to have amused themselves by dressing girls in this material, and walking with them in their gardens on moonlight nights.

[2] Belígh of Brusa, the biographer, who was also something of a poet,
predeceased Belígh of Larissa by twenty-nine years, dying in his native city
in 1143 (1730—1). The following are mentioned as his poetical works: Gul-i
Sad-Berg, 'The Hundred-leafed Rose;' comments on one hundred Apostolic
Traditions; Seb'a-i Seyyáre, 'The Seven Planets;' a series of seven na'ts;
Ser-guzesht-Náme, 'The Book of Adventures.'

'From the keen desire of office ne'er may the official win,
'Sore he striveth till Death gives him an appointment lasting aye.' [1]

His endeavours in this direction would seem to have been
successful, as we read that he held several important positions, and finally died as judge of Eski-Zaghra in 1172
(1758—9).

Belígh has hardly attracted that amount of attention from
the critics which might have been expected. Ziyá Pasha
although he includes two or three couplets from his Díwán
among the selections in 'The Tavern,' omits all mention of
him from the preface. He is not among the poets whom
Professor Nájí reviews in the series of essays to which
reference has so often been made, and Ekrem Bey is silent
concerning him alike in his 'Course of Literature' and in his
pamphlet upon the early poets. Fatín Efendi, again, following his wont, confines himself to a conventional compliment
about his being among the poets who by the eloquence of
their verse, have stamped their name for ever on the records
of the world, Tevfíq Bey, who in his "Caravan of Poets"
confuses him with Belígh of Brusa, is a little more diffuse,
though no more definite; while Von Hammer has through
some strange oversight omitted him altogether from his
History.

Jelál Bey, on the other hand, declares that the brilliant
imagery and daintiness of fancy which distinguish portions
of the work of this poet remind him of Nedím. And Kemál
Bey, when 'demolishing' 'The Tavern, criticises Ziyá Pasha
for having passed him over in his preface, and pronounces
his qasídas to be no whit inferior to those of his contemporaries Sámí and Muníf, whom the Pasha introduces with

[1]

اهـل منصب كاچـهمـر داعيةُ مصيبلن

جالشور تا عـلم آبادى اسـدنجه تـأسـد

deserved acclaim. Kemál goes on to tell a story, which he
says is well-known in literary circles, as to how, after the
poet Sumbul-záde Vehbí (whom Ziyá eulogises as the Muftí
of Art) had tried to 'parallel' the ghazels Nábí and Rághib
had composed with the redíf of mehtáb, 'moon-light,' he saw
Belígh's ghazel with this same redíf, whereon he exclaimed,
'I wrestled with Nábí and Rághib, but had I seen Belígh,
I had not spent my strength in an attempt so vain.' Why,
asks the Bey of the Pasha, do you ignore a poet whom
your 'Muftí of Art' declared to be stronger than himself?

Belígh is unquestionably a poet of some interest. His
language is at times scarcely less graceful than that of
Nedím, whom he farther resembles in frequently choosing
subjects of a delicate, and occasionally risky, character. But
it is with Sábit that his truer affinities lie; like that writer
he has a dash of humour in his nature, an element entirely
absent in Nedím, and like him he deals with his themes
in a robust and outspoken fashion, though without the
coarseness which disfigures so much of the earlier writer's
most characteristic work. Sábit too, rather than Nedím, appears to have been his model in the Turkicising of his
language; for although, as we have said, he occasionally
approaches the dainty charm of the latter poet's diction,
it is more often the idiomatic phraseology of the former
that he seems to have kept in view.

With the contemporary Persianist School Belígh had scant
sympathy; the trite moralisings of the followers of Nábí were
but little to his liking, neither was he inclined to seek his
teachers across the eastern frontier. It is true that he recognised the talent of Rághib Pasha, and went so far as to
write a 'parallel' to one of that poet's ghazels, but this, be
it noted, was one of the most Turkish of the Pasha's poems, one
of those in which he yielded most to the tendency of the age.

The foregoing remarks apply to Belígh's poems other than
his qasídas. His work in this form, which, as has been said,
retained its conventionality up to the end, is scarcely to be
distinguished from that of the most thorough-going Persianists
of his day. Here his favourite models seem to have been
Sá'ib and Shevket and, in a less degree, 'Urfí, he once
mentions Muhtasham [1] as though he admired him Belígh's
qasídas are generally harmonious and graceful, but they
cannot be described as brilliant, and being inspired from a
common source, they have much resemblance to the similar
productions of his contemporaries, and form the least characteristic and consequently the least interesting section of
his work.

The Díwán, which comprises all Belígh's literary work,
contains of course a number of ghazels These are of far
greater interest than the qasídas, for in them he allows far
freer scope to his individual idiosyncrasies. It is in the ghazels
that occur the pretty Nedím-like fancies and phrases to which
we have already referred, it is in the ghazels too that we
become aware of a latent strain of irony in the poet's temper,
which at times breaks out in terse and forceful expression.

But the real Belígh, Belígh the Romanticist, Belígh the
innovator, is seen most clearly and in his truest colours in
a remarkable group of four serio-comic poems, by virtue of
which productions it is that I have said that this writer
invented a new variety of poem. Whether this new variety
was worth inventing may well be open to question, but
the introduction of anything fresh into this poetry is a fact
of which few indeed can boast.

These four poems are in the form called museddes, and
consist of a succession of six-line stanzas, — nine in three

[1] Muhtasham of Káshán, a Persian poet of eminence who died in 996
(1587—8)

cases, twelve in the fourth. They are named respectively:
Hammám-Náme, 'The Book of the Bath; Kefshger-Náme,
'The Book of the Shoemaker;' Khayyát-Náme, 'The Book
of the Tailor;' and Berber-Náme, 'The Book of the Barber.'
They derive from the Shehr-engíz alike in subject, for
they all deal with the minions of the bazaars, and in style,
for they treat their themes in the playful and humorous
fashion proper to that variety of composition. The new move
here made by Belígh was the application of the familiar
half-quizzical half-laudatory tone of the Shehr-engíz to the
sustained account of a single type. The Shehr-engíz was, as
we know, a kind of catalogue of the young beauties of a
certain city, each of whom was mentioned by name and
presented with a combination of flattery and good-humoured
chaff in two or three couplets. Belígh took this style, which
he found ready to his hand, and choosing two or three
typical examples from the numerous entries (if we may so
call them) in the Shehr-engíz, expanded these into as many
separate poems, each of considerable length. The boys in
Belígh's poems are, however, nameless; and in all probability
are nothing more than fictitious representatives of certain
familiar types. They are moreover not so much described
as (so to speak) written round. We are not told much about
the lads themselves; they form, as it were, centres from which
the author flashes his witticisms in every direction, or pegs
on which he hangs his manifold pleasantries; but they themselves remain more or less nebulous throughout. It will be
observed that they all (except perhaps in the first of the
four poems) belong to the lower orders, they being the sons
or apprentices of a shoemaker, a tailor, and a barber, respectively, — boys whose position in life would necessarily
bring them into contact with the loafers about the bazaars.
This is almost invariably the case in poems of the Shehr-

engíz class, and is of course quite what we should expect. With us to-day analogous productions would discuss in piquant and rather free verses the typical barmaid or tobacconist's girl, just as our parallel to the Shehr-engíz would be a playfully written riming list of the principal courtezans of a city.

Belígh's half-humorous half-complimentary dissertations are, as has been said, somewhat vague in detail, though the general intention is clear enough They contain a liberal supply of the usual punning allusions to the lad's trade as well as of the usual proverbs and popular locutions. The vocabulary and phraseology are far more Turkish than in any other of the writer's poems, which offers another instance of that peculiar tendency which we have already noticed to regard humorous writing as the most appropriate field for the exercise of the native idiom. Being full of technical expressions, sometimes obsolete or local, these poems are exceptionally difficult to understand; in some lines indeed the meaning is so obscure that it can scarcely be even guessed at

The lead here given by Belígh was not, so far as I know, followed by any contemporary or subsequent poet. No one seems to have thought of writing 'parallels' to these works of his, or of adding any fresh portraits to his little gallery. So these four sketches of the Larissa poet remain unique in the literature, and on the whole this is perhaps as well.

Belígh has furthermore a Sáqí-Náme which both in tone and diction is modelled upon the earlier poems of the same class. In form it is what is called a Muʿashsher, that is a succession of ten-line stanzas, of which in this case there are thirteen. This work, which is of course very Persian in character, is graceful but lacks sincerity, and has the appearance of having been written as a literary exercise. In it, as here and there in the ghazels, Belígh plays with mystic ideas

and phrases, like so many other Turkish poets who used
the similes and metaphors of the old mystic writers as part
of their literary stock-in-trade, bringing them out from time
to time to serve as decorative points in their artificial productions without the slightest regard to, often with but the
dimmest conception of, the profound depths of their original
signification.

This ghazel is somewhat in Nedím's manner:

Ghazel. [375]

The red fez lieth on her locks, like rose-leaf upon jacinth rare:
The perspiration gems her cheeks, like dewdrops upon roses fair.

Since shone the cupbearer's bright chin, reflected in the brimming bowl,
Mine eyen on the wine are fixed, e'en like the bubbles floating there.

Behold how she hath knotted yonder flowing tresses musk-perfumed
Which bide as 'twere a sweet pastile upon her amber-scented hair.

The Typal Love is passed full soon by them who faithful tread the Path;
There lives no man on earth would choose to dwell upon a Bridge for e'er. [1]

Belígh, whene'er the steed, thy reed, doth caracole across the page,
Thy finger is the Hayder bold whom that Duldul doth onward bear. [2]

The next is in a different vein.

Ghazel. [376]

Look not thou for biding mansion mid this world where nothing stays:
Fashion thou thy tent of rushing whirlwinds mid its desert ways! [3]

---

[1] The reference is to the famous saying of the Mystics, المجاز قنطرة الحقيقة;
el-mejázu qantaratu-l-haqíqa, 'the Typal is the Bridge to the Real.' In mystic
terminology 'ashq-i mejází, or Typal Love, stands for love towards a mistress
or sweetheart, in distinction to 'ashq-i haqíqí or Real Love, that is Love
towards God, which is its consummation. The 'Path' in this verse is, of course,
the mystic Path.

[2] Hayder is 'Alí the Prophet's son-in-law; Duldul is the name of his
famous mule.

[3] i. e. 'Do not hope for, or strive after, any settled or permanent abode

Ever turns the Wheel of Heaven even as the fool would wish, —
Sooth, the very vilest beggar heeds his sightless child always!

Swelling up elate with fragrance from the loved one's sweetest wafts,
Reach the waves of floral odour e'en the topmost cypress-sprays [1]

All who view that lovesome Torment sore are dazed for dule and woe,
While athwart the facial mirror every thought, reflected, plays [2]

Naught of reverence I render to the gowned and turbaned fool,
Learned men esteem a sentence but for that which it conveys

Never leaves the Sphere to play these drunken turns and shiftings wild,
Ne'er hath stone of heart's dispraising cracked its blue enamel glaze. [3]

'Tis thy mole's reflection kindleth vision in the optic lamp,
Yea, the fulgent sun's the pupil its parhelion's eye displays

Let yon wanton on my spirit's tablet write her name, Belígh,
For 'tis to the letter's superscription that folk turn their gaze.

This is the "Moonlight" ghazel against which Sumbul-záde Vehbí held it vain to compete.

Ghazel. [377]

A-yearning for the sun of love, the moonlight watcheth all the night,
And filleth thus its bowl with milk from out the Selsebíl of light

Within its crucible the moonlight melts the shining sun's bright rays,
Displaying the alchemic art to all the stars the sky that dight.

For scarlet skirt the moonlight dons the halo, and sets forth a-field,
And fair within the sky performs the sacred Mevlevian rite. [4]

in this fleeting world, i. e. be ever moving on through this desert of life on thy homeward journey.

[1] The scent of the rose is conceived as rising up to overtake the sweeter fragrance of the locks which crown the 'cypress-form' of the beloved

[2] i e the affliction of her lovers is reflected in her sensitive, or 'mirror-like' face

[3] i e the stones of man's complaints in no wise touch or affect.'that inverted Bowl they call the Sky.'

[4] Referring to the mystic circular dance of the Mevlevian dervishes.

Meseems the moonlight strides, an archer-champion, o'er the heavenly plain;
The halo shines his thumb-stall, while the beams shoot down in arrow-flight.

The moonlight takes in hand its golden pen like Rúmí Mevláná,
And each night to the Sun's bright work it doth a parallel indite. [1]

The moonlight evermore the glory of the sun's elixir wins,
For vigil keeps it in the halo nightly till the dawn is bright.

The black of soul are aye the mortal foes of them of radiant heart;
And thus alway the moonlight doth the darkling thief dismay and fright.

Oh how should they who watch the livelong night depart the vale of Love?
For lo the moonlight turns its beams to chains for every weakling wight.

Let not that wanton fair this night illume the banquet of the moon;
For sore I fear me lest the moonlight-beams her tender frame may blight. [2]

If thou hast any slightest lack in the night-roaming art, my friend,
The moonlight will disclose thee mid the loved one's ward to all men's sight. [2]

Belígh, in honour of the noble feast of Rátib, Asaph-sage, [3]
The moonlight doth with golden pen these all-effulgent verses write.

The following ghazel upon a young dancer is in the spirit
and manner of the Book of the Tailor and its fellows. It
is an innovation, not only to use the ghazel-form in this
fashion, but to adhere throughout to any single theme.

[1] Rúmí Mevláná = Mevláná (our Lord) of Rúm, i. e. Jelál-ud-Dín, the author of the Mesneví and founder of the Mevleví order. The 'Sun' here refers, in the second place, to Jelál's friend Shems-ud-Dín (Sun of the Faith) of Tebríz, generally known as Shams-i-Tabríz. The Díwán of mystical poems known by his name is really the work of Jelálu'd-Dín.

[2] The notion that exposure to the moonlight is injurious prevails in the East as well as in Europe.

[3] Ahmed Rátib Pasha, to whom Belígh inscribes this ghazel, like the poet himself, was a native of Larissa, and was the son of the gallant and high-minded Topal 'Osmán Pasha ('Osmán Pasha the Lame). He became Grand Admiral, married a daughter of the Sultan, and finally died governer of the Morea in 1175 (1761—2). Several of Belígh's qasídas are dedicated to this officer.

Ghazel [378]

Whene'er that pretty dancer [1] 'gins on the castanets to play,
Did the sun and moon look down, they were each for envy rent a-tway. [2]

What time she falls a-dancing fair I may brook no more, in sooth;
For my heart it leaps along with her and my vision swoons away.

When the moon looks down on her what way may it fail to be scared of heart?
For that moon-face maketh a halo bright of her skirt of scarlet say.

In all of her motions and pauses, lo, what thrills of wild delight!
And she holds her frame a-quiver like to quick-silver away.

A-thrill for her figure's beauty roars the drum with a lusty voice,
And the tambour smites its breast the while that its bells cry Welaway!

And when that Fairy comes and prays for the coin that circles free, [3]
An one had hearts by hundreds, all he would throw in her tambour gay.

On gala days she decks her brave in the scarlet, O Belígh;
And she hath burned the soul of me, alack, the fire-bright may. [4]

[1] The dancer referred to may have been a boy, and not a girl, but as
there is nothing in the text to show which is meant, we shall give the poet
the benefit of the doubt. This, however, is an indulgence which he scarcely
deserves seing that he has the bad taste to say, though perhaps not quite
seriously, in one of his ghazels.

اولدەمز حسمله خوبانله دوابر فرلر قلبدر آنلرى مشاطه در آز بالدرلر

'Girls cannot equal fair boys in beauty;
'For they are made up, the tire-woman tinsels them a bit'
None the less, the bringing of the two sexes thus into line is a sign of the times.

[2] There is in this couplet an untranslatable pun between charpara 'castanets'
and chár pára 'four pieces.' Something of the effect, but not the sense, may
be given thus·
Whene'er that pretty dancer 'gins on the *castanets* to play
She doth *cast a net* for the sun and moon, and fain to be ta'en are they

[3] Naqd-ı Rewán means at once 'current coin' and 'the coin of the soul,'
here the first line suggests the first meaning, the second, the second.

[4] It will be noticed how in this ghazel the various 'properties' associated
with the street-dancer are introduced, — the castanets which she herself
plays, the drum and bell-encircled tambourine of her accompanists, the scarlet
skirt which she wears, while allusion is made to the peculiar vibratory motion
which forms so distinctive a feature of Eastern dancing.

Of the four serio-comic poems the Hammám-Náme or Book of the Bath is the least bizarre in language, though also the least characteristic. It is, however, a novelty, and gives an accurate though fantastic account of the modus operandi still in force in the Turkish public bath.

The Book of the Bath. [379]

Up from sleep awaking, rose yon winsome Torment blithe and gay,
Early in the morn toward the public bath he bent his way.
All the folk who saw him deemed the sun had risen twice that day.
When he came into the dressing-room he sate him like a fay.
 Sweat the windows from the glow that from his crystal neck did ray,
 Hot through yearning to embrace him waxed the bath in sooth straightway. [1]

Then his dainty cap, as 'twere a lover, from his head he threw,
And with many an air did he the belt which bound his clothes undo,
And he laid his garments each on each, that like a rose they grew. [2]
Thought they who beheld his silver breast when off his shift he drew, —
 From its wrap the silver mirror hath been bared and flasheth gay, [3]
 Otherwise hath the sweet almond, glowing, cast its shell away.

Through the ardour of the looks upon him bent his body glowed,
So the bathman turned the others out that coolth and calm abode.
When he saw him the shampooer, [4] wildered, strayed from off the road,
And the while he tied the pattens [5] down to yonder Idol bowed;
 When he did the musky towel [6] round about his waist display
 To its middle was the plenilune eclipsed, ah, wel-a-way.

[1] In this couplet there are two examples of husn-i taʿlíl: the windows studded with drops of water resulting from the condensation of the warm air in the bath-room are said to perspire in the glow of the lad's bright skin, while the bath, which is being heated, is figured as growing ardent in the expectation of embracing him.
[2] The articles of clothing laid one upon another are likened to a rose with its superimposed circles of petals.
[3] It being usual to keep metal mirrors in bags or wraps.
[4] That is the attendant who rubs and kneads the bather.
[5] High pattens are worn in the bath to protect the feet from the hot floor.
[6] A kind of towel, generally dark blue (whence here called 'musky' i. e. dark-coloured), is wrapped round the waist.

'When the young shampooer led him to the private chamber there [1]
'Twas as though the sun and moon together in one mansion were.
Like a jelly did his body tremble whoso touched it e'er;
So he [2] saw yon tender Rosebud [3] naught of massaging could bear
  Then the heat took the shampooer that he fainted straight away
  Till a youthful lad did o'er him water from the ewer spray.

When he sought to rub the musky bag [4] on yonder charmer free,
Writhed and wriggled sore the loofah, [5] melted swift the soap, ah me!
Then a little while to play here with the bubbles fancied he
Seeing him within the private-room, deem not him ranged [6] to be.
  Entering the bath, the moon hath all his freckles washed away, [7]
  Thou shalt see how bright his lustre at to-night's carouse will ray [8]

Flowed the water over yonder cypress-body to his feet, [9]
Freshly watered it his hyacinthine tresses long and sweet,
Yea, the water grew ecstatic, and its heart did throb and beat
When yon moon-face was reflected in the brimming bowl, I weet.
  Jealous of thy cheek's refulgence, did the windows flash, in fay.
  To the Sphere of Fire the bath-house cupola was turned that day [10]

[1] Some public baths are provided with private rooms
[2] The shampooer.
[3] The young bather
[4] The sort of bag which the shampooer puts on his hand like a glove,
and with which he rubs the bather's body.
[5] The mass of date-palm fibre used to make the soap foam.
[6] The original has موزون which is the Arabic equivalent to the Turkish
دورلمش, a word that sometimes replaces the more usual مشكلمس.
[7] There is a pun here, the spots or markings on the moon's face being
in Arabic called its 'freckles'
[8] The young bather being imagined as going to attend some party in the
evening.
[9] At one point of the performance the bather stands up and has water
poured all over him, which of course trickles down to his feet
[10] The windows of a bath-room are always in the roof, and form a kind
of cupola or lantern Here this cupola, lit up with the refulgence flashing
from the dazzling white skin of the bather, is likened to the Sphere of Fire
which in the Ptolemaic cosmogony is situated immediately within the Sphere
of the Moon and immediately without the Spheres of Air and Water by
which the earth is enveloped

When he found the bath was warm no more, that all its heat was spent,
Thence to hie him straight the heart of yonder restless Moon was bent.
By the radiance of his visage was the window's glory shent.
Having dried his mirror-body, to the outer room he went;
 There he donned his brilliant vestments even like the fancies gay,
 And he did his balanced figure like the hemistich array. [1]

Sheeny had the water made his tresses like the royal crest; [2]
And the waves of air his fragrant hyacinthine locks carest;
When the keeper felt the perfume that 'twas ambergris he guest,
For the comb e'en at that moment yonder sweetheart's tresses drest.
 Ambergris was shed on every side therefrom in fragrant spray,
 And the wafts of sweetest odour all around did breathe and play.

Now the coffee-cup to yonder sweetheart's dainty lip was set,
Lighted was the censer, sprinkled o'er him the rose-water jet. [3]
Since, Belígh, whoever entereth within the bath must sweat, [4]
Silver aspers [5] for the bath fee scattered yonder winsome pet.
 Then did he arise, whereon the mirror's breast was broke in twain; [6]
 Like the fire [7] yon Moon departed, and the bath was froze straightway. [8]

The Khayyát-Náme or Book of the Tailor is a much
better and more characteristic example of the peculiar style
elaborated by Belígh in his four humorous poems. But it is
impossible to present this work satisfactorily in translation;

[1] The bather's figure is here compared to a well-balanced hemistich, and
his gay garments to the brilliant fancies wherewith that is clothed.

[2] The royal crest means the Tugh or horse-tail standard.

[3] After the bather has had his bath and has resumed his clothes, he is
generally presented with a cup of coffee, and is sometimes fumigated with
incense and sprinkled with rose-water.

[4] One is made to perspire profusely.

[5] The aspers, small silver coins, being conceived as drops of perspiration.

[6] Just before leaving the bath-house it is usual to look at one's self in a
mirror in order to see whether one's head-gear and so on is tidy. Here the
mirror is supposed to be heart-broken at the lad's departure.

[7] The boy was like the fire both because of his ardour-inspiring beauty
and because he 'went out.'

[8] The bath 'remained frozen;' this is a common phrase and means 'was
dumbfoundered', rendered speechless and motionless, as if turned to ice.
Here, of course, the literal meaning, 'made cold,' is also kept in sight.

9

since, apart from its intrinsic difficulty, the effect at which
it aims is not of a nature to admit of exact reproduction
in another language. This effect is in part produced by the
apt citation, or at least suggestion, of certain well-known
proverbs and popular locutions bearing more or less on the
craft of tailoring. To achieve an analogous effect in English,
we should have to allude to or hint at the stitch in time
that saves nine, the needle in the haystack, the nine tailors
that are held needful to make a man, and so on; but to do
this would be to write a paraphrase or 'parallel,' not to
make a translation. In the following rendering, therefore,
I have attempted no more than to give the literal meaning
of the lines; though in some cases this is so obscure that
the translation is little more than conjectural, while in two
instances it has completely baffled all my efforts.

The Book of the Tailor. [380]

In the morn a tailor stripling, sweet an Idol debonair,
With his figure like a silver measure, [1] forth did gaily fare;
And he decked his shop within the market with his beauty's ware;
Full a quarter-length [2] his face was shrouded by his knotted hair. [3]
  Blood his needle-eyelash spilt, his glances they were shears of care;
  Yonder beauty shore my secret's stuff the while I laid it bare.

All from needle e'en to thread [4] my heart's plight to that fair I told;
Through his shift could I his body like to marrow soft behold;
Beat him not; it is but orphan trickery, [5] an he be bold;
Plucking-to his collar, do not yonder Torment tightly hold.

[1] The word used in the original is more especially a cloth-measure.

[2] Here again the word employed is correctly used only as a cloth-measure.

[3] His hair is tangled or knotted as thread might be; once more the word
is also the name of a measure.

[4] ايكنەدن ايپلكه وارنجه 'From needle to thread,' is a popular phrase
meaning 'entirely,' 'from beginning to end.'

[5] Orphanlike behaviour, i. e. naughtiness; the orphan having no parent to
rear him properly.

Even though the rival hap to win to favour with the fair,
Yet be sure the seam will hold not[1] with that cordless[2] wight contrare.

He, the bow-eyebrowed, a mighty trousered swimmer is,[3] I ween.
Lo, his lashes form the vest to clothe his glances swift and keen
Beauty's vesture is the mantle[4] cut to fit his form and mien
Press not, jacket,[5] let his silver bosom naked still be seen.
Ope the eye, but gaze on yonder sweet in purity, beware,
Close it not, for fear the rival seize the chance and rush[6] the fair

All so flushed with wine is yonder moon-faced beauty bright and gay[7]
That the tresses full an ell-length downward o'er his middle stray.
Since that yonder hips and knees from e'en his drawers shrink away,[8]
Round about yon hair-waist wind not thou thine arm, for pity, pray!

Tender is that sweetheart's body, squeeze him not then vest-like[9] there,
Ay, belike yon dear will fell it,[10] for he can't thy boredom bear.

[1] دیكمش طوبدرمك 'To make the seam hold,' another popular locution meaning so to arrange that a business may be successful or a thing answer its purpose.

[2] Ipsiz, a cordless or ropeless one, is colloquial for a good-for-naught, here it is playfully applied to the lad

[3] Shalwárli shináver, 'trousered swimmer,' I have been unable to find any explanation of this curious phrase. Perhaps it was a slang expression current in Belígh's time, with some such meaning as 'ruffler' or 'swaggerer.' Shalwár is the name given to the large baggy trousers formerly worn in Turkey.

[4] The qaftan (here translated mantle) is an upper gown or robe with long skirts and sleeves, the name was sometimes applied to the robe of honour given by sovereigns.

[5] The nim-ten (colloquially 'mintan') is a short round jacket with sleeves to the elbow only.

[6] There is a pun here 'lest the rival seize the chance and make a 'binish,' which last word means at once (here) an assault, and a kind of long full outer cloak worn by gentlemen in olden times.

مست می شونله كه چاقشبر گمی اول مه رو

I cannot place the words چقشبر گمی chaqshir-like, that occur in this line. Chaqshir is the name of a special kind of trousers that are fastened round the waist in folds with a band in a broad hem, and round the ankles by being sewn to light leather boots

[8] His skin is so delicate that he can hardly bear his clothes rubbing against it; as in the third verse of Nedím's ghazel [322] on p. 40 *supra.*

[9] The entari was a kind of short inner vest with long tight sleeves; the name is also given to a variety of long robe made of some light material

[10] Tegellemek means properly 'to fell,' i. e. to lay a seam or hem and sew

Loose not thou the cord of union,[1] there will issue naught but bane,
Thou wilt only vex his spirit, and he'll pull it to[2] again,
Heed thee, be not rough, elsewise the lace[3] will snap and break in twain,
Though yon musky braid be wroughten all of twisted silken skein
  Meet it were the line of light from eyes of those on him that stare
  Formed the rays of yonder sun upon his mantle[4] broidered rare.

Come, my silver-bosom, gather not thy cloak[5] about thee so,
Yonder vest[6] with gold bedizened through thy tunic's opening show;
Nay, nay, not yet all alone can he, the sweetheart, tear and sew.[7]
Haste thee, master,[8] round this Kurdish coat[9] a cord of red must[10] go.
  If thy measurements suffice not he, the dear, will make it square[11]
  Not unworthy are their actions who the fire of love do bear!

Ready is the cloth to make those blessed[12] drawers for the dear,

it down level with the cloth; but here it seems further to hint at some figurative sense, perhaps we should read 'will fell thee' for 'will fell it.'
  [1] That is the uchqur, the long broad band with which the trousers or
drawers were fastened round the waist.
  [2] The word here used, چلاتيرش, is, I am informed, peculiar to tailors,
and means to patch or mend
  [3] This and the 'braid' of the next line both refer to the uchqur.
  [4] The kerake was an outer coat or cloak, usually of light woollen stuff,
and often ornamented with gold embroidery and large buttons The word
tár is used not only for warp or thread, but for the line of sight or a ray
of light
  [5] The jubbe is an outer robe or gown, with full sleeves and long skirts,
and open in front.
  [6] The fermene (or fermele) is a short jacket or vest, rounded in front,
and ornamented with gold braid. It is like what is called called in England
a zouave jacket
  [7] I e he is still too young or too inexperienced to work without supervision.
  [8] This line is addressed to the master tailor
  [9] The kurdiyye or Kurdish coat is a kind of frock-coat with short sleeves
  [10] The name huseyní is given to a kind of red cord used for trimmings
  [11] This line is literally. If it (i. e. the coat or cord) come not out from
the lines (of chalk marked on the garment to indicate the fit) — i e. if the
material runs short — the sweetheart will make thee a cord, i e find thee
some clever device to overcome the difficulty.
  [12] The word here used, مبعوذ, expresses contempt in a vague way, with
something of the force of the words 'blessed' or 'blooming' in English slang,
but without their tinge of vulgarity.

(Never holy saint is made by turban and by frock austere.) [1]
Ne'er a purchaser will find such stuff as this [2] or far or near,
E'en brocade would not as good as sendal by its side appear. [3]
  Like to rosy satin nappy is yon glowing cheek, I swear. [4]
  Tell me, zealot, hast thou ever seen so sweet and coy a fair?

* [5]

Silken clad, he maketh every homespun-wearer felt to don; [6]
Work for us he's cutting out there on his bench, the wanton one;
Give the coin of life, for money may not buy this princely gown. [7]
  Whensoe'er that darling marketh with his chalk his mirthful air
  Fire of eagerness flat-irons straightway all my facial hair.

He, my needle-plier, doth my frame as 'twere his thimble smite,
Yet he never thinks to blame himself there-for, the frolic wight.
Yea, my mole-besprinkled princeling wants a royal robe and bright. [8]
Yesterday, Belígh, before him I unrolled that cloth, my plight;
  Then he measured it by guess-work, and he shaped it, did the fair;
  Ah, but it came out too little, so with skill he felled it there. [9]

In the poems of Nevres and his contemporary Hashmet,
of whom we shall hear more later on, another aspect of
romanticism is presented. The feeling for beauty which
inspires the work of Nedím, and in a less degree that of

---

[1] This proverb-like line has no evident connection with the context, and seems to be introduced here for no better reason than that it makes mention of the khirqa or frock and destár or turban worn by dervishes.

[2] The cloth mentioned in the first line of the stanza.

[3] The text has بلاقون brocade, which is evidently some special and valuable variety as it is said that beside the cloth referred to even this brocade would not appear as good as sendal, a light thin silky stuff.

[4] The down on the rosy cheek being compared to the nap on pink satin.

[5] There is here another line that I have failed to make out.

[6] Felt being worn by the poor.

[7] The qontosh was a special kind of richly embroidered robe worn by the Tartar princes and nobles of the Crimea; the word is used here figuratively.

[8] The khil'at or robe of honour formerly given to grandees by the Sultan.

[9] There was not enough of it (the cloth which figures the speaker's plight), so he had it skilfully felled; here again the 'felling' must have some secondary meaning. See n. 10 on p. 131 *supra*.

Belígh, gives place to a more personal element in the writings of these two poets. They both, and more especially
Nevres, regard their poetry as a vehicle for the expression
of their individual experiences and sorrows, a view scarcely
possible to the Persianists shackled with the fetters of precedent and conventionality.

We shall consider Nevres here, as he died shortly before
Rághib Pasha, the year of whose death I have adopted as
the boundary-year between the First Transition and Romanticist Periods, reserving our account of Hashmet, who sur-
vived the Pasha, till we come to discuss the poets of the
last-named age.

'Abd-ur-Rezzáq, whose pen-name was Nevres, was born
in the town of Kerkúk in the distant province of Baghdad.
He made his way to Constantinople where he studied for
the legal profession, and eventually became a 'circuit' molla.
But in the Shevvál of 1175 (1762) both he and Hashmet
were banished to Brusa on a charge of undue freedom of
speech, though in what direction this was exercised we are
not informed. His exile from Constantinople, where he seems
to have formed some very dear ties, broke Nevres's heart.
In his last poems he bewails his lot in the most pitiful
language, the sincerity of which admits of no gainsaying.
The shock must have been too much for him, as we are
told that he died suddenly not many days after reaching
his place of banishment

The little Díwán which contains all of Nevres's literary
work is of no very great account in the history of Ottoman
poetry. Its chief interest lies in the fact that it offers one
of the earliest examples of that phase of the Romanticist
movement in which the poet, disregarding the claims alike
of pleasure and of humour, finds in his individual circumstances sufficient motive for his verse, for, as I have already

said, it is his own personality that gives the keynote to
Nevres's poems. The individuality therein disclosed is of an
amiable, though somewhat melancholy and not very robust
type; and the despairing tone of the poems written on his
exile shows that he was completely unmanned by his mis-
fortune and points to a somewhat weak nature; unless,
indeed, as perhaps we may infer from his speedy death,
he was in ill-health at the time of his exile.

But if Nevres was weak, he was not without his good
qualities. With a modesty rare indeed among Turkish poets,
he says in one of his qasídas that he cannot vie with those
'Sultans of the realms of verse,' Ráshid, Vehbí and Rághib,
that he cannot attain to their 'pearl-bestrewing genius;'
though he adds, after his wont, that had he been as fortunate as they in obtaining the Sovereign's favour, he too
might have done wonderful things.

In his language and phraseology Nevres is quiet and rather
colourless. That he should have any share in the subtle
elegance of the Persianists was perhaps hardly to be looked
for; but he made only a feeble attempt to follow the brilliant lead of Nedím, while the introduction into his verses
of any of those homely but forcible Turkish words and
idioms such as were now just beginning to be used in poetry,
was too bold a step for this timid and retiring spirit. We
find in his poetry neither novel combinations of old materials
nor the introduction of any fresh invigorating element; but
a vocabulary of well-established respectability used with no
great artistic skill to depict not conventional emotions, but
his own feelings. When I say that he does not depict conventional emotions, I speak, of course, relatively; it is obviously
impossible that any writer or any school should at once win
wholly free from convention after so many ages of a literature
that knew little else.

Although Nevres is on the whole unheedful of beauty, he has one couplet which for the grace and harmony of its language is surpassed by few things in Turkish poetry; the underlying thought which it enshrines is moreover both profound and true: these English words convey the meaning, but the delicate charm of the original is gone

Yonder night whereon they decked the Khusrev's nuptial-chamber meet
'Twas with Ferhád's blood they henna-tinted lovely Shírín's feet [1]

This poet is sometimes called Nevres-i Qadím or Nevres the Elder to distinguish him from ʿOsmán Nevres Efendi, a poet of the time of Sultan ʿAbd-ul-ʿAzíz.

Here are two ghazels selected from his Díwán

Ghazel. [381]

What though dust are now the crown and throne of Káwus and of Key[2]
Back unto their first beginnings all things find at last their way [3]

---

[1] This couplet forms the first two lines of a rubáʿí or quatrain, the second couplet, though good in its way, is much inferior, and is without apparent connection
Never yet hath vest sufficed to clothe the form of high emprize,
Though they oft have sought the spheric satin with this hope, I weet

جلوه‌گاه خسروی اول شب که نرین ابتدنلر

خون فرهادی حنای پای شبرین انمدنلر

چیفمدی بر ندم دن مد بلمد همتـه

اطلس گردونی بر فاچ کرّه نخمن امدنلر

The Primum Mobile or Empyrean, the outermost of the Ptolemaic heavens, is called the Felek-i-Atlas, i. e. the Plain Heaven because there are in it no stars Atlas also means satin, and the poet plays on these two meanings
[2] Two legendary Kings of Persia belonging to the fabled Keyání dynasty, in whose time the hero Rustem is supposed to have flourished
[3] This line alludes to the well-known hadís —

كُلُّ شَيءٍ تَرْجِعُ إلى أَصْلِه 'Every thing returns to its origin.'

Even now he knows not how of Unity it sings the tale,
Ne'er shall the self-centred preacher understand the flute's sweet lay. [1]

Knew not I how it was plaining of the bitterness of fate;
Once I held the weeping gurgle of the wine for laughter gay.

Wine doth yield relief against the bitterness of fortune's cold;
Yea, the blazing fire subdues the rigour of December's sway.

Weeping makes Nevres to tell the stars all night till morning dawn;
Friends, declare his plight, for Allah's sake, unto his love, I pray.

Ghazel. [382]

No rose a rose, no garth a garth doth seem to be withouten thee;
But lone and drear were Eden's self, O love, to me withouten thee.

Dismay my fere and comrade dear, and dole my labour morn and eve;
With burning sighs is filled my heart, with tears mine e'e withouten thee.

My life and soul have bade farewell and parted from my frame at last;
O love, my dearest friends as alien folk I see withouten thee.

O how should I upon the garden of another's visage look?
Mine eyelashes are mural spikes, O darling free, withouten thee. [2]

Come nigh his pillow once, though it be only in a dream, O coy;
For sick doth hapless Nevres lie and anguish dree withouten thee.

The terkíb-bend, all of which, with the exception of the
first and last stanzas, is translated below, is the most prominent of the poems in which Nevres bewails his exile. The
distracted state of his mind is evidenced by his now upbraiding his beloved for neglecting him and now endeavouring

---

[1] The reed-flute of the Mevleví order of dervishes, typical of the mystic
and his visions and aspirations, incomprehensible to the common herd.

[2] There is here, apparently, a reminiscence of the following Persian verse
by Shevket of Bukhárá:

گلستان ی گل رویت برنگی تنگ بود امشب

که چون مژگان بهم خار سر دیوارها آمد

to excuse her to himself. The earlier period of 'strangerhood'
to which he refers is probably that of his departure from
Kerkúk and arrival in Constantinople.

Terkíb-Bend [383]

* *

O God, how hard it is from one's dear home exiled to be!
What to the soul it is to leave the body now I see
May punishment be made to taste of dole! O bulbul heart,
What need was there to sunder thee from yon rose-shifted she?
In separation's abject plight what shall I make of life?
Is't not unto the bulbul death to part him from the lea?
Ah me! will ever be vouchsafed in gladness to return,
To go unto my fair, and quit this den of misery?
Alas! alas! O soul of me, I've learned and know full well
How passing hard it is to me to be disjoined from thee!
What though this bitter severance constraineth me this wise,
Though to the soul it seem as forth the frame it fled, ah me!
  Will e'er the heart attain to peace while crying in dismay?
  While crying 'Home!' will it abide in this strange land for aye?

Where yonder hours when union's couch I did in joyance share?
Wherein I slept with yon moon-face free of all grief and care?
Where yonder hours when, drinking deep of union's vintage sweet,
Meet was I held to taste the grace of Love's cupbearer fair?
Where yonder hours when with the gracious fawns of Istambol [1]
I quaffed the wine and hand in hand o'er friendship's plain did fare?
Ere then had I full mickle dreed of strangerhood's duresse,
And fain the dolour of the stranger land did I declare
At length for separation's ill a medicine had I found,
The friend was I become of health's physician debonair,
At length had I won forth the narrow pass of strangerhood,
At length my face was set toward repose's meadow fair.
  Then Fate o'ertook and drave me forth an exile once again,
  And made my Fortune-smitten heart, alas, to wail and plain

[1] The 'fawns of Istambol' are the graceful young beauties of Constantinople.

Since forth I fared into the land of exile, O my queen,
This broken heart of mine nor rest nor peace from pain hath seen.
All night until the morning break the skies are sore distraught
By reason of the flames my burning sighs diffuse, I ween.
Remembering me of thine all-lovely cheek, o'erwhelmed am I
By this unceasing torrent poured from forth my weeping e'en.
Mine eye, like to the ring upon the door, [1] looks on the road
Awaiting tidings of thy welfare, O my love amene!
Thou hast not asked of my sad plight, nor hast thou soothed my heart;
Is't on this wise thou hold'st the pact that standeth us between?
Is't meet that thou should'st lie upon coquetry's couch, the while
For stress and bitterness of soul torn hath my garment been?
Ah yes! 'tis good that thou should sweetly smile mid all delight,
That I should wail and sigh, my love, in anguish and in teen!

   A charmer who in troth hath neither part nor share art thou;
   O my beloved, passing fickle and contraire art thou.

Through parting's stress my back is bent like to thine eyebrow high;
The shifts of changeful Time have made me languorous like thine eye.
Confusion hath deranged my wits like to thy ruffled hair;
The thought of thee, O Queen of grace, hath made my peace to fly.
O God, for this sad lot of mine the very mountains weep,
Not only sons of men on earth and angels in the sky.
Alas, alas, of none account am I before thy sight;
Ah faithless one, this bitter truth full sorely learned have I.
No letter hast thou writ to me, no greeting hast thou sent;
In brief, thou dost the claims of love and gratitude deny.
Thou never sayest mid the feast, 'I have an exiled friend;
'I marvel how he fares, if sick of absence he doth lie.'
She is not faithless, yon moon-visaged beauty of thine own;
So bear oppression's load, and burn, O heart, burn thou, I cry.

   Surely the God of all that is will pity my dismay;
   And this sad time of exile drear and lone shall end one day.

* *

---

[1] The ring-shaped knocker on the door; it is round like the (pupil of the) eye, and always looks out upon the road, awaiting the coming of a visitor.

CHAPTER IV.

Hashmet Fitnet Khánim. Kání.

Hashmet Efendi was the son of a Qádí-ʿasker named
ʿAbbás He studied for the legal profession, but before he
had passed through the several degrees of the muderrisate
he was banished to Brusa, at the same time as our acquaintance the poet Nevres, and on the same charge. Fatín says
that after he had resided in that city for a considerable
time, Hashmet's place of exile was changed to the island
of Rhodes, wheie he died in 1182 (1768—9). The biographer
adds that he was buried near the well-known tomb of
Murád Reʾís.

Hashmet was a man of a very different stamp from his
fellow-exile Nevres. He made the best of his position, and
during his enforced sojourn at Brusa formed the acquaintance of all the leading men of letters in the city. Among
these was a certain Seyyid Mehemmed Saʿíd Imám-záde,
who edited Hashmet's Díwán, prefixing to it an interesting
preface of his own In this preface Imám-záde tells us that
as he was on intimate terms with Hashmet, he was requested
by some of the notables of Brusa who had seen a few of
that poet's verses, to make a complete collection of these,
and arrange them in a díwán He therefore requested Hashmet
to supply him with copies of all his writings, but this the

poet was unable to do, as he had only a few qasídas and
some forty or fifty ghazels in his possession; the rest, he
informed his friend, might perhaps be procurable from various
acquaintances in Constantinople. Imám-záde therefore set to
work and, recovering all he could, formed them into the
Díwán which we now have. He then applied to Hashmet
for some personal details to place in the preface which he
proposed writing. These the poet refused to give, saying
that his friends were sufficiently acquainted with his circumstances. But the editor, anxious that posterity should
possess some particulars concerning the personality of so
remarkable a man, determined to write down what he had
himself seen and heard.

He begins by saying whose son Hashmet was, and then
proceeds with a eulogistic account of his poetry and other
literary work, to which we shall return by and bye. We
are next told that Hashmet was a great a marksman, alike
with bow and musket, and as great a swordsman as he was
a poet. One day he showed his skill with the musket in
the promenade of Abdál Murád, [1] outside Brusa, where he
hit the mark three times in succession at a distance of over
a thousand paces, an unheard of exploit which moved one
of the local literati who were present to compose a qit‘a
celebrating the event, which qit‘a was engraved on the stone
erected on the spot where Hashmet had stood. This stone,
adds the editor, is now known as Menzil-i Hashmet or
Hashmet's Range; and when men go out, he continues, to
practise with the musket, they stand half-way between this
and the target, and even then it is only with difficulty that
they can hit the mark.

[1] The Abdál Murád after whom this place is called was one of Orkhan's
companions at the capture of Brusa. His tomb, which is situated on a height
overlooking the city, is still a place of pilgrimage.

Imám-záde winds up his enlogy of his hero as an athlete with an account of a feat of swordsmanship which he himself witnessed. The people of Brusa, having heard from Hashmet's attendants of his wonderful skill in this art, prayed him to give them an example. The poet good-naturedly consented, and having asked them to procure a piece of felt, had this rolled up till it was thicker than a man's waist. It was then suspended in such a way that it dangled in the air. Hashmet then took his sword in his hand, and going up to the roll of felt, cut it in two at a single stroke, so that the one half fell to the ground, while the other remained swinging in the air. All who saw this were filled with amazement and shouted out 'Strength to his arm! Strength to his arm!' They then went up to the piece of felt and counted the number of plies Hashmet had cut through, and they found these to be one hundred and seventy five, whereat they all mar-velled the more, for even in the traditions the champions are not reported to have cut through more than seventy or eighty plies of felt. And for all of this Imám-záde vou-ches, as he himself saw Hashmet deal the blow, and he himself counted the number of the plies.

Imám-záde does not give the date of his compilation, but it was probably somewhere about 1180 (1766—7), as Hashmet had evidently been in Brusa for some time, and we know that he went there in 1175 (1761—2) It is very unlikely that the present collection contains everything that Hashmet wrote, he is almost certain to have continued composing verses after its completion, verses which being too late for insertion, and not having found any Imám-záde to record them, have now been lost byond recovery.

In the Díwán as we have it, Hashmet shows himself to have been a poet of considerable ability, bold as a champ-ion of the new literary movement, and versatile as an imitator of the various styles of poetry then in vogue. In his qasídas he has the good sense to take Nef'í as his model, many of his works in this form being indeed 'parallels' to poems of the master. That his qasídas possess no little merit and have at times something even of distinction, may be readily allowed; but to declare, as Imám-záde does, that they are superior to all other 'parallels' to Nef'í's, savours of permitting personal feeling to override deliberate judgment.

The ghazels of Hashmet may be divided into two classes about equal in extent; those in which the poet has deliberately imitated other writers, and those in which he has endeavoured to strike out a new line for himself. The first of these classes comprises the very numerous poems which he wrote as nazíras or 'parallels' to the works of other men, and here he shows a great deal of skill in catching and reproducing the characteristics of many widely dissimilar writers. For he measured his strength with all the greatest and most popular poets of the time, with Sá'ib, Shevket and Bídil among the Persians, with Nábí, Rághib, 'Asim, Ráshid, Muníf, Sámí, Neylí, Nedím, Vehbí, Belígh and a host of less important men among the Turks; he even went back to the days of the Second Persianist School and had a tussle with Ná'ilí and Fá'izí. This endeavour to surpass, or at least to rival, other writers on ground of their own choosing has at all times been a favourite amusement of Turkish poets, but few among them have carried the game so far as Hashmet, with whom it seems to have been almost a passion to wrestle with as many champions and in as many fields as he could find opportunity. That he should be uniformly successful in so many opposite directions is of course not to be expected; and Imám-záde's claim that his friend's works of this class are throughout of greater value than all other 'parallels' to the same models is on a par

with his statement regarding the qasídas. In some cases his
efforts in this direction may possibly be more successful
than those of other imitators, but this is assuredly not so
in all. Still taken as a whole, the emulative work of Hashmet
possesses considerable merit, and shows not only an extraordinary degree of imitative and assimilative power, but an
exceptionally wide range of sympathies.

Turning now to the second class of Hashmet's ghazels,
that consisting of his more original work in this form, we
find a vigorous, sometimes almost brutal, robustness to be
the salient feature here. This characteristic is apparent alike
in the sentiments of the poet and in his phraseology Instead
of whining over his lot in the fashion of Nevres, he attacks
with bitter scorn his high-placed enemies and turns with
contemptuous pity from those who court their favour. A
cursory glance through his Díwán is enough to show us how
likely Hashmet would be to get into difficulties through
giving his tongue too free a rein, and to incline us to sus-
pect that in his case at any rate, those who sent him into
exile may have been acting in quite justifiable self-defence.
Just as in his imitative work he attempts a score of different
styles, here too he has verses of every kind, religious, philosophic, amatory and bacchanalian, as well as invective and
satiric The boldness which distinguishes most of his work
leads him at times in his amatory poems to overstep the
bounds of propriety, and as he has none of the deft delicacy
of handling which enabled Nedím to touch without offence
upon risky themes, the result is, as we might expect, often
unpleasing

Except of course when he is imitating poets of the Persianist
schools, Hashmet's diction and vocabulary are markedly
Turkish. He is fond of using redífs consisting of a succession
of two or three different Turkish verbs in the same personal

form, a somewhat questionable device which complete success alone can justify. This is but one of a number of similar ventures, too technical to enter upon here, which other poets had experimentally tried, and which recommended themselves to the daring mind of Hashmet as new paths along which to seek poetic triumphs.

That his success was not greater arose from no lack of courage or want of enterprise, but from the fact that nature had not dowered him with all the qualities needful to make a great poet. It is true that within his limits he was a poet, and an interesting poet too, but for all his hardihood he was never able to win beyond the fifth, or perhaps the fourth, rank. Knowing the ways of such would-be critics, we may allow Imám-záde his statements as to how his friend's poetry on being studied shines with distinction and individuality, and as to how his gallant words and loverlike tones give fresh life to heart and soul, and fill all the captious throng with amazement and admiration. We can also easily believe him when he tells us how all the savants and scholars of Brusa held his noble speech to be of one value with the fabled gem called sheb-chirágh [1] which lights up the world, and yearned to inscribe his words with ink of musk on the pupils of their eyes. I say it is easy to believe that Hashmet was popular and esteemed in his place of banishment, for possessing, as he did, so many varied talents and accomplishments, his must have been an interesting personality.

Von Hammer has by an oversight omitted Hashmet from his History, as he has Belígh; in his account of Nevres,

[1] This is the account of the sheb-chirágh given in the famous dictionary called Burhán-i Qáti': — 'Sheb-chirágh (Night-lamp): This is a jewel which during the night-time shines like a lamp. They say that on certain nights when the water-bull comes up to land to graze, he brings this jewel with him in his mouth, and sets it down on the place where he would graze, and by the light of it does he graze.'

however, he mentions the name of the former, which he
erroneously writes Hischmet [1]

The Díwán of Hashmet opens with four Arabic poems,
the first two of which contain the names or titles of God
and the Prophet respectively. These are followed in the
usual way by the qasídas, chronograms and ghazels, among
which are inserted two or three sharqís, while a number of
acrostics and riddles brings the collection to a close.

Among the prose writings is the Intisáb-ul-Mulúk or The
Service of the Kings, in which Hashmet describes a vision
which he feigns to have seen on the night of the accession
of Mustafá III. The poet finds himself in a vast plain where
he beholds all the kings of the earth coming in state to
pay homage to the new Sultan and to crave permission to
serve at his court. The kings come up to Hashmet and tell
him the object of their journey, each announcing his desire
to receive some office connected with what was taken to be
the speciality of his country. Thus the Imám of Yemen hopes
to be placed in charge of the coffee-service, the Emperor of
China to be entrusted with the care of the palace china-
ware, the Czar of Russia to be appointed court furrier, the
King of Holland to be chief gardener, [2] the King of England
to be overseer of the powder-magazine, [3] and so on After
a good deal of persuasion they prevail upon Hashmet to
conduct them before the Sultan, who receives them graciously,
and to whom the poet recites a panegyric. Thereupon Mustafá,
in order to place him on a level with his royal companions,
names him King of the Poets, and promotes both him and

[1] [Though the Turks, I believe, pronounce the word *Hashmet*, the correct
Arabic form is, as Von Hammer writes it, *Hishmet* ED]

[2] Holland being famous for its bulbs.

[3] About this time the English were reckoned experts in the use of fire
arms, and English gunpowder was considered the best.

his father. Upon this, Hashmet declares that since fortune is so favourable to him, he fears the whole thing must be a dream; but the Sultan consoles him by saying that even if it be but a dream, it will assuredly ere long come to pass.

Hashmet has two other prose works: the Súr-Náme or Viládet-Náme, an account of the festivities held on the occasion of the birth of the Princess Hibet-ulláh in Rejeb 1172 (March 1759); and the Sened-ush-Shuʿará or Title-Deed of Poets, which he dedicated to Rághib Pasha, and in which he discusses certain passages from the Koran and the Hadís which fall into metrical form, whence he endeavours to prove that the poetic art must have been held in high esteem by the Prophet.

The following ghazels are from Hashmet's more original poems: the first is an example of his outspokenness.

Ghazel. [384]

'Tis lies that form the themes of all the grandees of the state;
And lies would fain on this poor tongue [1] likewise predominate.

We've washed our hands of yonder fountain-spring of truthfulness;
And lies do like the Rebel Stream [2] sweep through the world elate.

The legend on the signet-ring of truth is worn away;
'Tis lies that in our day ennoble them of high estate.

The only cause of poetry's disfavour standeth here:
That naught of lies the folk have left the poet to narrate.

Hypocrisy is loved of all, both high and low, Hashmet;
And lies compose the capital alike of small and great.

---

[1] That is, on the poet's own tongue.
[2] Nehr-ul-ʿAșí, the Rebel or Tumultuous Stream is the modern name of the Syrian river called in ancient times the Orontes.

Ghazel. [385]

What time the world-displaying bowl [1] of mirth and glee is trolled
The heart doth through the crane-eye wine [2] the whole wide earth behold.

The harvest of the orchard of the world is on this wise,
The fruitage of the tree of hope doth rot ere it unfold.

Upon the hunting-ground of longing's waste do vacant swing
The booty-straps of yearning's steed, their tassels flying bold [3]

The tears descend to earth as rain from out the clouds what time
The darkling smoke of bitter sighs around the world is rolled.

Although thou naught of union with thy love hast seen, Hashmet,
The heart doth through the crane-eye wine the whole wide world behold

Ghazel. [386]

Sans the searéd bosom ne'er may we the soul's desire obtain,
Ne'er withouten gold, O heart of mine, are any lovelings ta'en

Naught beside her rubies' kiss may close the bitter-plaining mouth,
'Tis with wax of red are sealéd missives and all these contain.

Show not off thy wares, but be thou heedful of the keen of sight;
Every flaw before the spy-glass of attention standeth plain.

Degradation's den his stead is who would scrape up Fortune's orts;
On the midden-heap the besom's flung, and there it doth remain

Wine it is that lifts the veil of bashfulness in union's hour;
Aye the blushing fair to seek protection from the bowl are fain.

Hashmet, they of mine acquaintance who are clients of the great
Underneath that shelter often eat their crust in mickle pain.

[1] The wine-cup, alluding the legend of Jemshíd's bowl.

[2] Crane-eye wine is yellow, or as we should say, white, wine. When he
drains the wine he sees the map of the world engraved inside the bowl, or
he sees this through the wine

[3] Dees or straps attached to the saddle for carrying game or other things,
such trappings were often profusely ornamented with silk tassels, etc

Ghazel. [387]

The scars of yearning in my heart are every one a burning lowe,
The roses in this garden-ground of Love are all aflame, I trow.

I poured out my heart long since like water 'fore a cypress-form,
What makes my tears to flow to-day is e'en that tale of long ago.

The tranquil-souled are they who truly garner merriment of heart,
While those whose hearts are filled with lust like bubbles on the wine-cup show.

O soul, be not heart-bounden, like as Mejnún was with Leylá's hair,
For God alone it is who makes thee o'er the wilds of Love to go.

Hashmet, did God create this tongue from hues of the Primaeval Wine,
Or else how comes it that thy words and speeches all so brilliant glow?

Ghazel [388]

Charmer moon-bright, yon disdainful frown within thine eyebrow free,
With the gleaming sword of beauty pierce and pierce the heart of me

Cast thy glance, I pray, O fair one, on my scar-strewn breast's expanse,
Open fling thy vision's window on the flower-besprinkled lea

Say'st thou, 'Let me sail no longer in the cramping bark of lust,'
Launch thou then the wine-skiff out into Renunciation's sea.

O, intoxicate with one swift glance the sick for absence drear,
Ope thine eyes, let Beauty's Tavern open to the sad heart be!

Draw no pigment o'er thine eyebrow; Beauty's zágh sufficeth there.
Dearest tyrant, let no rust besoil thy glaive, I pray of thee!

Suage, at least, with peaches¹ Hashmet's thirst for union, O my sweet,
Leave them not on beauty's salver, fill the helpless heart with glee.

Ghazel. [389]

Love doth come not with one scar of longing in the heart, in fay;
Spring is made not by one flowret, howsoever bright and gay.

¹ A peach (sheftálú) means also a kiss.

Like to Moses were the adept fain to meet the tongue of flame,
But the glory shineth not for each familiar of Sinai.

Springs the essence of the soul through severing of earthly ties,
Till are cut its leaves and branches sprouteth not the plane-tree, nay [1]

Though this Might would in one moment shatter all the worlds that be,
Yet the heart no sign of rent or rift, O Hashmet, doth display [2]

Not since the closing years of the Classic Period, when the lady Hubbí Qadın graced the literary world of her day, has our attention been claimed by any Turkish poetess This is not because such have been altogether absent, but because none among those who have appeared during this interval has attained a position of sufficient eminence in poetry to warrant her inclusion in a list that has of necessity to be selective. Of these minor stars the best known are probably Sidqí who died in 1115 (1703—4), and Fátima Khátún, whose pen-name was 'Aní, and who died in 1122 (1710—1) Both these ladies are said to have left díwáns, but that of the second appears to have been lost.

Far more richly dowered and far more famous than either Sidqí or 'Aní, or indeed than any of her sister-poets who have gone before, is the gifted authoress who now calls for our consideration Fitnet Khanım is the greatest poetess reared in the old school of Ottoman literature. To find her

---

[1] i e. Unless the plane-tree is pruned in the Autumn, it will not put forth new shoots in the Spring

[2] The first misrá' refers to a saying of the mystics to the effect that God is a Light which, if displayed, would consume the Universe; the second to the well-known tradition

لَا تَسَعُنِى أَرْضِى وَ لَا سَمَائِى وَ لٰكِنْ تَسَعُنِى قَلْبُ عَبْدِى ٱلْمُؤْمِنِ

'Neither My Earth nor My Heaven sufficeth Me, but there sufficeth Me the heart of my believing servant'

equal we must come down to modern times when the altered state of social matters renders it comparatively so much more easy for a Turkish woman to develop and express what intellectual gifts she may possess.

The article on Fitnet Khanim in Fatín Efendi's Tezkire is as usual of the slightest, and later writers such as Zihní Efendi the author of 'Famous Women', and Ahmed Mukhtár Efendi, who has compiled a little book entitled 'Our Poetesses,' have been able to add but little to his meagre details. This poetess, whose personal name was Zubeyde, belonged to a talented and distinguished family, her father, Mehemmed Es'ad Efendi, being Sheykh-ul-Islam under Mahmúd I, and her brother, Mehemmed Sheríf Efendi, holding the same high office under 'Abd-ul-Hamíd I. The father is said to have been skilled in music, an extraordinary accomplishment in a member of the 'ulemá, while both he and his son were gifted, though in far less measure than his daughter, with poetic talent. Fitnet was unfortunate in her marriage, her husband, Dervísh Efendi, who became a Qádí-'Asker of Rumelia under Selím III, being a man without ability and utterly unworthy of his brilliant wife. When it is added that Fitnet died in the year 1194 (1780), all that is known concerning her life-story has been told.

The unlucky union of the poetess with Dervísh Efendi has formed a text for more than one subsequent writer. Thus 'Izzet Molla, who flourished during the earlier part of the nineteenth century, when upbraiding the 'Sphere' in his Mihnet-Keshán for its ill-treatment of poets as a race, marvels why this malicious power should have made 'an ass like Dervísh Efendi' the husband of Fitnet, adding how unmeet it was that she should be the wife of that old man. Professor Nájí again quotes the following well-known lines of Nizámí in order to emphasize how exactly the reverse of what the old Persian describes was the case of Fitnet and her husband·

'Though the society of woman be to the man of pleasure
'The warrant of life and comfort, the bail of joy and delight,
'Yet with her the taper of converse may not be kindled,
'For while I talk of Heaven she talks of a thread ' [1]

Fitnet Khanım was celebrated for her wit, and many stories are told concerning her which are strangely at variance with current Western notions as to harem discipline, and which, if they contain, or even reflect, anything of truth, argue that poor Dervísh can have had no easy task if he endeavoured to control his sprightly wife Here is an example of these stories, which so far as I am aware, has never been published, though it is widely known in Constantinople. [2] Fitnet Khanım is in the square before the Mosque of Báyezíd, one of a crowd of people who are choosing animals to offer as sacrifices at the approaching Bayrám festival. Her friend the poet Hashmet, who is there also, comes up, and having saluted her, says, 'Why are you wandering about here?' 'I am looking for a sacrifice,' replies Fitnet. 'Take your servant as your sacrifice,' rejoins the gay poet, whereon the lady, perceiving the covert proposal in her friend's gallant

[1]
وصل زن هر جمد باشد پیش مرد کامجوی
روح و راحترا کعمل و عمش و عشرترا صمان
لمک با او سمع صحبت در نمی گمرد ارانک
من سحس از آسمان می گویم او از رسمان

The jingle, ásmán u rísmán = Heaven and thread, is a Persian locution to imply the confusion of incongruous things either intentionally or more usually, as here, through lack of discrimination [To talk 'cats and camels' (shntur u gurba) is another similar expression in Persian, used in the same way. ED].

[2] [In a later pencil-note the author adds, however, that it has been printed in a book entitled Newádiru'z-Zurefá (Anecdotes of Wits). ED]

phrase, wittily checks him by replying, 'There is some defect
about thy horns; to take thee as a sacrifice were not lawful.'[1]
That the English reader may see the point of Fitnet's answer

[1] As I believe this story has never been written down, I subjoin the words
of the conversation between Fitnet and Hashmet as I took them from the
lips of a Turkish friend. The Hashmet of this and the next story is, of course,
the hero of the hundred and seventy-five plies of felt, whose work we have
just been considering.

حشمت : نيچون گزيبيورسكز بورادە
فطنت : قربان آلهجغم
حشمت : بو قولڭزی قربان ايديڭز
فطنت : سنڭ بوينوزڭدە قصور وار سی قربان ايتمك جائز دگل

The following story, likewise about Fitnet and Hashmet, which I obtained
from the same source, must remain under the veil of the original. In it
Hashmet is represented as being what the Turks call a Kuse, that is a
beardless, or next to beardless, man.

حشمت بر گون فطنت خانمڭ قپوسنڭ اوكندن گيدرايكن
خانم حشمتڭ مروريني گورمش . در حال جاريه‌سنی ارسال ايدوب
استهزا ايچون "او لكلك آغزينه چوپلری آلمشده نريه گيدبيور؟"
ديمك حشمتدن صورديرمش و بو صورتله آغزينه چوپ آلوبدە
اوچان لكلكلره تشبيه ايتمك صورتيله حشمتڭ همان بر قاچ تلدن
عبارت صقاللی بوئنان بر كوسه اولديغنی ايماء قبيح ايله آڭلاتمشدر .
حشمت ايسه ينه ايماء قبيح ايله جواب اعطاسی ايچون جاريه‌يه
"خانمڭ بجاقلوبنڭ آرسنده يووا ياپمغه گيدبيورم" ديمشدر .
خانم ينه رد جواب ايدوب جاريه‌سنی تكرارًا بالارسال "او محل
صولبدر اوراده يووا تمل طوتماز" ديمشدر . حشمت ايسه ينه جواب
اعطاسنده عاجز قلميوب "بن او يووادە قيشلايه‌جك دگلم آنجـق
ايكی يمورطه چالقايـوب همان گيده‌جكم" جوابنی بالاعطا خانمی
قطعيًا الزام ايتمشدر .

it is necessary to explain that animals offered in sacrifice must be without defect or blemish, and that in Turkey to say of a man that he is 'horned' is to imply that he is a reprobate. [1]

Fitnet's poetical work is wholly lyrical and is all comprised in a not very extensive Díwán. Its principal distinctions are delicacy of sentiment and lucidity of expression Indeed there is so little that is weak or faulty in the language of this lady that Professor Nájí, who bestows on her the title of Queen of the Poetesses, declares that very many poets might well envy her in this respect. That her range of subject should not be very wide is scarcely a matter for astonishment, certainly not for reproach; limitation here has been too universal a rule among the poets to permit us to hope that a woman, whose field of observation was of necessity so much more restricted, should prove any exception. Consequently it is without surprise that we find Fitnet has practically but two themes, the one love, the other a simple philosophy of which the keynote is contentment. Not only does the poetess rarely get away from one or other of these two motives, but she is rather inclined to repeat herself even in her phraseology. Expressions and phrases, often in themselves both original and graceful, recur again and again in her verses, pointing to a somewhat limited command of language But this shorteoming also is shared by very many of the old poets, and in a writer of less merit and renown than Fitnet would hardly deserve remark.

These defects are after all but slight, perhaps under the circumstances inevitable, and do not seriously detract from the beauty of Fitnet's work or impair her position among

---

[1] Originally the term was applied, as formerly in the West, to the husband of an unfaithful wife; then, by extension, to a pander to his own wife, and so to any low-minded scoundrel

the eminent authors of the Romanticist Age. For Fitnet is a true Romanticist through the directness and spontaneity of her verse, though like most of her contemporaries she was largely affected by the influence of the Third Persianist School. Her admiration for the genius of her friend Rághib Pasha and the effect which his work produced upon her mind can be clearly traced in many of the philosophic poems which, as we have said, form one of the salient features of her Díwán.

It should be added that Fitnet's little volume contains several sharqís and a good many riddles.

The two following ghazels show the grace and delicacy which distinguish this lady's love poetry.

Ghazel. [390]

Whene'er that rosebud [1] smiles, the roses, shamed, are blushing red;
Whene'er those tresses wave, the jacinth, envious, bows the head.

Beneath the claw of love he'll fall, though he the ᶜanqá be,
Whene'er that falcon-glance of thine against the heart is sped.

That yet unopened rosebud fair shall smile as doth the rose
Whene'er the tears of hearts lovelorn are dew-like o'er it shed.

Thine every hair doth turn a snake [2] to guard the hoard of grace
Whene'er the comb doth o'er thy cheek the dusky ringlets spread.

An if thy purpose, Fitnet, be to yield thy life for love,
Then quit not till thou die the dust afore the loved one's stead.

Ghazel. [391]

Hearts are caught in yonder all-enchanting glance's deadly snare;
Lions fall the prey to yonder Fawns in beauty's field that fare.

[1] The rosebud is the beauty's mouth.
[2] In the East a snake or dragon is supposed to watch over and guard hidden treasure. Black locks of hair are often compared to snakes, and also to scorpions.

'Told they not of hue and perfume sweet of lovesome charmers' locks,
Who for gillyflower or jacinth mid the bowers of earth would care?

Myriad Torments [1] are tormented by one roguish glance of hers,
Bounden lie a thousand Hárút-heaits in every curling hair. [2]

Ever patiently they bear the rigour of the bow-eyebrows, [3]
Bravo for the strength of arm that falleth to Love's folk to shaic!

Fitnet, make thy body dust upon yon stately figure's path,
So thou'rt fain to kiss the ground beneath her gracious feet and fair

The next two ghazels are examples of Fitnet's philosophic manner.

Ghazel [392]

Contentment's heart-adorning feast is fraught with mirth and glee,
Contentment's ruddy wine from head-tormenting fumes is free.

Extinction's bitter blast will blight the rosebud of desire,
Contentment's rose alone from Autumn knows immunity

Each gleaming drop of modesty's bright perspiration shines
A sheen and lustrous pearl of price from out contentment's sea [4]

[1] That is, cruel beauties.
[2] Hárút and Márút are two fallen angels whose names are mentioned in the Koran. According to the legend, while still in Heaven, they scoffed at the moral weakness of man, whereupon God, in order to prove them, endowed them with human passions and sent them down to earth. Here they were led astray by a woman named Zuhre, who was transferred to the planet Venus, which was afterwards called by her name. In order to punish them, the two angels were imprisoned in a pit at Babylon, where they are hung up by their heels till the Judgment Day, and where they are said to teach the magic art to any one who applies to them It is in this latter connection that they are usually referred to by the poets Thus here the 'Hárút-hearts' implies, among other things, hearts that are skilled in magic, even such being impotent to escape from beauty's thraldom
[3] In this verse there is a double entendre (íhám), for chekmek means both 'to draw' and 'to bear,' while chille means both 'a bow-stiing' and 'the forty days' vigil' practised by dervishes as a religious austerity
[4] The modesty here meant is backwardness in asking for favours Compare n. 4 on p 84 *supra*, regarding the Eastern belief as to the formation of pearls

What though he would not purchase at one groat the Satin Sphere [1]
Who dealeth in contentment's fair and precious mercery!

The names of Sheref and of ʿIzzet will appear therefrom,
If one but read contentment's riddle hard right heedfully [2]

Look that thou never for a morsel press the ignoble crew,
The while contentment's board is spread with dainty fare for thee.

In very truth more spacious far than Fortune's plain, Fitnet,
Appears contentment's yard however strait and cramped it be.

Ghazel [393]

To crave or gift or favour of the losel Sphere were vain;
To look unto inverted bowl for draught of cheer were vain! [3]

Strive ever to adorn thyself with virtue's precious pearls,
Elsewise the anxious thought for glory's gorgeous gear were vain

Beware, the house-top edge a station is with danger fraught, [4]
The hope of rest upon the couch of rank to rear were vain.

The electuary of the dear one's ruby lip is health, [5]
O leech, to medicine the love-sick heart, I fear, were vain

[1] The Satin, i. e. the Crystalline or Starless Sphere, another instance of the favourite equivoque which we have met before See n. 1 on p 136 *supra*
[2] The words sheref = honour, and ʿizzet = excellence, are used as proper names. The riddles in the dîwáns of the poets usually conceal some proper name which is hinted at in a variety of ways, generally exceedingly subtle and obscure
[3] When, as is often the case, the vault of the sky is taken as the visible embodiment of the power which is typified by the Sphere, the comparison to an inverted bowl is not infrequent ["That inverted Bowl they call the Sky" is familiar to admirers of FitzGerald's rendering of the Quatrains of ʿUmar Khayyám ED.]
[4] People sometimes sleep in hot weather on the flat roof of an Eastern house, but as there is often no parapet, they are in danger of falling off if they go too near the edge Here the idea is that high place or rank is dangerous, the roof being of course the highest part of the house
[5] The word maʿjún, here translated 'electuary,' is applied to a medicated preparation of sugar, spices, etc something like a soft toffee In that prepared for the use of the Sultan and other very great people, pearls, rubies, emeralds,

The heart holds all the cruelty that comes from thee for grace,
So leave it off; thy cruelty, O wanton dear, were vain.

The wind-wafts of the grace of God will bear it safe to shore,
A pilot for the barque on yearning's ocean drear were vain.

The Typal path will surely lead at last to Truth's highway, [1]
Fitnet, upon the road of Love or guide or fere were vain.

The following museddes is very pretty and is well-known.

Museddes [394]

The vernal cloudlets scatter glistening pearls athwart the earth below,
And all the blossoms issuing forth, the radiance of their beauty show.
'Tis now the tide of mirth and glee, the time to wander to and fro,
The shady trees a fair retreat on all the winsome ones bestow.
    My lord, come forth and view the scene, the whole wide world doth
                                    [verdant glow,
    The sweet spring tide is here again, the tulips and the roses blow

Behold the roses blushing red as cheeks of lovesome beauties fair,
The fragrant hyacinths show like to youthful charmers' curling hair;
And see, upon the streamlet's marge the cypress-shapes of lovelings rare.
In brief, each spot doth some delight to gladden heart and soul prepare.
    My lord, come forth and view the scene, the whole wide world doth
                                      [verdant glow,
    The sweet spring tide is here again, the tulips and the roses blow

The garden flowers have oped, and all a-smile the roses shine for glee,
On every hand the lovelorn nightingales bewail the dule they dree.
How fair along the garden-walks are gillyflower and picotee!
The long-haired hyacinth and jasmine each embrace the cypress-tree
    My lord, come forth and view the scene, the whole wide world doth
                                      [verdant glow,
    The sweet spring tide is here again, the tulips and the roses blow

and coral reduced to a powder were occasionally mixed Here Fitnet compares
the beloved's red lips to this health-giving sweetmeat or confection into which
rubies enter
 [1] Yet again, 'The Typal is the Bridge to the Real'

Arise, my Prince, the garden-land hath wonder-joys in fair array;
And hark, the plaintive nightingale is singing on the rosy spray.
The tender bud will blush for shame whene'er it doth thy cheek survey.
Arise, and to the garth thy gracious air and cypress mien display.
My lord, come forth and view the scene, the whole wide world doth
[verdant glow.
The sweet spring tide is here again, the tulips and the roses blow.

Enow, thy lovers pain no more, of loyal plight the days are these,
Of mirth and joy upon the streamlet's margin bright the days are these,
So grasp the heart-expanding bowl in hand forthright, its days are these,
And, Fitnet, come, this couplet fair do thou recite, its days are these.
My lord, come forth and view the scene, the whole wide world doth
[verdant glow;
The sweet spring tide is here again, the tulips and the roses blow

One of the most singular figures in the Turkish literary
world of this period is the letter-writer and poet Ebú Bekr
Kání. This author, who owes his fame to the possession of
a peculiar playful humour, in virtue of which he occupies a
unique position in Ottoman literature, was a native of the
city of Toqad in Asia Minor, and was, when we first catch
sight of him, a member of the Mevleví order.

In 1168 (1754—5), when Hakím-záde ʿAlí Pasha was passing through Toqad on his way from Trebizond to assume
for the third time the office of Grand Vezír, he was presented
with a qasída and a chronogram by Kání, who was then
thirty-eight years of age, and who from his youth upwards
had been famous in his native town alike for his learning
and for his writings both in verse and prose. These poems
so pleased the old statesman that having obtained the
permission of the local Mevleví sheykh, he took Kání along
with him to Constantinople. Here, through his patron's
influence, the poet was at once entered among the Clerks
of the Divan, a good position in itself, and one which might
easily have led to something better But the restless nature

of Kání could not brook the routine of official life, and he had hardly received his appointment before he began to look about for some excuse to throw it up The opportunity was not long in coming, 'Alí Pasha's third tenure of the Grand Vezírate lasted only two months, and when it came to a close Kání resigned his post, and set out for Silistria as divan secretary to an officer who had been appointed governor of that place. Having lived a free and easy life for nearly forty years in an Anatolian provincial town, Kání not unnaturally found the formalities and ceremonies of Constantinopolitan official society unendurably irksome, and as the following passage from one of his letters shows, this was one at least of the reasons of his eagerness to escape. 'As this draggle-turbaned Kání is not of the same stamp as that stately company who, clad in sumptuous apparel, adorn the streets and market-places, he has been compelled to forsake Constantinople and find a peaceful abode for himself in this reptile-house of Islam called Silistria '

By and bye the poet passed over to Bucharest where he acted for a time as Turkish secretary to the Waywoda, as the tributary Prince of Wallachia was called, and where a portrait of him in company with the Waywoda Alexander is still preserved in the Museum

On the elevation of Yegen Mehemmed Pasha to the Grand Vezírate about the end of 1196 (1782) Kání returned to Constantinople on the invitation of that statesman who had been one of his most intimate friends in earlier years But Kání did not, or wonld not, recognize that the Grand Vezír was no longer the comparatively humble official with whom he had once consorted on terms of equality, and by the familiarity of the tone he still thought proper to adopt, and yet more by his indiscretion in speaking about certain things on which silence would have been better, he so enraged

the minister that his execution was determined on. Khayrí
Efendi, the Re'ís-ul-Kuttáb, was able to save him from death;
but he was banished to the island of Lemnos. Here he
suffered much distress, for as he tells his former patron the
Waywoda Alexander in a letter ostensibly written to recommend one Baqlawaji Sheykh, who was noted for his
humour, all the wealth and property he had been able to
earn during thirty years — even down to his freed slave-
girls — had been confiscated in the name of the Treasury,
though he had nothing whatever to do with the Treasury.
He seems even to have been in want, as in another letter,
written this time to a private friend, he says that when he
turns his eyes to the snake[1] which is twisted round the
silver head of its nargile, and has for some three months
and a half been longing for tobacco, he seems to see it
wriggle and writhe as it were indeed a coiled-up serpent.

Ebu-z-Ziyá Tevfíq Bey, from whose 'Specimens of Literature' most of the above particulars are derived, takes to
task the historiographer Edíb[2] and also the late Jevdet
Pasha, who in this case simply embodies the former's facts,
for omitting from their works every thing about Kání's exile
and for neglecting to inform us whether the poet ever returned from his place of banishment and even where he
died. All we are told is that before his death, which occurred
in the Latter Rebí' of 1206 (Jan[y].—Feby. 1792), he repented
of the recklessness and debauchery in which his life had
been passed, and returned to the bosom of the dervish
order in which he had been brought up.

---

[1] The Márpích or 'snake' is the long flexible tube of the nargile or water-
pipe for smoking, often called 'hookah' in England. Kání means to imply
that he has been for three and a half months without tobacco.

[2] The Imperial Historiographer Mehemmed Edíb wrote under Selím III.
He died in 1216 (1801—2).

As I have said, Kání is chiefly remarkable as a humorist,
and a strong bias towards fun of every description, very
unusual in a Turkish poet of old times, seems to have
characterized him during the whole course of his long life.
Indeed, we are told that even when he lay dying he pro-
voked to laughter by the droll things he said the sorrowing
friends who were gathered round him. There are of course
a number of stories current about Kání, one of which is
inserted in his Tezkire by Fatín, who, in reporting it, breaks
away for a moment from the monotonous and inventory-
like style in which he has elected to write his book. In this
story, of which Kání can hardly be said to be the hero,
the poet is represented as seated with one of his cronies,
a Christian, probably an Armenian, as the scene is laid in
Erzerum, to whom by way of jest he proposes the adoption
of Islam. At that time there was living in Erzerum a certain Sheykh Ibráhím Haqqí who stood in the highest repute
on account of his saintly life and of the wonders which he
wrought So the Christian replies to Kání with the question,
'If I adopt Islám, shall I become a Musulmán of the standing of Sheykh Haqqí?' On the poet's rejoining, 'To attain
to his degree of excellence were impossible,' his friend replies
'Then since I cannot attain to his excellence, what should
I gain by leaving my religion to become a Musulmán such
as you?' To which query, we are told, the poet was unable
to find any answer.

That religion, or at least conventional religion, had little
hold on Kání is shown by the celebrated words he uttered
but a brief time before his end. 'I am no beggar of Fátihas,'
he said, 'let not the word Fátiha be carved on my tomb-
stone.' We have often seen how it was the custom to cut
on the grave-stone a request to the visitor to repeat the
Fátiha, that is the brief opening chapter of the Koran,

for the repose of the soul of him or her who lies beneath.

'Shall the forty-years' Kání become a Yani?' [1] is a proverb often in the mouths of the Turks when they wish to express the difficulty of changing a habit acquired by long usage. Yani is the Greek form of the name John; so the proverb means 'shall the Kání (i. e. Musulmán) of forty years turn a Christian?' The phrase is said to have been originally pronounced by our poet in connection with himself on the occasion of a curious adventure that befell him at Bucharest.

When we turn to Kání's literary work, we find his prose to be much more interesting and more noteworthy than his verse. It is in his prose, which consists entirely of letters, that the humour, which we have seen to be his most striking characteristic finds freest scope. This humour of Kání's is quite unlike that of Sábit or that which we have noticed in works of the Shehr-engíz type; it is sometimes playful, as in the celebrated petition purporting to be presented by a kitten to her master; sometimes audaciously familiar, as in some of the letters addressed to Yegen Mehemmed Pasha; and sometimes it displays itself in heaping up huge piles of similar words and making long lists of things more or less closely connected. In this last peculiarity Kání resembles Rabelais, with whom his genius has more in common than with Piron to whom he is compared by Ebu-z-Ziyá Tevfíq Bey.

This critic, who inserts some of his letters in the 'Specimens of Literature,' has an appreciative notice of Kání's work, in the course of which he says that all of this author's letters and ghazels are charged with humour, a statement which, so far as the poems are concerned, appears a little beyond the mark. Speaking of the prose works, the same critic maintains that these are distinguished by a grandiosity

[1] قرق ييللف كأنى اولورمى يانى.

164

which may well delight the admirers of the old-fashioned
artificial style, combined with orderliness of thought and
facility of expression He then proceeds to state that in his
opinion had Kání but treated his work more seriously, he
would have been not only unrivalled among the authors
of his own age, but one of the most distinguished writers
in all Ottoman literature. As it is, he declares him to be,
so far as Turkish letters are concerned, among those whose
class is restricted to himself.'

In the preface prefixed to Kání's Díwán the editor, Núrí,
tells us that he made the collection at the desire of the
Re'ís-ul-Kuttáb, Mehemmed Ráshid Efendi, who was unwilling that the name and fame of a man possessed of so much
learning and culture as the lately deceased Kání should be
cast aside into the nook of oblivion and dwell alone in the
cranny of the silent The editor therefore set to work and
gathered all that he could find of Kání's poetical works,
but as the author himself had made no attempt during his
life either to preserve or to collect these, many of them
were irrecoverably lost. Had they all been forthcoming, adds
Núrí, they would have formed several volumes each as large
as a 'Complete Works of Nábí'!

Kání's verse is a long way inferior to his prose The
humour which is the strong point of the latter is far less
evident here. Often it is absent altogether, and when it is
present it appears rather in the way in which the author
uses words and phrases than in the actual things that he
says. None the less he does from time to time say things
in his verses that are really droll; lines containing such
occur even in his Hymns to the Prophet

Jevdet Pasha, however, who has a brief chapter on Kání
in his celebrated History, questions the fact of his having
really been a humorist at heart He says that the poet was

misunderstood by the simple-minded folk about him who
saw his funny verses and heard his wonderful tales, and
that they, judging only from such things, failed to appreciate
his true character. According to the Pasha, Kání's guile-
lessness and good-nature were the real cause of his writing
so much facetious poetry; persons in search of a little amusement would often come to him, saying, 'Kání Efendi, I
have thought on a line or a couplet with such and such a
rime; but the rime is a difficult one, how should we go on?'
whereupon he, being put on his metle, would in reply spin
off a number of burlesque or whimsical lines with the
same rime or redíf. And for this reason, adds the Pasha,
do his facetious writings outnumber the rest.

What Jevdet says here about Kání's readiness to complete
in ludicrous fashion poems brought to him by friends on
the quest of a laugh, is perhaps the explanation of the curious fact that many of the ghazels in his Díwán after opening seriously enough in the ordinary conventional manner,
suddenly dash off into the wildest buffoonery, sometimes
into downright nonsense. But the evidence supplied by the
poet's own writings is too strong to permit us to doubt
that the tendency to look on the funny side of things had
its roots deep down in his nature.

But whether or not he be true humorist, Kání is no true
poet; he is not even a poet in the old Turkish sense of
an artist in words. As Professor Nájí says, his verse is of
no great importance, and it would be vain to seek in it
anything like elegance or grace. He was a careless worker,
and does not seem to have thought it worth his while to
devote any serious attention to the artistic quality of his
poetry, with the inevitable result that his ghazels appear
rough and unfinished. He is, for example, very slovenly
with regard to his rimes; sometimes he repeats the same

rime-word two or three times in a short ghazel, sometimes
he uses a redíf without any rime-word at all, defects which
might easily occur in verses written in the impromptu fashion described by Jevdet Pasha.

His vocabulary and phraseology are often Turkish to the
verge of grotesqueness, if not vulgarity, although, as most
of his letters and some of his poems prove, he was a very
learned man and thoroughly versed in Arabic and Persian.
It is in those ghazels in which he is most negligent of the
conventional arts and graces that he is most Turkish in his
language, just as it is in those same poems that he gives
freest rein to his whimsical way of putting things, and to
a trick he has of bringing together into a single couplet a
string of words similar in spelling but different in meaning
and sometimes in pronunciation. In a word, it is in such
poems that he is most truly Kání.

Many of the poems are conventional enough in sentiment,
but in the more characteristic the author often lets his own
voice be heard, and when he does speak out, it is in tones
at once clear and vigorous But verse was not the true
medium of expression for Kání, from his Díwán alone we
could never have learned what manner of man he was, if
we wish to know him we must seek him in his letters.

The poems moreover are often very difficult to understand, not only does the author frequently use vulgar or
even slang terms and affect non-literary idioms, but he often
says things that no other poet would dream of saying, —
things that the student of conventional Turkish poetry is
scarcely prepared to encounter in the pages of a díwán. Of
course; all this makes for the burlesque, but it is rather
trying to the translator, who is not always certain that he
has really caught the writer's drift, and must in any case
despair of giving an adequate rendering of such verse.

The following couplets occur in a qasída which Kání presented to Mehemmed Ráshid Efendi, the official by whose instructions his works were collected after his death. The whole poem is more or less a travesty of the usual conventional style.

From a Qasída. [395]

O figure of my dear, no pose of love-delight hast thou?
O sapling fresh and fair, not e'en one berry bright hast thou? [1]
O blast, no zephyr gently breathing soft and light hast thou?
O weakling sigh, to work effect nor power nor might hast thou?
I wonder, wilt thou bend thee ne'er to union's side at last?
O prop of coquetry, [2] no bender left or right hast thou?
What time it saw thee naked, hair-like straightway grew the soul, [3]
Not e'en a girdle then, O hair-waist slim and slight, hast thou?
Each passing murmur of thy liplet's ruby's worth the soul,
Ah me, none other peerless gem of beauty bright hast thou?
O day of fast, on convent fashion [4] is thy festival,
O night-pavilion of dismay, no dawn of light hast thou?
Wilt thou not then bestrew the dust that lines the beauty's path?
O weeping eye of mine, no pearl with lustre dight hast thou?
Whine not, 'There is no place for me!' when parting presseth hard,
O misery, within the inmost heart no site hast thou? [5]
What meaneth all this sophistry anent the Typal Bridge?
No pass that straight unto the Truth doth go forthright hast thou? [6]

[1] Both these lines mean: 'With all the grace of form that thou hast, hast thou no grace of manner?'
[2] The beloved, or her figure, is meant by this curious term, which means 'buttress' or 'support' of coquetry
[3] The soul was overcome so that it could not bide erect [Does it not rather mean that it was wasted away with love till it became feeble or slender as a hair? ED.].
[4] I e. Austere He means that whereas the bayrám, or feast, which concludes the fast of Ramazán should be merry, it is instead sad and dreary.
[5] Addressing misery, the poet says 'Even though the thought of the beloved fills my heart, yet there is still room for thee.'
[6] Ridiculing the constant allusions of the poets to the proverb, 'The Typal is the Bridge to the Real.'

Curl not thy lashes, saying, 'Who can e'er my charms withstand?'
For yonder eyebrow-bow of thine no bender wight hast thou?[1]
O tree of hope, what mean those branches dry and bare on thee?
Hast ne'er been green? nor leaf, nor fruit of red or white hast thou?[2]
I marvel why the bubble's eye collyriumless should be,
O daughter of the vine, no friend to keep thee right hast thou?[3]
What may it be that is thine aim in hitting not the mark?
O arrow-sigh, nor plume nor wing to speed thy flight hast thou?
We have not tasted sweet the kisses of the ruby lip,
I wonder, naught of sugar in that casket bright[4] hast thou?
While that the Sphere doth turn its mill above thy grain-like head,
Here upon earth to turn thy head no plaguy plight hast thou?
So then, thou hast not winged thy flight toward some rosy cheek!
O nightingale, nor van nor plumery nor sprite hast thou?
What want I with the fables of Nesími and Mansúr?
No skin nor derrick known and seen of all with sight hast thou?[5]
I pray thee stop that brat, the heart, from squalling on this wise,

[1] As in Fitnet's ghazel the bender of the beauty's eyebrow-bow is the lover who compels her submission See n 3 on p. 156 *supra*.

[2] i e Hast thou always been dry and barren, never green and fruitful? Is no hope of mine ever to be fulfilled?

[3] By the eyes of the Daughter of the Vine are meant the wine-bubbles, which are unadorned with collyrium, though their lovers are many

[4] The casket is of course the beauty's mouth

[5] Kání refers on several occasions to the Turkish poet-martyr Nesími and his prototype Mansúr; thus·

بە منصورم نه بر دار سر زلف اولمغ اسر دل
دسمەی وار هٔله بورمکه لایف درم دوغدر

'I am not Mansúr, nor doth my heart desire to be gibbeted on her ringlet,
'Likewise I have not a skin worth the flaying like Nesími.'

And again

مادسلهٔ نسمسٔی فىلم حرامسدر کىلدی درىسی حنهٔ وحدت کسارہ

'Even as with Nesími of old,
'Their own skin is unlawful for the wearers of the gown of Unity'

The story of Nesími will be found in that portion of the present work which deals with the Archaic poets, Vol I, pp 343 et seqq Kání here affects to treat it and the history of Mansúr as legendary, and calls for something known and certain

O mole black-cored, no pepper-corn to hush the wight hast thou? [1]

＊ ＊

＊ ＊

Here are a few ghazels from Kání's Díwán. The first three are all characteristic of the author's peculiar style; the first of all is an instance of a ghazel which after opening in an ordinary and conventional manner, proceeds in a vein of burlesque.

Ghazel. [396]

Why still these coy coquettish airs, O maiden fair and free?
Will never any prayer, my love, avail to soften thee?

Thou'st stolen this little heart of mine, and left me lorn and lone;
Thou'st made it burn my patience up, — this lowe of love in me.

May ne'er the heart become the prey of beauty's falcon-claw;
May never God that portal ope again, petition we.

Since I have fall'n a-longing for thy figure rest I ne'er,
O cypress-shape, this tale becometh long, as thou dost see. [2]

What debt of bitter words is due the lover, O my Liege?
At times needs not the wailing heart a little butter, [3] eh?

Now open bare thy bosom, let yon magic mirror shine;
But shut thine eyes, uncover not those caves of coquetry.

---

[1] Parents in Turkey sometimes threaten to fill the mouth of a querulous child with pepper if he will not keep quiet. Kání here hints at the resemblance of the black mole (so belauded by the poets) to a pepper-corn, and suggests that it should be used to silence the wailing heart of the lover. To compare the heart to a child is a poetic common-place, and here, as throughout, Kání is turning the conventional language of the poets into ridicule.

[2] To say of a story or speech that it becomes long, is to imply that it is growing tedious. Here the idea of the length of the lover's complainings is associated with that of the length, i. e. tallness, of the 'cypress' shape.

[3] The original word is piyaz, and means hashed onions added to a dish to flavour it; in vulgar speech it is often used figuratively as here, when it stands for 'flattery', 'blarney,' 'soft sawder.'

Kání, those wanton little nooks, and those sweet bosses theie, — [1]
Yon fiolic rogue hath made me perturbation's thrall to be

Ghazel [397]

Concealing fez were vain, the rival soon would scent the han,
Just so, the heart wants no humbug [2] in union's pleasures fair

The down it is that with its kit two-stringed doth hold the heart,
Man doth not woman-like desire a mirror smooth and bare [3]

The yearning lover needs must bind his heart to yonder locks
Although forsooth the Sultan of the land of Fez he were [4]

'Tis fitting to be good to such as goodness' worth do know,
For though they gave the vulture sugar, nought therefor he'd care [5]

[1] It is impossible to render this line satisfactorily The word كِرِشمه
means in Persian 'a coquettish and enticing glance,' and is constantly so
used by the Ottoman poets, but it is also an every-day Turkish word meaning 'an entering,' or 'going in', and in the present instance stands for كيردى
'a recess' Kání here uses it first in the orthodox poetic sense, and then, by
way of a joke, calls up in the reader's mind its ordinary meaning by bracketing it with چقفدى, a very homely Turkish word which is applied to
anything that projects or rises from a surface The first word then, besides
meaning the coquettish glances of the girl, would also suggest the depres-
sions or concave features of her body, the چم or the dimples for example,
while the second word would hint at the more salient members, such as the
breasts But to employ such words as كِرِشمه in its Turkish sense and چقفدى
in the description of a beauty's charms, is merely an affected grotesqueness
[2] The very unclassical expression فلفس fel-fes is our 'humbug' in its
sense of 'deceit', 'trickery,' 'gammon '
[3] This couplet alludes whimsically, perhaps satirically, to a prevalent vice
The iki-telli qabaq, here rendered 'two-stringed kit,' is a kind of rude lute
played by Albanians The down, i e the faint mustachioes of youth suggest
the idea of the two strings of the instrument; the smooth mirror hints at a
quite hairless face
[4] The name of the Kingdom of Fez, i e Morocco, suggests the cap called
fez which covers the locks
[5] That is, goodness is thrown away on those who cannot appreciate it, as
sugar, the delight of the beautiful parrot, would be wasted if offered to the
carrion-loving vulture [Perhaps there is here a reminiscence of a Persian
verse — I think by Qásimu'l-Anwár — ريشک بطوطى افكن مردار پیمش کرگس
"Throw sugar to the parrot, carrion to the vulture " ED.]

Tell not to me the tale of bosom scarred and vitals burned,
Have grace on me, my lord, we want it not; forbear, forbear [1]

Go, fetch, and bring to me her fragrant tresses' odour sweet;
Then blow, an so thou list, O breeze, or. an thou listest, spare.

O Sphere, if thou could'st make my loved one yield her once to me,
Enow it were, nor further grace of thine I'd seek to share

The body of you Sprite should be stark naked in good sooth,
Who walks with head and rump unclad doth want not satins rare

Come, see thou make not game of us, thou mulish zealot fool,
But praise that Moon or not, as thou shalt please, it matters ne'er.

From forth the Idols' harem chaste no voice must ever sound.
Love's mysteries and lovers loyal seek naught of language e'er. [1]

The olden guards like Heart and Soul will well suffice therefor;
The ward of Love hath little need of novel guardian's care

Sufficient surely are these wounds, what need then for these scars [?]
The bosom-sepulchre no ventilators needs, I swear. [2]

Ghazel [398]

Although thou drum, the sluggard will not wake, his sleep alone he eyes,
He weeteth not that on the morrow blood will rain from yonder eyes [3]

'Twill profit not, although thou scratch thine inwards still with yearning nail;
For if the heart and breast were bared, all o'er the scars would ope their eyes [4]

[1] The Idols, i e. pretty women. The outside world must never hear a whisper of what passes in a well-conducted harem The verse would bear a mystical interpretation.

[2] Here the bosom is likened to a sepulchre in which is buried the heart killed by love, the wounds and scars are conceived as openings into this sepulchre

[3] Although thou beat a drum beside him, the sluggard will heed nothing but his sleep; he is ignorant that the indolent must eventually suffer for their sloth

[4] As heart and breast are already covered with scars, whose eyes (i e. marks) would be seen were they exposed, and as these have profited nothing, it were useless to wound one's self further.

172

Thou'lt be the flitter at the blithe and merry banquet of Iblís, [1]
The fire of sore amaze will laugh at thee the while thyself it fries [2]

Awake, the longer thou dost sleep, the lower sin will bow thy back,
Bethink thee now, I wonder how the hunchback crew the journey plies

Thou liest like a lazy ass the while thy real self is man,
Go, look upon the field, the very oxen, when they'd graze, arise

Will ever any speech avail to move thee, Kání, since the fair
Have o'er thee cast the spell of yonder stellar-bright cerulean eyes?

The next ghazel is in a somewhat unusual strain.

Ghazel [399]

Thy soul's a guest that in thy frame will brief remain, be kind thereto,
Thy heart's a bird that beats against its cage in vain, be kind thereto

Thine outer and thine inner senses [3] ever have befriended thee;
So deal thou by thy friends [4] as justice doth ordain, be kind thereto

These limbs and members came with thee, and with thee have they still abode
'Tis these the durance of thy weal and wealth obtain, be kind thereto

Since thou must surely from thy friends be parted, spite whate'er thou dost ·
Be Joseph-like, and though thy brethren work thy bane, be kind thereto [5]

I have commended thee to God, O thou dear Radiance of my eyes, [6]
Thy Kání is a traveller soon his rest to gain, [7] be kind thereto

[1] Iblís, i e Satan [Though otherwise explained by the Arabian philologists,
I believe it is now recognized that this word is simply a corruption of the
Gieek διάβολος ED]
[2] The noise of the frying is the laughter.
[3] The outer or external senses are five, viz sight, hearing, taste, smell,
touch, the inner or mental senses are also five, viz idrák = perception,
khayál = conception, vehm = fancy, háfiza = memory, mutasarrifa = the faculty
of ordering or arranging See Browne's 'Year amongst the Persians', pp 144—5
[4] That is, thy senses.
[5] Joseph was kind to his brethren when they visited Egypt although they
had sold him into bondage.
[6] 'Light of my eyes' is a common term of endearment
[7] He will soon reach his journey's end, i e. will soon die.

The following ghazel is a specimen of Kánf's more imaginative work, the Keshkúl or begging-bowl which supplies
~the motive, is the boat-shaped alms-dish which suspended
from a chain or cord, is carried by mendicant dervishes.

Ghazel [400]

Aloft within the vault the moon holds forth its olden begging-bowl, [1]
Although but ill accords with dervish-hood a golden begging-bowl

To-night the Sphere hath ta'en in hand the lunar crescent halo-dight,
And turned a dervish-wight who bears his arch-wise moulden begging-bowl

From this learn thou the Sphere is mean of soul nor knoweth of noblesse,
That ne'er by saint of worth thus shamelesely is holden begging-bowl

The sun stands o'er against the crescent moon within the eastern sky,
To lustrous sheykh by silver-bosomed fair is holden begging-bowl

As all would veil the secrets dear of mendicants of modest heart,
O Kánf, held from hand to hand is still the olden begging-bowl [2]

Ghazel. [401]

I saw that Scian girl, her cheeks are, oh, so ruddy red!
Her eyes are black, her lips of ruby glow so ruddy red
Bare foot, with brow unveiled, with breast and bosom too unclad,
Within the Skinker's hands the glasses show so ruddy red
Uprisen to the waists, nay, more, they frolic to the breasts,
Like rosy girdles do the sashes go so ruddy red
Ay, let the wine rampage and riot in the harem-jar,
Be all the streets lit up with lamps a-row so ruddy red
The daughter of the vine and Magian boy drink squabble's wine:
The Magian elder's household puff and blow so ruddy red

----

[1] Referring of course to the resemblance in shape between the new moon
and the dervish's alms-dish
   That is, the mysteries of dervish-hood, symbolised by the beggar-bowl,
are handed down from master to disciple from generation to generation

The sleighs have made the city-children mounted thereupon
In youthful glee, with rose-bud lips, to glow so ruddy red
With glaive of coquetry, as 'twere the dirk of Mars in hand,
Yon skittish rogues to luckless Kání show so ruddy red [1]

[1] [In a pencil-note the author expresses the opinion that this poem probably describes a festival of some sort in winter, with illuminations, wine-drinking, and skating or sleighing ED.].

CHAPTER V.

THE ROMANTICISTS (CONTINUED).

Sheykh Ghálib.

In this chapter we have to consider Sheykh Ghálib, the last of the four great poets of the Old School of Ottoman literature. We have already seen how the first of these, Fuzúlí, is distinguished by his tenderness of feeling; how the second, Nefʿí, stands pre-eminent through the splendour of his language; and how the third, Nedím, shines by his delicate and graceful fancy and his exquisite daintiness of diction. But far rarer than any of these qualities, at least among his fellow-countrymen, is the gift which has raised Sheykh Ghálib to the first rank in the vast army of Turkish poets. Originality of conception and power of imagination are not very common in the literature of any people, while in that of the Ottomans they are singularly rare; yet it is to these, and not to any artistry in language, that this poet owes his lofty rank.

Muhammed Esʿad, afterwards known as Sheykh Ghálib or Ghálib Dede, [1] was born in the district of Yeni Qapu, or New-Gate, in the west of Constantinople, in the year 1171 (1757—8). [2] His father, Mustafá Reshíd Efendi, was a clerk

---

[1] Dede = Grandfather, is a title sometimes given to certain Mevleví dervishes, much as Father is to some Christian priests.

[2] In one of his ghazels Ghálib gives this chronogram for his own birth:

ın a Government office, and also, accordıng to Von Hammer, a qudum-zen or kettle-drum player at the Mevleví convent ın hıs own dıstrıct of New-Gate. [1]

Núrí Bey,[2] the Imperıal Chronıcler, who wrote the annals of the Empire between the years 1209 (1794—5) and 1213 (1798—9), states ın the bıographical notıce of Sheykh Ghálıb whıch he inserts ın hıs work that though the latter receıved Arabıc lessons in hıs chıldhood from certaın professors, all the Persıan he learned was from hıs father, who taught him from the one book ın that language whıch he possessed, a copy of the Tuhfe or Gift of Sháhıdí. [3] The hıstorıan, who seems to belıeve that these were the only Persıan lessons Ghálıb ever had, regards, as well he mıght, the proficıency whıch the poet afterwards attaıned ın that tongue, as a kınd of mıracle But we know from other authorıtıes that a lıttle later on Ghálıb studıed under the celebrated teacher and poet Khoja Nesh'et, [4] whose more intımate acquaıntance

کـمـمقادر عـلاچ املـمگه حـکـم قضا در

تاریخی ادمش عالـب رارگه اثر عشف

"Who may ıemedy it? It ıs the decree of Destıny

"'Love's Work' must e'en be poor Ghálıb's chronogram (or, hıstory)"

The idea of the couplet ıs that Ghálıb's exıstence ıs the work of the Dıvıne Love, ın whose seıvıce ıt ıs therefore necessarıly spent

[1] The Mevleví orchestra, whıch plays durıng the performance of the semáᶜ, or mỵstıc dance, ıs composed of reed-flutes called ney and kettle-drums called qudum It is probable that Ghálıb's father, who was most lıkely affilıated to the order, played at the convent on Frıdays when publıc busıness ıs suspendcd such an arrangement ıs not unusual

[2] Khalíl Núrí Bey, who succeeded Fnverí Ffendı as Imperıal Chronıcleı, was grandson of the Grand Vezír ʿAbdulláh Ná'ılí Pasha He dıed ın 1213. (1798—9). Besıdes hıs Hıstory he left a Díván of poems. Possıbly he ıs the same Núrı who edıted the Díván of Kání ·

[3] Thıs ıs a well-known versıfied Persıan-Turkısh vocabulary whıch was composed ın 920 (1514—5) by Ibráhím Sháhıdí Dede, a Mevleví dervısh of Mughla ın Menteshe, who dıed ın 957 (1550—1)

[4] Thıs ıs exactly Dommıe Nesh'et, to translate ınto Scotch.

we shall shortly make. It was, as we shall see, the practice of the Khoja to confer on his favourite pupils a makhlas or nom de plume, which in the case of a chosen few was presented in a poem of his own composition. One of the most carefully written of these Makhlas-Námes, as the Khoja called such productions, is that in which he confers upon our poet the pen-name of Esʿad, which is somewhat equivalent to Fortunatus. For a little while the young writer used this name which is found in several of his earlier ghazels; but as it was very common and had been adopted by various poetasters without a spark of talent, he very soon discarded it in favour of the more distinctive style of Ghálib or Victor.

Ghálib at first essayed to follow his father's calling and entered the civil service, but this he soon abandoned to devote himself heart and soul to the dervish-life. He went to Qonya, the head quarters of the Mevleví order, with the intention of accomplishing his novitiate there. But he had presumed too far on his detachment from earthly ties, for ere long he became homesick, and unable, we are told, to bear the separation from his father and mother, he secretly implored the Chelebi Efendi [1] to allow him to return.

The answer of the Chelebi Efendi shows him to have been both wise and kind-hearted. 'Since', he replied, 'you truly purpose to abandon worldly pursuits and to approach nigh to God, there is no virtue in your electing thus to wear the weeds of poverty and endure the rigours of your novitiate in a strange land. What manhood and virtue demand is this, that you should return to Constantinople, your native city, and that there in the New-Gate convent in your own district, amongst the friends and comrades to whose society

[1] Chelebi Efendi is the title given to the General of the Mevlevís who resides at the headquarters of the order in Qonya.

and companionship you are accustomed, you should elect
the path of dervishhood and accomplish your novitiate.'

So Ghálib returned to the capital where, following the
Chelebi Efendi's instructions, he placed himself under the
direction of Seyyid 'Alí Efendi, who was the Sheykh or
abbot of the New-Gate convent. There he completed his
novitiate of a thousand and one days, and there he continued
to reside till the year 1205 (1790—1) when he was appointed
by the then Chelebi Efendi to be Sheykh of the celebrated
convent at Galata. It was during his residence at the New-
Gate convent, where, it is said, he continually enjoyed the
society of men of piety and culture, that he wrote his great
poem 'Beauty and Love'.

We can readily conceive that to bid farewell to his old
abode, to the quiet cloisters outside the city walls, where
he had spent so many years, where he had borne the hard
service of a dervish acolyte, where he had held high converse
with many a dear friend and had written many a noble
line, — to leave these familiar scenes, hallowed by so many
memories, and go to a new home in the midst of squalid
Galata, must have been no light matter to the sensitive and
tender-hearted poet. But though at that time falling into
ruins, the Galata convent was the most ancient and most
venerable of all the Mevleví houses in the capital It was
consecrated by many associations; within its walls had dwelt
Isma'íl Rusúkhí of Angora, the commentator of the Mesneví,
and many another equally famous in the annals of the order
To be Sheykh there was no mean distinction, besides, the
dervish must obey the bidding of his superior.

Ghálib, moreover, was probably aware that in becoming
the head of this house he would benefit his order. His
poetry had already attracted the favourable notice of Sultan
Selím the Martyr who no sooner heard of his appointment

than he ordered the crumbling ruin at Galata to be entirely and thoroughly restored, a graceful and meritorious act which the poet-Sheykh fittingly acknowledged in a beautiful qasída.

Sultan Selím, in whom was revived the old love of poetry and culture which had distinguished so large a number of his ancestors, showed in many ways his appreciation of the poet who has crowned his age with an undying glory. His desire to gratify the dervish-Sheykh was shown in the restoration of Mevleví convents in various parts of the country carried out at his own expense or that of members of his family; his admiration of the poet appeared in the magnificent copy of his Díwán which he caused to be transcribed, and of which the gilding alone cost three hundred ducats; while his affection for the man found expression in the appropriate and valued gift of a beautiful manuscript of the Noble Mesneví written by the hand of Jevrí the famous penman and poet of the preceding century. [1]

Ghálib passed the eight years of life that yet remained to him as Sheykh of the ancient convent of Galata where he continued to enjoy not only the personal regard and esteem of his sovereign, but the affection and respect of all with whom he came in contact, notably of his friend and fellow-poet Esrár Dede, whose death, which preceded his his own by two years, he mourns in a touching elegy which is among the most beautiful of his minor poems.

This last great poet of old Turkey died, after an illness of several months, at the comparatively early age of forty-two, just before daybreak on the 26th of Rejeb 1213 (5th January, 1799). [2]

[1] For an account of Jevrí see Vol. III, p. 297 *et seqq.*

[2] Such is the statement of the historian Núri Bey, Ghálib's contemporary, who himself died later on in the same year. Von Hammer, who does not mention his authority, says that Ghálib died and was buried at Damascus on his way home from the pilgrimage in 1210 (1795). This statement is not

The poetical works of Sheykh Ghálib consist of a Díwán and an allegorical mesneví intitled Husn u ʿAshq or Beauty and Love. It is on the second of these alone that his claim to greatness rests; the Díwán is relatively unimportant. But Beauty and Love is the crown and consummation of the Turkish mesneví. Born, as it were, out of time, this noble poem appears amid the trivialities and impudicities of the Romantic Age like a pure and stately lily in a wilderness of nightshade and hemlock.

But while this poem is exempt from the vices of its age, it typifies what was best in it: for here, as in no other mesneví in the language, the individuality of the author asserts itself. Sheykh Ghálib in his masterpiece treads in the footsteps of no Persian leader, neither does he look for guidance to any of his countrymen. Alike in subject and sentiment, in imagery and language, he is a law unto himself, acknowledging no master and no guide other than his own unaided genius.

It is, as I have already hinted, in originality and vigour of imagination that this genius is most clearly seen. Here the poet stands not merely above, but apart from all his predecessors. In originality, more than in any other quality, has Turkish poetry been deficient all along the course of its story; during the Archaic and Classic Periods there was practically none, while such as the Romantic School has introduced has hardly been of the kind that makes for elevation. There is absolutely no one who in this connection can be mentioned along with Ghálib. The lovely Leylá and Mejnún of Fuzúlí is indeed instinct with a pathos and human tenderness

borne out by any of the Turkish accounts that I have seen. The date is certainly wrong, as is proved by this obituary chronogram of Surúrí's which gives the sum 1213:

كچدى غالب دده جاندن يا هو

'Ghálib Dede hath passed from life, O God!'

for which we might search the later work in vain, but there
is nothing of originality there beyond what is involved in
the characteristic setting of the threadbare tale. But here we
have a story, slender in plot, it is true, but yet borrowed
from no predecessor, shadowing forth the noblest aspirations
of the soul and presented in a series of pictures which now
for weird terror, now for celestial radiance, recall the inspired
pages of the Divina Comedia.

One of the most marvellous things about this marvellous
poem is that it was written when the author was only twenty
-one years of age. [1] How came this youthful dervish to voyage
in such a wonderland, a wonderland undreamed of by any from
whom he could learn, a wonderland where, as Ekrem Bey truly
says, we meet with counterparts to certain of those touches
of exquisite sadness and certain of those visions of haunting
terror which have done so much to place the works of Victor
Hugo among the literary glories of the nineteenth century?

Von Hammer's assertion that the poet took as his model
Fettáhí of Níshápúr's prose romance called 'Beauty and Heart'
(Husn u Dil) is absurdly wrong. [2] The two works have nothing
in common beyond the identity of the heroine's name, and
the fact that both are allegories.

As Ghálib himself tells us in the epilogue, he speaks a

---

[1] According to some authorities, Ghálib was twenty-six when he wrote
Beauty and Love; but the question seems to be settled by the chronogram
(unless this be spurious) which he himself composed for his work and which
gives 1192 (1778—9) as the date of completion. This chronogram is:

غالب بو جريــدهٔ جفانــكڭ تاريخــى اولــور ختام الٗمـسٚـك

'Ghálib, of this register of suffering
'Is 'a musky close' become the chronogram.'

Khitám-ul-Misk = 'a musky close', is a well-known literary expression used
to signify that a matter has been brought to a fragrant or happy end.

[2] As I have said when speaking of their works, the Classic poets Ahí
and Lámi'í translated this book into Turkish.

different tongue from his predecessors, and though others may have adhered to the methods of the Genjeví, [1] he has been the follower of no man. These are no idle boasts on the lips of this poet, conscious of his own divine gifts, and bold with a boldness hitherto unheard of in the annals of his nation's poetry, he waves off every would-be guide, and looking neither to the right hand nor to the left, confidently and courageously goes on his way in the light of his own genius only. Mesíhí, 'Azízí, Sábit, Belígh, all showed courage in revolting against the fetish of precedent which enslaved Turkish poetry, but when these raised the standard of rebellion, it was to bring this poetry down to the common things of earth, Ghálib sought to raise it to the very Heaven of Heavens.

A little farther, on in the epilogue we are told that the poet derived his philosophy from the Mesneví, and no doubt his inspiration, taking that word in its vaguest sense, did in a measure come from the great work of the founder of his order But that is the extent of his indebtedness; nothing like his story, nothing resembling the strange scenes he conjures up, is to be found in the volumes of Jelál-ud-Dín, the Súfí system of philosophy, which he shares with countless other mystics, is all he owes to any but himself

Turning now to the question of literary style, we find that here too Sheykh Ghálib is the disciple of no master. He speaks with admiration both of Fuzúlí and Nef'í, but he copies neither. As imagination is the great distinction of his genius, so is dignity the foremost characteristic of his style. This dignity sometimes rises to sublimity, as in the opening hymn to the glory of the Prophet, where in one passage the

[1] That is, the celebrated poet of Genje, Nizámí the Persian, whose Khamsa or Quintet, was imitated by so many subsequent writers, both amongst his own countrymen and amongst the Turks

noble lines, each more majestic than the preceding, seem in
the phrase of Ekrem Bey, to tower ever higher and higher
as the peaks of a lofty mountain-chain soar one beyond the
other into the blue depths of heaven.

The well-considered and judiciously restrained phraseology
of Ghálib greatly assists in bringing about the dignity which
pervades more or less almost the whole of his poem. True
dignity was scarcely possible either with the lifeless pedant-
ries and laboured extravagances of the late Persianists, or
with the familiar colloquialisms, not to say vulgarisms, affected
by the extreme Turkicist School. Ghálib steers a middle course,
avoiding on the one hand the foreign affectations of books
like Nábí's 'Khayrábád' (partly as a protest against which
his own poem was written) and on the other those uncouth,
if forcible, words and expressions which give a grotesque
and bizarre appearance to the characteristic works of such
Romanticists as Hashmet and Kání.

The phraseology of this poet is as much his own as any
other feature of his work. He takes as his basis the Turkicised
idiom of his day, from which he eliminates whatever is trivial
or ungainly; to this he adds such Persianist turns of phrase
and expression as he feels to be in harmony with the spirit
of the Ottoman tongue, thus imparting to his language a
cultured grace and finish, which, raising it above the level
of everyday speech, render it a more befitting medium for
his lofty theme. In this way Sheykh Ghálib almost anticipates
the literary idiom of to-day; and the greater glory is his,
in so far as he had not, like the modern authors, either any
work, such as his own, which could stand as sign-post, or
any acquaintance with Western literature to serve as guide.

The same reticence and self-restraint which mark the
phraseology of this poet are apparent in his use of figurative
language. He cannot, it is true, win altogether free from

the fantastic and extravagant in this direction — such a feat has proved beyond the unaided effort of any Oriental poet — but even here his vagaries are comparatively few and venial. He very often arrests our attention by new metaphors and similes, inventions of his own, delightful in their freshness or startling in their boldness. Sometimes again he takes the outworn fancies of old time and, inspiring these with the touch of genius, presents them to us as living things.

But while this poem of Ghálib combines originality and dignity, perspicuity and reticence, in a degree up till now unapproached in Turkish literature, no absolute or ideal perfection is claimed for it. On the contrary, it undeniably contains not a few obscure passages and not a few trivial and strained conceits. The author too indulges freely, far too freely, in the metrical licences permitted by his time, an indulgence which materially detracts from the technical merit of his poem as a work of art.[1] But these, together with an occasional error of taste or lapse from the prevailing sobriety, are comparatively speaking but little matters, upon which it were as needless as it would be ungracious to dwell farther. They are, as Memdúh Bey puts it, of no more account than those tiny vaporous clouds we sometimes see upon the horizon on a bright clear moonlight night.

---

[1] For example, in the line:

هم دينده هم كفرده معذور

the words هم دينده and كفرده, which are correctly scanned $-\smile$ and $-\smile\smile$ respectively, have to be read as if the scansion were $-\smile\smile$ and $\smile-\smile$. Similarly, the Kesre-i Khafífa has to be omitted after the word فرد in the line:

بر فرد بونى هيچ ايشتنمـمشدر

and the word جان, properly —, must be scanned $\smile-$ in the line:

حيرتنده جان او چشم شهباز

Ghálib constantly makes movent the nún preceded by a long vowel; but he appears to follow no rule with regard to this and similar solecisms, using them or not as suits his own convenience.

Without one dissentient voice the Ottoman writers and
critics join to eulogize this splendid poem. Núrí Bey, the
historian, who was a contemporary of the author, thinks to
pay him the highest of all compliments when he says that
by his imaginative Turkish poetry he is the Shevket of
Rúm. [1] Ziyá Pasha, while censuring Ghálib for his attitude
towards Nábí, says that by his 'Beauty and Love' the Dede
Ján, or Good Father, as he calls him, did indeed, so far as
mesneví is concerned, snatch away the cap, or, as we might
say, bear off the bell; and adds very truly that putting all
his strength into this one poem, he wrote it in a manner
that is replete with charm. We have already seen how Ekrem
Bey maintains that certain passages in his work rival some
of the finest things in Victor Hugo. In many places in his
'Course of Literature' this distinguished writer refers to Ghálib
in terms the most eulogistic, bracketing him with Fuzúlí,
Nefʻí and Nedím, and often quoting from his poem to
illustrate such qualities as imagination and sublimity. Professor
Nájí, who speaks of Ghálib as being one of those most rarely
gifted with poetic genius, and no doubt having in mind the
lurid visions of "Les Nuits", ranges him in line with Alfred
de Musset, and gives it as his opinion that 'Beauty and
Love' is the finest mesneví ever written by a Turkish poet
of the Old School.

Von Hammer too, though he does not seem to realize
the full greatness of this poet, sees enough to perceive that
he is foremost among the writers of his time, and bears

---

[1] Ghálib might not have found this comparison displeasing; at least, when
speaking of the wonderful and delicate carving that adorned the Phantom
Castle, he says:

هب آنده‌كى خرد كار صورت باريك ايدى چون خيال شوكت

'All the minutely wrought sculptures there
'Were fine as the fancies of Shevket.'

willing testimony to the originality which distinguishes his
masterpiece. Although he is mistaken in saying that Fettáhí's
'Beauty and Heart' served Ghálib as a model, he discerns
clearly enough that the latter's style and treatment are entirely
his own. He likewise gives the Sheykh due credit for the
moderation observed in his descriptions and for the faculty
which he has of arousing the interest of his readers, and
winds up his remarks by saying that with the one exception
of Fazlí's 'Rose and Nightingale', [1] there is no Turkish mesneví
so well adapted for a European translation

Let us now look a little more closely at this poem which
is the last, as it is the most beautiful, of the old Turkish
mesnevís.

The author's strong innate bias towards the contemplative
life together with his condition as a devoted Mevleví rendered
it inevitable that all his serious poetry should be inspired
and dominated by that mystic philosophy to study and
cherish which is the one object of his order. The theme
then of this poem is that Divine Love which is at once the
life and the law of all creatures, and which draws to Itself,
their common origin and their common centre, with a might
ever greater and more irresistible the closer they approach,
all these seemingly separate and individual existences, even
as every material body in the physical universe is drawn
ultimately towards a single point by action of that law of
nature which we call gravitation. This teaching, which for
the Súfí and the dervish is the truth of all truths, as it
ever has been for the mystic in every age and in every
land, is here set forth by Ghálib under the form of an allegory
wherein the relations between the Divine Soul of the universe

---

[1] This Suleymanic poem, for which Von Hammer had a profound admiration
and of which he published both the text and a German translation, has
already been described. See vol III, pp. 110 *et seqq*

and the individual existence are shadowed in the adventures
of the dazzling maiden Beauty and the youthful hero Love.

The opening scene, the fateful night on which Beauty
and Love are born together, when terror shakes the earth,
and the heavens flame with strange portents, while the angelic
host, foreseeing alike the anguish that is to be and the final
blissful consummation, keep watch with mingled tears and
smiles amid the ever-shifting showers of darkness and of
light; — in this scene may well be typified that point in
the great cycle of existence when the Divine Soul impelled
to self-manifestation, first awoke to self-consciousness in matter, when the 'Hidden Treasure' that 'would fain be known' [1]
projecting Itself into a being of Its own creation, gazed for
the first time through his mortal eyes on Its own immortal
perfections, and started on that long and painful pilgrimage
of love whereof Its self-realization is the goal.

That God seeks man before man seeks God, that the
Divine Soul yearns for love ere the individual learns to love
It, is indicated by the longing and sighing of the girl Beauty
for the youth Love while he is as yet heedless of and indifferent to her. It is by the friendly intervention of the all-
wise elder named Sukhan, the Logos, that Love is made
aware of the affection of Beauty and is taught to see her
surpassing fairness and inestimable worth, whereupon he
becomes her devoted and impassioned lover. By this the
poet no doubt would teach that it is by the action of the
Word that the heart of man is brought to see and love God;
for this Logos, who existed before the heavens were made,
is none other than that Word which was in the beginning,
that Primal Intelligence or Element which was the first

[1] The often quoted answer of God to David's question why He had
created the world: 'I was a Hidden Treasure, and I would fain be known;
therefore I created the world so that I might be known.'

creation of God, which is ever present with Him, and through
which His voice is heard and His command conveyed throughout
the universe. Again and again, when on his long and perilous
journey to the City of the Heart, where alone is to be
found the elixir which must form the dower of Beauty, [1]
Love is borne down by the countless hardships and terrors
that beset the way, it is ever the Logos that comes to
succour him and inspire him with fresh strength and courage
to pursue the hard and bitter quest. And when at length,
having passed through the black wilderness of eternal cold
and swum the lurid sea of infernal fire, and having battled
face to face with dragons, fiends and other nameless horrors,
he finds himself in the Phantom-land where nought is real,
though all is goodly to the sight, and where he is like to
fall victim to the lures of the Phantom-princess who in
outward seeming is even as Beauty herself, it is once more
the Logos that cries to him to warn him of his danger and
tell him how he may win free from the accursed place. And
in the last scene of all, when, after one final desperate struggle,
Love reaches the celestial City of the Heart, where he is
welcomed by the shining legions of the Heralds of Sight, it
is still the Logos who is his guide and teacher, and who
there unfolds to him the mystery that this glorious place is
none other than the land from which he started long ago,
for Love is Beauty, and Beauty Love.

Simply and sublimely the allegory closes with Love at
the bidding of the Logos, who may go no farther, passing
within the veil which curtains the ineffable Beauty, for none
but Love, not even Eternal Wisdom itself, may penetrate
that sanctuary.

What has just been said is sufficient to indicate the general

[1] The dowry which in Muhammedan countries the husband must settle
on the wife before marriage.

character and purpose of the poem, though it conveys but
scant idea of the wealth of beautiful and suggestive detail
to which the work owes no little part alike of its charm
and its originality. Several minor characters are introduced,
such as Passion, Confusion, Modesty and Zeal, some of
whom play parts of considerable importance; Zeal, for
instance, being the faithful companion of Love throughout
his arduous journey. Similarly, there are many incidents
described to which no allusion has been made, as our subject
here has been, not the story, but the philosophy and teaching
of the poem.

This philosophy is, of course, none of Ghálib's conceiving,
as he himself declares, he derived it immediately from the
'Mesneví', but it is centuries older than Jelál-ud-Dín, older,
perhaps, than any written record Ghálib's work was to array
this old-world doctrine in the fashion of a modern age, to
teach this hoary wisdom of antiquity in the language of the
latter days, and to hold up to the ancient East, as of still
living and vivifiying virtue, those sublime thoughts and noble
aspirations which for unnumbered centuries had been to it
the bread of life.

With regard to the external form of his poem, Ghálib
was content to follow the model which ancient usage had
consecrated. The ground-plan of the narrative mesneví had
been handed down unchanged, almost unmodified, from the
days of Nizámí of Genje The book of 'Beauty and Love'
consists, therefore, of the usual three parts, — prologue,
story, and epilogue. These together comprise a little over
two thousand riming couplets. Enshrined in the story are
four short lyric pieces of much beauty, these, which are in
the same metre as the body of the work, are written in the
stanzaic form known as mukhammes, and take the place of
the incidental ghazels so general in earlier mesnevís.

The first and second cantos of the prologue are hymns to
God and the Prophet respectively, the third describes the
ascension of the latter, and is one of the finest of the many
poems that have been written on this subject In the fouith
canto Ghálib, like a loyal Mevleví, sings the praises of
Mevláná Jelál-ud-Dín, the founder of the order, in the fifth
he gratefully acknowledges the encouragement he received
from his superior in the prosecution of his work. The sixth
and last canto of the prologue is 'The Reason of Writing' [1]

The circumstances under which Ghálib here tells us he
was constrained to write his poem are very similar to those
under which, if their authors are to be believed, more than
half the mesnevís in the language have been produced. The
story then may very well be a mere conventional fiction,
on the other hand, it is so simple and so probable that it
may equally well be the relation of an actual occurrence.
It matters little which alternative be true This is what the
poet says: One day he finds himself in company with a
number of cultured and learned men The talk runs on
literature, especially on the Khayrábád of Nábí which is
eulogized by certain of the party in the most extravagant
and exaggerated terms, some of those present even going so
far as to say that no one could possibly write a 'parallel'
to it. This is more than the young Mevleví with his clear
critical insight can stand, and he at once arrests the speaker
and begins to criticise the much belauded poem. He admits
that it is a wonderful production considering the great age
of Nábí when he wrote it, but asks what right that poet
had to make additions to any book by Sheykh ʿAttár, as if that
great man (who was one of the most eminent mystics) were
likely to have left his work incomplete. He then goes on
to blame Nábí, and with perfect justice, for the ultra-

[1] It will be noticed that the poem is not dedicated to any patron

Persianism of his style in this poem, for the inadequacy and
meanness of his hyperbole, and for the carelessness with
which he wrote after his popularity had been secured. The
next point to which Ghálib takes exception is the somewhat
realistic account which Nábí gives of the nuptials of his
hero and heroine. Here, as I have said when speaking
of the 'Khayrábád', the later writer is hypercritical; for
although in a poem so lofty as 'Beauty and Love' any
remotest suggestion of such things would be impossible and
unendurable, passages of the kind were natural and appropriate in books like that of Nábí and had been sanctioned
by usage and tradition from the very earliest times. Ghálib's
objection that such a usage, borrowed from the Persian
voluptuaries, is no excuse would indeed be valid if urged
against a genius powerful and original as his own, and able
to soar into undiscovered heights; but if poor old Nábí is
to be condemned on this score, then nine tenths of the
imitative mesneví-writers must share in the condemnation,
to say nothing of the many Romantic poets who were far
more outspoken and had not even the excuse of following
an accepted model. When Ghálib censures Nábí for having
laboured in vain, taking a thief as one of his heroes, his
criticism, if still somewhat trivial, is at least more justifiable;
he asks indignantly whether the theme of Love was exhausted,
and whether any other theme were worthy of a poet What
though this has been sung a thousand times already? — one
does not refuse the wine that remains The whole world
is acquainted with the Grain of Love, beside which all else
is vain. If thou knowest of this road, he says, no thief will
spring out upon thy path. One of those present then expresses
his disapproval of what Ghálib has just been saying, but
the latter adheres to the strictures he has made, whereupon
the company call on him to make good his words by producing

a book which shall surpass the 'Khayrábád', asking him
whether God has bestowed on him while yet in his youth
that skill which the aged Nábí only barely reached Ghálib
therefore set to work upon his task, he confesses that his
book is not free from faults, but says that his claim to
superiority is not vain, for though the weaver of the silk
may be uncomely, yet it does not fall behind the stuff
of Aleppo. [1]

An outline of the story of 'Beauty and Love', which
follows the prologue, is given elsewhere. [2] It will be sufficient
to say here that the plot is very slight, and that the author
produces his effects less by the incidents of his narrative
than by the subtle and varying atmospheric setting in which
he presents the successive scenes. The thread of the story
is from time to time interrupted, especially at junctures
more than usually critical, by brief cantos in which the poet
calls on the cupbearer for wine to inspire and fit him for
his task Such appeals to the cupbearer, which take the
place of the Western poet's invocation of his muse, are
frequent in the old mesnevís, so .that the poet here, as in
all formal matters, follows in the wake of his predecessors.
In another short parenthetical canto, in his discussion on
the Logos, Ghálib gives us his opinion concerning certain
of the earlier mesneví-writers The Persians Firdawsí, Khusraw,
and Nizámí, he tells us, all found the glorious Word, likewise found the road thereto in the way of Newá'í. In our
own Constantinople did Nev'ízáde (i. e. 'Atá'í) run up and
down, a pedestrian, but how should he sing the same note
as Nizámí, or how can the chirp of the harp accompany
the Koran? The elegance of his genius may, indeed, not
be denied; yet are there very many like unto him, to each

---

[1] Nábí, as we have seen, wrote many of his poems in Aleppo
[2] See the Appendix to this volume.

of whom, adds Ghálib, be a thousand acclamations, and on
their detractors a thousand reproaches!

Following the established custom, as we have seen he
always does in such matters, Ghálib opens the epilogue with
a Fakhriyya or Self-Eulogy. But even in this, where most
writers allow themselves unbounded licence, the moderation
of this poet does not desert him. With the full assurance
of genius, quietly and simply, without bombast and without
extravagance, he begins:

> 'I have surpassed the style of my predecessors,
> 'I have spoken another tongue;
> 'I have been no follower of that host
> 'For all that Khusraw [1] conformed to the Genjeví.' [2]

Continuing, he proclaims how the words which he has
uttered are no commonplace words, and challenges the
would be critic to match them if he can. He asks him whether
he has ever seen any such ambushed valley, for this is no
Díwán way; [3] and adds that though he has taken but a
short time to write it, his work is not on that account ill-
digested. Next follows his declaration as to having derived the
philosophy of it from the 'Mesneví'; 'I have stolen', he says,

---

[1] For even Amír Khusraw of Dehli — born 651 (1253—4) died 725 (1324—5)
— whom Ghálib has already declared to have found the word, acknowledged
that Nizámí of Genje was his model in mesneví, and wrote a series of five
poems as a 'parallel' to the Khamsa of the latter.

طرز سلف تقدّم ایتـدم بر بشفـه لغت تکلّم ایتـدم [2]
بن اولـمدم اول کروهـه پیـرو اویمش بلکه کناجـوی یه خسرو

[3] The word here translated 'valley' means also 'manner', 'style', 'tenor', so
the 'ambushed valley' would mean a discourse in the tenor of which lurked
hidden things. Díwán Yolu = Díwán way, is the name of one of the principal
streets in Stamboul, here it also means the ordinary way or style of the
poetry in díwáns.

'but I have stolen what was public property, try thou too to comprehend it, find such a gem, and steal it likewise.'

Then, as it were by way of corrective and to show that all such praise of self is but a mere convention in his eyes, Ghálib breaks off to ascribe the honour and glory of his work to the author of the 'Mesneví'. 'O pen,' he exclaims, 'this work is none of thine; O night, this dawn is none of thine!' It is the sunbeams of the grave of that Guide of Rúm that have made his light visible on the horizon, that have inspired him even from his earliest days; for while yet a child his verses had become famous, without teacher, without instruction, he lisped in numbers. O God! what wondrous favour that a boy should be dowered with the gift of eloquence! But how? Grace reached him from Mevláná Jelál-ud-Dín, he learned many a lesson from the 'Mesneví'. Then taking as his text one of the parables in that great book, — a parable concerning a jackal which fell into a dye-pit and was so proud of the gay appearance he thus acquired that he bade all his comrades address him as a peacock, but when to try him these asked him to fly, he failing to do so, saw his claim rejected, [1] — taking this story as his text, Ghálib compares the 'Mesneví' itself to the dye-pit and his own heart to the jackal, all his friends, he says, flocked around him, and he gave himself airs before the very peacock of Paradise, [2] but, alas! he could not fly, so, like the flute, he had to wail in vain, and when he spoke only the taper wept.

The poem closes with the words:

'Whatsoever fire of yearning be in my soul,
'Whatsoever thrill of rapture be in my heart,

[1] Mesneví, Book III, story 3
[2] For the peacock of Paradise see Vol. III, p. 339, n. 1, here it is equivalent to the angels.

'Will remain in this vesture though, alas, I pass away;
'May God visit it with His saving grace!' [1]

I have dwelt at length, at too great length perhaps, on
this swan-song of the Asian Muse. But I hold this poem to
be the noblest utterance not only of the Romantic School,
not only even of the old poetry of Turkey, but of all that
vast Ottoman literature which derives its inspiration from
the East. By this poem, written almost on the eve of her
dethronement, has Asia justified the long despotism beneath
which she has enthralled the genius of Turkish poetry. For
here at last have the Ottoman Turks a poem worthy to
rank with the most brilliant triumph of the most brilliant
Persian; neither Nizámí, nor Saʿdí, nor Jámí, nor any other
of the great Íranians can point to any work of his more
lofty of purpose, more poetic in accomplishment than the
'Beauty and Love' of Ghálib.

The Díwán of Ghálib need not detain us long. The only
wonderful thing about it is that it exists at all. That the
man who, when but little past his twentieth year, gave to
the world a poem which is unique in Oriental literature
should in later life have cared to write the qasídas and
ghazels which fill this bulky volume is as amazing as it is
melancholy. It is not that these verses are worse than the
similar productions of other dervish poets; it is that they
are not better. If the master-poet of 'Beauty and Love' could
do no more therein than hold his own with the versifiers
of the time, he had looked better to his own fame by
altogether eschewing the 'Díwán Way.'

Some few of the occasional poems, such as the Elegy on

جانمده نـه سوزش ظلب وار كوكلمـده نـه نششه طرب وار [1]
بـو رسمه قـالور كيدرسم ايـواه تـوفيقنـه مظهـر ايـده اللـه

Esrár Dede, already mentioned, are really beautiful, some too of the qasídas, such as those addressed to the Sultan and other grandees who benefited the order, were necessitated by the circumstance of Ghálib being at once a poet and the Sheykh of Galata, but the vast majority of the poems in the Díwán were evidently composed merely for the gratification of the writer.

A strong Mevlevian tone pervades the volume, many of the qasídas are in honour of Jelál-ud-Dín and other illustrious members of the brotherhood; while the ghazels deal with little else than the Súfí philosophy, seen now from one point, now from another, but always through the eyes of a disciple of Mevláná. So far so good, the conceptions themselves, though unoriginal, are sublime, and had Ghálib continued to exercise here the same moderation and self-restraint as in his allegory, this collection would have been among Díwáns what 'Beauty and Love' is among mesnevís. But it was not so, poetry of this class was evidently unsuited for his genius, for here, instead of boldly carving for himself a path through regions none had ever trod, humbly and meekly he follows in the well-worn way of pedantry and extravagance, where whatever of verdure may once have been had long ago been trampled into clay by the coming and going of countless travellers.

A poet ranking beneath Nábí, beneath the Nábí whom he himself contemned, — such, according to one writer, would have been Ghálib's position had he left nothing beyond this Díwán Then Ziyá Pasha, speaking of him and his great allegory, says that he, the unique poet, came to the world only that he might write that one book. It is, of course, the surpassing merit of his mesneví that makes one look thus at Ghálib's Díwán. By itself this book would have given its author a respectable position in the third rank, and would have claimed our attention as a favourable example of Turkish mystical poetry; but it is the penalty of having once produced a work of the highest quality that the author may not thereafter descend to the level of the mediocre.

Besides the qasídas and ghazels, the Díwán contains a number of chronograms on current events, several 'parallels' to and glosses on verses of other poets such as Jelál-ud-Dín himself, Fuzúlí, Khayálí, Sháhidí, Nef'í, and, amongst the writer's contemporaries, Khoja Nesh'et and Pertev Efendi. There are also a few sharqís and stanzaic pieces, one or two short bits in mesneví, and a chapter of quatrains and unconnected couplets. A good many poems in the Díwán are in the Persian language.

In prose Ghálib wrote one or two Súfí treatises and a biographical work on the Mevleví poets.

It is with more than the usual diffidence that I offer the following translated extracts from 'Beauty and Love'. I am painfully conscious that, in the process of rendering these from the one language into the other, the subtle and incommunicable atmosphere which pervades and surrounds the original has been lost, and that they give but a dim reflection of the strong and glowing verse of Ghálib. Yet feebly as they represent the poet's power, the reader will discern in them a note unlike anything he has yet heard from any Turkish poet, and even through the veil of translation he will perceive the features of an unfamiliar style.

The first extract describes the birth-night of Beauty and Love.

From 'Beauty and Love'. [402]

Once on a night within this Tribe [1] befell
A passing wondrous thing and strange to tell.
The rolling spheres were each on other swept,
Some smiled among the angels, others wept
A clamour rang the vault of heaven round,
An earthquake shook the bases of the ground
A thousand terrors and a thousand joys
A din of cries, of tabors and hautboys
Now the thick darkness fold on fold was plied,
Now radiances flashed forth on every side.
Each leaf in adoration bowed the head,
The rivers, for amaze dissolving, fled,
Among the stars conjunctions dread arose,
A rain of joyance and a hail of woes
Amidst the darkness many a dreary cry,
And voices of the illumined lifted high
The sky pealed, echoing with the wild affray,
And earth through the strange turmoil lost her way,
This fear's contagion to each bosom came,
And peace of heart was but an empty name.
The spheres and all the air were filled with fright
A thousand destinies were born that night

This is one of the incidental lyrics, it is a lullaby sung
by his nurse over the cradle of the infant Love·

From the Same [403]

Sleep, sleep, and rest, for to-night, O Moon,
Shall the cry My Lord! on thine ear be thrown.
For all its design be yet unknown,
The decree of thy star this wise is shown
    Burned shalt thou be on the spit of pain!

[1] The allegorical tribe of the Beni Mahabbet or Children of Affection,
amongst whom Beauty and Love were born.

Sleep for this season without distress;
The Sphere against thee doth scheme duresse:
For cruel it is and pitiless;
Its aiding thee were an idle guess.
   I fear thou wilt mickle anguish gain.

O Narcisse of love, in slumber lie;
Clutch Fortune's skirt and for mercy cry;
With fear and dread ope the inward eye,
The end of the woe with heed descry:
   Thou'lt be as toy by disaster ta'en!

Rest, rest in the cradle peacefully,
A few brief nights from affliction free.
Oh think, I pray, what the end will be;
For milk it is blood shall be given thee:
   The beaker of harsh reproach thou'lt drain.

Sleep, Jasmine-breast, in the cradle here;
On this course will bide not the rolling sphere,
Nor will turn the stars on this wise for e'er;
See how they'll deal by thee, my dear:
   Thou'lt be the wheel on the stream of bane.

With wakefulness no communion keep;
If aidance come, it will come through sleep.
The Sphere will pledge thee in poison deep;
Thy work will be Ghálib-like to weep.
   The rebeck at dolour's feast, thou'lt plain.

The following is from the description of the Logos:

From the Same. [404]

An elder youthful-hearted, wise of thought,
Received as host them who that Pleasaunce sought:
His name the Logos, and his self full dear,
His life precedent to the ancient Sphere.
The souls of Love and Beauty well he knew;

And heat and cold stood open to his view [1]
The night-lamp of all knowledge was his mind, [2]
He shared the secrets lovers' hearts enshrined
Question alike and revelation he,
In him both miracle and prophet be
Unrivalled to beguile or lead aright,
In every fashion give or stint he might.
An so he pleased, without cuirass or spear,
He could make Peace waylay the path of war.
And he could make when dealing courteously
E'en Death and Life beloved and lover be
As fairy now, and now as fiend he strode,
Now of the sea, now of the land he showed.
A Khizr to direct who went astray,
A king to succour them withouten stay
As poet now, and now as sage he shone,
As zealot now, and now as wizard wan
Joy and Despair to his commandment bowed,
Hope and Desire submiss before him stood,
And ever by his order did there roll
Tears now of happiness and now of dole
He turnéd mourning into joy elate,
And intellect did he inebriate
The fashion of his mind no words may show,
And faculties are his which none may know
In need of him do all earth's folk remain,
Through him it is that man doth life attain
Kindler of beauty in the moon-faced fair,
Dust of their eyes who all their longings share
The joyful heart's companion dear and lieve,
The garb of mourning unto them that grieve
As is the woe, so he compassionates,
As is the mirror, so he radiates
What puissance in all he undertakes!
Yea, opposite from opposite he makes
Now is he bounden in the pit of teen,

[1] Heat and cold, i e all things, good and evil equally.
[2] For the 'night-lamp' see p 145, n 1 *supra.*

Now the grandee of Fortune's Egypt sheen [1]
All this beneath his glory still must be;
Beyond exaggeration standeth he.

Here are a few lines from the description of the Wilderness
of Dole through which Love and Zeal have to pass on their
journey to the City of the Heart:

From the Same. [405]

They lost the way amidst a desert drear,
Where winter-night doth reign and sudden fear.
A desert this — in God we refuge take! —
Whereof the jinn alway their tilt-yard make [2]
Together met were terror and despair,
It rained now darkness and now snow-flakes there.
What time the snow foregathered with black night
Fused in one mould was darkness and was light.
The moonbeams by the bitter frost were frore,
As dew quicksilver spread the desert o'er,
It turned to a white deer the gloomy dusk;
The waste was like to camphor midst of musk
The darkling night, surrounded by the snow,
E'en as the pupil of the eye did show.
Beshivered by the frost the enamelled sky
Seemed sprinkled o'er the desert's face to lie.

The next passage is from the picture of the Sea of Fire
with its waxen ships.

From the Same. [406]

Erewhile of this emprise heard tell had he, —
The waxen navy on the Fiery Sea
Now sudden on the way before him spread
That flaming ocean blighting hearts with dread

[1] Alluding to the Story of Joseph.
[2] It is said of a dreary and deserted place that the jinn or goblins play
at ball in it.

Building them ships of wax, upon that main
Had fiends full many habitation ta'en.
— For flames may work that people naught of woe,
As how should fire from fire anguish know? — [1]
These ever held their vessels in mid air
Scatheless for all the billows surging there
Vessels, but like to wedding-palms they showed; [2]
Ruddy of hulk, in shape as flames, they glowed.
Each seemed an island of disaster dire,
A blood-red carnage heap, a dismal fire,
Each rose a Mount of the Red Mere in view, [3]
Filled to o'erflowing with a fiendish crew.
A bier was every waxen ship, but none
Could tell their sepulchres who lay thereon.
Of the corpse-light that hangs o'er dead men's graves
Were all those ships and those drear fiery waves

The last extract which I shall give describes the marshalled
squadrons of the Heralds of Light who greet Love when
he reaches the City of the Heart:

From the Same. [407]

One company in robes of white so fair
That union's morn thereto might envy bear.
Lucent were they as any whitest fawn,
Each one a sun clad in the weeds of dawn.
A mighty host in golden mantles bright,
With golden vestments, golden crownals dight
Winged were they all and houri-faced, each one
From head to foot as life's elixir shone.

[1] The demons are said to have been created from fire as man from dust
[2] The wedding-palm was a pole decked with ribands and streamers of
bright colours which used to be carried in the processions that took place
on the marriages of great people.
[3] Kúh-i Surkháb = Red-Mere Mount, is a name given to several mountains,
notably to one on the south side of Tebríz in Persia where there are many
tombs and mausoleums. The demon ships are vast and red with fiery glow,
and are laden with corpses, — hence the metaphor

One troop thereof in azure panoply
Swept onward like unto the boundless sea.
Mid these the golden-clad were lost to view
Like the bright stars within the heavens blue.
　Another many clad in scarlet sheen,
Embraced of Paradise each one had been,[1]
Each one might put the sun and moon to shame;
Each one an Eden, yet a garth of flame
　Another throng, a blessed band, was there,
Arrayed in living emerald most fair.
A noble company, a sea of green,
Whose waves bestowed life on the souls of men.
　A troop thereof in raiment black bedight
Like flashing stars within the mirk of night.[2]
No need to tell of aught in this array;
As eve, but as the Ascension Eve, were they
　Each peerless band with glorious tints beseen
Was even as incarnate radiance sheen,
Their beams flashed ever hue on hue most bright,
Their rays phantasmal met in ceaseless fight.
Now every inch that fulgent City shrined
A mirror was clear as the scient mind,
From each reflection that was cast thereon
A hundred thousand reborn spirits shone.

I give four ghazels from the Díwán The first refers to the semá᷃ or mystic dance, which forms so striking a feature in the Mevleví rite that it has caused many European authors to designate the members of this fraternity as the 'Dancing' or 'Whirling Dervishes'. It is however only certain members of the brotherhood who perform the semá᷃.

Ghazel. [408]

While the lovers circle here in mystic dance[3]
Sun and moon travérse the sphere in mystic dance.

[1] Their robes were red as the roses of Paradise
[2] The angels were like the stars, their raiment like the dark night.
[3] The lovers are the Mevlevian dervishes.

Love's deep secret made the spheric heavens reel,
All the worlds do still appear in mystic dance

E'en as 'twere a whirlpool shows the weeping eye,
Casting pearls and spray as clear in mystic dance

Youthful Magians sweet about the Tavern go,
Like as pilgrims round in fere in mystic dance.

Lo, the reed ecstatic thrills, the Heavenly Birds
Dove-like beat their plumy gear in mystic dance. [1]

I am yonder vagrant Qays upon whose head
Whiles the nests do leap and rear in mystic dance

Ghálib, while the Sun of Love doth radiance pour
Mevlevís will mote-like veer in mystic dance.

It is, of course, God who is addressed in the next ghazel.

Ghazel. [409]

Those cries that sound throughout the fast as for the bowl are all for Thee,
Those songs and roundelays the which the minstrels troll are all for Thee

O world-illuming Sun, look down for once upon the rose of hope,
Those radiant beauties sheen as dewy aureole are all for Thee

O King, what though Thou deign'st to honour with Thy face the dervish poor? —
Those shouts of Háy! and Húy! that through this convent roll are all for Thee [3]

Intent to catch the lustrous pearls of Thy dear words those eager ears
That shell-like open wide and list from heart and soul are all for Thee

All single-handed how to clutch the skirt of my poor heart's desire?
Those cruel dagger-lashes fain to work my dole are all for Thee.

---

[1] The Heavenly Birds are the angels, these are here said to be so moved when they hear the Mevlevian reed-flute that they too break into the semá'.

[2] When Qays or Mejnún, the lover of Leylí, dwelt in the desert his only companions were the wild beasts and birds; the latter, we are told, used to build their nests in his long unkempt hair

[3] When in ecstasy the dervishes are wont to cry, 'Yá Hú! Yá Hú!' that is, Oh He! Oh He!" meaning God

The vines are scattered all around with purpose fair of quaffing wine;
Those shatterings of the cup, those cares to keep it whole, are all for Thee.

The while in Ghálib's walk there be no trace of aught suspicious seen,
Those reverences fore the Elder of the Bowl¹ are all for Thee.

Ghazel [410]

Out on this jugglery! by God' out on this idle snare'
Out on this pomp and circumstance! out on this glore and glare'

Since never pasha finds a rag to shroud his lopped off head,
Out on his flag of honour, his badge of horse's hair¹²

Since ever must the blast of death blow out the lamp of life,
Out on the useless candle that above the tomb doth flare'³

How often often have I traced it on the page of earth!
Out on this form of nights and days for aye repeated there'

A mansion whose foundation rests on sighs and bitter tears,
Woe for such show and bravery' out on such beauty fair!

From torment's furnace let them issue forth mid sweat of pain,
Out on them all, these regal pearls, these rubies pure and rare'

To those who, erst of high estate, their rank have forfeited
'Out on thee! groans the rumbling drum, and 'Out'' the tabor's blare ⁴

Since that the wedding-revelry must turn to mourning's gloom,
Pugh for the taper of the feast! out on the flambeau-glare'

O Ghálib, be thou dervish-souled, seek poverty's retreat,
Take flute in hand and play, then out on Fortune everywhere'

The while that at Our Master's gate I find my hopes I'll sing ⁵
'Out on the stress and anguish which from earth's duresse I bear'"

¹ I. e the superior of the convent
² The tugh or horse-hair standard that used to be the symbol of a
Pasha's rank
³ It is the custom on certain nights to light a lamp over the graves of holy men.
⁴ Alluding to the military band attached to the establishment of a Pasha.
⁵ Our Master, i e Mevláná Jelál-ud-Dín

Ghazel. [411]

We reached the loved one's blissful gate, but naught of her did sight,
We entered Paradise, but ah, we saw no Vision bright. [1]

E'en to the fourth sphere wandered we in quest of easement still;
Alas, no Jesus did we find to heal the ailing spright [2]

See how the circling of the o'erturned sphere hath dealt by us,
The very feast of Jem for us with brimming bowl's undight.

Like unto Mejnún have we journeyed to the Ka°ba fane;
Our prayers have passed, but naught of fair effect therefrom doth light

* *

The heart hath passed within the mirror shadow-like, and gone,
Amazed am I we ne'er have seen yon one, our heart's delight.

In such ascendant wills it not to scatter grace, we ne'er
Have seen the sun refulgent e'en the eastern skies ignite

O Ghálib, in sad sooth unread hath our petition bode,
To Love's Divan we've come, but ne'er have seen that Lord of Might

[1] The reference is to the Beatific Vision
[2] The fourth sphere is the 'station' of Jesus

CHAPTER VI.

The romanticists (continued).

Khulúsí Efendi. — Esrár Dede. — Khoja Nesh'et. Pertev Efendi.

Two at least of Sheykh Ghálib's brother dervishes at the Galata convent have earned for themselves a certain reputation as poets, — Khulúsí Dede and Esrár Dede. The first of these acted as chief cook at the convent during Ghálib's abbacy, and died in 1220 (1805—6). The second and much more important was that intimate and valued friend of the Sheykh, of whom mention has been already made.

Concerning the life of Mehemmed Esrár Dede there is little to relate. He was born in Constantinople, entered the Mevleví order, accomplished his noviciate at the Galata convent under the direction of Sheykh Ghálib, whose affection and esteem he gained, died before his master in the year 1211 (1796—7), and was buried in the convent graveyard by the side of the Mevleví poet Fasíh Dede. The most noteworthy point in Esrár's uneventful history is the close companionship which existed between him and his superior. In many of his poems he mentions Ghálib by name, and always in terms of the utmost admiration and respect. That his reverential attachment was truly appreciated is shown by the beautiful elegy in which the great poet bewails his comrade's untimely death.

208

The poems which make up the Díwán of Esrár Dede are
of the usual dervish type, though perhaps they display a
little more of purely human tenderness than is general in
such effusions. While many of his verses are quite clear,
even when symbolic, many others share the obscurity inevitable
in mystic poetry. To give a definite explanation of such is
impossible, they point to ideas so subtle or so vague as not
to be capable of adequate expression in definite language,
ideas to be conveyed only by suggestion. Such verses, though
not incomprehensible to those who have studied sympatheti-
cally the teachings of almost any mystic school, admit of
no absolute explanation, for even when their purport can
be expressed in ordinary language, their scope is so wide
that probably no two expounders would interpret them alike

Esrár Dede has not a larger proportion of such enigmatic
utterances than his neighbours, and indeed his book is on
the whole more intelligible than most dervish díwáns, yet
his poetry is of such a nature that it never could be popular.
It has its merits, it is the mirror in which is reflected the
soul of a gentle-hearted mystic, but it is the work of a
poet who held himself aloof, who dwelt apart from the busy
world of men who surged round his convent walls, and
whose struggles and pleasures alike were to him indifferent

He was therefore out of touch with the spirit of the
Romanticist age in which his lot was cast. So far as the
tone of his work is concerned, it might have been produced
in any Period of the past. In language only is he a true
child of his time, for though no follower of the Turkicist
school, his poems contain expressions that would not occur in
earlier writers, while in matters of versification he is as lax,
or as slovenly, as the most thorough-going Romanticist.

Professor Nájí singles out his rubáʿís or quatrains for
special commendation, remarking that he is one of the few

Ottomans who have excelled in this particular form of poetry. This is no doubt quite true; none the less I do not think that he can be justly held to have here equalled his predecessor Háletí.

I have translated two of his ghazels and two of his quatrains; all the four are wholly mystical.

Ghazel. [412]

Hast thou fallen in with Love's clear winsome Fair, O gentle breeze? —
For thy breath yon Darling's odour sweet doth share, O gentle breeze.

Thou hast tangled all the curling locks of her who holds the heart,
Thou hast made her lovers yearning's chain to bear, O gentle breeze.

Haply 'tis thy zephyr's aim to solve the riddle hard that lies
Hidden in the rosebud's bosom debonair, O gentle breeze. [1]

Sweet a rose-leaf wafted hither from the Heavenly bower above,
Jesus gained from thee his breath of virtue rare, O gentle breeze.

Hath the way thou camest led thee o'er the dust Our Master trod? — [2]
Lo, thou hast requickened Esrár with thine air, O gentle breeze.

Ghazel. [413]

All the universe is love-sick; O my Lord, what means this plight?
'Tis as 'twere the Day of Judgment, to Capella mounts the spright. [3]

[1] One aspect of the purpose of this couplet is expressed in Lord Tennyson's well-known lines :
        'Flower in the crannied wall,
        'I pluck you out of the crannies,
        'I hold you here, root and all, in my hand,
        'Little flower — but if I could understand
        'What you are, root and all, and all in all,
        'I should know what God and man is.'
[2] "Our Master" is Mevláná Jelál-ud-Dín.
[3] 'To mount to (the star) Capella', is to ascend to the highest heavens. The Day of Judgment, typical of turmoil and consternation.

14

Yonder cruel-dealing Beauty now hath thought hei to be kind ,
Blithe and gay the world rejoiceth, gladdened of this dear delight.

Standeth ready dight the banquet, circleth mid the guests the wine,
Flushed is toper and is loveling with the grace that there doth light.

Brimming are their bowls with radiance from the Heavenly Beauty shed;
Lo, the dregs thereof are blood-gouts of Truth's martyred Mansúr [1] wight.

Every overflowing goblet streams a flood of madness wild,
Every wine-retailing measure rolls a sea of wonders bright.

Every pose of the cupbearer fair a thousand signs reveals,
While her every movement doth from Love's Korán a verse recite.

Love, in truth, is an enigma, whose solution ne'er may be,
In bewilderment its birth is while its end is frenzied plight

Poverty is one with riches, malady is one with cure ,
He who understandeth needeth not with either to unite. [2]

Unto levellers who drink within the tavern of His Love
Bold and shameless words and ways are piety's clear mirror bright.

Lo, in forms His revelation, as in bright Epiphany,
The transgression of the Shadowless, Esrár, is e'en the right [3]

---

[1] [Huseyn ibn Mansúr al-Halláj ("the Wool-carder"), a favourite martyr
of the Súfís, to whom reference has been made repeatedly in previous pages
of this work ED]

[2] Experience is the only teacher, yet to him of understanding, to the
illuminate, experience is unnecessary

[3] In the first line of this couplet Esrár says that God reveals Himself as
truly in the forms of material phenomena as in the glories of such Theophanies
as that of Mount Sinai In the second he justifies a view calculated to offend
the orthodox by suggesting that what would be transgression in such as
them is true righteousness in himself and his fellow-mystics, a view expressed
in a well-known adage of the Súfís, "the virtues of the pious are the sins
of [God's] intimates" (i e the Súfís) The Prophet is said to have cast no
shadow, so that 'the Shadowless' will mean those holy as he, that is the
poet and his fellow-mystics

Quatrain. [414]

God's fire that in my breast doth flame is this;
The Adam worshipped with acclaim is this. [1]
Never may wisdom's Plato read it true, —
A brilliant riddle on Heart's name is this.

Quatrain. [415]

By wine of love of thee am I distraught;
Cupbearer, that hath my confusion wrought;
Give wine, and prate not of the morrow's dole,
The Day of Reckoning [2] in my eyes is naught.

When speaking of the early life of Sheykh Ghálib I mentioned that among his instructors was the celebrated teacher and poet Khoja Nesh'et, or, as I there ventured to translate, Dominie Nesh'et. This Nesh'et, who, though no great poet, was a somewhat remarkable individual, was among the most prominent figures in Constantinopolitan literary circles some hundred years ago. His personal name was Suleymán, and he was born in 1148 (1735—6) in the city of Adrianople, where his father, a courtier named Ahmed Reffá Efendi, was residing in temporary exile. Reffá Efendi, who had some skill both in poetry [3] and music, wrote a sharqí or song in which he bewailed his banishment and which he set to a touching air of his own composition. [4]

---

[1] Alluding to the legend concerning the angels worshipping Adam on his creation.

[2] The Day of Judgment.

[3] On the occasion of his son's birth he composed the following chronogram, which Nesh'et, when he grew up, had graven on his seal:

خدایا ایکی عالمده عزیز ایله سلیمدنی

'O God, in either world hold Thou Suleymán dear.'

[4] This sharqí begins:

مسکنمدن دور ایدوب غربتده سرگردان ایدن
قسمتمی طلعمی یوقسه جانا سنمیسین

This became popular, and eventually reached the ears of
the Sultan who, when he heard it and learned who was
its author, not only pardoned Refí'á but conferred upon
him yet greater favours than he had before enjoyed.

By and bye Refí'á was commissioned to accompany the
annual pilgrim caravan to Mekka in the capacity of Khaftán
Aghasi or Master of the Robes of Honour, as the official
is termed who has charge of the robes of honour sent by
the Sultan for distribution among the notables of the Holy
City His son Suleymán, who had now attained to years of
discretion, accompanied him on the pilgrimage, and when
passing Qonya on the homeward journey the youthful Hajji
was formally affiliated to the Mevlaví order by the Chelebi
Efendi.

Shortly after their return to the capital, Refí'á Efendi
died, and Suleymán began to devote himself with the utmost
assiduity to the study of Persian, and more especially of
the Mesneví He was assisted in his efforts by several learned
men, notably by Dáye-záde Júdí Efendi who bestowed on
him the pen-name of Nesh'et, which he offered to his pupil
in the following quatrain:

'As thou with all courtesy hast desired learning and letters,
'Ever hold converse with men of culture
'Devote all thine energy to the works of the ancients,
'Let thy learning-distinguished pen-name upon earth be Nesh'et ' [1]

'What is this that makes me wander, wildered, lonely, far from home? —
'Is it Fate, or is it Fortune, or can it be thou, my Love?'

[1] حویکـه علم و اد.ه انـدگ ادله رغـمت
دائمـا صاحـب عرفان الـه الـه حبیت
غمـرت طـمسی صـرف ان اثـر اسلافـه
مخلص معرفتگ اولـه جهانـده نشـأت

Possibly the manner of this presentation suggested to the poet a practice adopted by him when he himself became a teacher.

In the course of time Nesh'et acquired great repute as a Mesneví-Khán or Mesneví-chanter, as those persons are styled who intone passages from the Mesneví during certain portions of the Mevleví public service, and he began also to be much talked about as an accomplished and successful teacher of Persian. His residence in the Molla Kúrání ward [1] of Constantinople was frequented not only by many of the literary men of the capital, but even Persian and Frankish visitors; while the number of his pupils was so great that, as Professor Nájí laughingly says, his house might well have been the envy of many a medrese. Among those of his pupils who afterwards attained eminence were Ghálib himself, Pertev Efendi who subsequently edited his Díwán, the Beylikji 'Izzet Bey, and Khoja Wahyí.

Khoja Nesh'et was as skilled in the use of arms as he was in the interpretation of the Mesneví. He was moreover the owner of a fief, and therefore liable for military service. So when war broke out with Russia in 1768, the Khoja shut up his school, buckled on his trusty sword, and, joining the Imperial forces, took part in the defence of his fatherland. When, after having distinguished himself by his valour on the field, he returned to Constantinople, he re-opened his classes and began again to expound the subtleties of the Mesneví. But henceforward he adopted the extraordinary habit of always appearing when he delivered his lectures with his sword by his side, fully armed and equipped for battle. This practice was the more strange as it was against the custom for any Turk to wear a sword except when on a campaign or a journey.

[1] This ward (mahalla) is in the parish (semt) of Aq-Saray.

Nesh'et was connected with the Naqshbendí as well as with the Mevleví order, and is said to have advanced far in mystic lore. He died in 1222 (1807—8).

Brave, generous, and cultured, Khoja Nesh'et was a good example of the Turkish gentleman of the old school. That he had his share of the ready wit and kindly humour of his race is shown by many of the little anecdotes that gather round his name. He was always ready and eager to assist any one in distress, and used often to importune those in high places on behalf of such as sought his aid. His answer to one who thought to rebuke him for so doing is well known: 'Is it seemly,' said the would-be censor, 'to spend the sweat of one's brow in things like this?' 'Why' replied he, 'the sweat of one's brow won't turn a mill-wheel; it is in things like this that it is of use.'

The Khoja was among other things a great smoker, and the story is told how one of the 'unco guid' who happened to be in his company when he was indulging himself in this way, scandalized at the sight, gravely said, 'Sir, there is no fire in Heaven; whence will you light your pipe there?' Whereupon the Khoja, removing for a moment from his lips the mouthpiece of his huge chibuq, answered with a twinkle in his eye, 'From the stove where they are cooking kebábs for you.' [1]

On another occasion, we are told, a person of the same class, minded to reproach Nesh'et for devoting himself to furthering the study of the language of the heretical Persians, said, alluding to a vulgar prejudice widely spread among the ignorant and fanatical, 'Sir, they say that Persian is the

---

[1] To understand the point of the Khoja's reply it must be borne in mind that according to the notions of the ignorant pietists, eating and drinking will enter prominently into the delights of the blest in Paradise. Kebábs are small pieces of meat roasted on skewers.

language of hell; is it so?' 'If it is so,' replied the Khoja, 'it were as well to learn it; one can never tell where one may go, and suppose one should ·have to visit hell, to be unable to speak the language would be but a torment the more.'

Khoja Nesh'et was much more successful as a teacher than as a poet. His poetry never rises above mediocrity, though it very often falls below it. He is one of the most slovenly versifiers of this slovenly age; and so numerous and varied are his mistakes of every description that Professor Nájí says his Díwán might truthfully be entitled a Miscellany of Errors. Pretty phrases are certainly to be met with here and there in his verses; but such are, according to the same critic, merely accidental.

Although himself so indifferent a poet, Nesh'et was apparently an excellent teacher of Persian, able to inspire his pupils with enthusiasm for their studies and, what is more, with affection and respect towards himself. Many of his pupils outstripped him in poetry, and must eventually have felt how much beneath them he stood here; yet not one among them, though they often allude to him in their Díwáns, ever refers to him otherwise than with the reverence due from pupil to teacher.

Many of the poems in his Díwán are in Persian; but these reach no higher level than those in Turkish.

As I said when writing of Sheykh Ghálib, Nesh'et was in the habit of bestowing upon his more favoured pupils a pen-name conveyed in an original poem of his own composition. These poems, which he calls Makhlas-Náme or Pen-name Diploma, and of which several are included in his Díwán, are sometimes in mesneví-rime and sometimes in monorime, sometimes in Turkish and sometimes in Persian. No other poet, so far as I know, has a similar series of elaborate poems written for the like purpose; and in this series lies

the author's only title to originality. But such little originality as these works possess is exclusively that of occasion,
for in their scheme they differ hardly, if at all, from the
ordinary qasída The longer among them open with an
exordium of the general type; where the name of the patron
would come in the usual course, the pen-name of the pupil
is introduced, the panegyric is replaced by or diluted with
a string of counsels, and the poem winds up in the orthodox
fashion with a prayer for its subject's welfare. In this there
is scarcely any variation from the ground-plan of the qasída;
though of course the rime arrangement is different in such
of these versified`diplomas as are written in the mesneví
form Nesh'et's advice to his pupils consists for the most
part in recommendations to devote their best powers to
writing naᶜts in honour of the Prophet, to avoid everything
like satire, and (a counsel he might himself have profitably
followed) to study diligently the works of their predecessors

Most of Nesh'et's original ghazels are mystic in intention,
but he has a few written in the objective Romanticist style
His Díwán was collected and edited by his pupil, the poet
Pertev Efendi, in 1200 (1785—6).

The first of the following ghazels was written by Nesh'et
when he was at the wars

Ghazel. [416]

When o'er the meadows glowed the tears of yearning from mine e'e
As Yemen or the heights of Badakhshán was Rumelí. [1]

A wandering nightingale am I, forsaken of my dreams,
My home whatever stranger-land beneath my wing may be

[1] The tears of yearning are tears of blood, therefore red, so the hills and
plains of Rumelia, bright with these, resembled the high lands of Badakhshan
when rubies are found or the stretches of Yemen rich in carnelians.

As Jacob filled with grief, as Joseph banished far, am I;
The earth is House of Dole and prison dure alike for me. [1]

To cry aloud my weary plight in woful strangerhood
Each scar upon my breast hath oped its lips full bitterly.

Since I the yearning Jacob am of separation's vale,
The letter from the Joseph-fair e'en as the shift I see. [2]

Would that I knew if I alone am thus, or if all earth's
Delight and joy, like mine, are changed to pain and agony.

Nesh'et, my home is now the saddle, while the love I clip
Is e'en that silver-bodied fair they call the sword, perdie!

Ghazel. [417]

The rule of love is for the lover naught but wistful prayer,
Coquetry is the law of fascination for the fair.

Although the birds of high estate [3] should seek to soar aloft,
Within the sky of zeal, they still were geese both here and there.

Yon one who partridge-like doth pace coquetry's mountain-range [4]
Doth e'en as falcon through the chace of heart and spirit fare.

Alack that they most richly dowered with grace and beauty's charm
In faith and piety and pity should so scantly share!

The burning anguish of the moth that seeks the vision bright
The taper doth reveal, is to my thinking all a prayer.

At times meseemeth that the cock's loud clarion-call at dawn
Proclaims: 'O Lord, how long the night of absence drear doth wear!'

The gift of God to joyless Nesh'et in this cabaret
Is e'en the licence to be drunk with Love therein for e'er.

[1] The 'House of Dole' i. e. Jacob's dwelling-place after the departure of
Joseph; the 'prison dure', that wherein Joseph was confined in Egypt.
[2] The letter from some friend fair as Joseph is here compared to the shift
of that beautiful and saintly personage, which, being flung over Jacob's face,
restored sight to his eyes blinded with weeping.
[3] That is, the grandees of the state.
[4] The pacing of the partridge is held to resemble the graceful walk of a
coquettish beauty.

Mehemmed Pertev Efendı who, as we have seen, collected and edited hıs master's Díwán, was one of Khoja Nesh'et's most successful pupıls Among his fellow-students was a certaın ʿIzzet Bey, himself destined to acquire some dıstınctıon as a poet, wıth whom Pertev formed a close frıendshıp, and who eventually performed for hını the same servıce whıch he hımself ıendered to theır common master.

Both young men entered the government service, and both soon made theır way Pertev, whose lıterary gıfts were ındisputable, was for a tıme Imperıal Annalıst. In 1806 he was present ın an officıal capacıty wıth the Imperıal troops outsıde Sılıstrıa, and ın the followıng year, 1222 (1807), he dıed at Adrıanople, whıther the aımy had wıthdrawn ınto wınter quarters

It ıs said that when hıs friend ʿIzzet Bey brought to hım hıs poems carefully ordered and formed ınto a Díwán, Pertev took the cloak from hıs own shoulders and flung it over those of the Bey, ın ımitation of the actıon of the Prophet on a sımılar occasıon.

The poetry of Pertev, whıle conventıonal ın subject and tone, ıs carefully wrıtten. Hıs versıfıcatıon is ın marked and pleasıng contrast to the slıpshod work we have lately been consıderıng, and shows but few traces of that untıdy laxıty whıch ıs the bane of thıs Perıod and mars the work of some who as poets were ımmeasurably hıs superıors The ghazels of Pertev are, almost wıthout exception, dıstınguıshed by grace of fancy and neatness of executıon, and form pleasant enough readıng so long as one ıs satisfied wıth verse that ıs merely a pretty plaything. There are ın hıs Díwán frequent echoes from the earlıer poets, notably from Nedím, to whose works Pertev seems to have devoted much sympathetıc study

Thıs poet is frequently called Pertev Efendı ın order to

distinguish him from the statesman Pertev Pasha who gained some reputation as a poet in the earlier half of the nineteenth century.

Ghazel. [418]

Whiles unveiléd, whiles enveiléd, her fair face my dear one shows,
Whereby plenilune and crescent turn by turn doth she disclose. [1]

Now she feigns to heed not, now to weet not, now she wounds and chides,
Now she asks me of the anguish from her cruelty that flows.

Whensoe'er on wanton wise I seek to hint at union's joys,
With her dainty hand my dear one veils her face that crimson glows.

Now to union she provoketh, now she biddeth to depart,
Now doth she the futile order to abandon love impose.

Pertev, whiles have I, like loyal troth, no part in all her thoughts,
Whiles for sake of me with others doth she deal as with her foes.

Ghazel. [419]

Darling, whensoe'er the wine of pride inebriateth thee,
Every one who sees would deem thee drunken with the grape to be.

Loose not so thy locks, for should they fall profuse, O Sapling young,
Sore I fear they'll form a burden to o'ertax thee, Love of me.

O thou crescent-browed, while yet so young, this loveliness full sure
Maketh thee to shine the plenilune in beauty's galaxy.

Cruel, since thou'rt come to dwell within the mansion of the heart,
Ever of thy news do ask me all who yearning's anguish dree.

Chide not thou the wildered Pertev, O thou houri-envied fair;
Truly 'twould thyself dumbfounder, could'st thou thine own beauty see.

[1] The yashmaq or veil worn out of doors by Turkish ladies is so arranged as to leave an opening for the eyes somewhat in the shape of a crescent moon. The plenilune in the verse refers of course to the unveiled face.

CHAPTER VII.

Fázil Bey. — Sunbul-záde Vehbí. — Surúrí.

Turkish Romanticism culminates in the work of Fázil Bey. Revolt against traditional authority, assertion of individuality, local colour, unbridled license alike in matter and in manner, whatever in short distinguishes this movement from the Classicism which precedes and the Modernism which follows, is here present in fullest measure, inspiring and permeating the works of this author, and placing them at once among the most interesting and the least beautiful in all the range of Ottoman poetry.

Yet this writer, the most stalwart champion of the Turkish spirit in Turkish poetry, was, save by education, no Turk at all. Fázil was by race an Arab of the Arabs. His grandfather, Táhir 'Omer, who was descended from an Arab of Medína, Zídán by name, who had settled in Syria, had been a man of great ability and much ambition, and had held the district of Acre and Safed almost as an independent prince and in defiance of the Ottoman Sultan But in 1190 (1776—7) when the famous admiral Ghází Hasan Pasha, who had been sent from Constantinople to bring this Arab rebel to his knees, appeared under the walls of Acre, Táhir, finding that his Barbaresque mercenaries refused to fire upon

the forces of the Khalífa, resolved on flight. But it was
then too late; as he was leaving the town he was shot dead
by one of his own soldiers. The Imperial forces entered
Acre, and Fázil and his younger brother were carried off
to Constantinople by the Turkish admiral. Fázil's father,
ʿAlí Záhir, who had been outside the town endeavouring
to collect men to aid in the defence, fled into the interior,
and was there treacherously slain the following year.

Fázil himself, who had been born at Safed, was on reaching
the capital placed with his younger brother in the Imperial
Seraglio, where they were to be educated as Turkish gentlemen. The younger brother, whose name is variously given
as Kámil and Hasan, died in the palace, apparently soon
after his arrival. The education offered to the youths who
were admitted to the Seraglio was, so far as culture went,
the best then obtainable in Turkey, and of this young Fázil
took full advantage. Nothing seems to have escaped unobserved
by the quick-witted Arab lad; and it is most likely that it
was during his residence here that he obtained from eunuchs
and others familiar with the more recondite mysteries of
the imperial pleasure-house many of the curious details which
he afterwards embodied in his works. In these works he
gives some interesting particulars concerning his life in the
Palace, notably of his love-adventures, disappointment with
the result of one of which, he says, induced him to quit
the Imperial residence in the year 1198 (1783—4). [1] Whether
this be strictly true or not, we know from other sources
that Fázil left the Seraglio during the reign of ʿAbd-ul-
Hamíd I who was on the throne at that date. Under Selím
III Fázil was named administrator of the mortmain properties

---

[1] The word Enderúní, meaning connected with the Enderún or Seraglio,
is often prefixed to the names of persons brought up in the Palace; thus
our author is frequently called Enderúní Fázil Bey.

in Rhodes [1] and received the rank of Khoja or Master-Clerk. For a time all went well and Fázil served in various official capacities of greater or less importance, devoting his leisure to the composition of his curious and unique poems. At length in 1214 (1799—1800) on account of some complaint against him, the nature of which is not mentioned, he was exiled to the island of Rhodes which he does not appear to have visited before. Here he was afflicted with some eye trouble through which he became at least temporarily blind. This according to ͨAtá, the historian of the Seraglio, was brought about by his constant and excessive weeping for the murder of Sultan Selím; but Fatín with more plausibility attributes it to his anxiety lest he should share the fate of his old patron Rátib Efendi, who was just then executed in the same island of Rhodes whither he had been banished three years before. [2] But Fázil was more fortunate; he was permitted to return to the capital, where he resided first at Eyyúb and then at Beshiktash where he died in 1224 (1809—10), after having been confined to his bed for seven years, if Fatín Efendi speaks the truth. In one place in his History the late Jevdet Pasha says that Fázil Bey recovered his sight; but this is unconfirmed by any of the other authorities.

Fázil Bey was no true poet; in his writings there is no reflection, however faint, of that light that never was on sea or land; and so these writings are without attraction for the modern Ottoman critics, who simply ignore them, regarding them, if they deign to regard them at all, as little better

[1] Such positions no longer entailed the personal supervision of the holder, the latter usually employed a deputy to do the work, while he himself drew the emoluments.

[2] Ebu-Bekr Rátib Efendi was a well-known poet and statesman who had held the office of Reͦís-ul-Kuttáb (chief secretary) under Selím III from 1209 to 1211 when he was exiled to Rhodes; he was there executed in 1214. Fázil's Khúbán-Náme is dedicated to him.

than an insult to the fair name of Poetry. But though Ekrem
Bey and Professor Nájí may deem this daring and original
writer beneath their notice, for us his works are full of
interest. For in these we have not only the revelation of a
marked individuality, but a veritable treasury of the folk-lore
of the author's age and country. Many are the curious customs
and traditions that are mentioned, sometimes described in
detail; and besides we have here, what we get nowhere
else, a full and clear account of the way in which the old
Turks, while yet absolutely uninfluenced by Western ideas,
viewed the various nationalities with whom they had come
in contact, whether within or without the frontiers of their
Empire. The plain matter of fact way in which Fázil says
what he has to say, while hurtful to his work on the poetic
or artistic side, is an additional advantage from our standpoint;
for by means of this, vagueness and conventional generalities
are avoided, and precision and definiteness are attained.

Fázil's works consist of a Díwán; three mesnevís named
respectively Defter-i 'Ashq or 'Love's Register', Khúbán-
Náme or 'The Book of Beauties', and Zenán-Náme or 'The
Book of Women; and of a poem in four-line stanzas entitled
Chengí-Náme or 'The Book of Dancers.'

The Díwán of Fázil, where alone among his works the
proprieties are treated with due respect, is much on a par
with similar contemporary collections, though perhaps the
workmanship is on the whole a little more careful than is
usual about this time. The most original poem in it is an
ode in praise of the much-reviled Sphere. It contains besides
a number of fairly successful love ghazels, several religious
poems and a long elegy on Sultan Selím the Martyr, in
which several details of his murder are given, including the
names of the assassins. But the Díwán is the least interesting
part of Fázil's literary output, and until we turn to his

other works we find but little to mark him out from the crowd of his contemporaries

The earliest written of the mesnevís is the Book of Beauties, the date of which is given by a chronogram as 1207 (1792—3). This was probably very soon followed by the Book of Women, which Fázıl declares in the introduction to have been written as a companion or pendant to it. Love's Register would thus be the latest of the three, the date of its composition being incidentally mentioned as 1210 (1795—6) Although thus slightly later than the others in chronological order, it will perhaps be best for us to take this last-named book first, as in it Fázıl fully expounds his theory of love, some acquaintance with which will assist us in understanding the motive underlying the bulk of his work.

In the Defter-i ʿAshq or Love's Register the title of which suggests its contents, Fázıl chooses a subject which, as he himself asserts, is absolutely new in Turkish poetry, namely a detailed and circumstantial account of the successive love episodes by which his career has been marked This at least was the author's purpose, but as a matter of fact we have only four of such love affairs bringing the story down to the year 1199 (1784—5), at which point the book ends abruptly without any formal conclusion. We are therefore constrained to assume that the work as it has come down to us is only a fragment of what the author originally projected, but for some reason or another never brought to completion.

As was to be expected, the objects of the poet's love are all youths Fázıl was a man of the Romantic Period and far from insensible to the charms of the fair sex, as his Zenán-Náme abundantly testifies But he lived a century too early to place woman in the front rank, at the time when he wrote the old tradition handed down from ancient

Greece and medieval Persia was yet potent, though no one
in his day dealt it a more deadly blow than did he himself.
In order to reassure us that the 'amorous enthusiasms' he
is about to record were purely Platonic, Fázil opens hi
book with a description of beauty and love, as he conceives
them, which is immediately followed by a description of
the true lover.

While there is, of course, nothing new in these introductory
verses, they are not without a certain nobility. Beauty, we
are told, wherever it is seen, whether in humanity or in the
vegetable or mineral world, is God's revelation of Himself;
He is the all-beautiful, those objects in which we perceive
beauty being, as it were, so many mirrors in each of which
some fraction of His essential self is reflected. By virtue of
its Divine origin, the beauty thus perceived exercises a
subtle influence over the beholder, awakening in him the
sense of love, whereby he is at last enabled to enter into
communion with God Himself. Thus God is the ultimate
object of every lover's passion; but while this is as yet
unrealised by the lover, while he still imagines that the
earthly fair one is the true inspirer and final goal of his
affection, his love is still in the 'typal' stage, and he himself
still upon that allegoric 'Bridge'.

So Love, says Fázil, is the guide to the World Above,
the stair leading up to the portal of Heaven; through the
fire of Love iron is transmuted into gold, and the dark clay
turned into a shining gem. Love it is that makes the heedless
wise, and changes the ignorant into an adept of the Divine
mysteries; Love is the unveiler of the Truth, the hidden
way into the Sanctuary of God. [1] And as for the true Lover,

---

[1] [I can recall no finer expression of these ideas than that contained in one
of the introductory cantos of the Persian Jámí's *Yúsuf u Zulaykhá*, of which a
translation will be found at pp. 125—128 of my *Year amongst the Persians*. ED.]

226

he is pure of heart and holy of life, worldly things are of
no account with him, dust and gold being equal in his eyes;
generosity and gentleness distinguish him; carnal desire stirs
him not, indeed if his beloved approach, he begins to tremble
in all his limbs while he dares not look upon the fair one's
face or display sign or emotion. Do not, says Fázil, addressing
the materialistic age in which he wrote, think that such
words are vain; if you will not believe me, search the ancient
books, for this of which I speak is the 'antique love'. But
now, he adds, another kind of love is studied. Then follows
a description of the sensualist, which the poet closes with
the words: "Such an one I call not lover, I call him lecher."

Having thus cleared the ground by explaining what he
means by 'love' and 'lover', Fázil, after a brief panegyric
on the reigning Sultan, Selím III, goes on to set forth the
considerations which induced him to undertake this work.
Ever since the eyes of his understanding were opened, he
says, he has been the prey of love; he has fallen from snare
into snare, and has sought out sorrow after sorrow; his poor
heart, which is a rosebud of love, has been the spoil of the
hand of love; his heart-jewel has been trodden under foot,
has been made a plaything by many a child. The throne
of his heart, be continues, has been as a tilt-yard whence
King has driven King; never has the realm of his bosom
been unoccupied, there lord has succeeded lord; but these
have not acted like other Kings, neither have they obeyed
the ancient laws; yet this dynasty has lorded it in his bosom
to the number of twenty-two. [1] Wishing to give this line of
sovereigns a name, he will call it the Dynasty of Shaʿbán;
some of the princes were cruel, some were just, some were
wise, some were foolish, but his desire is to enumerate them

[1] Thus in the printed editions, but in a MS. in my collection the line
in question is altered so that the number is not mentioned.

all, and thus to write a new history, — in a word, to describe every beauty who has held sway over him since first he fell a victim to Love. He further swears that he will set down the whole truth concerning them, and relate everything exactly as it happened, so that his work may be a memorial of these days and at the same time a Sháh-Náme for the dynasty of Sha'bán.

The purport of the book having been announced as above, Fázil proceeds to tell his story. He begins by saying that in the year 1190 (1776—7) the storms of the sea of destiny drove him from the Arab lands to Rúm, where he was placed in the Seraglio, being enrolled in the second company of the Imperial Pages, that known as the Khazína Odasi or Treasury Chamber. Then comes the account of the four love-adventures already referred to, an account which it is unnecessary to follow in detail, but which brings the story of the author's life down to 1199 (1784—5). There is one point, however, of importance as helping to fix the order of the works, that is, the incidental mention in the account of the third of these adventures of the year 1210 (1795—6) as that in which the poet is writing the book. In the account of the fourth adventure Fázil takes advantage of an incident to introduce a long and detailed description of Gipsy wedding customs, which is full of interest from a folk-lore point of view. As I have said, the Dafter-i 'Ashq comes to a sudden termination with this fourth episode; the closing passage is curious and striking, the author tells us how some six years after the events just narrated he unexpectedly came across that particular object of his admiration vilely and foully metamorphosed, and how terrible was the shock which he received from this encounter.

In the Khúbán-Náme, or Book of Beauties, and the Zenán-Náme, or Book of Women, we have the ultimate outcome of the Shehr-engíz. Mesíhí and his imitators gave us in their poems playfully written catalogues of the fair boys or girls of a certain city; Fázil gives us in these two books playfully written descriptions of the boys and girls of all the races of mankind. That style which has all along characterised poems of this class, whether of the original type or modified as in the works of Belígh, that whimsical and quizzical yet complimentary style bristling with proverbs and puns which we have learned to associate with such productions, is here adopted by Fázil with marked success.

As their general scheme is the same, these two books can, up to a certain point, be considered together. The Book of Beauties describes the boys, and the Book of Women the girls of the following countries and nationalities: India; Persia (including Central Asia); Baghdad; Cairo; the Súdán; Abyssinia; Yemen; Morocco; Algiers and Tunis; Hijáz (including the Bedouins); Damascus and Syria generally; Aleppo; Anatolia; the Islands of the Archipelago; Constantinople; the Greeks; the Armenians; the Jews; the Gipsies; Rumelia; Albania; Bosnia; the Tartars; the Georgians; the Circassians; the Franks of Constantinople (i. e. the Levantines); the Bulgarians, Croats; Wallachians, and Moldavians; France; Poland; the Germans; Spain; England; Holland; Russia; America. [1]

Now while Fázil was no doubt a man of much experience, and though he may have been only exaggerating when he said that if he saw a boy in the bath (i. e. stripped of his distinctive costume), he could tell his nationality before he heard him speak, yet it is obviously impossible that he can have been on intimate terms with individuals of both sexes belonging to all the races just enumerated. But the Imperial

---

[1] It is curious that Italy should be omitted from the list.

Seraglio, where the poet was brought up, was mostly peopled by foreigners. Within that portion of this assemblage of gardens and palaces which was set apart for the household of the Sultan, and which formed a little world by itself cut off from all direct communication with outside, there was, especially in earlier times, hardly a single native Turk. [1] The four chambers of pages, the two corps of eunuchs (black and white), as well as the harem, used all to be recruited, like the regiment of Janissaries, either from non-Turkish subjects of the Empire, or from foreign captives. At one time or another doubtless representatives of all the nationalities mentioned by Fázil have found their way within the Seraglio walls. In the old days when hostilities were chronic between Turkey and Christendom forays were continually being made along the ever-shifting northern frontier, and Frankish ships were constantly being taken and Frankish coasts raided by Algerine corsairs. On such occasions as many young persons of either sex as could be laid hands on were seized, and the most beautiful among them sent to the capital. There the most promising were, as in the case of Fázil himself, placed in the Seraglio and educated as Turks. In this way representatives of many races must during a period of over three centuries have passed through the Imperial household. It is most probable that traditions concerning the characteristics of these would be preserved, and if such were the case, Fázil, who was very intelligent and took a keen interest in collecting out of the way information, would undoubtedly have availed himself of his excellent opportunities to become acquainted with them.

But the description of the features, physical and moral,

---

[1] An account of the organisation of the Imperial Seraglio in old times, contributed by myself, will be found in the fourteenth chapter of the volume on Turkey in the 'Story of the Nations' series.

of the various races that he passes in review forms only a
portion, and in some cases a small portion, of the poet's
account of these. Whatever he has been able to pick up
regarding local peculiarities or the manners and customs of
foreign peoples, is here set down, with the occasional embel-.
lishment of a very obvious 'traveller's tale', which, as a rule,
the writer offers for what it may be worth. What confers
a special interest on Fázil's treatment of these matters, already
interesting in themselves, is that here, and here alone, we
have presented in a series of pictures, many of which are
drawn in considerable detail, the various nations of the
world as these appeared to the educated Turks of olden
times. For though the author was an Arab by birth, he felt
as a Turk and wrote as a Turk, he depreciates his Syrian
birthplace just as a native Turk might, and when he speaks
about the Russians it is with the hatred engendered by
centuries of wrongs

Fázil's attitude towards the two sexes may at first sight
appear strange He is much more reticent in dealing with
his boys than with his girls. The physical merits or demerits
of the former are almost invariably referred to in the most
vague and general way, and the author's attitude is on the
whole one of respect. But he deals with the girls in very
different fashion, their personal charms being discussed without
reserve, sometimes with a wealth of detail that is almost medical

The reason of this is not hard to divine. To an Oriental
of those days it was an accepted fact, indisputable and
undisputed, that a noble-minded man might, and often did,
entertain for a boy an amorous affection in which the pro-
foundest admiration was conjoined with the most perfect
purity, an affection, moreover, the cultivation of which tended
above all things to the moral advancement of the lover,
calling out whatever was best and highest in his nature. On

the other hand, if a man desired a woman, it could be for one thing only. So Fázil perfectly logically dwells most, when discussing his boys, on the way in which these are likely to appeal to the aesthetic instincts of his readers, and when describing his girls, on the degree of their suitability for the one purpose for which he conceives they can be desired. Thus in this pair of books we have presented to us more clearly than anywhere else in Turkish literature the attitude of the typical Eastern poet-lover towards the sexes, that attitude which is the direct antithesis of our own, through virtue of which what with us is reckoned shame was accounted honour, and what we hold for our glory and our boast was esteemed disgrace. And yet it is but in the object through which the sentiment of love is evoked that the difference lies; in their highest conceptions of true love with its soul-transforming power East and West are one.

But although Fázil's appreciation of womanhood is thus poor and inadequate, that he should have written a Zenán-Náme at all is a long step in the right direction. The physical beauty at any rate of woman is now admitted as a fit theme for poetry; no future 'Atá'í will ransack Qámús and Burhán to overwhelm with obloquy another Baqá'í; the work begun by Sábit and Nedím with timid and hesitating hand is here taken up by Fázil and carried boldly on; other poets are ready to push forward where he leaves off; and at last woman as woman is free to meet her ancient rival, the androgynous beauty of old-world tradition. And thus the minds of men are being prepared for the great change which the coming years shall bring, so that when in the fullness of time the poets of the Modern School arise and enthrone woman as the one fitting object of every true man's love, the consummation thus effected is hailed with universal enthusiasm, and those through whom it is accom-

plished are enrolled among the benefactors of their nation.
The Book of Beauties opens with a few lines praising
God who has given such beauty to humanity, and calling
attention to the marvellous diversity in creation through
which no two individuals are exactly alike. This is followed
by a short prayer for the prosperity of Sultan Selím, after
which Fázil goes on to tell how he came to write the book.
A few sentences (afterwards to be expanded in Love's Register)
inform us that while still young he was cast by the sling
of Fate from land to land, and that wherever he has gone
he has been the slave of Love, so that his heart has come
to be like a seal-engraver's register for the number of beauties
names that are stamped on it. [1] This introduces us to the
poet's flame for the time being, who is represented as praying
the author to write a book describing from his vast experience
the peculiarities of the youths belonging to different peoples,
a request to which a favourable answer is at once returned.
This incident is almost certainly fictitious, for apart from
the extreme unlikelihood of a person such as is described
desiring a book of the kind, in a few verses at the close
of the volume Fázil presents it as an offering to the statesman Rátib Efendi. But the invention of such stories to
account for the genesis of a book was a very venerable
tradition, and here at any rate Fázil seems to have approved
of the conventional usage.

The author then goes on to tell us how admirably fitted
he is to undertake such a work, alike through his studies
and his experience. The book, he says, is written throughout
in simple language so that the lad, for whom he professes
to have written, may easily understand it; it is moreover

---

[1] It is usual for a seal-engraver to keep a register of impressions of all
the seals he cuts, the seal bears the name of the owner, and its impression
used to serve as signature.

free from all padding, nor is there as much as one place
where the envier may lay his finger. A chronogram at the
end of the section fixes the date of composition as 1207
(1792—3). [1] In the section which follows Fázil sets to work
to make good his claim to erudition. Under pretext of
instructing the boy, he lets us see that he knows all about
the old mathematical and astrological geography which still
passed for science in Turkey, the ostensible reason for the
discourse being the influence exercised on the inhabitants
by the several 'climes' and their ruling planets.

Then come the descriptions of the 'beauties' themselves,
or more often of the various peoples to which these 'beauties'
belong, they being frequently but an excuse. Interesting
though it would be to examine these sections in detail, to
do so would occupy so much space that I am reluctantly
compelled to pass them over.

The descriptions are followed by a brief epilogue addressed to the lad for whom the poem is supposed to have
been written; this is succeeded and the work brought to a
a close by a short qasída in which Fázil presents the book
to the luckless Rátib Efendi, who was presumably his patron
at the time.

The plan of the Zenán-Náme, or Book of Women, [2] is
nearly identical with that of the Book of Beauties. [3] After

---

[1] The chronogram is خوبان مجشسة = The Assemblage of Beauties..

[2] In 1879 M. Leroux of Paris published, under the title of Le Livre des
Femmes, what professes to be a French translation of Fázil's Zenán-Náme.
This so-called translation is the most hopelessly and pitifully bad piece of
work of the kind that I have ever seen. It is seldom indeed that the would-
be translator, M. Decourdemanche, has understood two consecutive couplets
of his author; and no reader can possibly gain from his little volume the
slightest idea of what Fázil Bey has said.

Von Hammer has translated portions of all the sections; these are of course
infinitely more correct, but from their fragmentary nature quite inadequate.

[3] Von Hammer suggests that Fázil may have modelled his Khúbán-Náme

a short preface praising God the Creator of the two sexes, we have a long section in which the youth at whose instigation the former work is said to have been written is again introduced. He visits Fázil, thanks him for that book, and then prays him to write another in which he shall do for the girls of the several nations what he has already done for the youths. After what he doubtless considered as a modest and becoming hesitation, the poet agrees to do as he is asked. In a few lines at the close of the section, addressed to the reader, Fázil alludes to the originality of his work by declaring that this treatise is indeed a virgin, born of the bride called _ thought whom he has taken to his bosom, none of his predecessors having conceived an idea such as this, while these two books of his are, as it were, the one a fair youth and the other his sister. The next section, which is interesting through the many allusions it contains to the customs of the time, is of the nature of an Ars Amandi, in it the youth is instructed with considerable detail as to how he must dress and deport himself in order to win the admiration of the fair sex

Then follows the series of pictures in which the girls of the different countries are portrayed. These we must unfortunately pass over for the same reason as in the former case. Let it suffice to say that the Persians, the Greeks, the Circassians and the Georgians come in for the largest

and Zenán-Náme on two Arabic books named respectively Elf Ghulám ve Ghulám = The Thousand and one youths, and Elf Jánye ve Jánye = The Thousand and one Damsels These two books, the latter of which Von Hammer says was modelled upon the former by Muhammed bin-Rize(?) bin-Muhammed el-Huseyní the defterdár, contain, according to the same authority, descriptions of boys and girls of different countries and ages, and connected with different trades There is, however, no evidence that Fázil ever heard of these works, which are very little known, nor do I think that there is any occasion to assume them as the source of his inspiration when the familiar Shehrengiz type is at hand and amply sufficient meed of praise; that the Western nations, Fázil's knowledge of whom must have rested mainly if not entirely upon hearsay, are spoken of in flattering terms, while the Jewesses and Armenians are treated with contempt, and the Russians with loathing. The descriptions of the nationalities are succeeded by a few odd sections concerning various things connected with women, but unrelated to the proper subject of the book. In these are discussed such matters as the inconveniencies of marriage, the pranks that go on in women's public baths, and the evil effects that result from lack of self-control.

The book is wound up by an epilogue addressed to the youth whose request is represented as having been the occasion of its composition. Here Fázil again reverts to the originality of his subject, and adds that even if his work be copied in the future, that will not affect his merit, as it is easy to kindle a taper from the lamp another has lighted. [1] He then praises his own talents as a linguist; and closes with a complaint as to his unfortunate circumstances. No date of composition is mentioned, and there is no dedication to any patron.

Fázil's remaining work, the Chengí-Náme, or Book of Dancers, [2] is much shorter than the others, from which it differs in being composed not in riming couplets, but in verses of four lines, the first three of which rime together, while the fourth has the same rime throughout, the book thus being in form like an extended murebbaᶜ of the variety styled muzdevij. As regards subject, it is a descriptive list of the principal public dancing boys of Constantinople. The

---

[1] [Or as Tennyson says: —
       "All can grow the flowers now,
       For all have got the seed." ED.].

[2] The book is sometimes called Raqqás-Náme, which has the same meaning.

author declares that he once joined a party composed of
cadis and other learned personages who were engaged in
an animated discussion as to the merits of such-and-such
youths of this class. Fázil, who was recognised as an authority
on matters of the kind, was at once appealed to for his
judgment, this book or treatise formed his answer. Perhaps
the answer was framed to suit the audience, but whether this
be the case or not, the Chengí-Náme is infinitely more offensive
than any other of the author's works. Here all reticence
is cast aside and all pretence of Platonicism abandoned,
the wretched creatures, forty-three in all, are introduced by
name, and described in a way that is indescribable. They
are almost all Gipsies, from which people the ranks of the
profession have at all times been most largely recruited
Many of the names on Fázil's list are fanciful such as Darchin
Gulı, Cinnamon Rose, and Qanárıya, Canary, others are
Greek as Todorı (Theodore) and Yorakı (George) This little
book affords a view, as seen from within, of what has ever been
one of the darkest phases of life in Eastern cities, and so
far it may perhaps claim a certain instructive value. That
apart, it is worse than worthless, for though it was doubtless
written as a joke, it is but poor pleasantry and in the vilest
taste. It is without date or dedication

These four works, the Defter-ı ꜥAshq, the Khúbán-Náme,
the Zenán-Náme, and the Chengí-Náme form together a
small volume containing about 2,650 couplets, the fate of
which is to be alternately printed and suppressed in the
Turkish capital From the account which has been given of
the contents of this volume it will be seen that Fázil is no
poet, but a versifier whose claim on our attention rests
partly on the circumstance that he gives us much first-hand
information, elsewhere unobtainable, not only on local manners and peculiarities, but on the opinions and ideas then

current in Turkey on a great variety of subjects; and partly because his work exemplifies in perhaps a more marked degree than that of any other writer the peculiar phase through which Ottoman poetry was at that time passing.

It might be thought that prose would have been a more suitable medium than verse for the discussion of subjects such as Fázil's, but Turkish prose was just at this juncture in a somewhat uncomfortable condition. The grandiose but perspicuous style of the great Classic writers had been succeeded by the monstrous affectation and studied obscurity of the later Persianists; this proving alike intolerable and incomprehensible, had given way to a new and more Turkish and natural manner which, despite the gallant and individually successful efforts of a few talented men, was still in an unsettled and inorganic state, so that the average Turkish prose of the period was little more than a succession of vague and incoherent phrases loosely strung together.

By selecting verse as his medium, Fázil escaped the danger of this vagueness and incoherence. His couplets are each a sharp and clearly defined entity conveying a definite statement, often neatly, sometimes smartly, expressed. Similarly, his style, while destitute of all the higher poetic qualities, is, on the whole, witty, sparkling, and vivacious, the occasional introduction of familiar or colloquial words and phrases imparting a lightness of touch and playfulness of tone well suited to the subjects treated. This last-mentioned feature, the employment of conversational idioms in certain styles of poetry, became very popular about this time; tending as it did towards simplicity and directness, it was in harmony with the spirit of the Romantic Period.

The works of Fázil are noteworthy for yet one more reason; in them we have the last word of the Shehr-engíz type of poetry. There are no more riming lists of profes-

sional beauties, nothing at least beyond one or two mere
skits dressed by way of pleasantry in the ancient form The
later poets of the Romantic Age evidently felt that they
could not cope with Fázil in a field he had made so specially
his own, while in the following period the taste changed,
and things of this kind became impossible.

I have translated two of the descriptive sections of the
Zenán-Náme, these dealing respectively with the Greek and
English women The first is an example of the detailed
way in which Fázil deals with the races known to him at
first hand, the second of the vaguer and more general
manner of his treatment when he has to rely on hearsay
evidence alone Both sections are translated in their entirety.

From the Zenán-Náme.

Description of the Greek Women [420].

O thou, the bell within the church of grame,
Of all the Christian folk the name and fame! [1]
If woman be thy fancy, life of me, [2]
Then let thy love a Grecian maiden be,
For by their code whose taste is pure and clear
There's leave to woo the Grecian girl, my dear [3]
Treasures of coyness are the Grecian mays,
Most excellent of women in their ways [4]
How slender yonder waist so slight and daint!

[1] The opening couplet of every section is addressed to the youth for
whom the book is nominally written The imagery here chosen is intended
to be appropriate to the section as descriptive of a Christian people. Fázil,
however, several times speaks of and to this person, real or imaginary, as
though he were a Christian and a Greek

[2] 'Life of me', a term of endearment addressed to the same lad.

[3] That is men of taste, while rejecting the women of most other races,
regard the Greek girl as worthy of being taken as mistress

[4] The qualities about to be enumerated are not merely conventional com-
mon-places, but are really characteristic of the Greek girls

How yonder rosebud-mouth is bright and daint
How yonder speech and grace the heart ensnare!
How yonder gait and pace the heart ensnare!
How yonder shape is lithe as cypress-tree, —
On God's creation-lawn a sapling free!
What mean yon gestures gay and sly of hers?
What means yon languid ebrious eye of hers?
Those ways and that disdain are all her own,
That accent and that voice are hers alone.
With the tongue-tip she forms the letters fair, —
That winsome speech with many a lovesome air.
Strung are the royal pearls of her sweet speech,
Melting, as 'twere, soon as her mouth they reach;
So when she hath a letter hard [1] to say,
In her fair mouth it is dissolved straightway.
Her mouth doth unto speech refinement teach,
In sooth her mouth is the conserve of speech.
Yes, 'talking parrots' are they, gay and bright,
And so the 'birdies' speech', is theirs by right. [2]
With thousand graces saith her rosebud-lip:
'Ze wine, most noble lord and master, sip.
'Filled let ze emptied, emptied ze filled be;
'My Pasa, drink, and be it health to zee!' [3]
Her charms new life upon the soul bestow;
In truth, 'tis meed a loved one should be so.
E'en the old pederast, should he but sight
Yon infidel, would wencher turn forthright.
From head to foot her frame's proportioned fair,
As 'twere a balanced hemistich full rare.

[1] That is, a guttural or harsh letter. The Greeks, as a rule, pronounce Turkish with a peculiar accent of their own, one of the features of which — alluded to a line or two further on — is the substitution of an s sound for that of sh, which they seem to experience a difficulty in forming.

[2] The 'speaking parrot' we have often seen as a metaphor for a prattling beauty. 'Bird language' (qush dili) is a term given to any secret or fanciful language made by adding a syllable to, or otherwise modifying, the words of ordinary speech; this is a favourite amusement with girls in Turkey just as it is with children here.

[3] These three lines in the original are spelt in accordance with Greek pronunciation, all the sh sounds being replaced by s; thus Pasa for Pasha.

To copy her are other women fain, [1]
So meet it is pre-eminence she gain.
How winsome yonder step, yon stature tall!
Shapes fair and feat of fashion have they all.
Along the ground she's lief to draw her train,
To burn her lovers' hearts she lays a train! [2]
Yon diamond aigrette awry she wears;
Yon merry, tripping, mincing ways and airs!
What of those ways of hers, O heart of me?
Full daintily on tiptoe treadeth she. [3]
'Tis e'en as though her path with fire were laid,
And she to burn her feet were sore afraid;
Belike upon her road her lovers' hearts
Lie scattered and therefrom the flame upstarts.
Just as the women of the Greeks are good,
So are their boys evil of mind and rude;
But though their boys are obstinate and bad,
Their maidens ever make the lover glad.
Though stubborn, yet she still subdued may be;
Though fiery-souled, yet soft of temper she. [4]
Alack, O rosebud-mouth, O rosy-breast,
Smile not, while weeps thy lover sore distrest.
O radiant Sun, for whom dost rise and shine? [5]
O Flame of hope, around whom dost thou twine?
Ah, in what slough art thou as mire, sweet wight?
Ah, of what bordel shinest thou the light?
Say, on what arm is written thy dear name? [6]
Say, in what hearts is pictured thy fair frame?
Art common property, O Angel fair?

[1] Fázil says elsewhere that the Armenians and others try to copy the airs and graces of the Greeks and fail grotesquely.

[2] Train—train, in imitation of a pun in the original.

[3] Some Greek girls are fond of moving about on tiptoe in an affected manner.

[4] Suyu yumshaq = soft of temper, properly refers to a superior quality of steel, figuratively it means good and kind-hearted. In the phrase 'fiery-souled' there is a reminiscence of the employment of fire in the tempering of steel.

[5] The following lines are addressed to the typical Greek courtesan of Constantinople.

[6] Lovers in Turkey sometimes tattoo their beloved's name on their arm.

Who doth yon midmost hidden treasure share?
Ah, who is he hath scaled this 'Maiden Tower'? [1]
Of whose bombardment hath it felt the power?
I marvel, in whose snare is this the deer?
Before whom doth her vacant plain appear?
The while herself as Kokona they know, [2]
What perfumes from her tangled tresses flow!
Upon the ground her sash doth trail amain,
For it likewise to kiss her feet is fain.
For envy of her henna-tinted hand
Is the 'red egg' with blushes crimson-stained. [3]
Paynim, thou art a reason-reiving Woe; [4]
What manner Plague thou art I ne'er may know.
Art fairy, or art sprite? I cannot tell;
What thou'rt to Mary bright I cannot tell.
Art thou of ʿImrán's [5] Mary the young rose?
The light that in the monastery glows?
Thou show'st not as the Greekish folk, I trow;
Meseems a houri or a genie thou!

From the Same.

Description of the English Women [421].

O thou, whose dusky mole is Hindustan,
Whose tresses are the realms of Frankistan! [6]

[1] Qiz Qullasi = The Maiden Tower, called by Europeans 'Leander's Tower', built on a rock at the entrance to the Bosphorus opposite Scutari. It is of Byzantine origin, hence the appropriateness of the reference when speaking of Greeks. Here of course the Maiden Tower is a metaphor for the person or body of the girl. The same idea occurs in an untranslated quatrain of Sábit (p. 21 *supra*), by which this passage was perhaps suggested.

[2] Kokona means Madame or Mademoiselle in Greek, and is the title usually given to Greek ladies in Constantinople. In the second line there is a pun on this word and the Turkish qoqu ne! meaning, 'what a perfume!'

[3] [Easter eggs are called 'red eggs' in Turkey. ED.].

[4] Here again the typical Greek beauty is addressed.

[5] ʿImrán is the name given in the Koran to the father of the Virgin Mary, whom the Christians call St. Joachim.

[6] Hindustan is mentioned here on account of the connection between the English, whom the author is about to describe, and India, Fázil's practice

16

The English woman is most sweet of face,
Sweet-voiced, sweet-fashioned, and fulfilled of grace
Hei red cheek to the iose doth colour bring,
Her mouth doth teach the nightingale to sing.
They all are pure of spirit and of heart,
And prone are they unto adornment's art
What all this pomp and splendour of array !
What all this pageantry their heads display ¹ ¹
Her hidden treasure's talisman is broke,
Undone, or ever it receiveth stroke. ²

Amongst the most prominent of the central group of Romanticist poets is the author who is generally known as Sunbul-záde Vehbí. The patronymic Sunbul-záde ³ is that of a family of some distinction belonging to Mer'ash, a town in the province of Aleppo, and is commonly prefixed to the pseudonym of this poet in order to distinguish him from that other Vehbí — Seyyid Vehbí — whose namesake he is said to be.

Our present subject, whose personal name was Muhammed, was the son of a learned and accomplished gentleman called Ráshid (or according to some, Reshíd) Efendi, who at the time of our author's birth at Mer'ash was at Aleppo, where

being, as I have said, to compliment in the opening couplet of each section the person for whom he writes, in terms connected more or less remotely with the people he is going to discuss

¹ Some hint must have reached Fázil of the extravagant headdresses worn by English ladies toward the close of the eighteenth century

² [I do not know whether it was the author's intention to say anything more about Fázil Bey, or to give specimens of his Díwán or Chengí-náme Though this section seems to end rather abruptly, I find no trace of any continuation, and I think it likely that these two works were purposely ignored, the Díwán on account of its mediocrity, and the Chengí-náme on account of its very objectionable character ED.]

³ The name is pronounced Sumbul-záde, and means Hyacinth-son, I have been unable to discover its origin. Von Hammer is in error in stating that Hayátí in his commentary on Vehbí's Tuhfe says that the poet received this name on account of his predilection for hyacinths; the commentator says nothing of the sort, and, indeed offers no explanation of the name

he was acting as assistant to the poet Seyyid Vehbí, who was then cadi of that city. It so happened that just when the news of the young Sunbul-záde's birth reached Aleppo a son of Seyyid Vehbí died, whereupon the cadi besought his assistant to give his own pseudonym of Vehbí to the new-born child, so that, as he said, his name might abide for a little longer in this fleeting world. And thus it came about that the poet of the house of Sunbul-záde bears the same pseudonym as he who wrote the inscription for Sultan Ahmed's fountain. Such at least is the story told by Hayátí Efendi the commentator, who professes to have had it from the poet himself.

Sunbul-záde Vehbí received his education at the hands of the ʿulemá of his native town of Merʿash; but, thinking to better himself, he repaired to Constantinople where by means of his qasídas and chronograms he made himself known to certain persons of influence, through whose assistance he entered the order of cadis. His literary skill gradually became known, and several important state documents were given to him to draw up. These he executed with so much ability that he attracted the attention and gained the patronage of two powerful and discriminating statesmen, ʿOsmán Efendi of Yeni-Shehr and the Reʾís-ul-Kuttáb Ismaʿíl Bey. These gentlemen brought his work under the notice of Sultan Mustafa III, as a result of which Vehbí was soon promoted to the class of Master Clerks.

Early in the reign of the succeeding Sultan, ʿAbd-ul-Hamíd I, in consequence of a dispute between ʿOmer Pasha, the Ottoman governor of Baghdad, and Kerím Khán-i-Zend, the then de facto ruler of Persia, it became necessary to send to the court of Isfahán an envoy well acquainted with the Persian language. Vehbí was chosen for the duty, and so he visited Persia in the capacity of Turkish envoy.

While stopping at Baghdad on his return journey, he wrote
to the Porte with the information that the misconduct of
'Omer Pasha had been the real cause of the difficulty. This
coming to the governor's ears, he on his part wrote to
Constantinople to the effect that Vehbí had been won over
by Kerím Khán and had sacrificed the interests of the Empire
to those of his new friend, adding that the envoy had earned
the contempt of the Persians by behaving when in their
country in a riotous and disgraceful manner little becoming
the representative of the Sublime Empire The Sultan, who
was highly incensed when he received the Pasha's report,
despatched a special messenger with orders for the immediate
execution of the unlucky Vehbí. But the latter's friends
'Osmán Efendi and Isma'íl Bey sent him by a secret emis-
sary, who met him between Baghdad and Mosul, a sum
of money and a letter telling him how things stood and
bidding him, immediately on its receipt, give the slip to
his suite, disguise himself, come with their messenger, to
Scutari, hide there in a certain place, and secretly send
them word of his arrival All this Vehbí did. He reached
Scutari disguised as a courier, and saw his friends, who told
him to set to work on a qasída praising the Sultan and
describing his mission While the poet was busy on this
task, the truth about 'Omer Pasha was discovered, and it
was found that Vehbí was guiltless except in so far as he
had enjoyed himself somewhat too freely while in Persia
So when the two statesmen presented to the Sultan the
poem which has become famous under the name of the
Tannána or 'Resonant' Qasída, His Majesty was fully app-
eased, and granted a free pardon to the poet-envoy.

Upon this Vehbí resigned his position as Master Clerk
and returned to his former profession of cadi. At one time
he served as deputy-judge of the town of Eski-Zaghra (in

what is now Eastern Rumelia), and when there his dissolute habits so scandalized the citizens that they seized him and shut him up in prison. Surúrí, the poet and famous chronogrammatist, happened to be Vehbí's assistant at the time, and he too, on the presumption that he shared the tastes of his superior, was likewise cast into gaol. They were both released before long; but the incident seems to have been the starting-point of Surúrí's half playful, though wholly ribald, attacks on the elder poet, whose replies in kind round off an extraordinary and not very creditable episode in the literary history of the time.

Among the cadiships which Vehbí held was that of Rhodes, where he wrote another celebrated qasída, that known as the Tayyára or 'Volant', on the execution in that island of the unhappy Sháhín Giráy, last Khán of the Crimea.

When the poet-loving Sultan, Selím III, ascended the throne, he lost no time in arranging for Vehbí's comfort and well-being, an attention to which the latter responded by collecting his Díwán and dedicating it to the kindly monarch. For the rest of his life the poet seems to have been amply provided for, and, till his health gave way, to have divided his time between versifying and merry-making. He died in Constantinople, over ninety years of age, on the 14th. of the First Rebí', 1224 (28th. April, 1809).

It is said that several years before his death his constitution broke down; gout attacked him, his eyes were affected, and according to some his reason was impaired. For seven years he was confined to his bed. There is a story told by Suleymán Fá'iq Efendi how three days before he fell ill, Vehbí invited his friends and intimates to a feast at the close of which he addressed them as follows: 'I am now more than eighty years of age, and death is at hand for me. One of these days I shall die suddenly or else be stricken with some mortal malady. Whichever may happen, I pray you now to absolve me for the Hereafter.[1] They say many things concerning me, that I have been most dissolute and wicked, and I forgive them all. Do you bear witness before God that I have ever been a loyal Muslim, and of the Hanefí rite' His friends, thinking to comfort him, tried to turn the matter into a joke, telling him he was setting up as a prophet. But he replied that he knew something of the science of medicine, had studied his own case, and was certain of what he said, and so he prayed them to accede to his request

It is further told that on one occasion, after Vehbí's illness was come upon him, his friends the poets Surúrí and 'Ayní went to see him The sick man was much gratified by their attention, and prayed Surúrí, who was very famous for such things, to extemporise a pathetic chronogram for his death. His friend did so in these words·

'O God, may Vehbi rise with Imru-ul-Qays'"[2]

which pleased the old poet, who answered, 'What lets? Imru-ul-Qays was no little man.'

Sunbul-záde Vehbí wrote a good deal of poetry, his works include a bulky Díwán, a humorous mesneví entitled Shevq-engíz, or The Provoker of Mirth, a didactic poem called Lutfiyya, modelled on the Khayriyya of Nábí, and two riming vocabularies dealing respectively with Persian and

---

[1] On death-beds, or before battle or long separations, it is usual among Muhammedans to mutually forgive all that may have been unjustly said or done.

[2] امرء القيس ادله حشر اولسون الهى وهبى

The chronogram gives the date 1219; perhaps that was the date of the poets' visit. Imru-ul-Qays was one of the most famous poets of ancient pagan Arabia, [and, according to the Prophet, "their leader into hell-fire" In the charming history known as al-Fakhrí it is related that the Arabs were wont to say that their poetry "began with a King and ended with a King," alluding to Imru-ul-Qays and the Omayyad Yezíd ibn Mu'áviya. ED].

Arabic words. Besides these productions, which are all in Turkish, he left a small Díwán of Persian poems. [1]

Individuality is the keynote of this age, and nowhere is it more in evidence than in the works of this poet. Vehbí's personality breathes in well-nigh every line he wrote. Two subjects appealed to him above all others, and inspire directly or indirectly all that is most characteristic and most interesting in his work; of these the first is pleasure, the second himself and his own adventures.

As will have been gathered from the foregoing sketch of his career, Vehbí was notorious for the profligacy of his character, a profligacy which he was at no pains to conceal, and which on two occasions at any rate got him into positions of serious difficulty. To say that Vehbí was at no pains to conceal his profligacy, is to considerably understate the facts. He went out of his way to magnify it, and it tinges more or less the greater part of his poetry. Few indeed are the ghazels in at least one couplet of which the master passion of his nature does not display itself, sometimes, it is true, decently draped and veiled, though more often flaunting naked and unashamed. It riots in the witty shameless pages of the Shevq-engíz, where the fantastic imagination of the Eastern voluptuary revels unrestrained. Vehbí was no hypocrite; he wrote of the things that pleased him in the way that pleased him, and self-control was as little to his mind in literature as it was in daily life.

Vehbí's misdemeanours in this direction supplied Surúrí

---

[1] There occurs in the Persian Díwán a poem in mesneví verse which is passed off by Vehbí as his own, but the greater part of which, beginning with the line:

شبی با نو جوانی کفت پیری

is stated by Ziyá Pasha to have been appropriated from Mírzá Nasír, as whose work it is quoted in the Persian „Lives of the Poets" called ʿAtesh-Kede or The Fire Temple.

with an ample store of excellent material when that poet
fell to lampooning his brother-craftsman. These lampoons
which were penned in play, not in anger, and are as amazing
in their audacity as they are revolting in their ribaldry, were
answered in the same sort by Vehbí, so that there ensued
between the two poets a sort of mock scolding-match, in
which each tried to outdo the other alike in the ingenuity
and the coarseness of his attack. Trials of wit of this kind,
in which the disputants, without ceasing to be good friends,
bespatter each other with the foulest abuse, exist in most
early literatures. In Scottish medieval poetry, for example,
they are well known under the name of 'Flytings;' and
Shání-záde, [1] the historian, compares the duel between Vehbí
and Surúrí to the famous vituperative contests between the
old Arab poets Jerír and Farazdaq. [2]

Turning now to Vehbí's second subject, — himself; we
find that he is never tired of discoursing on his own doings
and his own experiences. His journey to Persia especially,
and what he saw and did there, forms a never-failing fountain
to which he returns again and again, till, as Professor Nájí
says, he fairly exhausts the patience of his readers. But
although this Persian journey is continually cropping up,
and is thrust upon us with a wearisome re-iteration, a good
deal of what Vehbí has to say on the subject is interesting,
and would be still more so, could we but be sure how much
is fact and how much fiction. He similarly favours us with

[1] Shání-záde Muhammed 'Atá-ulléh Efendi was Imperial Historiographer in
succession to ᶜAsim Efendi, the famous translator of the Qámús and the
Burhán-i Qátíᶜ. As he was affiliated to the Bektashi Order, which was closely
connected with the Janissaries, he was, on the destruction of that corps by
Sultan Mahmúd II in 1241 (1826), exiled to Tire near Smyrna, where he
died in the following year 1242 (1826—7).

[2] [My colleague Professor Bevan, of Trinity College, Cambridge, has long
been engaged on an edition of the voluminous *Naqá'iḍ*, or "Flytings", of
these two celebrated poets of the Omayyad period. ED.].

his opinion of Rhodes and Scio, an opinion which is highly
flattering to those islands, and above all to the fair maidens
who inhabit them. Then he is himself the hero of his two
most celebrated qasídas; for the Lutfiyya is, in the main, a
record of his own experiences of life; and so on, in greater
degree or less, with much of the best of what he wrote.

Taken as a whole, the qasídas which, as usual, open
Vehbi's Díwán are of but little account as poetry. The two
to which I have alluded as being the most celebrated are
those to which he gives the singular names of Qasída-i
Tannána and Qasída-i Tayyára, which may respectively be
rendered as The Qasída Resonant and The Qasída Volant.
The first of these, which, as we know, the poet wrote when
hiding in Scutari on his unceremonious return from Persia,
is dedicated to Sultan ʿAbd-ul-Hamíd I who is praised sky-
high in the orthodox fashion, a fashion which by this time
had become purely conventional, and was as silly as it was
extravagant and mendacious. This duty performed, the poet
proceeds to tell the story of his reception by Kerím Khán,
taking care to contrast every point connected with the
Persian court with its counterpart at that of the Sultan,
always of course to the glorification of the latter and the
disparagement of the former. In the same strain he goes on
to mention the various cities that he visited and objects of
interest that he saw in Írán, always comparing these unfa-
vourably with some more or less corresponding places within
the Ottoman dominions. Though not poetical, the work is
interesting; since, making allowance for extravagance and
partiality — due in some measure no doubt to the circumstances under which it was written, — it gives us at once
an Ottoman envoy's account of his reception by a famous
Persian ruler, and the impression which the classic land of
Írán produced upon an intelligent Turk of the old school.

The second qasída received from its author the title of
Tayyára or Volant because of the name of its luckless subject,
Sháhín (i. e Falcon) Giráy. This unhappy Prince was the
last Khán of the Crimea, and one of the countless victims
of Russian ambition and treachery. Weakly yielding to
Muscovite threats and bribes, he had renounced his allegiance
to the Sultan and proclaimed himself the vassal of St Pe-
tersburgh. But he was not long in finding out how Russia
deals by those who trust her. Continually insulting and
degrading him before his own people, his oppressors succeeded in compelling him to abandon his country and leave
it wholly in their hands. Unfortunately for himself, Sháhín
sought refuge in Turkey, for 'Abd-ul-Hamíd was incensed
at his betrayal of his allegiance and at his abandoning
without a blow a Muhammedan people to the cruel persecutions
of the most barbarous among the Christian nations, and so
Sháhín was sent a prisoner to Rhodes, where he was shortly
afterwards put to death. He was a Prince of considerable
culture, and wrote Turkish verse with skill and feeling. [1]

At the time of Sháhín's banishment Vehbí happened to
be cadi of Rhodes, and as such he was brought into contact
with the ill-starred Prince. The Volant Qasída is his account
of the tragedy so far as he himself was concerned It is dedicated to the Sultan, who is praised in the usual fulsome manner, while the wretched fugitive is in corresponding measure
vilified and abused. This was perhaps inevitable, yet it does
not tend to present the writer in a pleasant light. The
signification of the Prince's name Sháhín (Falcon) gives the
keynote for the imagery of the poem which is throughout

---

[1] Among the curiosities of Turkish literature is a 'circular' ghazel (ghazel-i
mudevver) by Sháhín Giráy. This ingenious composition is reproduced as the
frontispiece of my *Ottoman Poems translated into English verse*, published
in 1882, and the text (transliterated) is printed a few pages further on

connected more or less closely with birds, whence the peculiar
title Tayyára which, as we have seen, means Volant or
Flying In poetical value this 'Volant' qasída is about on a
par with its pendant the 'Resonant'.

Vehbí's powers as a poet were unequal to a sustained
effort Some of his qasídas are indeed of inordinate length,
and are monuments to his industry and his conscientious
· study of the dictionary, but they are absolutely uninspired,
and as pedestrian and prosaic as they are long-winded He
had a better chance with the ghazel where each couplet is
a practically independent unit attached to its fellows by a
purely formal bond. Here he is consequently more successful,
and so we find in his ghazels, amongst much that is trivial
and in bad taste, many couplets that are bright with wit
or beauty, or embellished with fancies novel and picturesque.
Yet on the whole we feel little difficulty in agreeing with
Ziyá Pasha when he prettily and happily compares our
author's lyric poetry to the scentless mountain rose.

The same critic pronounces Vehbí to be as a mesneví-
writer second only to Nábí, and indeed this poet does to a
certain extent remind us of the illustrious founder of the
Third Persianist School, alike by his extraordinary facility
in versifying whatever subject he chooses to take up and
by the lack of genuine poetic feeling which pervades his
work. Ziyá Pasha considers the mesnevís to be better than
the ghazels; but they are so in one direction alone Vehbí
was a very learned man, and his learning is more in evidence
in the former than in the latter, and so far there is a
superiority. But erudition is not poetry; and, little poetical
as are the lyrics, the mesnevís are still less so. The subjects
alone of these last are almost sufficient to condemn them.
a ribald story, a series of lectures to a youth as to what
he should study and how, when grown up, he should rule

252

his household, together with two riming vocabularies designed
to serve students as a sort of memoria technica — could a
more hopeless set of themes be presented to any poet?
They were too much for poor Vehbí at any rate; but though
he failed to make a poem out of any one of them, he none
the less acquitted himself creditably with them all.

Let us look first at the Shevq-engíz or Mirth-Provoker.
Here Vehbí has a subject with which, from the peculiar
bent of his temperament, he was exceptionally fitted to deal.
The poet whose love of fun and frolic of every sort made
Sháni-záde compare him to the old Turkish merryman Injili
Chawush, [1] was in his true element in a field where restraint
would have been a hindrance, and where audacity and
ingenuity were the first conditions of success. The work is
a mesneví of nearly 800 lines. It is without date or dedication,
the only piece of information concerning its genesis vouchsafed
by the author is that it was composed in the town of
Maghnisa when he himself was advanced in years. [2] It has
been called a story, but that designation is somewhat mis-
leading, as it contains very little action, being almost entirely
descriptive It is really nearer to the Munázara or 'Contention'
of Classic times than to the ordinary narrative poem In
the opening lines we are introduced to the two personages
whose dispute forms the occasion of the work. These are
represented as the two most dissolute reprobates in Constantinople, the one a debaucher of women, the other a
pederast, but each notorious for his devotion to and proficiency
in his special form of wickedness This worthy pair are then
described, the one after the other, in great detail. These

---

[1] Injili Chawush was a famous Turkish jester, concerning whom many stories
are current He flourished about the beginning of the seventeenth century

[2] The Shevq-engíz is usually printed and bound up along with Fázil Bey's
four mesnevis

descriptions, which form the first part of the book, are much
in the manner of Sábit's humorous poems, they are amazingly
clever, almost every line contains some more or less suggestive pun or allusion, or some ingenious and often amusing
simile; the proprieties are of course outraged at every turn,
but that is part of the game.[1] The two scoundrels meet,
and the discussion which ensues between them regarding
their respective hobbies makes up the second part of the
book. Each in turn exalts his own and attacks the other's
ideas of beauty and pleasure, and attack and defence are
both conducted with as much wit and as little reticence as
are shown in the descriptions. Unable to come to any
conclusion as to which has the right on his side, they agree
to go to the Sheykh (or, as we might say, the High Priest)
of Love, argue their case before him, and pray his judgment.
This interview forms the third part of the poem. Having
sought out the Sheykh of Love, who is described as an
aged and pious man who has abandoned the world and
lives a life of holy contemplation, the pair lay their dispute
before him and ask him to pronounce whether girl or boy
is the more fitting object for the lover's devotion After
listening patiently to all they have to say, the Sheykh
administers to each in turn a most severe rebuke, censuring
the baseness of their thoughts and the wickedness of their
lives. He tells them they know nothing of love, but only
of carnal desire, which they must leave behind if they would
understand what true love is. Then answering their question,
he says that it matters nothing whether the object of pure
love be girl or boy, noble love for either will eventually
lead to that higher, that true and absolute Love, to which
it is but the 'bridge'. The Sheykh then exhorts them to

[1] The names of the two blackguards are themselves suggestive; the one is
Su-Yolju-záde, the other Qazıqjı-Yegeni

forsake their evil ways and pursue the True Love, and his wise and gentle words produce so deep an impression on the two libertines that they then and there abandon their sinful courses and enter the band of the holy man's disciples. And so even this book, for all the ribaldry with which it opens, closes with a tribute to the Love that is eternal and undefiled, which is the ultimate theme of nine-tenths of all the Eastern poetry in existence.

The Lutfiyya, which derives its name from the author's son Lutf-ulláh, for whose behoof it was written and to whom it is dedicated, is confessedly modelled on the Khayriyya of Nábí It is, like its prototype, a versified book of counsels composed by the poet for the guidance of a beloved son. The general scheme of the two works is the same, though of course the advice given differs somewhat in each. Vehbí lays greater stress on educational points, he carefully indicates which sciences should be studied and which left aside' Among the former he recommends medicine, as most of the physicians of the time are untrustworthy, and logic, which he regards as the basis of every science, he would dissuade from mathematics, from philosophy, because of its futility, and from the astrological astronomy of his day, seeing that it deals with things impossible to be known. All the occult sciences come similarly under the ban While he admits that music is pleasant to hear, he says it is unbecoming a gentleman to sing or play any instrument History and literature ought to be studied, when speaking of poetry he gives his son the bad advice to cultivate the 'enigma', which he says is very popular in Persia. In prose the 'new style' is to be followed, that of Veysí and Nergisí being out of date. Calligraphy is recommended. Chess and draughts are discouraged as being too absorbing. Profligacy and debauchery are forbidden, as are hypocrisy, sanctimoniousness, and many

other vices and evil qualities, while the corresponding virtues
are extolled and urged. Vehbí counsels his son, as Nábí did
his, against seeking to attain the high offices of state, pointing
out how precarious is the position of those who hold such,
and how hard it is for a man so placed to live an honourable
and upright life. Nábí had recommended a Khojaship (Master
Clerkship); Vehbí does not, he had himself tried it and was
.but too pleased to give it up and return to his humbler
calling of cadi, things, he declares, have changed since the
days of the elder poet. Much sound practical advice is given
as to the conduct of every day life, as to regulating expenses
according to resources, and so on. Vehbí's advice in the
matter of marriage is exactly the opposite of that of Nábí;
the latter had recommended his son to abstain from bur-
dening himself with a wife and to remain content with
concubines as the law allows, Vehbí on the other hand
advises Lutf-ulláh to marry a well brought up lady of his
own position, as slave-concubines are often unfaithful, besides
being ignorant and ill-mannered, if, however, such are necessary, Vehbí recommends like Nábí that Georgians should
be chosen in preference to any other nationality. Great care
should be shown in selecting servants, and these ought to be
treated kindly but without undue familiarity. All intoxicants,
including opium and hemp, are to be eschewed, even coffee
and tobacco are to be used sparingly. The poet winds up
his admonitions by advising his son against the fashionable
crazes of keeping birds and rearing flowers, which he regards
as vain and frivolous pursuits, the former being moreover
cruel, as it entails the imprisonment in cages of creatures
that ought to be at liberty

In an epilogue, still addressed to his son, Vehbí says
that he wrote the whole poem within a week and at a time
when he was very unwell, in consequence of which the style

is not so poetical or the composition so careful as might
have been. In his time, he continues, he has seen much of
the world, has travelled in many lands and mixed with all
manner of people; he has known the ups and downs of
fortune, and in the course of his career has found out most
of what is to be found out. What he has embodied in this
book is his own experience, he has himself tested most of
the counsels given, and so he can with the greater confidence
recommend them for his son's guidance. An 'enigmatic'
chronogram, in a different metre from the book, gives 1205
(1790—1) as the date of composition. [1]

Although through being second in the field, the Lutfiyya
necessarily lacks the quality of originality possessed by the
Khayriyya, it is quite as interesting. It presents an equally
faithful view of the age in which it was written, and the
picture that it gives of the social life of the time is to the
full as vivid, and is drawn with rather more detail. The
personality of the author, too, is more in evidence, and the
allusions to his own varied experiences which he is so fond
of making lend an individual interest which is without
counterpart in the earlier poem. But it is the work of a lesser
man; regarded from a literary point of view it is far inferior,
and, though the ill-health of the author may have been in
some measure responsible for this, it is more than doubtful

---

[1] اولدی تاریخیده خـال رخ زیبای خیـال
احسن وجهله لُطفیّـه نو بـولدی ختنـام

'So the moles on the fair cheek of fancy are its chronogram:
'In the best of fashions hath the fresh Lutfiyya been completed.'

By saying that the moles on the fair cheek of fancy are the chronogram
of his book, the poet means to hint that the date of its composition will be
found by adding together the numerical values of the dotted letters that
occur in the following line, leaving out of count the undotted letters, which
in the usual course would have been included.

whether Vehbí, even under the most favourable circumstances, could ever have rivalled his predecessor here.

From the whole tone of the book as well as from every definite precept it contains, it is evident that the poet desired and hoped for his beloved son a nobler and more creditable life than his own had been. But poor Lutf-ulláh did not live for very long to put in practice his father's counsels. An obituary poem in Surúrí's Díwán tells us that he died of the plague in his twenty-seventh year, in 1210 (1795—6), that is five years after the Lutfiyya was written and ten years before Vehbí's own death. His mother had predeceased him, as Surúrí thus prettily indicates:

'Entering the grave beside her, he rejoiced his mother's heart;
'But he left his father bowéd down with parting's weary woe'. [1]

Of the two riming vocabularies, the one known as the Tuhfe-i Vehbí, or Vehbí's Offering, is an earlier production than the Lutfiyya, the other, the Nukhbe-i Vehbí, or Vehbí's selection, a later. Both belong to a class of works which has numerous representatives in Ottoman literature, and which has for object the assistance of the memory by presenting information embodied in easily remembered lines of verse. The Tuhfe contains a large number of Persian, the Nukhbe of Arabic, words and phrases along with their Turkish equivalents conveyed in lines of this description.

The Tuhfe, which, although Vehbí does not say so, is clearly modelled on the well-known work of the same name by the sixteenth-century writer Sháhidí, [2] was an outcome of the author's Persian journey. In the preface he tells us

قرب مادرده گیروب قبره سوندردی اثی   ثكن آلام فراقیله پدر اولدی دوتا [1]

---

[2] The Tuhfe-i Sháhidí, or Sháhidí's Offering, was written in 920 (1514—5); it is the best known work of the class after Vehbí's, which superseded it. Sháhidí died in 957 (1550—1).

that when in Trán he paid much attention to the language,
and found that there was often considerable difference in
signification between the same words when used in Persia
and in Turkey. He found two main dialects in the country,
that of Isfahán, which he calls Derí, and that of Shíráz,
which he calls Pehleví and which he regards as the better.
Unwilling that the fruits of his observations should be lost,
he resolved to embody them in a book, primarily for the
benefit of his son Lutf-ulláh. The result is this Tuhfe, which
is dedicated to the Grand Vezír Khalíl Hamíd and his two
sons, and which, as a chronogram at the end informs us,
was composed in 1197 (1782—3). [1] In 1206 (1791—2) an
accomplished scholar named Hayátí Efendi wrote an excellent commentary on the Tuhfe, which is still highly esteemed
for the valuable information it contains on points connected
with the Persian language. [2]

In the Nukhbe, Vehbí does for Arabic what in the Tuhfe
he had done for Persian. This second vocabulary was not
written till many years later, as is shown by a fanciful
chronogram such as the author loved, which gives 1214
(1799—1800) as the date of composition. [3] In the preface,

[1] بحمد اللّه بو زيبا تحفهٔ وهبى تمام اولدى

'Praise be to God, this fair 'Offering of Vehbí' has been completed.'

[2] Hájji Ahmed Hayátí, who was a contemporary of Vehbí, was a native
of the town of Elbistan in the sanjaq of Merʿash. He was a man of great
learning, well versed in Arabic and Persian. He wrote a good deal both in
verse and prose, including a commentary on Sháhidí's Tuhfe. He died in
1229 (1813—4).

[3] آب كوهرله عطارد لوحهٔ تاريخون يازر   اخىمهٔ نگين زادايى ايلدى وهبى تمام

With jewelled water doth Mercury (the scribe of the sphere) write on the
tablet the chronogram hereof:

Vehbí hath completed the brilliant 'Selection.'

Here again it is the dotted letters of the second line that are hinted at in
the 'jewelled water' of the first.

after dilating on the success and popularity of his Tuhfe, and praising the skill with which Hayátí had expounded it, Vehbí says that as old age crept upon him he felt distressed at the thought that all his learning should die with him. He therefore resolved to complete his lexicographical labours by making an Arabic vocabulary which should be a companion, or as he calls it, a twin, to the Tuhfe. And so we have the Nukhbe, which is probably one of the last of its author's works. Hayátí commenced a commentary on this volume also, but as he died before he had finished it, the work had to be completed by his son Sheref.

From the account that has just been given of his works, it will be seen that Sunbul-záde Vehbí was a voluminous and versatile writer. As he shows us in many places, he was well up in most of the sciences of his time; in the Shevq-engíz he makes great display of his knowledge of logic, in the Lutfiyya he has the whole circle of the sciences for a theme, while the Tuhfe and the Nukhbe prove him to have been no ordinary master of the classic languages of Islám. He was moreover an enthusiastic student alike of Persian and Turkish poetry. Of the Iranian masters his favourite seems to have been Háfiz, whom he frequently quotes and sometimes imitates. He has many 'parallels', takhmíses, and so on to poems by Sáʾib, Shevket, and Saʿdí amongst the Persians, and Nefʿí, Báqí, Sábit, Nábí, Nedím, and Sámí amongst the Turks.

Vehbí was one of the first Turkish poets to write what we should call 'occasional' verses. Thus, a girl passing in the street takes his fancy, so he records the circumstance and the thoughts it suggests to him; a young lady, Sara by name, comes with a petition to the Turkish camp outside Nissa in Servia, Vehbí sees and admires her, and the incident is versified and enshrined in his Díwán. Vehbí's poems of this class are not numerous, but they are highly characteristic; they are always more or less humorous, and have for subject some beauty and his own feelings regarding her.

In the technicalities of his art Vehbí was well equipped; he rarely transgresses the formal rules of poetic composition, and his versification is in general more correct than that of some who were immeasurably greater poets than himself It is impossible not to admire the skill and dexterity with which he manipulates the most unpromising material, and fashions it into forms which, if not, beautiful, are at least ingenious Had he possessed a sufficient measure of the critical faculty to enable him to choose and discard with wisdom and good taste, he would, with his great gifts of industry and skill, have left a more worthy legacy. As it is, Professor Nájí has to pronounce his work to be in all things save extent inferior to that of his name-giver Seyyid Vehbí.

The following ghazels from Sunbul-záde Vehbí's Díwán will give a fair idea of his usual manner

Ghazel. [422]

How distant to the barque of yearning seemed the shore, alack !
This blast from furnace-fires to furnace-fires me bore, alack !

With parchéd heart hope-thirsty for a drop of heavenly dew
I bode, as tulip, many a scar my bosom wore, alack !

The ruthless flower-gath'rer plucked the rose and went his way,
A thousand times the mourning bulbul plainéd sore, alack !

Behind her o'er the waste of passion pressed the lover-throng,
Yon fair gazelle hath fall'n a hound in heart before, alack

For all that Vehbí is the mine of culture, like the gem,
He bides within the rock, unpraised, unprized, forlore, alack!

The next ghazel is an example of a curious practice very
popular about this time; this consisted in choosing as redíf
some peculiar and poetically unpromising phrase and writing
to this a number of couplets, on widely different subjects,
but each closing with it in an appropriate and effective
manner. Other poets, seeing such a ghazel, would endeavour
to outdo it by themselves composing 'parallels' to it. As a
result we find in many contemporary díwáns ghazels having
the same curious redíf, and with the same rime and metre,
though as a rule there is nothing to show which poet started
the game. Ghazels of this sort cannot be satisfactorily translated, as the redíf calls for a different rendering in nearly
every couplet. Thus in the following ghazel, although the
redíf has been given throughout by 'coil on coil', such phrases
as 'curl on curl', 'fold on fold', or 'bend on bend' would in
some cases have been more suitable; but to have varied
the translation in this way, would have been completely to
ignore the purpose of the poet.

Ghazel. [423]

Within her cap are twined the locks of yonder fair in coil on coil,
In sooth as 'twere the snake at rest within his lair in coil on coil.

For hinting that his waist hath passéd through the gauge-plate is the wire
In yonder wanton silver-drawer's fingers yare in coil on coil. [1]

[1] The ḥadda or 'gauge-plate' of the silver-wire drawers is a steel instrument
pierced with several holes of different sizes through which the wire is drawn
according to the degree of fineness desired. Vehbí here fancies that the silver-
wire which the fair young craftsman is twisting and turning about in the
process of his filigree-work is being thus tortured for having suggested the
idea that the slenderness of his waist may be owing to its likewise having
passed through the gauge-plate, and for having in so doing presumed to set
up a comparison between that slender waist and itself.

As 'twere the dragon keeping watch unceasing o'er the Shaygan hoard, [1]
Her trouser-knot's a mighty talisman and rare in coil on coil. [2]

By straight, uncrooked ways may any win the peak of high estate?
The road is like the mountain-path that windeth e'er in coil on coil. [3]

The statesman is head-bounden aye unto the orders of the King,
And so he doth the Khorásání turban wear in coil on coil. [4]

The zealot fain would show himself upright as yonder minaret;
But I have searched the caitiff's heart, and all is there in coil on coil.

This feeble body through the flame of absence from yon dearest one
Doth ever show, Vehbí, as 'twere a fire-scorched hair in coil on coil.

Ghazel. [424]

Wilt take thy lovers for thy union's festal sacrifice?
Wilt give one kiss, dear heart; and take the heart in me that lies?

In secret raising on thy shoulder yonder henna'd feet,
O zealot, dost e'en thou take blood upon thy neck this wise? [5]

[1] As has been said before, the Sháyagán hoard was one of the eight
treasures of the old Persian king Khusraw Pervíz, and is in the legendary
lore of the East what the Nibelung hoard is in that of the West. That
hidden treasures were guarded by snakes or dragons is among the most ancient
and wide-spread of traditions. ‚بيتنده گنج شايگان فرج جانان ديمكدر.

[2] The trouser-knot is the knot of the string or cord by which the ample
trousers of the old costume were fastened round the waist. In this characteristic
couplet the loops of this knot are considered as the coils of the treasure-
guarding dragon.

[3] As it is by a winding road that one reaches the summit of a mountain,
so lofty rank and high place can be attained only by tortuous and crooked ways.

[4] 'Head-bounden' means simply 'bound to obey', but Vehbí here keeps in
view the literal meaning, whence the second line. The Khorásání turban,
or rather bonnet, was the distinctive head-dress of the Khojas or Master
Clerks. It contained more than an oqqa's weight (2. 83 lbs.) of cotton covered
over with cloth of different colours, and round the foot of the cap ran
a border of muslin folded in such a way as to form a row of diamond-shaped
squares: it is probably this to which the poet here alludes. The Khorásání
is scarcely distinguishable from the qafes or 'cage', which was worn by the
Re'ís-ul-Kuttáb.

[5] To take blood upon one's neck, means to take upon one's self the guilt
of some wicked action, i. e. to commit it. The henna-stained feet are, of

I've heard the tidings that the price thereof's the coin of life,
Dost think to buy for little cost her union's merchandise?

With them of understanding seek no traffic, O thou Sphere,
Wouldst buy, though for one groat they sold, the pearl of wisdom's prize?

Again hath Vehbí sought thy ward in strangerhood; 'Wilt thou
Receive him for thy guest within thy secret court?' he cries.

Ghazel. [425]

At times the rival and at times her guardian grey doth hindrance be,
At yonder portal some vile wretch to us alway doth hindrance be.

Th'acacia blooms a rose for him who seeks the Kaʿba-shrine of Love,
No thorn unto the bare-foot throng who press that way doth hindrance be. [1]

Although I loose her sash and drag yon wanton fair to union's couch,
Alack! her trouser-knot to fond desire's allay doth hindrance be

I've fall'n on evil luck, the zealot's come and made his dwelling here,
And ever rising with his staff, he to my play doth hindrance be.

The premisses of hope yield no conclusion, have I found, Vehbí,
If but their statement I conceive, the same straightway doth hindrance be [2]

course, red; hence the connection This first line alludes to what is called in Turkish جمال سكمشى, which is much the same as what the French describe as "faire la crapaudine" Other varieties are سوبورکه سمكمشى; جابيرار سمكمشى; شادروان سمكمسى; قايلوبغه سمكمشى. In the Sheıq-engíz Vehbí repeats this fancy in almost identical words, when Qazıqjı-yegenı is rating his opponent he says·

انمه پیای محتادی سدوش دوینفه قایی آلور صاحب قوش·
Raise not the henna'd foot upon thy shoulder·
Does the man of understanding take blood upon his neck?

[1] This, in the original, is a beautiful couplet The mughílán of the text is the Egyptian or Arabian thorn, the *acacia arabica* of botanists, a kind of spiny mimosa or acacia which abounds in the deserts traversed by the Mekka pilgrims When these enter the sacred territory they abandon their boots or shoes and assume a special sort of sandal which leaves the instep exposed The meaning of the verse, of course, is that pain itself, far from being a deterrent is a pleasure when encountered for the sake of love
[2] This couplet is expressed in the technical terms of logic

The following is modelled on one of the best known of the ghazels of Háfíz. [1]

Ghazel. [426]

Here with the olden wine to me, freshly fresh and newly new;
Call up, cupbearer, our ancient glee, freshly fresh and newly new.

Though but a child, that wanton gay hath stolen my will and my wits away;
An elder needeth a youngling free freshly fresh and newly new.

E'en as the rosebud fresh and fair, they freshen the scar that our bosoms bear,
When they loose the veil on the flowery lea freshly fresh and newly new.

What do they do, these ancient lays, to call up again the olden days?
Minstrel, sing me in sweetest key freshly fresh and newly new.

Rosy-bright must be yon ghazel that is cast in an ancient mould known well;
Vehbí, it must for freshness be freshly fresh and newly new.

This is the ghazel included in the Resonant Qasída; the travels of the author form the subject of that poem, hence the list of place-names here; as is usual with qasída-ghazels, some real or fictitious beauty is addressed.

The Ghazel from the Qasída Resonant. [427]

What though for yonder musk-diffusing mole I gave Shíráz away? — [2]
Nor India nor Cashmere nor Khoten such a grain might e'er purvey. [3]

---

[1] That beginning:

مطرب خوشنوا بگو تازه بتازه نو بنو باده دلکشا بجو تازه بتازه نو بنو

Sweet-voiced minstrel, here, and sing freshly fresh and newly new;
The wine that is heart-expanding bring freshly fresh and newly new.

[2] An echo from Háfiz:

اگر آن ترک شیرازی بدست آرد دل مارا

بخال هندوش بخشم سمرقند و بخارارا

"If yon Shirazian Turk would take this heart of ours within her hand,
I'd fain give for her Hindu mole Bokhárá, aye, and Samarcand!"
By the 'Shirazian Turk' is meant some cruel beauty of Shíráz; her mole is 'Hindu' because it is black.

[3] India, the country of the blacks, is mentioned because the mole is black;
Khoten, the native land of musk, because it is sweet-scented; Cashmere, perhaps to fill up the line.

In Aden never have I seen a pearl to match thy pearly teeth,
To Badakhshán I went, but found no rival to thy rubies' ray [1]

This beauty and these lovesome charms would lay the Moon of Canaan low, [2]
I marvel, in that well, thy dimple, doth the Moon of Nakhsheb stay? [3]

In Kábul met I not, nor yet in Sind, nor China, nor Ferkhár [4]
A fair like thee with ruffled locks, so dark of hair and mole, and gay

I've tendered the Red Apple for thine apple chin, but woe is me! [5]
Not Portugal itself might buy thy orange breasts, my winsome may [6]

As thanks for all the sugared speech that floweth from thy candy lips
Hath Vehbí given Samarcand and Candahár with their array [7]

Surúrí, the associate of Sunbul-záde Vehbí, occupies a
unique position in Ottoman literature. From early times
the chronogram had been a favourite field with the poets
for the exercise and display of their ingenuity, and during
the eighteenth century its popularity has, as we have seen,
been continually on the increase, until the number of the
chronogram-writers has practically come to be the number
of the poets. But over all the mighty throng of poets and
versifiers who have composed such things, whether among
his precursors or his successors, Surúrí stands in unquestioned

[1] Aden is famous for pearls, Badakhshán for rubies 'Thy rubies' are thy lips
[2] The Moon of Canaan is a title of the beautiful Joseph.
[3] The Moon of Nakhsheb was a false moon which the impostor al-Muqanna᷄
(Moore's 'Veiled Prophet of Khorassan') is reported to have made to arise
from a well near the town now called Qarchi, but formerly Nakhsheb, in
Transoxiana
[4] Ferkhár is one of these semi-legendary cities of the far East that were
renowned for the beauty of their inhabitants.
[5] The 'Red Apple' i e Rome, as we have seen before
[6] In Turkish the word portuqal' means both an orange and the kingdom
of Portugal, hence its employment here On account of its shape and size
the orange is a favourite figure with the poets for the firm breasts of a well-
developed girl.
[7] In this verse it has been possible to retain the puns of the original in
'candy', 'Samarcand', and 'Candahár'.

and unapproached pre-eminence, by virtue alike of the vast number of his chronograms, and of the skill and felicity with which so many of them are expressed. And so he has come to be known emphatically as Sururí-i Mu'errikh or Sururí the Chronogrammatist.

Seyyid 'Osmán, such was the poet's personal name, [1] was born in the town of Adana in 1165 (1751—2). In 1187 (1773—4), when about twenty-two years of age, he began seriously to work at the art of chronogram-writing. It is said that his taste for this was awakened by the singularly simple and happy way in which he managed to introduce into a chronogrammatic line the names of six Adana students who had died of the plague.

'Velí, Ahmed, Hasan, Músá, Suleymán, Mustafá are gone.' [2] Nothing could be more simple, more natural than that, yet the numerical values of the letters in this line, on being added together, give the sum 1187, which is the year in which the young men died. It is to the absence of anything like forcing, to, one might almost say, a seeming inevitableness like this, that Sururí's great fame as a chronogrammatist is chiefly due.

The abilities of the young poet, who had devoted much of his time to the study of Arabic and Persian, attracted the notice of Tevfíq Efendi, the deputy-judge of Adana; and when this official was promoted, he persuaded the poet, who was then twenty-eight years old, to accompany him to Constantinople. They arrived in the capital in 1193 (1779—8), and in the same year the poet, on the recommendation of his patron, discarded the pseudonym of Huzní, which he had hitherto used, in favour of that of Sururí, under

---

[1] That Fatín Efendi is mistaken in saying it was Mustafá, is proved by a verse of Sururí's quoted by Professor Nájí.

[2] ولي احمد حسن موسى سليمان مصطفى كتدى.

which it is that he has acquired his reputation. On their arrival in Constantinople Surúrí lived as the guest of Tevfíq Efendi, through whose influence he was appointed a cadi, and by whom he was introduced to many of the great men of the day. But though Tevfíq eventually became Sheykh-ul-Islám, he did little more for his protégé, who never attained any position beyond his cadiship.

As we have already seen, Surúrí served at one time as assistant to Sunbul-záde Vehbí, whose junior he was by some forty years, and when they were at Eskı-Zaghra was made, though innocent, to share the punishment inflicted on his superior by the scandalised citizens. The facts of the case are not very clear, but it would seem that on his return to Constantinople, Vehbí accused Surúrí of having incited the Eskı-Zaghra people against him, and that this (presumably false) accusation was the cause of the younger poet attacking the elder in the series of lampoons which inaugurated the long scolding-match that ensued between them

As Surúrí wrote chronograms on every possible occasion, we get from his Díwán several isolated fragments of information concerning himself and his doings. Thus we are told that in 1193, the year of his arrival in Constantinople, he heard of the death at Adana of his father, Háfiz Músá, through whom he had inherited his sayyidship. Then he tells us that in 1200 (1785–6) he married a lady called Nefíse Qadın, whom he soon afterwards divorced, and who died in 1208 (1793–4) Another wife, 'Ayıshe Qadın, died in 1222 (1807—8). In 1206 (1791—2) he built himself a house in Constantinople In the following year he lost his mother But as his career was an uneventful one, he has little of interest to chronicle in this connection. He died in Constantinople on the 11th of Safer 1229 (2nd. February 1814), and was buried by the side of his old friend Vehbí outside the Cannon Gate.

'Surúrí's death had been the cause of anguish to his friends.' [1]

Such is the obituary chronogram written for this greatest of Turkish chronogrammatists by the poet 'Izzet Molla.

Ebu-z-Ziyá Tevfíq Bey, in an excellent little monograph on 'Surúrí the Chronogrammatist', says that he has heard from some persons who remembered the poet that he was a man of tall stature and stout build, whose appearance struck those who saw him for the first time as being little in keeping with the wit and culture for which he was renowned. He was, moreover, according to the same reporters, quiet and silent when in society, rarely speaking unless spoken to, but always expressing himself when he did speak in correct and well chosen language.

Surúrí was not a poet as Nedím and Ghálib were poets, he was hardly even a poet as his friend Vehbí was a poet; he was a chronogrammatist, but as Turkish chronograms are practically always in verse, he was of necessity a versifier. With him the composition of chronograms was a passion almost amounting to a mania. He must have written many hundreds, possibly thousands, of these. He has a large Díwán, as bulky as that of Vehbí, filled almost entirely with chronogrammatic poems of all lengths from qasída-like productions of forty or fifty couplets down to single distichs, the real ghazels being all huddled away into a little corner near the end. Every kind of event, important or unimportant, public or private, was seized upon by this insatiable versifier as material for one or more of his beloved chronograms. Not content, like any other chronogrammatist, with the occurrences of his own day, he went back into the past and wrote chronograms for all the Sultans from old 'Osmán downwards. Displeased with the work of contemporary poets,

[1] سرورینك وفاتی باعث حزن اولدی احبابه .

he composed new chronograms for events that had happened before his birth or during his childhood.

Even more extraordinary than the immense number of Surúrí's chronograms — although there too he is facile princeps — is the truly marvellous felicity of so many among them. To write a good chronogram must obviously be no easy task; seeing that in addition to the universal rules of the poetic art as to rime, metre and so on, which must be observed here as strictly as in any qasída or ghazel, the sum of the numerical values of the letters in the line (or that part of it which forms the actual chronogram) must of course be neither more nor less than the date required. To do all this, and yet to preserve the crucial line from all appearance of being forced, to keep it natural, and still more to make it telling and impressive, requires a skill, which, though not necessarily indicative of poetic power, is surely neither to be despised nor ignored That it is painfully conscious art is true, but seeing how five-sixths of the poetry of the East is little else than painfully conscious art, we are in no way surprised that most of the Turkish poets should have tried their hand at this particular feat of literary legerdemain, and that success in it should have been accounted no mean achievement.

But while it was with others but an interlude or a pastime, this was with Surúrí the main business of his life, and so here, on his own ground, he meets and overcomes men of far higher literary standing than himself, and fully deserves, as Ebu-z-Ziyá Bey says, to be described, so far as this particular art is concerned, as the Imám of the poets of Turkey. Most men when they write a chronogram, even a bad one, have to sit down and work it out with no little care and labour; but Surúrí had the extraordinary power of improvising such things on the spur of the moment, a most marvellous gift which would suggest that the numerical value of a word or phrase was as obvious to his perception as its sound or signification, and which may perhaps bear some relation to those abnormal faculties which enable the possessor to play at once half a dozen games of chess without seeing the boards.

It so happens that the numerical values of the letters in the word Táríkh, which means 'chronogram,' and of those in the name Seyyid ʿOsmán Surúrí, alike give the sum 1211, a curious coincidence which naturally filled the poet with delight, and which made him declare that chronogram-writing was manifestly the special gift of God to himself. When the year of the Hijre 1211 (7 July, 1796—26 June, 1797) came in, Surúrí is reported to have said, 'This is ʿchronogram' year, so it is my year; during it I shall hold the field of literature.' But as Jevdet Pasha says when telling the story, in the art of chronogram-writing this poet holds the field in every year. That he is the greatest chronogram-writer in all Turkish literature is beyond dispute; does there exist in any literature one greater or as great as he?

Surúrí is famous not only as a chronogrammatist, but as a humorist. Had he never written a single chronogram, he would yet have made his mark in Ottoman literature by his comic poems. It is as writer of humorous verses alone that Von Hammer knows him. So strong was the bias of his temperament towards humour that even in his professedly serious poems the comic element is continually coming to the fore. Many of his best chronograms are wholly humorous, some even of those that he wrote on the deaths of friends cannot be read without a smile.

The avowedly comic poems, which are grouped together under the title of Hezeliyyat or Facetiae, are not included in the Díwán, but form a volume apart. In this volume the author hardly ever employs his usual pseudonym of Surúrí, but almost invariably calls himself Hewá'í. There is much that is clever and a good deal that is really amusing in these Facetiae of Surúrí, but for the most part they are exceedingly offensive to modern taste, depending for their point but too often upon the most filthy ideas and language Vehbí is frequently licentious; Surúrí is less licentious than obscene. In this direction Rabelais himself would have had to own that here he had met his master. 'Intolerable evils' is how Professor Nájí describes these verses, while he adds that no censure passed upon the author for having produced such things can be too severe. In this volume, the proper title of which is Mudhikát-i Surúrí-i Hezzál or The Drolleries of Surúrí the Wag, are collected the lampoons on Vehbí along with a number of similar pasquinades directed against others among the author's contemporaries, but none of these other victims are of any note, save perhaps ʿAyní the poet.

One might be inclined to marvel on reading some of the many scurrilous jests here made at his expense, how Vehbí could ever again address a friendly word to the lampooner; but apart from the consideration that an immeasurably greater licence of speech was not only permissible, but customary, in those days, it is easy to perceive that, at any rate in the vast majority of instances, the writer was inspired, not by any feeling of malice or ill-will, but by sheer love of fun and a desire to outdo his rival. Many of the things Surúrí says are too preposterous ever to have been taken seriously, had such been his intention, the very extravagance of his statements would have inevitably defeated it. Again, in many of his comic verses he speaks of himself in terms to the full as disrespectful as any that he employs in connection with Vehbí. Indeed it is impossible to regard some of those ghazels where he speaks in the first person as anything beyond mere whimsical conceits and fancies thrown into this particular form in order to give them more point and force; and exactly the same thing may be said of the lampoons. And therein lies the great difference between the pasquinades of Surúrí and the satires of Nef'í; the later poet is even coarser and grosser than the older, but he has none of that venom which turned every one of the "Shafts of Doom" into a poisoned arrow that rankled in its victim's breast, so that, whereas Nef'í roused in those whom he attacked a hatred to be quenched only in his blood, Surúrí, Vehbí and 'Ayní remained good comrades to the end. None the less it is, as Ebu-z-Ziyá Bey puts it, a matter for sincere congratulation that contests such as that between Surúrí and Vehbí are no longer possible amongst men of letters.

It is worthy of note that several of Surúrí's humorous ghazels are comic 'parallels' to professedly serious ones that occur in his Díwán, having the same metre, rime, and redíf as these; and as these themselves are most often 'parallels' to similar works of contemporary poets, those facetious ghazels of Surúrí may be looked upon as burlesques on the whole series.

Surúrí's gift of humour made him a popular guest at many great houses. In those times the jests and jokes of a humorist like the poet were all, as the author recently quoted says, that men had to fill the place of the comic papers of to-day. And so Surúrí was an ever welcome addition to a party. His appearance would be greeted with such questions as, 'Well, what is new with you to-day?' or 'Have you had another row with Sunbul-záde Vehbí?' and he, partly to amuse the assembly, and partly because he himself enjoyed a joke, would say something which would set the whole company laughing.

But neither the buffoonery of Surúrí nor his chronograms, which were eagerly sought after by all manner of persons anxious to obtain such memorials of incidents in their private lives, did much towards advancing his material prosperity. Alike from the grandees whom he entertained and from the people for whom he wrote chronogrammatic verses he never received anything beyond the little presents with which from time immemorial it had been the custom to reward such services But Surúrí was a man easily contented, and though, as he often lets us see, he naturally preferred a full purse to an empty one, he seems to have gone happily enough through life, making jokes and chronograms, and not allowing his want of professional success to weigh too heavily on his mind

It is, of course, impossible to give by means of a translation any just or satisfactory idea of Surúrí's chronograms, for although the verbal meaning of the lines might be adequately rendered, there would necessarily be lacking the numerical values of the letters, the real raison d'être of the composition. [1] Moreover, that very simplicity and naturalness, which in the original is rightly regarded as so great a merit, could hardly fail in a translation, whence every suggestion of its real purpose has vanished, to appear bald and uninteresting, if not indeed trivial and prosaic.

I shall therefore not attempt to represent this, the most important side of Surúrí's work, by more than one example,

---

[1] [The difficulty of making chronograms in the European languages (excepting Greek) is increased by the fact that only seven of the Latin letters (viz I, V, X, L, C, D and M) have recognized numerical equivalents, but such chronograms were not uncommon in England in Elizabethan times, and several very good ones are given in Puttenham's *Art of Poetry* Hermann Bicknell ("Hájji 'Abdu'l-Wahíd") has some very neat translations of chronograms by Háfiz of Shíráz The well-known chronogram on the death of that illustrious poet — خو تاریخس از خاك مصلّی, in which the last two words give (A H) 791 he renders —

"Thrice take thou from 'MOSALLA'S EARTH' 'ITS RICHEST GRAIN'", where MLL (= 1100) minus three times CIII (= 309) gives the same date, 791. ED].

the obituary chronogram which he wrote for the poet and humorist Kání who, as we have seen, was noted alike for his wit and for his devotion to all sorts of amusements. The verses appear both in the Díwán and in the 'Drolleries'.

Chronogram on the Death of Kání. [428]

Let the gay forego their laughter, let them vaunt their tears, for now
Gone is yonder mine [1] of merriment the silent feast to share.

Round the town he'd go a-tambourining as at wedding-feasts,
And he'd dance as none had ever danced before him anywhere. [2]

Many were his jaunts and junkets, so that were they all described,
Of their stock were very many scores of ink-shops emptied bare.

He would have made even Avicenna his toad-eater be,
Though the Toqat Turks are most-wise dolts and simpletons full rare [3].

Free and easy he in converse, yet when he did silence keep
Would his courtesy and bearing put to shame the people there.

Little recked he of this filthy carrion they call 'the world';
In the Everlasting Mansions may he find a home for e'er!

Stricken with death's ague, passed he from his place on earth away;
May the Lord make Heaven's eternal bowers to be his blest repair!

Lo, his bowéd form was e'en the bandy in the hand of Fate,
So she smote him 'gainst that ball, the globe of earth, in wrath contraire. [4]

[1] An allusion to the name Kání, which means 'he of the mine'.
[2] This couplet is a humorous and doubtless exaggerated allusion to Kání's predilection for merry-making.
[3] Kání was a native of Toqat; the Turks from many parts of Asia Minor are looked upon as country bumpkins by the Constantinopolitans.
[4] The bowed form of the aged Kání is here very curiously compared to a curved bandy or polo-stick with which Fate or Death is supposed to strike the earth. The metaphor is not good, as Fate did not strike the earth with this crook, but struck it into the earth; in other words, the worn-out body of the old poet was buried.

Whensoe'er we sight the stone that standeth there to mark his tomb,
Strike our arrow-sighs yon marble mark for sadness and despair.

O Surúrí, for his chronogram let wits and poets say. —
'Gone is Kání, he whose every word's a mine of jewels fair' [1]

This ghazel occurs in the Díwán, so we must presume
that it is to be considered as 'serious'.

Ghazel [429]

The purse of gold's appearance makes the pious beggar wight to smile [2],
What virtue doth the saffron boast to make the sad of spright to smile? [3]

How should the masters [4] not rejoice and laugh for fill of earthly gear?
A toy doth make the child whose play is all of his delight to smile

[1] Another reference to the meaning of Kání. This is the chronogrammatic
line and yields the sum 1206.

[2] Poor devotees go round to the houses of great men during Ramazán,
when they get a meal (within the lawful hours) and often a present of money.

[3] This alludes to an old notion that saffron possesses the virtue of making
the eater smile, a notion to which Nábí refers in a well-known passage in
one of his ghazels ·

روی زردم یسمه لبدستهسین خنـدان ابـدر
زعفران حمس نسانٹک خواحـه دصر الدعنمـر

'My sallow face maketh her lip-bounden pistachio (i. e. closed mouth) to smile
'Saffron is the Khoja Nasr-ud-Dín of the vegetable world.'

Khoja Nasr-ud-Dín is the famous old merryman mentioned a little further
on Surúrí here associates the present of gold with saffron because (1) of
their yellow colour, (2) of their power to evoke a smile [The following citation from the *Notting Hill High School Magazine* of March, 1899, copied
in pencil by the author, was found attached to this page "Saffron has a
sweetish, penetrating odour, and a warm, pungent, slightly bitter taste It is
possessed of stimulant qualities, though in no marked degree, and was much
used in the early days of medical science in conjunction with other drugs
An Elizabethan herbalist asserts that 'the moderate use of it is good for the
head, and maketh the senses more quick and lively It shaketh off heavy
and drowsy sleep, and maketh a man merry' Great virtue was assigned to
it in consumption, and it was highly valued in cases of surfeit " ED]

[4] 'Masters' is here used, in imitation of the word in the original, to mean
both 'great men' and 'boys belonging to the upper classes.'

What though in union's night the lover weep for very stress of joy,　　　·
When tickling her, he makes the darling fair he claspeth tight to smile

Why should they not invoke God's ruth thereon when mentioning the heart[?]
Its doings, like to Khoja Nasr-ud-Dín's, the folk incite to smile [1]

My genius laughs at those who fain would follow it along these ways,
The crow's deporture makes the pacing partridge for despite to smile [2]

The Khoja Nesh'et at these fancies of Surúrí deigned to laugh,
A Solomon is he the meanest ant's harangues excite to smile [3]

The next two ghazels are from the 'Drolleries', and, as
is usual with works in that collection, are signed Hewá'í in
place of Surúrí.

---

[1] When mentioning the name of a dead person held in esteem it is customary to add the phrase 'the mercy of God on him!' Surúrí here anticipates
his own death, and implies that he has afforded his contemporaries so much
amusement that when his heart (i e he himself) comes to be mentioned, he
will be as much entitled to the benedictory phrase as Khoja Nasr-ud-Dín, the
Turkish Joe Miller, who is credited with endless comical sayings and doings

[2] Referring to the proverb فارغه ككلكه تعلمك اندركن دوربشى شاشورمش
'the crow lost his own walk while imitating the partridge,' which in its turn
is taken from the fable of the crow who, admiring the gait of the partridge
(the type of a graceful walker), sought to imitate it, but did so in a fashion
so awkward and ungainly as to call forth the derision of his model, while
he forgot his own proper walk into the bargain. Belígh cleverly applies this
fable in the following couplet

فارسى شعر سپار رومنده شاعر مثلا
روشن زاغ اوسودر كنكه اندركن بعلمك

'The poet in Turkey who writes Persian verse is even as
'The crow that forgets his own walk while imitating the partridge'

[3] Khoja Nesh'et, the well-known poet and Persian teacher whose life and
work have been considered in the last chapter. The Khoja's personal name
was Suleimán (i e Solomon), hence the allusion to the legend of King Solomon's conversation with the ants, the ant here being of course Surúrí
himself.

Ghazel. [430]

We ever roam the world's expanse, a-sighing, passing dolefully;
A vagrant strange are we, in truth the wind-chaser of earth we be. [1]

Not once hath wit or understanding deigned to stop and lodge with us,
Although on earth's high-road we ever stand like any hostelry.

No dealings have we in the market-place of learning and of skill,
But day and night we stone the hounds without the city's boundary. [2]

The carnal mind [3] doth never cease to seek to make our head to reel;
We're like the sling in children's hands who play therewith full merrily. [4]

What wonder if thy savour's strong, Hewá'í, to the cultured folk?
Since we're an onion grown in ignorance's field in verity.

Ghazel. [431]

It will not bide, to liquid streams will turn this snow full quietly,
'Twill melt before the fiery sun's caloric glow full quietly.

Deliberation e'en in quarrels needful is, so ere the dog
To bark and bite begins he snarleth hoarse and low full quietly.

So tired am I upon the road of dole that had I e'en an ass,
Right gladly would I mount thereon and ride him now full quietly. [5]

That ne'er the Sheykh Efendi hear within his convent fast asleep,
Upon his tender pupil fair a kiss bestow full quietly.

[1] The 'wind-chaser' (in Turkish, yel-qowan), the Bosphorus shear-water, a bird which flies in large flocks up and down the Bosphorus without appearing ever to rest.
[2] Vagrants and others who find themselves outside the walls of Eastern cities have sometimes to throw stones at the dogs that prowl around, in order to keep them off.
[3] The 'carnal mind', that is the 'commanding flesh' (Nefs-i-emmáre), is the technical term in Muslim ethics for that state of the soul when the lusts of the flesh rule unrestrained.
[4] Children in the East sometimes play with a sling which they swing round, thus, as it were, making its head to reel.
[5] It was held beneath the dignity of a man of consideration to ride an ass.

Hewá'í, lest the spying rival see and come upon thee, off
And speed thee after yonder darling sweet to go full quietly.

Ghazel. [432]

Like nightingales the rivals sang, for all that crows are they,
For all they are the biggest owls that nest midst earth's deray.

The heart beheld yon partridge fair and from its love it flew,
Alack! although an eagle strong it failed to catch its prey[1]

Doth e'er the buzzing in our house grow less or cease, although
The spider weaves his web intent the flies to snare and slay?

O trickster, how should any deal with thee in the bazaar
When all thy work is but to cheat and swindle night and day?

"Here, Master, buy me hose!" the 'prentice plants his foot and cries,
And yet but battered shoon and tattered socks his old array[1]

Again I've had a tussle with Hewá'í the buffoon,
When yonder clown, for all his wit, was silenced straight away

[1] That is, in spite of his former poverty and misery, no sooner does the apprentice find himself in service than he begins to make all sorts of demands

CHAPTER VIII.

The Poets of the Later Romanticism.

Wásif. — ʿIzzet Mollá

The literary tendencies of this critical period are well exemplified in the writings of the celebrated poet Enderúní ʿOsmán Wásif Bey. As the term Enderúní, which is often associated with his name, implies, Wásif Bey was brought up in the Imperial Seraglio, his admission to which he probably owed to his connection with the family of Khalíl Pasha, the Albanian Grand Vezír of Ahmed the Third The gieater part of his life was spent in the Palace, where he latterly held the post of Kilar Kyahyasi, or Comptroller of the Buttery, an office of considerable importance in the Sultan's household. He finally retired on a pension, and lived quietly at his private residence till 1240 (1824—5) when his uneventful life came to a close. [1]

Wásif Bey, besides being one of the most characteristic writers of his time, is among the most generally popular of the older poets. Like his famous contemporary, ʿIzzet Mollá,

---

[1] Von Hammer has confounded the poet ʿOsmán Wásif Bey with the Imperial Historiographer Ahmed Wásif Efendi who died in 1221 (1806—7). [I find in the margin of the manuscript a pencil note [by the author to the effect that, from a passage in the Mihnet-Keshán of ʿIzzet Mollá (p. 98 of the edition used by him), it appears that Wásif's house at Top-Kháne was burned in a conflagration during the week in which the Mollá left Constantinople for Keshán, that is in Jumádá II, 1238 (= February, 1823). ED.]

he endeavoured to write verse in a simpler and more natural manner than had hitherto been accounted literary, and
to use by preference native Turkish idioms, when this could
be done without offence. Wásif indeed went so far as to attempt
to write verses in the language as it was actually spoken in
Constantinople.

That this bold venture was not wholly unsuccessful is
proved by the favour with which the public has ever since
regarded his sharqís, that section of his work where it is
most in evidence. That he did not achieve a more sure
success and win for himself an undying name as one of the
great leaders in the development of Turkish poetry, is probably, as Kemál Bey suggests, due to his lack of courage
in not substituting for the Persian metres that purely syl-
labic system of scansion which the Turks call parmaq hi-
sábí or 'finger counting', and which alone is really in
harmony with the Turkish language, where, properly speaking, there is neither quantity nor accentuation.

Wásif's sharqís, which are very numerous, form the most
important division of his work. On reading through them
we are struck by two points: the one, the extreme pretti-
ness of the verses as a whole; the other, the astonishing
inaccuracies of the writer. Many of these little poems are
appropriately written in unusually short metres, which im-
parts a charming lightness and lilt to the lines so that
it seems at once easier and more natural to sing than to
read them. Few poets, again, have so happy a gift of
stringing together pretty words. In many of the sharqís we
get line after line consisting entirely of words pretty alike
in themselves and in their associations, till the little song
comes to resemble a dainty nosegay composed of delicate
and sweet-scented flowers. His favourite, indeed almost exclusive, subjects are love and beauty; and his treatment of

these, if without much depth or spirituality, is at least free
from the voluptuousness that tinges so much contemporary
work. In short, it may be truly said that the sharqís of
Wásif form delightful reading so long as we are content to
be lulled by pleasant cadence and harmonies of sweet-
sounding words, and are satisfied with a vague, dream-like
consciousness that the vision suggested is a thing of beauty.

But so soon as we look below the surface, the charm
vanishes. Technical faults of every description, feeble conceptions, and incoherent ideas confront us in nearly every
poem, beneath the wakeful eye of criticism the whole en-
chanted fabric melts away. And so the popularity of Wásif,
great as it has been and is, is a popularity confined to the
half-educated and the very young, that is, to those classes
who are incompetent to judge critically. The poet wrote
in a dialect easy to understand, he wrote in it with much
grace, composers set his songs to music, and hence his
name is a household word.

But the critics see him in a very different light. Ziyá
Pasha allows him to be a graceful poet, and admits that
he wrote with much ease and fluency, adding that he did
so entirely through the force of native talent. This criticism
is controverted by Kemál Bey who holds, surely somewhat unwarrantably, that while there is* not in Wásif's
verses a single word which would point to absence of culture, more than half his Díwán is disfigured with lines
which betray nothing else than downright poverty of language Professor Nájí goes a step further and denies to
Wásif fluency and learning alike, quoting passage after
passage from the Díwán to make good his words The
Professor is in general a just critic, but it seems to me
that in this instance he has allowed his zeal for accuracy
of workmanship somewhat to prejudice his judgment. It

cannot, indeed, seriously be disputed, notwithstanding the remark of Kemál Bey, that there is much in Wásif's work that looks like either imperfect education or gross carelessness, but this ought not to blind us to the real merit that is no less certainly there. The extraordinarily felicitous selection of metres for the sharqís is evidence of true artistic instinct, as is also the rare and exquisite taste with which the poet has chosen his vocabulary. The charge of poverty of language has no basis, unless it be that having found the words which best suggest the idea he wishes to evoke, he uses them again and again in poem after poem. This, which is the result of constantly playing upon the same string, might justly bring upon the poet a charge of monotony; but seeing that he has elected to say the same thing over and over again, it is surely less his fault than that of the dictionary that he is unable to find a new set of equally suitable words for each occasion. The poetry of Wásif may be likened to the work of a decorative artist of good feeling but limited range and very uncertain craftmanship.

It may be that the Turkicising spirit, which had been gathering strength ever since the days of Sábit and which is so potent in the writings of Wásif, had something to do with that poet's neglect of the technicalities of his art. It may be that he thought that by disregarding the conventional rules he was taking a step towards making poetry more truly national. Much might have been said in favour of this, had he only had the hardihood to go to the root of the matter and wholly ignore the Persian metres which are essentially alien to the genius of the Turkish language. So long as he retains these artificial metres, a poet must needs observe the artificial laws which regulate their use, on pain of giving to the world a hybrid production offensive to every student of literature.

Although the foregoing remarks are made more particularly with regard to Wásif's sharqís, they apply in greater or less degree to his whole Díwán. The qasídas, ghazels, chronograms, and so on, are all distinguished by the same general features, beauty of language marred by slovenliness of workmanship and sometimes by feebleness of thought.

Besides the sharqís and those other poems of the usual conventional type, there are in Wásif's Díwán two works of an altogether unique character and of very great interest. There are two poems, consisting respectively of thirty-three and thirty-two five-line stanzas, composed in the harem dialect used by women of the middle classes in Constantinople in the author's time Although these two pieces, being wholly humorous in intention, are greatly exaggerated, they are of much value as offering what is probably the only written example of the Turkish language as it was actually spoken in the harems in old times, and as throwing considerable light upon the ideas and beliefs as well as upon the home-life of Turkish women before the days of high-heeled boots and western education. The two poems are supposed to form a dialogue between a mother and her daughter who is just emerging from childhood into womanhood. In the first the elder woman counsels the girl as to how she must conduct herself now that she is growing up, and the advice she gives is on the whole excellent, though sometimes conveyed in terms that are harsh even to grossness. In the second the daughter makes reply, and proves herself to have a will of her own. She revolts savagely against the social custom which compels her to pass her life quietly within doors, whether the house be that of her parents or of a future husband, the mere thought of such imprisonment renders her incapable of speaking to her mother or about a husband without bitterness and abuse;

she is determined to assert her freedom in defiance of them all. The whole of her so-called answer is little else than one long tirade against her mother, whom she looks upon as embodying the principle she detests, broken here and there by remarks addressed to friends or relatives supposed to be present. A good deal of dramatic power is shown in the alternations between tenderness and anger in the mother's tone as the daughter is supposed to listen with attention or impatience to her words, as well as in the way in which the girl works herself up into fury, imagining every one to be in league against what she regards as her natural freedom. In this, as in his subject and his manner of treating it, Wásif gives evidence of true originality, and makes us regret that his work of this nature is so limited. Wásif's mother and daughter are not to be taken as types of Turkish ladies; they are women of the lower middle class, as is shown by the fact of their doing their own cooking, washing and so on; this accounts for many of the things they say and in great measure for the coarseness of the language they employ. Like all Turkish women, they are constantly quoting proverbs, of which they have an inexhaustible store at their fingers' ends. These verses do not make the slightest pretence to be poetry; they are the veriest doggerel, and were written partly by way of a joke, partly as a tour de force. And so, although faithful in the outlines, the picture they present must, as I have already hinted, be toned down considerably if we wish to catch a glimpse of things as they really were.

On account of the exceptional interest of these two works I have endeavoured to translate them both. This has proved no easy task, since so many of the words and expressions belong neither to the literary dialect nor to the language as it is generally spoken. They are consequently

entered in no dictionary, and had it not been for the assistance of a well-informed Turkish friend, I should have
been compelled to abandon the attempt as hopeless. Even
as it is, there are a few passages the true meaning of which
remains doubtful; for the feminine phraseology of a by-gone
generation is not always readily comprehensible. The form
of both works is the mukhammes with recurrent refrain. [1]
Here are five of Wásif's sharqís.

Sharqí [433]

Whoe'er her ruby lips hath known
Doth, bounden by her tresses, groan
'Tis meet her nightingale I moan
A lovesome Scian Rose is blown [2]

Unrivalled she with waist so spare,
With fashions sweet beyond compare,
With ways than e'en herself more fair·
A lovesome Scian Rose is blown.

The roses like her cheeks are few,
To rosy pink inclines their hue,
This summer ere the roses blew
A lovesome Scian Rose is blown.

---

[1] A metrical translation of these two poems along with a preface and
the text as it appears in the printed edition of Wásif's Díwán was issued
anonymously in 1881 by the late Sir James W Redhouse The pamphlet is
lengthily entitled   A Mother's | Advice to her Daughter | and | the wild
Daughter's | Undutiful Reply | Two Humorous Turkish Poems, | in the
Harem Dialect of Women, | and in Pentastich Strophes, | with Recurrent
Chorus. | by Wásifi Endeiûnî. | Metrically tianslated into English | Pri-
vately Printed | 1881. | The translation, which is very free, and was made
without any assistance, is in many instances mere guesswork, and consequently
often defective.

[2] The Rose of Saqiz or Scio is the name of a choice variety of the flower.
Here the allusion is to some girl from that island, possibly the same to
whom the poet refers in another sharqí the refrain of which is

گوڭلی بنك ادمدی بر سڊر كلی

"A Scian Rose hath bound my heart"

The bulbul to the rose is thrall,
The bulbul weeps the rose withal
Her smile were worth the world and all
A lovesome Scian Rose is blown

O Wásif, on the rosy lea
Yestreen the bulbul sang to me: —
'Be gladsome tidings now to thee:
'A lovesome Scian Rose is blown '

Sharqí. [434]

Fair a Moonbeam hath unveiled her face to-night,
With her cloudy hair had she her visage dight,
Never have I seen her peer, a sun of light;
  Like a brilliant gleams and glows her beauty bright

As the garden-land her night [1], her cheek is day
While her crimson lips a ruddy ruby ray,
I have seen yon wanton darling blithe and gay
  Like a brilliant gleams and glows her beauty bright.

She had her kerchief wrought with golden lace
And hath set it as a foil to grace her face [2]
Yesterday I watched her all a goodly space.
  Like a brilliant gleams and glows her beauty bright.

Silver-wristed, like a diamond flashing sheen,
Such art thou that ne'er the sphere thy like hath seen
Winsome darling, she's a jewel-flower, I ween [3]
  Like a brilliant gleams and glows her beauty bright.

---

[1] This phrase probably means that she has adorned her dark hair with
flowers.
[2] That is, like the thin leaf of metal sometimes placed beneath precious
stones to increase their brilliancy
[3] The 'jewel-flower', jevher chichegi, is what we call the dahlia, but its
more common Turkish name is yıldız chichegi, 'star-flower', the former name
is chosen here because the girl is compared to a brilliant.

She hath donned a robe of rich smaragdine shawl,
So her lissom form is grown a cypress tall
Wásif, graceful in their grace her motions all.
Like a brilliant gleams and glows her beauty bright.

Sharqí [435]

With waist so spare,
Beyond compare,
Meet praises rare;
 So passing fair

Thy visage glows;
Thy face, the rosey
Thy like who knows?
 So passing fair

Come, sweetest, best,
Entwine my breast,
By naught distrest;
 So passing fair.

With winsome ways,
Thou charm'st always,
Most worthy praise,
 So passing fair

O figure slight
Of beauty bright,
My eyes' delight,
 So passing fair.

Sharqí. [436].

Since, O wanton bright and gay,
Thou hast led my heart astray,
Cast these scornful airs away,
 Blithe and merry let us play

When thou drinkest of the wine,
And thy cheeks as roses shine,
Like the nightingale I pine,
  Wailing for my sad dismay.

What, O jasmine-bosomed one,
Cam'st thou to the feast alone? —
Thou wilt list not, — I'm undone, —
  Gad-about, howe'er I pray.

Yea, the festal robe for thee
Of the rose's leaves must be;
For to thee, O fair and free,
  Heavy were the broidered say.

See thy lover Wásif, sweet;
Pity him and kindly greet.
Were this cruel usage meet
  Any lover any day?

Sharqí. [437]

A charmer full of mirth and glee
I've chosen for my dear to be.
The wine her lips doth jealous see.
  A moonbeam passing bright is she.

Her neck is white, her bosom clear;
If thou would have yon bosom clear,
Then give thy gold, words weigh not here.
  A moonbeam passing bright is she.

Who gives yon slender waist his sprite
Shall burn as doth the flambeau-light;
So I'm become her servant wight.
  A moonbeam passing bright is she.

Her clapping castanets resound;
In ever heart is oped a wound,
May any balm there-for be found?
  A moonbeam passing bright is she.

Were't not for yonder Grecian fair,
Of life the wedding-feasts were bare,
So·oft to her the folk repair   1
A moonbeam passing bright is she.

The quatrain of which the following is a translation is a
good example of Wásif's happy knack of bringing together
a collection of pretty words

Rubáʻí. [438]

Around her let yon rosy-frame a shawl of crimson bind;
And let the ends, e'en like my heart, be trailed her steps behind.
Ay, he may vaunt who clips in his alcove yon slender waist,
He, Wásif, who his arms around yon cypress-shape may wind.

The following is the translation of the two humorous
pieces written in the harem dialect which have been described.

Mukhammes [439]

The Mother's Advice and Counsel,
the same being written in the phraseology peculiar to women.

List, girl, to my advice, in all thy words be true, my sweet,
Win thou thy husband's father, be his handmaid deft and feat.
Who'd bid thee go a draggle-tail through mud and mire and wet?
Be not a canting prude, but neither be thou indiscreet.
A street-broom 2 be not thou, my girl, be lady-like and neat.

Someone will see thee, go not out with girlish yashmaq drest· 3

1 She is a Greek public dancing-girl, whose performances are in much request for weddings and similar entertainments
2 Soqaq supurgesi, 'street-broom', is a common term for a prostitute.
3 The qız yashmaghı or 'girl's veil' is or was a special style of face-cover-
ing worn by young girls. Vehbí, when describing the woman-lover in the
Shevq-engız, says·

* * * * * * * * * * * * * * * * * * *¹

Play not the flirt; but honour every visitor and guest,
Or with their looks they'll eat thee up alive, thou plaguy pest!
A street-broom be not thou, my girl, be lady-like and neat

Get not with child by Bıkr Basha², gadding at the spring,
A maiden pure art thou, do not from thee thy virtue fling;
He'd enter and defile, but never midwife to thee bring
Befoul thee not, but hang my counsel in thine ear as ring
A street-broom be not thou, my girl, be lady-like and neat

And cling not, like a baby's pot, to every youthful beau;
Nor cur-like fawn on everyone thou seest high or low,
Nor lay thee, like a bed, before each dandy thou mayst know,
Nor, slut, to henna nights, as to a perch, for ever go.³
A street-broom be not thou, my girl, be lady-like and neat.

سمر ابلوب ناشده‌کی فر دشمغی دوس ابدردی اکلوب بشمعنی
'He would observe the girl's veil on her head,
'And bow down and kiss her shoes'

¹ The second line of this verse is a puzzle. In the printed edition it stands thus·

اشرمه دولاك آشمر آوه کاه بربری

So far as this is comprehensible, it appears to repeat the injunction of the preceding line The girl seems to be told not to pass over (her head) دولاك (the usual meaning of which is 'girth', through apparently it here refers to the 'girl's veil'), but to pass over it something else The بربری is perhaps here a vituperative term

² Bıkr Basha· this is a proper name and perhaps conveys an allusion to some story, in any case it stands here to typify a rake

³ The festivities in connection with a Turkish wedding extend over five days, from Monday to Friday, each one of which is devoted to some special function It is always on the Thursday evening that the bride and bridegroom meet for the first time, and the term 'henna night' is applied to the evening which immediately precedes this, that is of course the Wednesday evening. It is so named because on it the hands of the bride are stained with henna, and this performance is made the occasion of a great gathering of the female friends of the bride's family who usually indulge in so much fun and merry-making as to have given rise to the proverb دنا گیجه‌سنده گمی گولمك, 'to laugh as on the henna-night'

Get married to a youth and do whate'er he biddeth thee,
And give him trotters five or six to feast on merrily; [1]
The husband will supply the lack of them that lacking be
With indoor slippers rushing out, O hussy, hark to me, —
 A street-broom be not thou, my girl, be lady-like and neat

O girl, thy lover were dumbfoundered should he see thee so,
Who once should clasp thy waist would live a thousand years, I trow
So sit not idle, but be up the household work to do,
Thy husband will divorce thee else, though but a beggar low.
 A street-broom be not thou, my girl, be lady-like and neat

Weave no deceits, a-taking youthful slave-boy of thine own,
Undo thy cloth at need [2], but see thou loose thy sash for none
For woe betide thee, if thou turn with yielding face to one;
For then, my maiden fair, thou wilt most surely be undone
 A street-broom be not thou, my girl, be lady-like and neat

See now thy eldest sister is became a blooming bride, [3]
Came thou too with thy sister and they nurse and maid aside,
And all united, to the chaperones thy hand confide, [4]
And seek some youthful lord and let him hug thee to his side.
 A street-broom be not thou, my girl, be lady-like and neat

On seeing others finely dressed, O stupid, do not fret,
Thy dad, — long life to him! — for thee the same will surely get
So be not naughty, thou'rt no longer little, O my pet;
To them be thanks who nurtured thee, thou'rt now quite tall and great.
 A street-broom be not thou, my girl, be lady-like and neat

[1] Sheep's trotters, cooked in various ways, are a favourite dish, and are supposed to have an invigorating effect. This line has further a figurative sense depending on the double meaning of the word pácha, which signifies both 'trotters' and 'trousers'. بش آلدى دفعه پاچه کسلسر یعنی
.شلوارینکی جوز یعنی جماع ادت

[2] The original has here بدجمككه در چور کوجهککه . Here بدجمككه is for
کوجك حسشکك.

[3] The original has, 'Thy elder sister has become a bride at (or in) کوجك توبه', which last term I do not understand

[4] The 'chaperones' (بسكه قادنملر) are the old women who in Islám take the place, up to a certain point, of our bridesmaids.

292

See, 'Atike [1] is wedded now, — her millet on thy head! — [2]
There by the Maiden's Pillar [3] she has entered someone's bed
See that thy thoughts be not with tambourines and dancers fed, [4]
For now into thy thirteenth year, my flirt, thou'st enteréd
  A street-broom be not thou, my girl, be lady-like and neat

I would that to some wealthy judge thy dad had given thee,
Then we'd have gone to visit at thy villa by the sea
Shun bare-legged rogue, nor seat upon thy carpet such as he,
Let not thy fancy after either fop or sloven flee.
  A street-broom be not thou, my girl, be lady-like and neat

With silken thread the spangles bright sew not thy cap about
To hook to thee, heed what thou dost, some worthless drunken lout.
Slip off, nor snatch another's handkerchief good cause without [5]
Let be, thy head will turn, this running round will tire thee out.
  A street-broom be not thou, my girl, be lady-like and neat.

Thou dolt, in cambric fringe that jangles not what good is there? [6]
I'll get for thee a silken dress that thou shalt joyous wear
So stray not out at night, like to a prowling thief, my fair;
The neighbours will thy father tell, so stop at home, my dear
  A street-broom be not thou, my girl, be lady-like and neat.

[1] 'Atike is the name of some girl friend
[2] Darisi bashine! May his (on her) millet fall on thy head! is a common expression meaning 'may thy turn come next!'
[3] Qiz Tashi, the Maiden's Pillar, is the name given by the Turks to the ruined column of Marcian in Constantinople It gives its name (Qiz Tashi) to the ward in the parish of Sháhzáde where it is situated.
[4] Referring to the musicians and dancers who perform at wedding feasts. The line means Do not be always thinking of gaieties and frivolities
[5] Youths and girls sometimes try playfully to snatch one another's handkerchief, the idea being that he or she who does so wishes the owner as lover The mother here warns her daughter not to do this unless she really wishes to marry the young man
[6] There is here a side reference to the gold or silver fringe which usually forms part of the nishán or engagement-present sent by the bridegroom to his fiancée, or to the veil of narrow threads of gold or silver worn by new-made brides, other fringes being in the mother's opinion profitless for a girl The word translated 'dolt' is literally 'camel', and is generally applied to a heavy and slow person.

Yield not to stranger men, for such thy corset ne'er unlace;
Nor cast thy hapless husband on his bed to weep thy case.
So ere before the eyes of all thou dost thyself disgrace,
The hand of neighbour Daddy kiss and hearken what he says, —
   A street-broom be not thou, my girl, be lady-like and neat.

Learn broidery, nor be by wiles of others led astray,
That those who see thy work may still 'How sweetly pretty!" say.
If warping looms suits not thy taste, my Pembe Khanim gay, [1]
Then union-tissue [2] weave and therewithal thy hub array.
   A street-broom be not thou, my girl, be lady-like and neat.

Now, girl, be off, nor buzz like a mosquito round me so,
Nor like a dancing slave-girl swing thy body to and fro.
For very shame would thy goodman hide like a mole, I trow,
Then tethered like a donkey thou wouldst bide, full well I know.
   A street-broom be not thou, my girl, be lady-like and neat.

Were't seemly thou should'st go and beg from neighbours bread and meat,
Be sure thy lad will hear of it, and soundly he'll thee beat.
So hie thee to the kitchen in God's name, and cook as meet,
And set thee to prepare for supper something nice to eat.
   A street-broom be not thou, my girl, be lady-like and neat.

Thou'st got thy due [3], thou would'st not listen to advice from me!
Well, let him whack thee, hussy, he will pay my debts to thee.
For others, whosoe'er they be, my cares for thee can see.
So let my counsels in thine ear as pretty earrings be.
   A street-broom be not thou, my girl, be lady-like and neat.

---

[1] Pembe Khanim, Miss (or Madame) Cotton, is a proper name for ladies; it is also used as a pet name or nick-name for any plump little girl or woman. It seems here to be really the name of the girl, as in her Reply she calls herself by it. [It is also used as a woman's name or sobriquet in Persia: see my 'Year amongst the Persians', p. 461. ED.]

[2] Halálí, 'union-tissue', is a tissue of silk warp and cotton, flaxen, or woollen woof, canonically lawful to be worn by men to whom pure silk is forbidden, — a prohibition to which little attention is paid.

[3] When thy husband beats thee.

O tender rose-bush mine, let not thy tears like dewdrops flow,
'Wherever the school-mistress strikes do fragrant roses grow.' [1]
Be studious, lest the monitor should beat thee harder though.
Nor idle sit, my learned madam, come now, that will do
   A street-broom be not thou, my girl, be lady-like and neat.

Soil not thy name. Time better than the present there is none
Get dad to buy thee sky-blue silken stuff to make a gown.
High time it is that thou wert wedded to some lad, my own;
'Tis shame that still in prayer-cloth wrapped, thou runnest up and down [2]
   A street-broom be not thou, my girl, be lady-like and neat.

My God! mayst thou not live, [3] O girl, so good-for-naught to be!
Thou'rt now grown up and big, thou baggage, sit thou still a wee
Rampageous hast thou broken loose, thou minx, O woe is me!
Thou art a parrot, [4] keep the house, lest hawks should seize on thee.
   A street-broom be not thou, my girl, be lady-like and neat.

From windows see thou chaffer not with men, my girl, I say,
But help thy nurse at times by working thou too, blithe and gay.
So let the fat thy mammy's heart in fold on fold o'erlay; [5]
And learn from childhood's years within thy home content to stay
   A street-broom be not thou, my girl, be lady-like and neat.

Because thou show'st thyself, though but for once, behind the door,
Behold how every day there come the viewers score on score [6]

[1] This is a proverb (slightly modified in the text) خواجـــــهنک اوردیغى بردہ گل بتر 'where the school-master strikes, roses grow,' meaning that good comes from the reprimand of the good, or that a severe experience may have good results. There is perhaps in the proverb an echo of the well-known fancy of comparing wounds to flowers.

[2] Little girls, instead of wearing the regular yashmaq or veil, sometimes run about in the cloths that women place over their heads when at prayer.

[3] Yetushme or yetushmesi, 'mayst thou not grow up!' is an expression often used by women to naughty children

[4] We have many times seen the term 'parrot' applied to a pretty woman

[5] That is: make her happy and content. بورہکى قارش قارش بلع باغلادى 'Fat has enclosed the heart fold on fold,' is a popular phrase

[6] The 'viewers' are female relatives or friends of would-be bridegrooms, who go round to the houses where there are known to be marriageable girls,

With shifts and towels and prints and painted handkerchiefs galore
Cram full thy chest of cypress-wood, [1] thy wedding-trousseau store.
  A street-broom be not thou, my girl, be lady-like and neat.

To pleat it, let the tailor have thy crimson satin rare; [2]
Around thy dainty fez entwine a spangled kerchief square.
'According to his measure give not cloth to each,' [3] my dear
At times sing ballads, and at times embroider purses fair.
  A street-broom be not thou, my girl, be lady-like and neat

On baby's head black cummin seeds and garlic see thou tie, [4]
And get the charm for sleep, and fasten it the cradle by,
Put out the charcoal, that afar may bide the Evil Eye.
Sit down, thou plague, and work, what shouldst thou do a-gadding? — fie
  A street-broom be not thou, my girl, be lady-like and neat.

Invite not to thy house the fortune-tellers' lying crew,
Ne'er look from folk like these, thou trull, to learn the future true;
With cheats like these inside and outside tally not as due;
Take care a slave-girl's bastard drive thee not ill deeds to do.
  A street-broom be not thou, my girl, be lady-like and neat

Now trim with fringe of golden thread thy flowered robe so gay,
And go and see thy friends and mates upon the trotters' day, [5]

inspect them, and report upon them to the man in whose interest they made their inspection.

[1] Wedding-chests are often made of cypress-wood, which is durable and sweet-scented.

[2] This may perhaps refer to the red silk which the bridegroom's mother presents to the bride, and which the latter gets made into a pair of trousers

[3] Alluding to the proverbs هر كسك آرشوننه گوره بز ویرونر 'cloth is not given to each according to his measure,' i. e. every one does not get all he asks for.

[4] As charms against the Evil Eye.

[5] The 'trotters' day' is the day immediately following the actual wedding-day (and therefore always a Friday), when it is the custom for the newly married couple to partake of a dish made from sheeps' trotters, — whence the name. It is the occasion of a gathering of the relatives and friends of both bride and bridegroom at the house of the latter, and is the last of the wedding festivities

Thy tresses bind, and off, and at the money-throwing [1] play,
Perhaps some youth may see and fancy thee in such a way
    A street-broom be not thou, my girl, be lady-like and neat

Begrime thee, laughing merrily, then wash thee fair and clean, [2]
To-morrow the old lady's son will send the ring, I ween; [3]
Put on thy jewels, don thy trousers, O my diamond sheen; [4]
Thank God, through generations seven good our house hath been [5]
    A street-broom be not thou, my girl, be lady-like and neat. -

And hang around thy neck thy strings of coins in row on row,
And send the rakes away heart-sick with many a bitter throe,
But heed thee, daughter fair, to tribade's tricks no leaning show;
Elsewise thy aunt will see and run a knife through thee, I know
    A street-broom be not thou, my girl, be lady-like and neat.

Ha! ha! just let me laugh a while at thy sublime conceit!
I'll squeeze a radish, [6] baggage, for thy mincing ways so sweet
I'll salt thee, stink not. [7] O poor goose, I'll settle thee as meet!
A thousand times thy foster-mother prayed of thee, I weet, —
    A street-broom be not thou, my girl, be lady-like and neat

Thou stiff-necked whore! draw not thyself up in defiance there,
To shower abuse like 'Stones upon my mammy's head!' forbear.
Alack for all the toil and labour that for thee I bare!   -
If now the lads should shoulder thee, why, who, I pray, need care?
    A street-broom be not thou, my girl, be lady-like and neat.

[1] Part of the Wednesday's function consists in showering small coins,
millet, and so on, over the bride

[2] كولە كمرٲن كولە كولە 'get thyself dirty laughing the while,' is an expression
used by female attendants at public baths to their lady clients, the impli-
cation being of course that the latter may soon have occasion to re-visit the
bath. The phrase is here used merely playfully, without any distinct
meaning

[3] The ring which usually forms part of the engagement-present.

[4] 'My diamond' is a common term of endearment to apply to a girl.

[5] i. e. We can trace our family through seven generations.

[6] 'I'll squeeze a radish!' is an expression of contempt something like 'a
fig for you!'

[7] طورلایمله دوئمسس 'I'll salt you that you stink not!' is another
impolite speech sometimes addressed to persons who talk impudent nonsense.

Stand not like statue ¹, loose thy tongue, but do not rant and rave!
I'm worried! hush that dotard, may he bellow in his grave!²
'O David, cozen thine own heart,'³ good deeds from no one crave,
From others learn to work and win the food thy life to save
    A street-broom be not thou, my girl, be lady-like and neat.

Before that Wásif breaks the string of abstinence,⁴ I say,
Put on thy drawers, nor show thy legs unto the folk, my may
Now cease to prate, shut down the lid upon the box, I pray.
Hast thou not heard the order which was issued yesterday? —
    A street-broom be not thou, my girl, be lady-like and neat.

The Pearl of a Girl's
Most Dutiful Reply ⁵ [440.]

If once again she preach at me, I'll bind her to a stake,
And with a stick burnt in the fire her head and eyes I'll break.
And then upon my own account a job I'll undertake,
I'll first go pray a friend to aid, and then my course I'll take, —
    I'll seek a romp of fifteen years and him my sweetheart make

Old dotard, may I ne'er grow up if I attend thy screed!
Thou sleep'st each night with dad, but I'm to have no love indeed!
No more I'll roast myself within the kitchen, that's agreed
I'm not to chat with any pal, or any comrade heed!
    I'll seek a romp of fifteen years and him my sweetheart make

¹ I e silent
² The 'dotard' is probably the speaker's husband and the girl's father
'May he bellow in his grave!' is an imprecation, and alludes to the belief
concerning the examination of the dead in the grave by the two angels
Munkar and Nekír who, if the answers they receive are not satisfactory, beat
the sinner on the temples with iron maces so that he roars out so loudly
that he is heard by all beings except men and genies
³ داود گوگلكّى آووت 'David, dandle (or soothe) thy heart!' is a proverbial expression addressed to one who hopes for something he is not
likely to get.

⁴ By the curious term 'string of abstinence' جلّه باغّى Wásif probably
means the uchqur, that is, the string by which the trousers are fastened
round the waist.
⁵ This title is of course ironical.

Just hear her speak! well might one cry, — a fig for her, the scum!
When thou wast young, didst thou for ne'er a reason stop at home?
The neighbours all are gone in coaches forth to ride and roam !
O nurse, whene'er Sha'bán is here, nay, ere Rejeb is come, [2]
    I'll seek a romp of fifteen years and him my sweetheart make.

Instead of droning, babbler, like a spinning-wheel all day,
Go work thy loom and weave thy web and make some coin, I pray
'The bastard 'tis who spoils the market,' [3] so at least they say;
So what if all the pots and pans to sell I sneak away,
    And seek a romp of fifteen years and him my sweetheart make?

Once in a way, 'Here, girl, thy husband comes,' she says to me
The measles take thee! shriek not like a wench who wails for fee. [4]
Burn up, thou and my husband too, like withered corn-cob be! [5]
While life is in my body left I'll to the streets, thon'lt see,
    And seek a romp of fifteen years and him my sweetheart make

With washing greasy rags and clouts my nails are worn away.
May daddy crack his boxwood spoons upon thy pate, I pray [6]
Thou mak'st me stuff thy cronies first who come here day by day,
And then clear up the litter after they have gone their way
    I'll seek a romp of fifteen years and him my sweetheart make.

[1] In old times coaches were reserved almost exclusively for the use of women, who sometimes went in them to the Valley of the Sweet Waters and other places of resort.

[2] Rejeb is the name of the seventh, Sha'bán that of the eighth month of the Muhammedan year The girl is supposed to be speaking in some earlier month, perhaps in the sixth, the Latter Jemází, and to say that she means to be off and enjoy herself before Sha'bán, before even Rejeb, comes, — i. e immediately.

[3] The proverb in full is بيار پارار حلالزاده بوزار پارار حرامزاده 'the bastard spoils the bargain, the lawfully born makes the bargain ' The first phrase is used of one who causes any project or arrangement to fall through; the second, of one who causes such to succeed.

[4] That is, a hired mourner.

[5] There is a popular expression اولمش كمى دوحان دورونوب 'he (she, it,) is dried up and become like a corn-cob,' i. e is become very feeble.

[6] Spoons made of boxwood are very hard; they used to be highly esteemed. [They often bore suitable inscriptions, such as the following on a spoon of this kind which I bought in Constantinople in 1882 —

My summers and my winters have in tittle-tattle past [1]
"The plaintiff's off to Brusa gone," [2] and so I'm free at last
With sitting still at home my thighs are stuck together fast
Before my wisdom-teeth are cut I'll make thee stand aghast, —
   I'll seek a romp of fifteen years and him my sweetheart make

The viewer, if she comes, will make me fifty times too old;
She'll say, 'Her nose and mouth are big, her teeth are wide and bold,
'No, no, her age, I see full well she's fifty summers told.'
So now for once I'll off and squander whatsoe'er I hold,
   And seek a romp of fifteen years and him my sweetheart make.

Shall I as nightly task four hanks assort, I wonder, eh?
And work instead of sleep, forsooth? Go, lick thy palm! [3] I say
If I've turned out light-headed, look at yonder drab, [4] I pray
Now, auntie dear, let go my hand and hold me not, nay, nay, —
   I'll seek a romp of fifteen years and him my sweetheart make

If e'er I ask a pretty thing as Bayram gift, [5] saith she —
'Thou whore, a pity for the salt they sprinkled over thee!' [6]
See yonder mopsy! pity on my youth! O woe is me!
O sister mine, before I'm thirty years, as thou shalt see,
   I'll seek a romp of fifteen years and him my sweetheart make.

'Twould seem she'd bought me with her coin, like any slave-girl fag,
She'd like to shove me down into the kitchen, filthy hag

!٠٨٨

[ED بو قاشعله دسمز اولدى تمام بمورك خانهمر اى همام بمورك سمه

[1] There is a proverb دسلى دوننله عمر كتچمرر 'he (or she) passes his (or her) life in tittle-tattle,' i e in silly or frivolous pursuits

[2] دعواحمكك دبروسمديه كنلى 'Thy accuser (at law) is gone to Brusa,' is another proverb, meaning that one is free to go or do as one likes, there being none to hinder

[3] 'Lick thy palm,' a popular expression meaning, 'don't you wish you may get it?'

[4] That is, her scold of a mother, the girl is here supposed to be addressing some third party, perhaps her 'auntie dear'

[5] Bayram is the great festival; a Bayram gift is equivalent to a Christmas present with us

[6] It used to be, and perhaps in some out of the way places still is, a custom to sprinkle salt over new-born infants.

But I, I'll throw thee off as though thou wast a greasy rag.
At dawn upon the morrow I'll be up, nor ever lag,
   To seek a romp of fifteen years and him my sweetheart make

Is't needful I should learn to wash those dirty clouts of thine?
I cannot wind the balk up with these cotton hands of mine. [1]
Is't fitting me to weave at looms, and threads of silk to twine?
Go now and to the cupboard comb and distaff both consign
   I'll seek a romp of fifteen years and him my sweetheart make.

Of making wafer-cakes and macaroni do not blare;
Of pastry-work and cakes and sweets I know naught whatsoe'er.
But one or two wee dishes rough and ready I'll prepare,
And to invite him to the feast to-morrow forth I'll fare,
   And seek a romp of fifteen years and him my sweetheart make.

'Is't he who longest lives or travels most who most doth know?' [2]
Unless I move about a bit, I'll never learn, I trow
Both men and women, when they see my face, do praise it so
I'll give myself a touch up in my glass, then off I'll go
   And seek a romp of fifteen years and him my sweetheart make

'The orphan cuts its navel-string itself,' [3] so stand aside,
Nor meddle with thy chatter — Babbler, shall I mateless bide?
I'll serve thee that thou'lt tear thy hair with rage, thyself beside,
I'll softly ope the neighbour's door, and slyly in I'll slide,
   And seek a romp of fifteen years and him my sweetheart make

Just see, to spite thee, I'll be off with some right gallant beau,
Who seeth, needeth not to carp at sun and moon, I trow; [4]

[1] 'Cotton hands,' i. e. white and delicate hands, 'lily hands,' as we might say

[2] This again refers to a proverb, چوق گزن چوق بیلمر چوق نشانان چوق 'he knows not much who lives long, he knows much who goes about much.' Sometimes this is quoted in metrical form

بیلمر افندی چوق نشانان چوق گزن بیلیر

[3] اوكسوز چوحقنی گوبكنی كندی كسر 'The orphan itself cuts its navel-string,' is a proverb meaning that those who have none to help them must help themselves

[4] By the sun and moon the girl here means herself and her lovers.

Let them who see his jaunty ways exclaim 'Oho! Oho!'
His step, and air, and figure too, I say, Bravo! Bravo!
  I'll seek a romp of fifteen years and him my sweetheart make.

Now, Esmá Khanim, [1] rouge my face and trim my locks, I cry.
Hush! ne'er a word! for off to see a comrade dear am I.
It is not for a full-moustachioed gaffer that I sigh,
But for a frisky youth with sprouting down and fez awry.
  I'll seek a romp of fifteen years and him my sweetheart make.

Come, fork out a five-hundred, buy a slave-girl deft and feat,
And make Emíne Tútí teach her dancing as is meet. [2]
Don't loiter near the barracks of the sailors of the fleet, [3]
But take a boat from Yagh Qapani to Stamboul, my sweet, [4]
  To seek a romp of fifteen years and him my sweetheart make.

I will not marry and bring home a ram, I tell thee nay;
So if thou wilt, come on and with a blunted knife me flay.
Now, now, my mother-gossip dear, just let me be, I pray.
If others talk, why more's the fun; but I will off to play
  And seek a romp of fifteen years and him my sweetheart make.

The house doth ring through emptiness from selling of our gear.
The life within me thrills and bounds if e'er a man appear.

  [1] Esmá Khanim, Miss (or Mrs.) Esmá; here the name of some friend of
the girl. It is usual for female friends to assist at one another's toilettes.
  [2] In this verse, the first two lines of which have no connection with the
rest, the girl is speaking to herself. In the first couplet she imagines herself
rich, and proposes buying a slave-girl for a large sum of money, the word
'sequins' being probably understood after 'five hundred.' Emíne Tútí was
most likely a well-known dancing-mistress of her time. The title Tútí (literally, Parrot,) is sometimes given to elderly ladies.
  [3] The Qalyonji Odasi, or barracks of the men-of-war's men, was situated
between Pera and Qásim Pasha, in the quarter still called Qalyonji Qulli-
ghi or the men-of-war's men's guard-house. The qalyonjis (galleon-men) or
men-of-war's men of old times were a rough wild set, so that even this very
independent young lady thought it as well to keep clear of them.
  [4] The yagh qapani, or oil weigh-house, was situated in Galata on the
Golden Horn. Formerly all the oil, butter, etc. brought into the capital
used to be taken here to be weighed and taxed before being sold in the
market. The name still survives in that of the landing-stage called yagh qapani iskelesi.

My name may turn to copper rather than bide golden here; [1]
So when 'tis eve I'll out o'er hill and dale afar and near,
   And seek a romp of fifteen years and him my sweetheart make

My heart's set on yon spun-silk stuff upon the hedge, I trow. [2]
I'm roasted in the sun, I'm sick of tramp and trampling so;
I'll take a parchment fan in hand and in a boat I'll go,
And slipping off with none to see, towards the bay I'll row, [3]
   And seek a romp of fifteen years and him my sweetheart make.

A young and tender palm am I in beauty's garden fair.
Through singing songs amid the bowers I've lost my voice, I swear
With spangles will I trim my newest fez, and that I'll wear,
And stepping up into the coach with coy coquettish air,
   I'll seek a romp of fifteen years and him my sweetheart make.

From Túti [4] will I beg her robe of Scian scarlet bright, [5]
And I will wind her yellow shawl around my waist so slight,
I'll comb my dotard daddy's beard with these my fingers white, [6]
And like the graceful cypress swaying to and fro as right,
   I'll seek a romp of fifteen years and him my sweetheart make.

To Aydın on some work our governor [1] is gone to-day,
Up, Chidem Usta, [8] run, my girl, and tell my friends, I pray,
Well then, thou'st spread my bed upon the belvedere, I say?
To-night the moon's a fortnight old, just full to light our play.
   I'll seek a romp of fifteen years and him my sweetheart make.

آلتون آدی باقر اولدی [1] 'His (her, its) golden name is turned to copper,' is a proverb meaning 'his (her its) fair fame in tarnished' Sunbul-záde
Vehbí says, referring no doubt to some contemporary.

آلتون آدنی قرل باقر ابلر بولورسه گر صاری داك اوغلی گبی فرومایه بكلكی

   'He will turn its golden name to red copper,
   'Should a wretch like Sari-Bey-Oghli get the Beyship.'

[2] Some stuff she sees hung out on a hedge to dry
[3] The Golden Horn is probably meant by 'the bay'
[4] Túti, the name of another friend
[5] The scarlet dye and the scarlet cloth of Scio are well-known.
[6] To wheedle him
[1] Her imaginary husband, the master of the house.
[8] In this verse the girl imagines herself well married, that she has several

There's someone knocking at the door, la, who can that be now?
Just pull the string; [1] O here's our sister, stop that horrid row!
Thy husband ne'er says aught to thee, a lucky lass art thou;
Ta-ta, just now I cannot listen to thy why and how
  I'll seek a romp of fifteen years and him my sweetheart make.

My passion is gone out to a fair sun, [2] dost ask my plight? —
For love of him the vitals in my breast are melted quite,
Cold water's running down my head, I can't tell left from right,
Indeed I've sworn that ere my youthful days have winged their flight,
  I'll seek a romp of fifteen years and him my sweetheart make

The charge for the head basin has left naught for bather's fee, [3]
I'm sore perplexed for tips to give the bath-maids, woe is me!
If like the bath-mother [4] should come my beastly hub, thou'dst see
Before the fool could pick up comb and bowl [5] away I'd flee
  And seek a romp of fifteen years and him my sweetheart make.

If to the tank for water, grumbling, came his ma next day,
Why, smash her crock and with a cudgel crack her crown, I'd say,
It's precious little fun to hear her buzz and buzz away,
I shall not stop and listen to her droning on for aye,
  I'll seek a romp of fifteen years and him my sweetheart make.

servants is implied by the title usta, which is given to the chief female servant in an establishment, and which she here adds to the name of her attendant Chidem or Crocus.

  [1] The door being unlatched by a long string leading to the room
  [2] That is, a handsome youth
  [3] The 'head basin' is the best basin in a public bath; the charge for the
use of it is so high that the girl would not have enough left after paying
this to give the superintendent and the bath-servants their usual tips.
  [4] Hammam Anasi, 'the bath-mother', is the directress of the bath
  [5] طاس طراغی طوپلامقف 'to gather up bowl and comb,' is an expression
something like 'to clear out bag and baggage.' 'Kání has a verse

كرمانهٔ وصلنده باسلدق او پریسك كای ننبشور دبوشمرهلم طاس طراغی

  'We have swooned in the hot-bath of union with that fairy;
  'Kání, it is enough, let us get together bowl and comb'
The bowl and comb are used in the bath, hence the conjunction.

So we must ask a husband's leave! What's next? I'd like to know.
And so the indoor groom for things like this will angry grow!¹
Or what? — Has some new law been issued that we must do so?
A shove behind, and down the well head-over-heels he'll go!
I'll seek a romp of fifteen years and him my sweetheart make.

That aye uncanny is a midden in the house I knew,
So over everything I thrice have whispered 'tu, tu, tu'.²
I wonder, is there no one here to sweep the place as due?
I'll tackle fast to me a herd of colts,³ that's what I'll do,
And seek a romp of fifteen years and him my sweetheart make.

My Pasha⁴, come at five to-night, now do not say me nay;
Come underneath the balcony, and 'Hullo Pembe'' say,⁵
But do not shout aloud lest Khani Dudu⁶ hear, I pray,
While I beguile the babbling fool with gossip as I may
I'll seek a romp of fifteen years and him my sweetheart make.

Let's stop the squabble, mammy, and let's ask of Wásif there
If thou'rt a trollop or if I'm a baggage, that is fair;
I'm sure he'll say, 'If I am asked, you're both a precious pair'
Now summer's come, is't likely I shall stick at home for e'er? —
I'll seek a romp of fifteen years and him my sweetheart make.

The famous statesman and poet, Kecheji-záde Mehemed
'Izzet, who is generally spoken of as 'Izzet Mollá, was the
son of a Qadı-ʿasker of Sultan ʿAbd-ul-Hamíd I named
Sálıh Efendi, and was born in Constantinople in the year
1200 (1785—6). He entered the learned profession, and in
1238 (1822—3) was made Mollá of Galata. But in the same

¹ A newly-married man who goes to live with his bride at the house of
her parents is called an 'indoor bridegroom', ich guwegisi As his position
in the household is a subordinate one, he is expected to show himself com-
plaisant.
² As a charm.
³ That is, a lot of wild young fellows
⁴ To her (imaginary) lover
⁵ The girl here speaks as though Pembe were her own name
⁶ Khani Dudu, perhaps her nurse, the name suggests an Armenian.

year his friend and patron the imperial favourite Hálet
Efendi [1] met his well-deserved fate, and his fall brought
disaster to all his clients and protégés. At first ʿIzzet escaped, but the resentment he felt at what he conceived to
be the unjust treatment of his friend impelled him to satir-
ize those who had brought about his ruin, [2] an injudicious,
if generous, action which entailed his banishment to Keshán,
a little Rumelian town situated between Rodosto and the
Lower Maritza. It was in this town, for which he started
about the middle of the Latter Jemází of 1238 (February,
1823), and where he remained for a year, that he wrote
practically the whole of his well-known poem called the
Mihnet-Keshán Soon after his return to the capital he won
the good graces ʿof Sultan Mahmúd who, himself something of a poet, was well able to recognize literary ability
in others. In 1241 (1825—6) ʿIzzet obtained the Mekka
Molláship, and the following year saw him in the lofty position of Judge of Constantinople The Mollá, who was an

---

[1] This Hálet Efendi was a conspicuous personage in his day. He was in
the civil service, and in his official capacity was brought into personal contact with Sultan Mahmúd, whose confidence he managed to gain His influence become great, but unhappily he used it solely to further his own
ends, and in so doing involved the state in serious trouble His removal
having become imperative, he was, through the exertions of certain patriotic
statesmen, exiled to Qonya, where soon afterwards he was executed He was
affiliated to the Mevleví order, and it was with the Chelebi Efendi that he
sought refuge when sent to Qonya His head was brought to Constantinople
and buried within the precincts of the Mevleví convent at Galata, for which
he had built a library and fountain. He was also fond of poetry, and left a
Díwán of his own verses.

[2] Jevdet Pasha says in his History that the verse which particularly excited
the wrath of the Grand Vezír and was the immediate cause of ʿIzzet's banishment was the following

حالمكڭ جانى حڧ مانى آلدى مسرى
مالـدى اهل حسـده خانه ادله كبرى

enlightened and patriotic statesman, vehemently opposed
the persecution of the disastrous Russian war which resulted
in the Treaty of Adrianople This roused against him the
hostility of the war-party in Constantinople, and through
their machinations he was in 1245 (1829—30) exiled to
Siwas, where very soon after his arrival he died — through
the traditional cup of poisoned coffee, if popular report tells
true 'Izzet Mollá was the father of Fu'ád Pasha, the famous
statesman of Sultan 'Abd-ul-'Azíz's time, who died at Nice
in 1285 (1868—9) The Mollá often mentions his little Fu'ád
in the most affectionate terms in the Mihnet-Keshan

'Izzet is the author of two mesneví poems, one of which
is entitled Gulshen-ı 'Ashq or the Garth of Love, the other
and much more celebrated being the Mihnet-Keshán.

The Gulshen-ı 'Ashq is a comparatively juvenile work,
having been finished in 1227 (1812—3) when the poet was
in his seven-and-twentieth year and still feeling' his way
along the paths of literature. It is a short mystic romance,
built entirely on the old Persian lines The inspiration of
the little work is that of the Archaic and Classic ages, its
philosophy that of Mevláná Jelál-ud-Dín, to whose order
the poet, like so many of his brother-craftsmen, was affiliated.
In it 'Izzet shows himself an idealist pure and simple, and
gives no hint of the intense realism which is to characterise
and render famous his later volume. The scheme of the
Gulshen-ı 'Ashq is poetically conceived, and, despite one
or two errors in taste, due to an insufficiently controlled
imagination, the allegory is gracefully and pleasingly presented The story, of which the following is an outline, is
slight but, I believe, original.

The scene opens on a beautiful morning in the Garth of
Love where the lovers of old time — such as Mejnún and
Leylá, Ferhád and Shírín, Wámıq and 'Azrá — are discov-

ered conversing among the flowers on the wonderful ways of Love. The Nightingale, who seems to be in charge, notices that ʿIzzet is not present in the assemblage of lovers, and despatches the Gardener to seek and bid him come After some trouble, this messenger finds the poet in the market-place of Dolour. ʿIzzet, however, refuses the invitation, as he fancies his beloved, without whom he cannot live, will not be present. The Gardener returns and reports his failure to the Nightingale, who then sends Mejnún, but with no better success. The third envoy, who is Ferhád, is able to persuade the poet to accompany him by assuring him that his beloved will be there. They set out, but mistake their way, being misled by the lying inscription on a fountain, and find themselves in a frightful valley infested by snakes Here Ferhád dies of sheer terror, and ʿIzzet, left alone, flies for refuge into what appears to be a cavern. This turns out to be the mouth of a dragon, who swallows the poet, but is so incommoded by his burning sighs that he goes mad and begins to waste the land and destroy the people. Heaven in pity determines to cast the dragon into the flames, so he is drawn up to the Sphere of Fire, when ʿIzzet, conscious of the monster's impending doom, prays for deliverance, and straightway finds himself in a garden on the earth Here he remains a long while in a state of bewilderment till he is accosted by an aged man, from whom he asks for directions as to the Garth of Love. The elder tells him that that Garth is a phantasm, and enquires the name of the poet's beloved. ʿIzzet answers that his dear one's name is Love Then the aged man, who declares himself Mevláná Jelál-ud-Dín, replies that he can so far aid his quest as to inform him that Love is only to be found through suffering. He then disappears After a long period of many pains and woes, ʿIzzet is at last conscious of the

presence of a glorious and more than earthly Radiance,
which possesses and permeates his whole being, and which
is none else than the Light of Love. In this Radiance
lover and beloved alike disappear, and Love itself is all in
all, till it too is merged in the refulgence of God, which
alone abides eternal. The poem concludes with the author's
acknowledgment of his indebtedness for all his lore to Jelál-
úd-Dín and the Mesneví.

In his second mesneví, the Mihnet-Keshán, a name which
may be read and understood to mean 'The Suffering one',
'The Sufferers', or 'The Sufferings of (at) Keshan', [1] ʿIzzet
is emphatically a son of his age. The mystic poet, it is
true, discloses himself here and there, but this is, as it
were, accidentally; the true purpose of the book is to give
a circumstantial account of an episode in the author's life,
namely his banishment to the town of Keshán. In this
work, which comprises somewhere about seven thousand
couplets, we have a most graphic account of contemporary
life. Everything is here set forth in detail; the circumstances of the poet's arrest in Constantinople, all the stages
at which he stopped on his enforced journey, the conver-
sations he held with his guards and attendants, the stories
told him by the country-people, even the fancies and day-
dreams in which he indulged as he was jolted along in his
springless ʿaraba. Then we have an account of Keshán and
the local notables, of ʿIzzet's intercourse with these, of the

---

[1] In order to have this last meaning the name would have to be read
Mihnet-i-Keshán. But the Turks generally speak of the work as Mihnet-
Keshán, and that they are correct in so doing is proved by the following
verse :

ديار كشـاندن ويروب جون نشان آنـكَ نامى قونمشلدى محنتكشان

where the metre requires the title to be read Mihnet-Keshán. This couplet
however proves likewise that the third meaning is kept in view.

excursions he made to the neighbouring villages, together with many details of his every-day life. A considerable portion of the latter half of the book is taken up with the recital of a curious incident that happened at Keshán during the writer's sojourn, in which the principal actors were a Greek woman, a Muhammedan youth and the poet himself, who, according to his own account, played a part in the little tragedy more prominent than admirable.

Though all in the Mihnet-Keshán is told with perfect good-nature, and often with a kindly playfulness, it is easy to perceive how sorely the exile yearned after his home and the much-loved family he so often mentions; and many a time he lets us see how bitter was his disappointment as month succeeded month and the longed-for pardon was still delayed. At length his hopes were fulfilled, and ʿIzzet returned to the capital by way of Adrianople, re-entering his native city about the middle of the Latter Jemází of 1239 (February, 1824), after an absence of exactly one year.

The interest of the Mihnet-Keshán is twofold; on the one hand it offers a picture of provincial life in European Turkey in the closing years of the old régime, on the other it affords us the opportunity of making the intimate personal acquaintance of an eminent and famous Ottoman official. For ʿIzzet is not content with giving merely an account, however detailed, of his travels and experiences, he avails himself of every opportunity that crops up to express his own views and opinions on all manner of subjects. The poem thus in some places partakes of the character of a common-place book, as in others it resembles an itinerary or even a diary, a state of matters which naturally results in medley so far as subject is concerned. This ʿIzzet perceives and congratulates himself upon, either unconscious of or indifferent to its fatal effect upon his poem as a work of art. He prefers to regard his book as a sort of museum in which specimens of every variety of poetry may be studied. It does not treat, he says, like other poems, of but a single subject; whatever matter one may bring forward, it will be found discussed here. And indeed, while a central thread connects and holds them all together, there are in the volume not only examples of diverse forms, such as qasídas, ghazels and chronograms, but passages narrative and descriptive, mystic and amorous, philosophic and didactic, plaintive and humorous. The book in short reflects the varying moods of its genial and learned author, who, no doubt found in its composition his greatest solace during his weary months of exile. The idea of writing it, as well as the title Mihnet-Keshán, was, ʿIzzet tells us, suggested to him by a scholarly and accomplished Afghan called Talʿat who visited him at Keshán not long after his arrival. The poem, which was completed in 1239 (1823—4), probably soon after the author's return, was arranged and edited in the following year by two literary friends named Husám and Wahíd; it was lithographed and published in Constantinople in 1269 (1852—3).

From a literary and artistic point of view the Mihnet-Keshán is no advance upon the Gulshen-i ʿAshq, perhaps rather the reverse; but in every other way it is much more interesting. In place of a mystic romance, which might have been written by anyone possessing sufficient culture at almost any time during the preceding four or five centuries, we get here a work full of the individuality of its author, and permeated with the spirit of the age in which it was written. On it rests ʿIzzet Mollá's claim to remembrance, a claim little likely to be challenged when we consider that nowhere else do we find a picture at once so comprehensive and so detailed of Turkish life and sentiment at the moment when Sultan Mahmúd the Reformer was about to change for ever, at least in its outward aspect, the old half-Asiatic half-Byzantine Turkey which had carried down into the nineteenth century many of the scenes and not. a few of the principles of the days of the Seljúqs and the Paleologi

ʿIzzet's lyric poems are arranged in two separate Diwáns, which, according to Fatín Efendi, bear respectively the special titles of Behár-i-Efkár or Fancy's Spring, and Khazán-i Ásár or Labour's Autumn The first of these, judging from the chronograms, comprises the poems written up to 1240 (1824—5), the second, those composed from 1241 onwards This latter collection may have been made after the author's death. It contains a pitiful qasída, which must be one of the last poems the Mollá ever wrote, as it is addressed from Siwas to a pasha at the court of Constantinople whose intercession it earnestly implores.

Although one of the most eminent and celebrated men of Sultan Mahmúd's reign, ʿIzzet Mollá does not hold a very high position as a poet in the estimation of the modern critics. Ziyá Pasha, it is true, has nothing but praise for this lord of the moderns, as he styles him, this eloquent merry-maker who expresses himself gracefully in every path, and at whose culture none can cavil Especially does the Pasha applaud the patriotism of the poet-statesman, who, as he says truly enough, sacrified his life for the welfare of the Empire. To this Kemal Bey rejoins that a man may be a very good patriot without necessarily being a good poet, and while he admits that the Mollá was the first, he emphatically denies that he was the second The critic's chief cause of quarrel with ʿIzzet is his practice of using high-sounding phrases without due consideration of their significance, a practice which results in his lines some-

times turning out to be very like nonsense when one begins to analyse their meaning.

Such strictures apply with more force to the lyric poems
than to the mesnevís, in which, and especially in the Mihnet-Keshán, the language is sufficiently explicit and precise.
The most serious defects in these poems arise from a want
of taste which manifests itself chiefly in the imaginative
vagaries already referred to, and from the lack of a due
sense of proportion, through which relatively unimportant
matters are brought into such prominence that the true
values are at times in danger of being obscured.

Like Wásif Bey, ʿIzzet rendered yeoman's service in the
work of Turkicising the poetic vocabulary and dialect. Although the Mollá nowhere condescends to the colloquialisms,
not to say the vulgarities, of the Mother and Daughter
Dialogue, there are in the Mihnet-Keshán numerous passages written in vigorous idiomatic Turkish which suffice to
secure for the author a distinguished place in the ranks of
the reformers. Still ʿIzzet was more beholden to the Persians than was his talented contemporary, and often sacrificed
the genius of the Turkish language to the exigencies of the
poetic art, so that his work, if measured by the conventional standard which still ruled in his day, may perhaps be
said to be the more successful. He struck a compromise,
the time not yet being come when it was possible for a
poet to turn his back upon the Persians and still produce
work of the highest artistic quality.

The following is the opening section of the Gulshen-i
ʿAshq; it is of course the Deity who is addressed.

From the Gulshen-i ʿAshq. [441]

O Thou who mak'st Love's fragrant garth to blow,
O Thou who bidd'st Love's fiery furnace glow,

Thy power can opposites in one unite,
Lo, here the heart, there the beloved bright!
'Tis Thou who mak'st the darling's eyes to beam,
'Tis Thou who mak'st the burning flame to gleam.
Thou channelest the bosom for that fire,
And mak'st the tears to flow for anguish dire
With fire-commingled tears, O Lord of might,
Thou waterest the wound-rose day and night
Whate'er Thou wouldest, that same dost Thou do,
In making me forlorn what makest Thou?
Through love primeval of the Ahmed-Light [1]
Well wott'st Thou of the wistful lover's plight
'Tis Thou whose wisdom over all doth reach,
Who love to lover and belov'd dost teach
Thou mak'st the hapless victims weep and plain,
Thou likewise art the balm to heal this pain.
The mystery of Love is Thy heart's core,
Thy virtues make to laugh, to weep full sore
Thine awfulness constraineth lovers' tears,
Thy graciousness in beauties' smiles appears
O sadly altered, Lord, our fortune shows,
Our life is overwhelmed beneath our woes
What may this fire of Love betoken, God?
Naught knoweth he who bears Love's woful load
Is it indeed a fire to burn the soul?
Is it the wine of the Primeval Bowl? [2]
Our hearths and homes are burned to earth thereby,
O God, take Thou our spirits, let us die!
Love's lesson Thou hast made full hard, Dear One,
Then questioned and examined us thereon,
Some read it 'Leylá', other some, 'our Lord,'
The sense is one, the diff'rence but of word

---

[1] The 'Ahmed Light' (Núr-i Ahmed) figures that conception of the perfect
or ideal being, which God is said to have formed in the beginning, and having formed, to have loved, and for the realisation of which, it is held, the
universe was created
[2] That is the wine of the Primal Banquet, the nourishment of the soul
ere yet the individual was separated from the universal

Then others shoulder mattock and stride forth
To raze the mighty mountains to the earth; [1]
Some like the nightingale bewail and plain,
While some in silence bear their bitter pain; [2]
Some like the lion chained and fettered lie,
Some like the arrow to the desert fly,
Some in the tavern quaff the heady wine,
Some drunken with their own heart's blood recline,
Some are mid crumbling ruins fain to hide
(And Love is with such mad ones fain to bide),
Some weep, O Lord, and some laugh joyous forth;
What means this woe, and what this glee and mirth?
O God, by yonder blessed martyr Qays! [3]
By the black dust where sepulchred he lies!
By true affection and by faithfulness!
By Wámiq's and by ʿAzrá's bitter stress!
By tears that flow from blood-bestrewing eyes!
By mourning heart's impassioned wails and sighs!
Restore, O God, the ruined heart in me!
Restore it, as it hath been burned by Thee!
Make me the moth and make my love the flame,
Unite us ere the fire consume my frame.
Deal by me, Lord, howe'er Thou dost approve,
But part me not from yon Dear One I love!

The remaining extracts [4] are all from the Mihnet-Keshán.
In the first ʿIzzet playfully alludes to the reflection of himself shown in the pieces of mirror which, according to an
old fashion, decorated the interior of the ʿaraba or coach in
which he travelled to his place of banishment. The ghazel
introduced, the imagery of which is suggested by the circumstances, is partly philosophic, partly mystic.

[1] Alluding to Ferhád.
[2] Alluding to the moth.
[3] Mejnún.
[4] With the exception of the first, these are all paraphrased in the late Sir
James W. Redhouse's pamphlet on Turkish Poetry.

From the Mihnet-Keshán: [442]

My comrade an eloquent man was, and good, —
Was none to have leave to enliven my road?
A marvellous poet, of language sublime,
A great rhetorician, the mage of his time,
A man all-accomplished, and skilled, and polite,
Of kind heart and nature, and waggish of sprite,
The wisest of all in the wide world was he,
My equal he was, if indeed such there be!
He showed like to me both in manners and face,
Likewise in his sapience you ʿIzzet could trace.
He tall was, with thin beard, and big frame, and strong,
His peer you would find not, though sought you for long.
I bowed me to him, and he bowed him to me,
And then at the same time discourse opened we
Wherever I glanced, there he too turned his eyes,
Looked I at a girl, he would sin in like wise
Him also the Sultan had doomed to exile;
Indeed we were both of us one in our guile
I looked at him there in the glass in the wain,
And pitied the poor wight again and again
I sighed deep for him, and for me did he sigh,
'Twould seem I were he and that he sooth where I.
His pen-name was likewise ʿIzzet, so you see
The substance was I while the form it was he.
Whenever my reed a ghazel would indite
He straightway a parallel thereto would write,
So whether he wrote this relucent ghazel,
Or I dashed it off, there is none who can tell

Ghazel.

That forms are but a passing shade the mirror doth asseverate
With silent eloquence it doth upon this subtlety dilate.
Undimmed the pure of soul by aught reflected from phenomena,
The mirror still the spirit of the men of heart doth illustrate

Debating like Sheykh Gulshení [1] the mystery of unity,
The mirror doth upon the text: 'All things shall perish,' commentate. [2]
Can e'er the Associate of the Pure his elemental nature change? —
The mirror doth this dark enigma for the fitting few translate.
'Tis folly to impute our good or evil temper to the sphere:
Imagine not the mirror fair or loathly features can mis-state.
No trace of the sojourner's loveliness or vileness bides on earth:
How well the mirror doth this mundane hostelry delineate!
The mirror looks on Beauty's fair díwán, and straight, like 'Izzet's soul,
It doth a 'parallel' to yonder dear one's eyebrow-line create. [3]

The following lines were prompted by 'Izzet's love for
the pen, which, he says, had been his constant companion
since boyhood, and was now his friend and comforter in
exile. The immediate occasion of the passage was the poet's
pleasure with a qasída, addressed to the Sultan, which he
had just finished, and by means of which he vainly hoped
to obtain his pardon. The pen referred to is of course the
reed-pen used in the East.

From the Mihnet-Keshán.
The Eulogy of the Pen. [443]

The Pen was the medium for B and for E,
Whence started the sequence of all things that be.
Doth He in His scripture divine swear in vain
Who guided the reed that inscribed, 'By the Pen'?
And had not the Pen traced the letters of might,
Unknown were the mystery, — 'And what they write.' [4]

[1] The celebrated mystic teacher of the early sixteenth century, mention of
whom has been made in a previous chapter.

[2] 'Every thing shall perish except His face.' Koran, XXVIII, 88.

[3] 'Beauty's fair díwán' seems to mean the fair face of a beauty; when this
is reflected in the mirror the eyebrows are of course repeated or 'paralleled',
as the lines in a díwán might be by some poet.

[4] These first three couplets refer to the Koranic verse in which God swears
'By the Pen and what they write!' (LXVIII, 1) and to the following myth

Concealed in this darkness doth Life's Water bide, [1]
Yea, here in its ink surges Life's Water's tide
'Tis not of this Fountain of Permanence fair
That each Alexander is given to share.
Though swarthy indeed is the line of its face,
On high like the sun ever mounteth its grace
A traveller circling the wide world alway,
A story traversing the ages for aye
By it are the feasts of earth's sovereigns sung,
It needeth no truchman, it knows every tongue
This envy of Jem ranges o'er all the lands,
But yet 'tis in Persia its capital stands [2]
'Tis ever the judge whose decisions remain,
And through it the Mollás to glory are fain
A patron symbolic it is, who may say
With yon slitten tongue either 'Yea' or else 'Nay'
It opes not its mouth for the fool or the low,
But only for him who is wise and doth know.
If ever a dunce by mischance doth it take,
Its trembling creates on the page an earthquake.
Although for fair wisdom its head it would yield,
It only will fluster if fools should it wield.

by which that oath is explained. When God before the beginning of time had resolved on the creation of the universe, the first things that started into existence were this Pen and what is known as the 'Hidden' or 'Preserved Tablet' (Levh-ı Mahfúz). On this latter the Pen straightway inscribed the two letters ك ن, meaning 'Be!' in Arabic — the Almighty's fiat to creation 'And what they write' would thus apply primarily to the Divine command, and secondarily to its consequences, namely, all that has since happened and will yet happen There are, it should be said, other accounts of the Preserved Tablet, according to one of these it contains the original of the Koran, according to another, it bears inscribed the acts and destinies of all created things ʿIzzet refers here to this verse and myth as being flattering to the genus 'pen'.

[1] The 'darkness' refers to the colour of the reed, which is a deep chocolate brown, or to the blackness of the ink, the 'Life's Water' Both this couplet and the next allude to the old fable of the Water of Life in the Land of Darkness and Alexander's Quest thereof

[2] Persia was of course the fountain-head of literature and culture for the old Turks, it is also the native-land of the reeds of which pens are made

'Tis somewhat capricious of temper withal,
Its speech doth now brief and now garrulous fall.
For all that it laudeth the locks of the fair,
At times it is sorely distressed by a hair. [1]
Its virtues and excellence none may gainsay,
And the eloquent look to its mouth every day. [2]
Coeval of all of the cultured and wise,
'Tis present wherever discussions arise.
The tongue may not tell of the works wrought by it,
Nor intellect reckon the tomes it hath writ.
And yet while its virtues by all men are seen,
And earth through the stream of its bounty is green,
Its dark inky fountain at times runneth dry,
And sore for a drop of cool water its sigh; [3]
And then till the life-giving draught it may drain
It sticks in the mud of the ink full of pain;
And yet doth the poor wight have naught but the dole,
Of that which its lips hold the page takes the whole;
If haply one drop in its mouth still remain
That straight as its share by the scribe's lip is ta'en; [4]
The penwiper too for its portion applies: —
Behold here the lot of the learned and wise!
May Allah reward him! how noble his word
When Sa'dí the pearl of this verity bored:
'This proverb is famous the city throughout, —
'The better a man is, the worse is his lot.' [5]

[1] A hair in a pen's nib is an annoyance familiar to everyone.

[2] To look to a person's mouth, means to look to him for instructions. Here writers look to the pen's work, i. e. to what others have written, and gain knowledge therefrom.

[3] To understand this couplet and that following it must be remembered that the ink of the East differs much from that which we use. Eastern ink is a compound of lampblack, gum, and water. The inkstand is provided with a certain quantity of the rougher fibres of silk found on the exterior of cocoons. This absorbs the ink and prevents its too rapid evaporation; but the ink from time to time becomes too thick, and requires a few drops of water to restore its requisite degree of fluidity.

[4] Sucking a pen is a common trick everywhere.

[5] These two closing couplets are in Persian; the second is evidently quoted from some work of Sa'dí.

In the next passage the reed-pen is supposed to answer
the poet

From the Mihnet-Keshán.
The Pen's Reply. [444]

It said [1] May thy favours continue for aye!
May all culture's foes be o'erwhelmed with dismay!
From sticks like to us what of virtue may come?
Wherein do we differ from staff or from broom?
To tutor us had not the erudite deigned,
To open our lips had we ever attained?
If we in the reed-bed had bode frail and weak,
Had ever the heart learned of knowledge to speak?
What I, but a reed, power to claim as my right?
In the hands of the learned alone have I might
Alone through their words my renown shineth forth,
The words of those kings 'tis that conquer the earth.
How many the ill-fated sons of our kind
Whom women in threads of their tyranny bind! [2]
But Allah hath made you the means blest for aye
To save us from such cruel tyranny's sway.
We've dipped in the ink of the sages our head,
With that holy water ablution we've made,
Our brow thus is worthy the prayer-rug to press, [3]
And God hath vouchsaféd our worship to bless
For had not the sages first laved us, howe'er
To touch the divine word of God should we dare? [4]
Becoming the clients of scholars again,
Escape from destruction as fire-wood we gain,
Our bodies were fuel the fires to light,

[1] It said, that is the reed-pen said
[2] Weavers, who are often women, use reeds as bobbins in their shuttles.
There is of course a suggestion of the bonds of love in the 'threads of
tyranny'.
[3] The page is here meant by the prayer-rug.
[4] The unwashed may not lawfully touch the Koran.

The ignorant therefore had burned us forthright.
Did Life's blessed stream in the reed-jungle flow? —
Then why naught of respite from thirst could we know?
For even while yet tender shoots, did we sigh,
Our hearts scorched and seared by the heats of July.
We crackled and hissed, soul and body aflame,
But no one to bring us a draught ever came.
What then though we're eager to serve sages thus? —
The Khizrs are they of Life's Water for us.
The clients of great men had we not become,
By reed-riding child to be strid were our doom. [1]
We're some of us flutes in the Mevleví's hands.
  * * * * * * * * * * * * * * * * [2]
To us men of heart [3] do their secrets outpour,
Though they who look on deem us pipes and no more.
The cultured and noble have tutored us fair,
Allowing us still in their councils to share.
May God of His mercy establish them sure,
And save us for aye from the hands of the boor.
With kindness the saintly do us ever treat,
In holding with us converse secret and sweet.
Were't not for the learned, we still should remain
As birds without portion in nest or in grain;
They give us the pen-case for home and abode,
Therein do our little ones find rest and food.
What we, reeds, that we should pronounce Yea or Nay? —
The learned 'tis still are our patrons for aye.

The next and last extract is the Mollá's humorous description of the foppish Muftí or official counsel of the

---

[1] As has been before observed, children in the East sometimes amuse
themselves by bestriding a reed as if it were a horse.

[2] The line that should come here is misprinted in the published text
where it reads:

موالیه بندن صغیر وكبیر

which is meaningless.

[3] Here the Mevleví dervishes, in whose rites the reed-flute plays so important a part.

little town of Ergene or Uzun-Koprı (Long-Bridge) not far
from Adrianople, who paid him a visit during his banishment at Keshan.

From the Mihnet-Keshán. [445]

Of Ergene's muftí I oft had been told;
He looked quite the bachelor though he was old. [1]
To follow the practice he might not attain, [2]
And so 'twas his aim like a youth to remain
He wound soldier-fashion his gay turban shawl, [3]
Concealing his learning and skill therewithal
Bemusing his beardlessness still and again,
To gaze on his visage my heart waxed fain.
This quatrain by way of a letter I wrote,
Then sought for a courier meet for my note.

   O beardless muftí, all whose thoughts are signs, [4]
   Know of this ʿIzzet sad of heart, that he,
   For all these months since to Keshán he came,
   Yearns for thy face, and waiteth still for thee!
It happened that Talʿat was then setting out, [5]
So he served as courier to carry my note.
My reed is a fountain whence sweet waters run,
My letter arrived at Uzun-Kopri town.
My note reached its place in the month of Shaʿbán,
He came in the month of Forgiveness for man. [6]
What think ye I saw? — this amaze of the day

[1] There is in this couplet an untranslatable pun between Ergene, the
name of the town, and the word ergene, the dative case of ergen, bachelor.
[2] The sunnet or practice of the Prophet here alluded to is that of wearing
the beard The muftí was what is called in Turkey kose, that is either
beardless or with a very slight growth of hair on the face
[3] He wore a gay shawl turban like a janissary instead of a sober white
one like a legal functionary.
[4] By 'signs' miracles is meant The reference is to the muftí's reputation
for learning
[5] Talʿat was ʿIzzet's Afghan friend
[6] That is Ramazán, the following month

With head bravely turbaned, right jaunty and gay.
He seated himself, brisk and boyish his pose;
Moustachios and eyebrows as 'twere slender bows;
Begirt with his sabre, the foeman's affray, [1]
The Rustem of legend he seemed to portray;
Those Arnawut pistols with silver bedight [2]
Were ready to slaughter the fell Muscovite.
His speech testified to his rare merits high,
For all that his countenance gave them the lie.
He versed was in every science in truth,
No duper through show of fair fashions in sooth.

* * * * * * * * * * * * * * * * [3]

The canon full earnestly studied had he
Although in demeanour so easy and free.
For two nights or three as my guest he abode,
And then for Uzun-Köpri took he the road.
Such man with such qualities never was seen;
The laughing-stock he of all creatures, I ween.
The sphere ne'er will show us the like of this wight;
Could any behold him nor smile at the sight?
Whate'er man of sense hears his history true,
Although he have nought in Rumelia to do,
Delaying for none, either Pasha or Bey,
To gaze on this doctor will straight wend his way.

---

[1] It was unusual for civilians to go about armed with sword and pistols.

[2] Arnawut or Albanian pistols are often beautifully decorated with silver-work.

[3] There is here a couplet which in the published text is misprinted thus:

رفاعیلرڭ مرشدی شیخِ کامل   طریقتنده هادیٔ خیرِ سبیل

the general meaning of which is obviously that the mufti was an eminent member of the Rufá'í dervish-order. [It seems to me that by reading كُلّ for كامل we give the line both sense and metre. It will then mean: "The director of the Rufá'í's, the sheykh of all, a guide unto the 'best of ways' in his order." ED.]

CHAPTER IX

THE ROMANTICISTS (CONTINUED).

The Rival Vezírs, ʿAkif Pasha and Pertev Pasha.

Among the most prominent figures in the Turkish official world in the time of Sultan Mahmúd were the rival statesmen ʿAkif and Pertev Pashas, of whom the former, ʿAkif Pasha, occupies a position of great importance in the history of Ottoman literature. It was, however, in the development of Turkish prose that this writer rendered the most signal service, evolving, as we shall see, by the sheer force of his own genius and without any extraneous aid, a style of writing which, though faulty in many ways, has led directly to the up-building of the powerful and flexible literary idiom of to-day. Although himself a poet and the author of a small díwán, his services to poetry were less direct, for while there is in his verses a certain freshness, they contain absolutely nothing revolutionary, and but little that gives any hint of advance or even points in the direction of change. In these later days the development of prose has preceded that of poetry, it has only been after the former has found itself firmly and securely planted on its feet that the latter has ventured to make a move and step forward in the same direction And so, by directly helping the development of prose, 'Akif Pasha has indirectly helped that of poetry; and this, though he never knew it, is his truest service to the art.

On the fifteenth day of the First Rebí᷄ of the year 1202 (26 December 1787), long before any glimmer of Western culture had reached even the capital, there was born to a certain Cadi 'Ayntábí-záde Mahmúd in the town of Yuzghad, deep in the heart of Anatolia, a son whom he named Mehemed, and who was destined to become famous in the future as Hájji 'Akif Pasha. When about six years old, the boy accompanied his father on the pilgrimage to Mekka, thereby earning the title of Hájji, which is often prefixed to his name. On his return to Yuzghad, 'Akif set to work and studied diligently till he made himself master of such learning as the age and locality could supply. This learning was, of course, exclusively Oriental, and therefore to all intents and purposes medieval, a circumstance which sadly handicapped 'Akif when he came to have dealings with trained European diplomatists, but which renders his literary achievements all the more remarkable and the more creditable.

The young man's first employment was as secretary to one Jebbár-záde Suleymán Bey, a local notable, on whose death he went to Constantinople, where he arrived in 1228 (1813). Here the influence of a paternal uncle called Mustafá Mazhar, who held the position of Re'ís Efendi, got him into the office of the Imperial Divan. His abilities were soon recognised, and promotion quickly followed, till, after having held various important offices, such as Amedji and Beylikji, he found himself in his uncle's old post of Re'ís Efendi.

Among the revolutionary changes with which Sultan Mahmúd so profoundly modified the outward form of the

Ottoman government, and brought it, externally at any rate, more into line with those of other European states, was the reconstruction of the Sublime Porte; a proceeding which involved the abolition of many ancient offices and titles, and the creation of a number of fresh ones modelled more or less closely on those prevailing in the West. Among the titles thus suppressed was the time-honoured style of Re²ís Efendi, and as in later years the most important of the functions discharged by the officer so designated had been the direction of the foreign relations of the Empire, the substituted title was Umúr-ı Khárijiyya Náziri, which is simply a translation of Minister of Foreign Affairs This change was affected in the Zí-l-Qa°de of 1251 (March 1836) when °Akıf was Re²ís Efendi, and as he continued to hold the office after the change of designation, he became the first so-called Foreign Minister of the Ottoman Empire. But before many months had elapsed, °Akıf Pasha was deposed through the intrigues of his inveterate rival Pertev Pasha, who was in charge of the Home Department, and bore under the new dispensation the title of Minister of Civil Affairs [1]

The immediate cause of the Pasha's dismissal, was what was known as the Churchill affair, a miserable little dispute which would have been forgotten long ago but that it supplied the occasion for °Akif's most noteworthy literary effort. An English merchant named William Churchill [2] had, while quail-shooting at Cadı-Kyuy, unluckily wounded a Turkish child who was feeding a pet lamb. This infuriated the mob, who were at the time excited against the Franks,

---

[1] Umúr-ı Mılkıyye Názırı

[2] A few years later, in 1256 (1840—1) this Mı Churchill founded the semi-official Turkish newspapeı called Jeríde-i-Hawádıs ("the Journal of Events").

so that, after handling Mr Churchill somewhat roughly, they dragged him before a magistrate, who cast him into prison A peremptory demand from Lord Ponsonby the British ambassador for the immediate release of Churchill was met by a refusal on the part of the Pasha to liberate him before he had stood his trial. On this, the ambassador, partly because he lost his temper and partly because of a mutual misunderstanding, broke off communications with the Ottoman Foreign Minister. Here ʿAkíf's purely Oriental education had brought him into difficulties, he had been unable to communicate directly with Lord Ponsonby, and had been compelled to depend entirely on unprincipled Levantine dragomans. These persons, according to the detailed account of the incident which ʿAkif himself has given, acting in the interest of and in collusion with his rival Pertev Pasha, deliberately fostered the misunderstanding until Pertev was able to persuade the Sultan to dismiss a minister with whom the British ambassador refused to deal It was not long, however, before Sultan Mahmúd discovered the pernicious intrigues of Pertev, who was in his turn summarily dismissed and banished to Adrianople, where, as we shall learn a little further on, he straightway paid the penalty of his deeds. ʿAkif, who, whatever his mistakes might have been, had always acted loyally in the interests of what he conceived to be the honour of the Empire, was thereupon recalled and entrusted with the office of his old rival, the title being then changed from Civil Minister to Minister of the Interior, [1] which it remains to the present day This occurred in the Latter Jemází of 1253 (September 1837).

When Reshíd Pasha returned from the London embassy to resume charge of the Foreign Office in 1255 (1839), at

---

[1] Umúr-ı Dákhılıyya Názırı

the very beginning of Sultan ʿAbd-ul-Mejíd's reign, ʿAkif
Pasha was compelled to retire from the government, his
old-fashioned Oriental notions being incompatible with the
changes seen to be necessary by Reshíd who when in the
West had learned, first among Ottoman statesmen, to grasp
the real position of Turkey in relation to the great powers
of the modern world.

The rest of ʿAkif's life was spent partly in retirement and
partly in exile, now at Adrianople and now at Brusa. At
length in 1263 (1847) he started on the Mekka pilgrimage
for the second time in his life, but on his return journey
he fell sick at Alexandria, and there died in the Rejeb of
1264 (early summer 1848).

ʿAkif Pasha was a man of many gifts, of an amiable and
affectionate disposition, and of unswerving loyalty to what
he believed to be the right, but his early education, together with a certain impliability of temper, tended to unfit
him in a measure for the part he was called upon to play.
Sultan Mahmúd held him in high esteem and summoned
him to his councils, not because he shared the imperial
enthusiasm for reform, but because the Sovereign knew his
unflinching fidelity and relied upon his sterling honesty.
Regarding as he did the dicta of old Arab and Persian
writers as the final pronouncement not on statesmanship
alone, but on every question, ʿAkif was necessarily out of
sympathy with the Europeanising tendencies of his day,
while his personal experiences of European officials were
not of a nature calculated to inspire him with either admiration of their methods or respect for their candour.

But while ʿAkif Pasha was thus rather reactionary than
progressive in his views on politics and the art of government, in literature he was the leader of a revolution. This
faithful disciple of the old classic teachers, who neither

knew nor cared to know a word of any Western language, whose notions as to the conduct of affairs were so antiquated as to necessitate his removal from a government which meant to face the situation, was yet moved — such was the pressure of the reforming spirit in those days — to cast aside the old cumbersome phraseology which swathed and shackled Ottoman prose, and to create for himself a style at once simpler, freer, and more natural, which he handed down as a priceless legacy to his successors. This style, as its creator left it, is a curious medley, to the formation of which both the official language and the current literary style, duly modified to suit the circumstances, were laid under contribution; but none the less its creation marks definitely the emancipation of Ottoman prose from the strangling grasp of that involved and lumbering fashion of writing which Turkish writers emphatically call 'the Bureaucratic style'. [1] Subsequent authors, with greater opportunities for the most part, and under happier auspices, have carried forward and perfected the good work; but to old ʿAkif belongs the honour of having dealt the first blow in the struggle which has led to freedom.

The most remarkable and best known example of ʿAkif's special style is the treatise which he called Tebsire, that is, 'The Elucidation'. [2] This work, which was never completed, is ostensibly the author's account of the Churchill affair; essentially it is an impassioned attack on his rival Pertev Pasha. That the latter was a not over-scrupulous intriguer, and that he did his best to undermine the position of the colleague, whose public spirit he was probably incapable of

---

[1] Usúl-i Qalem.

[2] It has been well translated into French by M. A. Alric, the Dragoman of the French embassy at Constantinople, and published by Leroux of Paris in 1892 under the title of 'Un Diplomate Ottoman en 1836.'

comprehending, may be allowed, but ʿAkif's onslaught, though absolutely free from the grossness wherewith earlier writers were wont to assail their enemies, is too embittered wholly to command our sympathies and, if we may judge of other charges by the somewhat childish criticisms passed on Pertev's literary works, too prejudiced to carry with it complete conviction.

As I have said before, it is in his prose alone that ʿAkif Pasha ranks with the reformers, in his poetry, the amount of which is small, he is content to proceed upon the old lines He was a learned man, according to the learning of the ancients, and his learning is manifested in his verses. None but a scholar and a thinker could have written his most famous poem, the 'ʿAdam Qasídasi', the 'Qasída of Nothingness' This well-known poem is perhaps the most terrible in all Turkish literature, the 'Chute des Feuilles' of Millevoye has been called the Marseillaise of the Melancholy, this qasída of ʿAkif Pasha might be styled the Marseillaise of the Pessimists, it is the very paean of despair. Other poets have found delight in singing of beauty and of love, others again have lost themselves in ecstasy dreaming of some far-off union with the Divine, but ʿAkif can derive no comfort save from the fondly cherished hope that for him and all existent things there comes after a brief season eternal annihilation Life has so dealt by this man that the very idea of it in any form is hateful to him, the life of this world is an intolerable burden, the existence of the blessed in Paradise is a weary strain, even the vague impersonal state of Being which is the mystic's goal is more than he can bear, in absolute extinction only does he hope to gain the longed-for rest This qasída is a qasída in form alone; it is dedicated to no Sultan or Vezír, it eulogises no one, here the qasída merely happens to be the particular verse-form in which the poet has chosen to embody his aspirations. [1]

With one exception, none of ʿAkif Pasha's other poems call for special attention. This one exception is a very tender and pathetic little elegy on a dearly loved granddaughter who died in girlhood. In its purity of sentiment and poignancy of tone, as well as in its simplicity and directness of language, this little poem anticipates the work of the Modern School.

The following verses from the Qasída of Nothingness will give an idea of the poem. The word ʿadam, which has throughout been rendered by 'Nothingness', is in reality rather stronger. The idea it expresses is the negation of existence, an idea for the expression of which we have to use some compound such as non-existence or not-being.

From the Qasída of Nothingness. [446]

To muse upon the draught of Nothingness fresh life on man bestows;
Is life's elixir, then, the elixir Nothingness's glass bestows?
When with the eye intent one scans the entity of Nothingness
To man the plain of Nothingness like Paradise's garden glows.
But nay, I err; how were it meet to liken this to Paradise? —
Far other are the bliss and peace the realms of Nothingness disclose.
For let us grant that there in Heaven all manner of delights abound,
The gifts of Nothingness need not enjoyment's weary stress like those.
If anywhere, 'tis there alone, and if not there, 'tis nowhere, no; —
Then yearn and long for Nothingness, if so be thou desire repose.
Nor grief nor woe, nor pain nor pang, nor any stress of hope or fear; —
Right fitting were it did the world the quest of Nothingness propose.
If but for once its billows surged, straightway were all existent things
O'erwhelmed within the boundless deep of Nothingness that silent flows.

---

[1] [The qasída has been, however, since the eleventh century of our era at any rate, the usual vehicle wherein the didactic poets, like Násir-i-Khusraw, have developed their philosophical, ethical and religious ideas. ED.]

The nourice-Fortune would provoke the children of the sphere [1] to pride
Did not the tutor-Nothingness continual chastisement impose. [2]
It may not be contained within the ring of space; what knoweth he
Of Nothingness's realm sublime who 'neath the Empyrean goes?
Idle and vain the zealot's brag of being while the iron grasp
Of Nothingness is clutching fast his collar though he little knows.
Through graving of the writer [3] turns the seal, I pray, a writer too? —
Meseemeth here a hint of Nothingness to them existent shows.
Let not that inexistent heart fret over earthly wants or cares
While ready the provision vast that Nothingness doth aye expose.
Its own existence unto every being is a load of bane,
But Nothingness's subjects dwell at peace from all distress and woes.
Spend forth thy being then if thou be wise in truth, go, and be naught;
Ay, yearn and long for Nothingness, if so be thou desire repose. [4]
We were but infants when we came to this sad land of being, else
To leave the old familiar home of Nothingness we ne'er had chose.
We'd known of rest in sooth, had but the world into non-being sprung
While in its stead the far-extending plain of Nothingness arose.
Asunder had I rent the robe of life full many a year agone
But that upon its train the stamp of Nothingness embroidered glows.
So weary of existence I that to my sorrow-laden heart
The dreary waste of Nothingness as my beloved home-land shows.
The dayspring of the morn of everlasting life before my eyes
Is pictured by the darkling floods that Nothingness's night compose.
The star of my desire o'erclimbeth ne'er the far horizon-line,
Though Nothingness's pregnant night brings forth each day a thousand shows. [5]
Could any bear with this, could any soul endure this bitter strain,
But that the physic-Nothingness relief from life at length bestows?

This is the little elegy referred to:

Elegy on a Grand-Daughter. [447]

Ne'er shall I forget thee, O my child most fair;
  Not though months and seasons and years may pass away.

[1] I. e. mankind.   [2] By destroying them.   [3] The seal-engraver.
[4] This line is repeated from a previous couplet.
[5] 'The night is pregnant,' the well-known proverb we have met before.

Bitter is thine absence, hard for me to bear
  Shall thy sweet words ever cease with me to stay?

Scarcely would we let us thy dear form embrace, [1] —
Yet in what sad plight is now all thy sweetest grace!
When I muse amid the bowers upon thy rosy face
  Well might the roses turn through sighs of mine to ashes grey! [2]

O'er thy frame of silver changedness hath crept,
Hath thy radiant forehead those dark brows still kept?
By thy golden tresses is the black earth swept?
  Lie the locks I once caressed now in sad disarray?

Hath the sphere its cruel ruthlessness displayed?
Hath it bid thy rosy cheek's blooming beauty fade?
And, Oh! are they turned to dust, are they all decayed, —
  Those dear hands so soft and white wherewith I used to play?

ᶜAkif's rival, Pertev Pasha, who was, like himself, a poet,
was born in the village of Daricha, which lies not far from
the town of Izmid   He repaired to the capital where he
entered the civil service, in which he gradually made his
way, becoming Reʾís Efendi in 1242 (1826—7)   In 1245
(1829—30) he was dismissed, and remained for a time in
retirement.   He was afterwards sent on a special mission to
Egypt, and on his return was again actively employed.   In
1251 (1836) he received the rank of vezír and, as we have
seen, was named Minister of Civil Affairs.   But on his intrigues coming to light, he was in 1233 (September 1837)
again dismissed, and on this occasion banished to Adrianople.   Shortly after his arrival in that city Pertev received
an invitation to dine with the governor Emín Pasha   When
the repast was finished, Emín presented to his guest the

---

[1] Lest we should hurt thee, so tender wert thou
[2] This line contains an untranslatable equivoque between گل gul = rose,
and کل kul = ashes.

imperial fermán which condemned him to death. This Pertev read without emotion and, asking for the poison, quietly drank it off, laying down the cup without uttering a word except the name of Allah. As the effects of the poison were not sufficiently rapid, four servants brought in the fatal bowstring, and to these Pertev surrendered himself without a murmur, meeting his death with the courage and resignation of a good Muslim of the old school Such at least is the account of Pertev Pasha's end given by Messrs Jouanin and Van Gaver in their work on Turkey, and in substance at any rate it is doubtless true.

Pertev Pasha's poetical work is of considerably greater extent than that of his rival, but although it too bears witness to the erudition of its author, it is lacking both in the distinction and in the personal note which impart so much of interest to the more remarkable of ʿAkif's works. The Díwán of Pertev is a good example of the style of poetry that became fashionable in Sultan Mahmúd's time, alike in its trivial though inoffensive treatment of threadbare themes, and in its almost aggressively Turkish vocabulary.

The Sharqí and Mustezád [1] which follow are both recommended by Kemál Bey.

Sharqí [448]

Let groups of merry revellers once more the garden grace,
'Tis rose-time now, so let the rosy wine go round apace,
Let water Jemshíd's beaker's mouth, let us carouse a space,
    'Tis morn, away let yonder merry Rosebud slumber chase,
    Let blush the mirror-wine [2] for shame to see her rosy face

---

[1] For a description of the verse-form called mustezád, see vol. I, pp 87—8
[2] The wine in the bowl mirrors the face of the drinker.

Amazed the narcisse at her dark and languid eyen rare,
Amazed the hyacinth before her tangled clustering hair,
Amazed the rosebud when she doth in hand the goblet bear, [1]
  'Tis morn, away let yonder merry Rosebud slumber chase;
  Let blush the mirror-wine for shame to see her rosy face

When 'scape her roguish locks from 'neath her fez and fall adown,
A sigh escapes with every breath from every stricken one,
The bulbul-soul begins within the body-cage to moan
  'Tis morn, away let yonder merry Rosebud slumber chase,
  Let blush the mirror-wine for shame to see her rosy face.

With flute and wine alone for feres have we retired to-night,
The flute accompanies our sighs, the wine partakes our plight [2]
Come, Pertev, let us with the plaining nightingale unite.
  'Tis morn, away let yonder merry Rosebud slumber chase;
  Let blush the mirror-wine for shame to see her rosy face

Mustezád. [449]

All night I woke and slept by turns with bitter yearning ta'en,
    (Of yonder beauty fain,)
I dallied with the thought and dream of her for plaything vain,
    (Till morning beamed again)

Blood wept I as I drank the wine of separation's feast,
    (Sans cupbearer's behest,)
Empty and brimming o'er by turns, cup-like, did I remain,
    (Bedyed with every stain.) [3]

I wildered and dumbfoundered moth and taper both this night,
    (With yearning's ardent plight,)
Burned sore, to stumble on with sinking steps, full hard the strain,
    (Consumed with fiery pain)

  [1] The twig bearing the bud is sometimes compared to the arm with the hand carrying the goblet
  [2] Being bitter
  [3] In this and the foregoing line the poet means to imply that he was tossed about between hope and fear.

No strength have I to bear those cruel tyrannies of thine,
   (O floating Angel mine!)
I gave my heart, and thought that thou to show thee kind would'st deign;
   (But now of life I plain.)

 wandered earth while in my hand the coin of soul I bare,
   (Accosting many a fair,)
Still seeking, Pertev, for this friendless heart a friend to gain,
   (And won but endless bane.)

CHAPTER X.

THE ROMANTICISTS (CONTINUED).

The Poets of the Reaction.

Hasan ʿAyní Efendi. — Dánish Bey. — Jávíd
Bey. — Saʿíd Bey. — Táhir Selám Bey. —
Leylá Khánim. — Sheref Khánim. —
ʿArif Hikmet Bey, Sheykh-ul-Islám.

Hasan ʿAyní Efendi, whom we have met as a friend of
Sunbul-záde Vehbí, although not a writer of any great
eminence, deserves a brief notice in our review of Ottoman
poetry. This author was born in 1170 (1756—7) in the
town of ʿAyntáb where he seems to have passed his youth.
At least it is not till 1205 (1790—1) that we find him in
the capital studying for the legal profession. Failing to get
the promotion expected, he abandoned the lawyer's career,
and in 1247 (1831—2) was appointed teacher of Arabic and
Persian to certain government officials. In the same year
he was decorated with the Nishán-i Iftikhár or Order of
Glory, the earliest of Ottoman orders of knighthood, created
by Sultan Mahmúd but abolished by his successor in 1267
(1850—1). ʿAyní died in the Safer of 1254 (May 1838), and,
as he had been associated with the Mevleví order, he was
buried in the courtyard of their famous convent at Galata.

The best of ʿAynī's poetical works is his Sáqí-Námc or Cupbearer-Book. In this poem, which was the work of his old age, having been finished in 1247 (1831—2), he-has expressed the conclusions to which he had come concerning things in general during the course of his long life Although ʿAynī chose the time-honoured name of Sáqí-Náme for this work, his poem is in no wise modelled upon the earlier productions so entitled The poet's subject is no material carouse, but the purpose of creation and the destiny of man, the title but gives the keynote for the imagery derived from the wine-feast, the ancient symbol of that knowledge of God wherein stands eternal life, an imagery which is consistently maintained throughout the poem. The cupbearer to whom the poem is addressed, and who is from time to time apostrophised, is no doubt a purely imaginary being. The author's philosophy is of course that of the Eastern thinkers who, so far as Turkey is concerned, have all along been most typically represented by the members of the Mevleví fraternity Although there is nothing essentially new in the poem, the conceptions and expressions are at times bold and original, the language, as becomes the theme, and perhaps in part owing to the re-actionary tendency which was now beginning to make itself felt, is more Persian than has been usual of late, considerably more so than in any of the writer's other and earlier works. In form the book is a mesneví, with a few incidental lyric pieces, it consists of about fifteen hundred couplets.

Besides the Sáqí-Náme, ʿAynī left another mesneví, unnamed, and a Díwán of ghazels, for the most part 'parallels' to works of contemporary poets, and a great number of chronograms. The unnamed mesneví is in a way the counterpart to the Sáqí-Náme, as it deals with all matters connected with a wholly literal carousal, the different kinds

of wines, the qualifications of the cupbearer, the merits of
the various musical instruments, the characteristics to be
desired in the guests, and numerous other similar details.
This production is interesting as showing what was the
ideal of the Ottoman bon-vivant; but it can hardly claim
to be reckoned as poetry.

'Ayní has further a number of Na'ts or poems to the
glory of the Prophet, which, according to Fatín Efendi,
bear collectively the title of Nazm-i Jewáhir, 'The String
of Gems.'

A great part of 'Ayní's literary career fell within the
heyday of Romanticism, and the gay defiant note of that
hedonistic time echoes bravely enough in many of his
pages. Thus the whole of his earlier mesneví is simply one
long eulogy of material pleasure. But the writer lived to see
the rise and feel something of the effect of that more or-
derly and sober spirit which was eventually to chase away
the Sardanapalian visions of the poets.

This extract from the Sáqí-Náme will give an idea of the
character of the work; it describes the 'making of man'
as conceived by the Oriental poets, the descent of the soul
from its celestial home being traced through the nine heavens and the three spheres, of fire, air and water, with which
the Ptolemaic scheme encircled the earth.

From the Sáqí-Náme.

My Descent to the Banquet of Humanity. [450]

> The Hidden Tablet [1] was my royal abode,
> Through which high state inebriate I bode.
> I looked on nature's feast, and there saw I

---

[1] The 'Hidden Tablet' (Levh-i-Mahfúz), on which at the beginning of all
things all that was to be was recorded, has been already repeatedly mentioned.

The heat, the cold, the humid and the dry [1]
I won the lofty Empyrean dome, [2]
And downward gazed upon the earth therefrom.
I served the Magian Elder a brief while,
Then sate me on the throne in regal style. [3]
I saw the twelve bowls of the Zodiac, [4]
And drunken, I forgot the pathway back
I wandered all the Seven Heavens through, [5]
My heart grew wise the hour when drunk I grew.
I hob-a-nobbed with Saturn merrily,
And bode a space with him in mirth and glee
With Jupiter a while I held debate,
And bade the reeling stars to coruscate
I made Mars drunken mid the planets roll,
And tutored the Fifth Sphere to quaff the bowl
The Solar beaker in my hand I seized,
And sighed remembering the Primal Feast. [6]
I bade the lovesome Venus chant her lay
And the Third Heaven dance upon his way
I learned right goodly lore of Mercury,
And sage and poet turn by turn grew I.
I drained the Crescent bowl, a sun I turned,
Through this hilarity with light I burned
The Sphere of Fire a tavern-house I deemed;
To me its wayward flashes goblets gleamed
The Air exhilaration found through me,
I dashed the Waters with the wine of glee [7]
I reeled into the cloud's carouse elate,

[1] That is, the many and varied phenomena displayed in nature.
[2] This represents the Ninth Heaven, the Primum Mobile, or Starless Crystalline Heaven (Felek-ul-Eflák or Felek-i-Atlas), the farthest from the earth of the series.
[3] This couplet is figurative, and probably means that at this stage the soul got an insight into the truth, which made it free
[4] In the Eighth Heaven, that of the Fixed Stars.
[5] The seven planetary heavens
[6] The oft-mentioned Feast of L-lest.
[7] The Spheres of Fire, Air, and Water, which immediately surround the earth, being between it and the first planetary sphere, that of the Moon.

I took the life-bestowing rain to mate.
Drunken, I gazed upon earth's stage astound;
And drunk, dead drunk, made I the blessed ground.
Within the seedling's heart the cup I drained,
And drunken there a twain of days remained.
In the wheat-stalk I strong and goodly grew;
In the grain's heart myself for fair I knew.
I quaffed for nourishment clear wine and bright, [1]
I turned to chyme, and pleasant was my plight. [2]
In hours of grossness wine-dregs I became;
In hours of pureness, spirit pure as flame.
From chyme was one within the liver made,
The other in the father's loins was glad.
At length did I wine seminal become
And lie within the runlet of the womb.
For nine months in the dungeon-womb immured,
What blood I drank! what anguish I endured! —
Then issued to this exile. What should I
But seek the regions where my home doth lie?

The second extract, which is from ʿAyní's other Mesneví, is taken from the passage in which he describes the model cupbearer, that minister of pleasure, who figures so largely in the works of Eastern poets.

Description of the Cupbearer. [451]

Polite be the cupbearer and discreet,
Of sunny cheek, moon-visaged, angel-sweet.
The fashions of the feast she well should know,
And all the fancies of the rev'llers too;
How some pure undiluted wine require,
While others mingle water with the fire.
A maiden should she be in boyish dress, [3]

---

[1] Wine here of course means the water the plant lives on.

[2] 'Chyme' in Turkish 'Keymus', here stands for sap.

[3] ʿAyní here declares that the ideal sáqí or cupbearer is a girl dressed like a boy.

Unmatched and peerless in her loveliness.
Gentle and simple should her wit enthral,
Neither untutored nor ill-bred withal.
In minstrelsy and wines she skilled should be,
From all disfigurement and blemish free,
Of sugar-lip, sweet-tongued, and gay of soul,
Of fourteen years, like to the moon at full, [1]
That all the party through her airs be bright
And in her voice the revellers delight.
Her silvern hand the crystal bowl doth bear, —
Radiance on radiance! radiance everywhere! [2]
When to the banquet comes she like the moon,
Her beauty should add splendour to the sun,
That archly stepping like the peacock fine
She deck with lively hues the feast of wine
As yon fair Torment passeth to and fro
A wild sensation should the banquet know,
And should she drain a cup, her eyen bright
Would smite the royal falcon in his flight

A passing mention must suffice for Dánish Bey, Jávíd Bey, and Sa'íd Bey. Of these, Dánish and Jávíd were both Constantinopolitans by birth, and both employed in the civil service. The former died in 1245 (1829—30), in his twenty-fifth year, the latter died in 1250 (1834—5). They were both influenced by the re-actionary spirit that marks the close of this Period. Both were imitators of the Persian-ists, and more especially of Nef'í But the lesson of Rom-anticism was not entirely lost on Dánish at any rate, as he tried with fair success to infuse something more of the Turkish element into the grandiose style of his master.

---

[1] The moon is in its splendour on its fourteenth night.
[2] This alludes to Koran XXIV, 35. So Nesímí (see Vol I, pp. 336 et seqq) says —

مرا صاچكڭ كه طلمانلده در نور آنسك آدىدرر نور علمى نور

Khizr-Agha-záde Sa'íd was brought up in the Seraglio, where, thanks to the beauty of his voice, he served for a time as mu'ezzin or caller-to-prayer. He afterwards held various official appointments till his death in 1252 (1836—7). His literary reputation rests chiefly on the score or so of sharqís included in his little Díwán; but the fact of his social qualities having gained for him a large circle of friends may perhaps have had something to do with procuring for him a wide celebrity hardly justified by the intrinsic merit of his work.

Táhir Selám Bey, another Constantinopolitan civil official, was a poet of more note than any of the three writers just named. He died in 1260 (1844), leaving, besides a complete Díwán, a translation of the famous Maqámát or Séances of the old Arab Harírí, and a commentary on Ahmed el-Qudúrí's celebrated Mukhtasar or Compendium of Jurisprudence.

With the single exception of Fitnet, Leylá Khanim is unquestionably the greatest Turkish poetess of the older school. She is a gracious and interesting figure, standing here at the close of the last purely Oriental period of Turkish poetry, her bright and mirthful spirit shedding a farewell radiance on the old Eastern fashions and fancies, as in her own Stamboul the setting sun lights up the Asian hills with a parting glow ere he disappears below the western horizon.

The life of a Turkish woman is never very much before the public, and so the details that we possess concerning Leylá's career are naturally few. She was the daughter of a cadi-'asker called Morali-záde Hámid Efendi, and was born in Constantinople. Among her relatives or connections was the famous 'Izzet Mollá whose life and work we have already considered, and from him she received, in considerable part at any rate, her literary education. She never forgot the debt she owed to this early instructor, or ceased to hold him in veneration and esteem; and when she learned of his tragic end at Siwas, she embalmed his memory and her own sorrow in a beautiful elegy. While still quite young, Leylá was married; but the irrepressible spirit of the poetess could ill brook the fetters of wedlock, and within a week, if Fatín Efendi speaks truly, husband and wife parted to meet no more. Having won free from wedded thraldom, Leylá gave herself up entirely to the cultivation of literature and the pursuit of pleasure, between which engrossing occupations she divided her time until she died in 1264 (1847—8).

Many stories are current bearing on the gay doings and ready wit of this vivacious lady, some examples of which are given by Zihní Efendi in his work on Famous Women. Thus he tells us that Leylá once conceived a fancy for a handsome boy who acted as assistant in a wax-chandler's shop in the bazaar, and would very often make excuses for going to his shop so that she might have the pleasure of looking at him and speaking to him. The boy, however, was very bashful, and would blush deeply but make no answer. The shrewder among the neighbours soon noticed this and at once divined the truth, whereon one of them composed the following line which he taught to the boy bidding him answer the lady with it when next she spoke to him: —

'Look not on my cheek's bright taper, lest with fire consumed thou be.' [1]

---

[1] The boy's line: شمع دخمه دقّت ايله باقمه ينارسين

Leylá's reply: خطّك كلبجك سنده بنى موملە آرارسين

Shortly afterwards Leylá came up and addressed him as usual, whereupon he straightway made reply as he had been told. Without a moment's hesitation the poetess turned the tables on him by improvising in the same metre and rime:

'When thy beard doth sprout, with candles wilt thou come to seek for me.[1]

Leylá's temperament is reflected in her Díwán; she is fond of fun and cares little for the world's opinion, she is determined to enjoy herself and let others say what they will. But strong as was her character and marked as was her individuality, not even this poetess could escape the fatal conventionalism of which her school was dying. And so we sometimes find in one and the same ghazel verses as trite or as forced as those of any old Persianist alongside of others instinct with her own strong and ardent vitality. None the less her Díwán forms very pleasant reading; her verses are graceful both in substance and in expression, her language is lucid and fluent, and everywhere we have the

---

Zihní has further the following story bearing on the Lesbian proclivities which he says were generally imputed to the poetess. A certain bookseller called Hátif Efendi once raised a laugh at the lady's expense by causing the following verse which he had composed to be repeated in her hearing in some public place:

لیلیٔ پیشین ایدی خیمه‌زن روزگار

شمدیکی لیلا خانم مهرٔزن روزگار

'The former Leylá was the nomad of her age,
'The Leylá Khanim of to-day is the burnisher of her age.'

In the translation the point, such as it is, of this verse has entirely disappeared. It lies in the parallelism between خیمه‌زن and مهرٔزن; the first of which words, literally 'tent-striker', but in practice 'tent-dweller' or 'nomad', is applicable to Mejnún's Leylá, the desert beauty; while the second, literally 'shell-striker', but in practice '(paper-)burnisher', that is, one who by rubbing paper with a shell puts a gloss on its surface and so renders it suitable for writing on, is meant to hint at certain of Leylá's reputed pranks.

[1] See the note on page 343.

charmıng feelıng that we arc dealıng wıth an artıst who seeks to produce her effects by the sımplıcıty and correctness of her work, and not through the aıd of a meretrıcıous ornamentatıon.

Thus Leylá's style ıs clear and straightforward, she dıd not go out of her way to create dıfficulties and stud her verses wıth enıgmas, on the contrary, she was careful to selcct the words and phrases whıch best expressed what she desıred to say, and so successful was she that there are but few passages ın her Díwán whıch have to be read a second tıme ın order to be understood, — an exceedıng great and rare merıt wıth a Turkısh poet of the Old School. Her vocabulary ıs, no less than her idıom, simple and corrcct, ındeed, it is almost classic ın its purıty, beıng free from any tinge of the exaggerated Turkıcısm of recent years and from all taınt of an affected Persianısm.

These happy results wcre no doubt partly owıng to the instructıon whıch the poetess receıved from her gıfted teacher, but they were probably brought about ın greater measure by that trend away from the exaggeratıons and extravagances of the past, and towards a greater sobrıety and moderatıon, whıch we have seen to be the most dıstınctıve feature of the close of the Romantıcıst Perıod.

Leylá Khanım's poetry ıs wholly lyrıc, and ıs all comprısed ın her Díwán

Here ıs a hıghly characterıstıc ghazel of this poetess.

Ghazel. [452]

The merry feast prepare, let them say whate'er they wıll.
Sıp the wine wıth yonder fair, let them say whate'er they wıll

In dreams by nıght the loʋer fondly kıssed and stroked a whıle
Her [1] dusky scented haır, let them say whate'er they wıll

[1] In these poems, seeıng that the wrıter ıs a lady, ıt mıght be better,

The darling one hath fettered with her tresses' chain my heart;
And I still the longing bear; let them say whate'er they will.

What the harm although my comrades chide and carp at me to-day? —
In the end will all appear; let them say whate'er they will.

Only let my darkened visage on the Judgment Day be white;
While on earth I onward fare let them say whate'er they will.

To me while here below what doth matter praise or blame? —
So my comrades joyance share, let them say whate'er they will.

Leylá, seek a nook apart, fall at yonder fairy's feet,
Unto her thy troth declare; let them say whate'er they will.

Again in the same strain:

Ghazel. [453]

Drink of wine upon the lea; let them say whate'er they will;
See thou pass thy days in glee; let them say whate'er they will.

Doth yonder cruel deem that my flowing tears are dew? —
Like the rose, a-smile is she; let them say whate'er they will.

I'm thy lover, I'm thy thrall, I'm thy loyal slave, O fair,
Till the Latest Day shall be; let them say whate'er they will.

Come and lie within my breast if the rival seek thy side;
Wherefore no? — pshaw! out on thee! let them say whate'er they will!

Leylá, play and frolic fair with yon moon-faced beauty bright;
See thou pass thy days in glee; let them say whate'er they will.

Among Leylá's sharqís there is a pretty little poem of which the following is a translation:

when translating, to use the masculine in place of the feminine pronoun;
but the highly conventional character of all the poetry of this school must
be borne in mind. The Turkish language, as I have elsewhere said, ignores
gender.

Sharqí. [454]

Beware, bid not me ope my mouth, for fires within me glow;
O cruel, make me not what hides within my breast to show!
Deny not that which thou hast wrought, dost doubt thee that I know?
    O cruel, make me not what hides within my breast to show!

No healing is there for my heart smit sore with love of thee,
Ah, never shall this parting in Love's world forgotten be!
If lovers are so rife with thee, is there no fair for me?
    O cruel, make me not what hides within my breast to show!

Dost thou yon loathly rival then a human creature name?
One day, O wanton, wilt thou tire of her too, just the same?
Thou'lt soon repent thee of thy deeds and blush for very shame!
    O cruel, make me not what hides within my breast to show!

I'll bear with patience every pang thou causest, loveling bright;
So let thy wont with Leylá still be rigour and despite,
These sighs and wails of mine must surely win to move thy spright.
    O cruel, make me not what hides within my breast to show!

The following is a mukhammes built by Leylá Khanım
on a ghazel of Báqí. The reader will recollect that in com-
positions of this description the lines of the earlier poem
are used as a base on which the superstructure is reared,
thus in this instance the fourth and fifth lines of each
stanza are the several couplets of Báqí's ghazel. It will be
noticed that in the lines she has prefixed to these, the
poetess has endeavoured to reproduce the style and imagery
of the Classic writers.

Mukhammes on a Ghazel of Báqí. [455]

Yon darling of the soul it is who all my sense and wit o'erthrows,
My waving Cypress 'tis who spreadeth fieshness through the garden-close
My bird-like heart my gardener is in Love's fair parterre of the rose
    'The eye-field with thy cheek's reflection bright, my flowery pleasance shows,
    'My soul doth all this while the image of thy palm-tree form enclose'

As prison cells appear to me the meads where-through I loved to stroll;
For love o' thee my heart wins naught but many a grievous wound to thole;
From hour to hour thine absence makes my tears like rushing waters roll;
  'The heart makes moan through grief for thee, and ever weepeth sore the soul;
  'The fountain of this garden-land from mine unceasing weeping flows.'

Although thou kenn'st my lot through fire of love of thee is naught but woe,
My smiling Rosebud, wilt thou ne'er a glance of ruth to me-ward throw?
Behold my sighs and tears, and but for once do thou compassion show!
  'By gazing upon rose and garth my soul repose shall never know;
  'The ward wherein my loved one dwells alone can yield my soul repose.'

What time I call to mind thy box-tree shape in sorrow's night-tide drear
The tales of Mejnún and Ferhád were 'fore mine own forgotten sheer.
My groans and sighs and prayers ascend alway to heaven, and so 'tis clear
  'For ever with my sighing's fiery sparks yon steely bowl, the sphere,
  'Goes round a-night my gold-bestudded beaker at the feast of woes.' [1]

Recall each hour to thy sad heart the glance of yon bewitching e'e;
When flow thy bitter tears adown, O Leylá, name not Oman's Sea.
Aneath thy shade my own heart's blood is all the favour gained by me:
  'My tears an ocean roll; therein the branch of coral, O Báqí,
  'Is th' image of my slender Judas-tree that in my mem'ry glows.' [2]

The last example is a mustezád:

Mustezád. [456]

My sighs set all the world aflame when mounting toward the sky;
    (My love doth naught descry;)
Yon Sovran still to this bewailing heart doth ruth deny.
    ('Fore God I burn thereby!)

---

[1] In this couplet Báqí means imply that the stars damascening with gold
the steel-hued bowl or vault of heaven are sparks from his burning sighs,
and that this bowl, which is none other than the sorrow-bringing sphere, is
his nightly cup, and that the feast of woe is the banquet to which he is
ever called.

[2] Here the Judas-tree, besides symbolising redness (the coral branch) as
usual, plays the part of the cypress or box-tree, and represents the graceful
figure of the beloved.

Longing and pining for her locks have made me wode to be,
    (Her eyne ensorcelled me.)
Once more this erring heart doth forth into the desert fly.
    (For aid on God I cry)

Blood weep I, thinking on thy lips, O sweetest soul and dear,
    (Yet thou dost nothing hear.)
On all the road of Love there is not one to help me nigh;
    (Nor friend nor fere have I).

Were I to pray yon Moon to visit this my hut of woe, [1]
    (She would refuse, I know.)
Could e'er the moon for e'en one night in unmeet house aby? —[1]
    (Till dawning greet the eye?)

Smit to the death hath Leylá been by one, a fawn-eyed fair,
    (With jasmine-scented hair;)
And now to her a plaything grown's the bitter morning-sigh,
    (Ah me, till dawn be high!)

Another noted poetess of this time is Sheref Khanim, whose father Nebíl Bey, himself something of a poet, was the son of the historian Núrí Bey. Of this lady even less is known than of Leylá; we are told that she was born in 1224 (1809—10), but the date of her death is unrecorded. Ahmed Mukhtár in his little book entitled 'Our Poetesses' tells us that in 1273 (1856—7) a sister of Sheref died leaving a little girl called Naqiyya whom the poetess adopted as a daughter, and educated with the greatest care and affection. This Naqiyya herself became a poetess, and when Ahmed Mukhtár wrote in 1311 (1893—4) she was employed as a teacher of history and Persian at the College for Muslim Ladies in Constantinople. [2]

Sheref's Díwán is larger than Leylá's and contains a num-

There is here an allusion to the 'houses' or 'mansions' of the moon.
[2] This college, which is called Dár-ut-Taᶜlímát, is in the Qosqa quarter.

ber of religious poems, including a series of elegies on Huseyn and the Martyrs of Kerbelá which are reckoned the
finest things she wrote. One of her most pleasing works is
a poem addressed to her little niece Naqiyya. [1]

The Sheykh-ul-Islám ᶜArif Hikmet Bey Efendi, a brief
consideration of whose work will bring to a close our survey
of the Romanticist Period, is at once the last poet of eminence reared under the exclusively Oriental culture which
has prevailed from the beginning up till now, and the last
member of the ᶜulemá, of that faculty whose vocation has
hitherto been regarded as emphatically, if not exclusively,
the Learned Profession, to obtain any real distinction in
the ranks of poetry.

As we shall see when we come to look more closely
into the matter, this coincidence is in no wise strange. The
curriculum of the ᶜulemá, revolving for ever in the same
old circle, had no place for that new alien culture whose
vivifying breath was to inspire with fresh vitality the mor-
ibund literature of Turkey, and the study of which, being
the sole avenue to the truer learning and purer taste of the
future, was henceforward to claim the allegiance of all who
were noblest and most gifted in the Ottoman literary world.

But ᶜArif Hikmet came too early to have art or part in
the new learning. He was born in Constantinople in the
Muharrem of 1201 (November, 1786), being the son of
Ibráhím ᶜIsmet Bey, a cadi-asker under Selím III. His legal
studies were begun at the tender age of ten. In his thir-
tieth year he was made titular mollá of Jerusalem; the

[1] [Presumably the author intended to give specimens of this poetess's
work, but none are contained in the manuscript. Though the pages are num-
bered consecutively in pencil, additions were evidently contemplated, for I
find a pencil-note in the margin, "Put Ghálib Bey here after Sheref". ED.]

molláships of Cairo and of Medína soon followed, and in 1242 (1826—7) he was named Judge of Constantinople In the following year he was sent into Rumelia to superintend the census that was being taken, and on his return was appointed Naqíb-ul-Eshráf, that is Dean of the Sherífs, as the descendants of the Prophet are called Up till this time ʿArif Hikmet had resided in a charming villa at Quzghunjuq on the Bosphorus which he had inherited from his father, but his fortunes now became temporarily clouded, and he was obliged to retire to a house in the quarter called Eski .Hammam (Old Bath), in Scutari, which soon grew to be a favourite resort of scholars and men of letters, just as his villa on the Bosphorus had been in more prosperous days. Things, however, soon improved, and in 1249 (1833—4) Hikmet Efendi found himself back in favour and holding the high rank of Anatolian Cadi-Asker Upon this he re-signed his deanship and gave himself up to study. In 1254 (1838—9) he was promoted to the Rumelian Cadi-Askerate, and in the following year, on the accession of ʿAbd-ul-Mejíd, was made a member of the Council of Justice, and soon afterwards, of the Military Council At last in 1262 (1846) he was appointed Sheykh-ul-Islám, which high office he retained for over seven years, retiring in 1270 (1854) to a villa which the Sultan had presented to him at Rumeli Hisár on the Bosphorus, where he gave himself entirely up to study and devotion. His intention was eventually to re-move to Medína, where he had founded and endowed a library, and there spend what remained of his life near the tomb of the Prophet from whom he claimed descent; but his death, which occurred on the 16th of Shaʿbán 1275 (11th March, 1859), prevented the realisation of this project. He lies buried at Scutari in the district called Noah's Well (Núh Quyusi).

ʿArif Hikmet, who, so far as literature is concerned, may be looked upon as the last of the Old Turks, was the most learned and scholarly man of the eventide of Eastern culture. Fatín Efendi, who wrote Hikmet's Memoirs soon after his retirement from the position of Sheykh-ul-Islám, speaks of him in terms quite unusually enthusiastic, describing him as being a peerless sage distinguished by piety and devotion, whose poetry would have filled Sáʾib and ʿUrfí with admiration, and whose prose would have made Nergisí and Veysí bite on the finger in wonderment.

The critics of the new school are, of course, somewhat less extravagant. Kemál Bey while declaring that Hikmet was an imitator of his predecessors, admits that he did his imitating in a learned fashion; and Professor Nájí pronounces his verse to be but mediocre, though he grants him to have been singularly accomplished for a Sheykh-ul-Islám.

In 1282 (1865—6) Seyyid Mehemmed Saʿíd Zíver, a personal friend and warm admirer of the poet, edited his Díwán, to which he prefixed an interesting and appreciative · preface. [1] From this we learn that the Seyyid, whose acquaintance with Hikmet dated from 1245 (1829—30), had often seen the manuscript of a valuable prose work on which the latter was for long engaged. This was a series of biographical sketches of the learned men of his own time, starting from the year 1200 (1785—6). Most unfortunately on the author's death this manuscript disappeared, and no one seemed to know in whose possession it was or what had become of it. In 1307 (1889—90) when Professor Nájí wrote, its whereabouts was still unknown, so it is to be feared that it must either have been destroyed or lost beyond recovery.

[1] The Díwán was lithographed in the following year, 1283.

'Arif Hikmet's Díwán is in itself a sufficient witness to
its author's erudition. It is in reality composed of three
distinct díwáns, one of Arabic poems, one of Persian, and
one of Turkish, of which the last alone concerns us here.
This Turkish Díwán is typically representative of the last
stage in the Romanticist movement It marks the definite
triumph of the reaction against the debauchery of the noon-
tide of Romanticism. Here in the pages of the greatest poet
of the close of the Period, the effrontery of language, the
unauthorised prosodial licenses, the aggressively, almost bar-
barously, Tartar vocabulary of the earlier phases have all
disappeared, and in their place we have a beseeming reticence of speech, a formal correctness of versification, and a
carefully studied and irreproachable diction, proving how
thorough has been the awakening from the opium-eater's
dream

But although respectability has been regained and a due
sense of decorum is once more in evidence, the gain stops
here. Hikmet's poetry, though academically good, is without inspiration and without originality. When, revolted by
its excesses, the poets turned their backs on the Romanticist spirit, which after all was the national spirit, they in
reality cast from them their only hope of salvation from
within. So Hikmet, when he turned from the Turkicism
which had been outraged by his predecessors, was forced
to fall back upon the worn-out paraphernalia of the Persianists. Had it not been for the light which gleamed from
the Western horizon just at this critical moment, when the
Turkish torch had spent itself and the poets were feebly
struggling to re-kindle the battered lamp of Persianism, instead of the story we have now to tell of advance and
progress, we should have had to record a monotonous succession of 'Arif Hikmets and Ghálib Beys. How near things

23

were to coming to this pass we shall see when we glance
at the next Period.

It must not be thought that Hikmet Efendi's poetry,
though it sets the seal on a hopeless reaction, is devoid of
merit; on the contrary it offers much that in its own way
is very good. There are many verses in his Díwán which
are truly beautiful both in substance and expression, and
which would do no discredit to poets of far loftier pretensions. Again, it must be said to Hikmet's honour that he
threw the whole of the great influence he possessed into
the struggle against the licentiousness which had degraded
Turkish poetry, and that no small share of the ultimate
victory was due to his example.

Although it is impossible wholly to commend a movement which, had it been altogether successful, must have
resulted in stagnation, in this one particular of purging
away the excesses of Romanticism, the abortive Persianist
revolt in which Hikmet played so prominent a part rendered a real service to Ottoman poetry. Unhappily the
literary leaders of those days were unable to distinguish
between use and abuse. To their eyes, it would appear,
there was no alternative between a corrupt Turkicism on
the one hand and a dead Persianism on the other. Possibly
all things Turkicist were contaminated for them by the
orgies of their immediate predecessors, and the only hope
lay in a complete reversal of all their ways. But be this
as it may, their failure to gather up the tares without at
the same time rooting up the wheat led to their would-be
revolution falling still-born; but by their success in cleansing
the Augean stables of Romanticism they fitted Turkish
poetry the more readily to receive and the more truly to
reflect the purer radiance flashed from the star of that
other revolution yet to come, and in this way these last

representatives of this expiring school corrected and completed the work of their predecessors, who, by breaking
the Classic Tradition, had rendered poetry susceptible to
influences other than Persian.

This movement, wherewith ʿArif Hikmet is so closely
identified, has been spoken of as abortive, and so it was in
so far as it failed to turn again the stream of Turkish
poetry into Persian channels. But it was by no means
without direct effect, since, apart from its preparing the
soil for the reception of the new seed, it determined the
lines to be taken by such purely Oriental poetry as was
still to be written. Those backward spirits of the coming
Periods who, while unable or unwilling to adopt the new
culture, yet desire to express themselves in verse, will turn
for guidance not to the brilliant daring writers of the meridian
of Romanticism, but to that more modest and humble band
whereof ʿArif Hikmet is the centre, and the work of Nefʿi
and his congeners the model.

The first of the following ghazels is that quoted by Fatín
in his Memoirs:

Ghazel. [457]

So bathed in floods of radiance is the garden-close to-night
A knosp of sheeny moonlight gleams each opening rose to-night.

To rouse it at the dawn will e'er my prayerful cries avail? —
So deep the sleep wherein doth evil luck repose to-night.

The moon's illuminations gay have made the reason drunk;
As cup the tulip shines, the dew as vintage flows to-night.

The moon with shoulders squirrel-mantle dight hath made the sky [1]
And all the evening-land a lamp that brilliant glows to-night.

[1] Mantles trimmed with grey squirrel-fur were formerly worn by certain

In darksome plight the mirror bright of genius lieth low, [1]
For tyranny's the only firefly-gleam that shows to-night.

O Hikmet, with these heart-enkindling fiery words of thine
Effulgence o'er the comrades' feast the taper throws to-night.

Ghazel. [458]

The draught of evil is the rosy wine of pleasure's bowl;
The draught of evil, — nay, the false mirage that cheats the soul.

The fever in the bosom lit by fire of love of thee
Doth make the lovers thirst to taste thy watered dagger's dole. [2]

By hope's exhilaration flushed at this wild earth's carouse
Inebriate each man doth grope for some phantasmal goal.

Since men have brought the charge of borrowed grace against the moon,
The sun is now the type whereby their judgments folk control. [3]

Mis-state not in their presence who are men of lore and wit;
For error 'tis correcteth the arithmetician's scroll. [4]

dignitaries; in this line the poet means to suggest that the moon is surrounded by light clouds.

[1] The 'mirror of genius' is no doubt the man of genius.

[2] The dagger of the beloved is often referred to by the poets; its mention does not necessarily imply that the wearer is a youth, for as D'Ohsson says, Turkish ladies of distinction used to wear little daggers the hilts and sheaths of which were often beautifully decorated with precious stones. Similar weapons were worn by the Princesses of Wallachia and Moldavia when in state costume.

[3] Did Hikmet know anything of the new astronomy, or have we here a merely fortuitous figure of speech implying that the pretensions of some hitherto respected person have been exposed and that honour is now given where it is really due? [I do not quite follow this note, for of course the old Astronomy was well aware of the fact that the Moon's light was borrowed from the sun. ED.]

[4] Error may be said to correct the arithmetician when he finds that his calculations yield a wrong result, and is therefore compelled to revise his work.

One breath would in one moment bring to naught its cupoles nine, —
A bubble o'er the sea of haps the mighty sphere doth roll

Of old my eyes were wont to see the world a rosy mead, —
The season sweet of youth is life's spiing-tide of joyance whole.

Hikmet, for him who knoweth of the many, many schools,
A book the best companion is seclusion to console.

APPENDIX.

First lines of the Turkish Text of the Poems translated in Volume IV.

[٣١١] خوشا فرخنده اختر ليلۀ معتاز و مستثنا

[٣١٢] گل ای گوڭل اولەر دل کشود چشم شهود،

[٣١٣] صدر اعظم آلدی گندی سنجق پیغمبری

[٣١٤] دبیرستانه آلمق جهد ایدر اول طفلی روز و شب

[٣١٥] ستر ایچون زاهد آلفته منش بادەسی

[٣١٦] ثقلتی آشکار در کمرگ

[٣١٧] دیدی ای هلدم مسیحم خصال

[٣١٨] گل ای رخش کلک سخن گیر و دار

[٣١٩] ایلدی بر ایکی پیمانه ایله سرگردان بزی

[٣٢٠] هر طرّەسنده بیگ شکن دلرباسی وار

[٣٢١] گردن صافی بیاض اویله که کافور گبی

[٣٢٢] مست نازم کیم دوینندی بویله بی پروا سی

[٣٢٣] رواق مهری شکسن ایتدی سینۀ صافک

[٣٢٤] عشقه دوشدم جان و دل مفت جوانان اولدی عب

[٣٢٥] زلف و کلاہ وبردی خلل مغربی قسه

[٣٢٦] ساق و سرین و غبغب و لب مشربەجه در

360

¹ [٣٥١]

[٣٥٢] ضعفدن كوى عنادە كيم دل شيدا بانور

[٣٥٣] غم عشق دل آشوبى زمين و آسمان چكمز

[٣٥٤] دم اولماز كيم بو شيون خانەدە آه و انين اولماز

[٣٥٥] انجمن گاه ازلدە عشقە قابل در ديو

[٣٥٦] يا رب بو معنايى بيلير هب علم

[٣٥٧] كيمسەدنك سرمايۀ آرامى غارت اولسون

[٣٥٨] دگلە نيدن كيم حكايت ايلەور

[٣٥٩] نطق جان بخش لبكدر مايۀ عشرت بكا

[٣٦٠] اگر جان گورمك استرسەڭ بدنسز

[٣٦١] ديار دلدە بكا هزبان بولنمدى غيبى

[٣٦٢] سبك سامان تقليدە حقيقت جلە پوش اولمز

[٣٦٣] خراباتى گورنلر هر برى بر حالتى سويلر

[٣٦٤] آزادگان قيد امل سرفراز اولور

[٣٦٥] مباهات ايلمز رندانە مشرب هر خصوصندە

[٣٦٦] مطلبك ني ايلە مخلوقە مدارا ويرمز

[٣٦٧] پيچ و تاب سبنەدن افكار كنديين گوسترر

[٣٦٨] كنج فراغە گرچە كه همت قومز سنى

[٣٦٩] صائمە منشور خرد يا عفت و تقوى يورور

[٣٧٠] شاهنشه عالى نسب سلطان ممدوح الحسب

[٣٧١] بنت العنب كە گل گبى رنگين بكتلى در

[٣٧٢] بانئز او غرۀ مست بها جان سپارينە

¹ In spite of all my efforts, I have so far been unable to discover the text of this quatrain, either in the author's note-books, or in any of his manuscripts or printed books.

[۳۷۳] دوشمش محنته دحی نورس جوان ایکن

[۳۷۴] مکنمی ننک زلف سه باندن خلاص

[۳۷۵] اول آل قس کاکل اوزره درگ گلدر سنبل اوسنده

[۳۷۶] بائه دهر بی ثبانک منزل و مأواسنه

[۳۷۷] هوای قبض مهر عشق ابله شبگیر اندر مهناب

[۳۷۸] اله آلدهجه او حمگی گورب چارپاره

[۳۷۹] اوناوب ایلدی اول قنه حوابده قام

[۳۸۰] صبحدم بو بت تری بجه شمربیمکار

[۳۸۱] دوله خاك اولدبسه تاج و تخت كاوس و كبك

[۳۸۲] نه گللر گل نه حود گلزارلر گلرار در سمر

[۳۸۳] نه مشکل ایمش الهی وطندن آیرلف

[۳۸۴] اولش کبار دولته ورد زبان دروغ

[۳۸۵] حام جهان نمای طرب هزنه دم نوزور

[۳۸۶] سیمه پر داغ اولمسه گیرمر اله مطلوبلر

[۳۸۷] دلمه داغ داغ حسری سوز آشنا در هب

[۳۸۸] ابروانك جبن اسنعندن ای مهپاره اچ

[۳۸۹] دلده نك داغ هوسله عشق بار اولر بدید

[۳۱۰] گللر قرارر شبرمله اول غنجه گولمجه

[۳۹۱] اولده دللر ربودی غمزه جادوسنه

[۳۹۲] پر شوی و طرت برم دلآرای قناعت

[۳۹۳] حرج دنیدن اننمه رجای عطا عبس

[۳۹۴] سحاب نو بهاری عالمه گوهر نثار اولدی

[۳۹۵] ای دد بار سبودلرك توبیدر سنك

[۳۹۶] ای دختر سنوه سنم نه ادجون بو ناز

363

[۴۲۱] ای که خال سیهی هندستان

[۴۲۲] کشتیِّ کامه دور گورندی کنار حیف

[۴۲۳] عرق چکیننده اوئش طرّهٔ دلدار ‌پیچاپیچ

[۴۲۴] عشّاق عید وصلكه قربان آلورمیسک

[۴۲۵] گهی دربانی منع ایلر گهی اعجبار اولور مانع،

[۴۲۶] کهنه شراب ویر بگا تازه بغازه نو بنو،

[۴۲۷] نوله شیرازی ویرسم بن اول خال عنبر افشانده

[۴۲۸] ختکی قویسرون طرفا گریهدن اورصون دم کیم

هرِ سوزی معدن جوهر ایدی گتندی کانی ١

[۴۲۹] ظهورِ ضرّهٔ زر صوئیّ جزاری گولدردی

[۴۳۰] دمادم عرصهٔ عالمده آه ایله دوانر بز

[۴۳۱] یاتوب قالئز اولور بو قارئر آب آهسته آهسته

[۴۳۲] بلبل گبی رقیبلر اوئش غراب ایکن

[۴۳۳] کیم گورسه اول لعلی ملّی

[۴۳۴] رونما اولدی بو شب بر ماهتاب

[۴۳۵] بر ایناجه بلّسن بك بی بدّلسن

[۴۳۶] چونکه ای شوخ فدائی گوگلمی ایتدگ هوائی

[۴۳۷] بر دلبر پرِ آب و تاب، ایتدم جهانده انتخاب

[۴۳۸] او گل اندام بر آل شاله بورنسرون بوربیوسن

[۴۳۹] قز دگله نصح و پندیمی فولگده صادق اول

[۴۴۰] پند ایلر ایسه بر دخی آغاجه صارریم

[۴۴۱] ای طراوت نمای گلشن عشق

¹ In this case I give the first verse instead of the first half-verse, because the second half-verse contains the chronogram (A. H. 1206) which is the chief point of the poem.

Lightning Source UK Ltd.
Milton Keynes UK
UKHW012051280219
338158UK00006B/173/P